Understanding Your Refugee and Immigrant Students

An Educational, Cultural, and Linguistic Guide

Jeffra Flaitz, Ph.D.
University of South Florida

Ann Arbor
THE UNIVERSITY OF MICHIGAN PRESS

Acknowledgments

I would like to thank the following individuals for generously giving their time and attention to this project, for checking on facts and details with friends and family, often via transcontinental phone calls, for sharing their memories and perspectives with me, and for showing me over and over what "love of homeland" means: Cacilda Barros, Vikramaditya Bhide, Vamsi Chikkam, Kathleen Coskran, Chaitanya Damle, Jane Downey, Tasnim Fidali, Andrea Freidus, Perlita Fuentes, Rodolfo Gandara, Vi Ganesan, Irella Gurdian, Denys Harasymiak, Su-lieng Ho, Sara Jaramillo, Alen Janjus, Nally Jorloba, Farah Khorsandian-Sanchez, Diana Kliss, Carmen Koly, Oretha Kossigbo, Abina Kouya, Nataliya Kovalch, Evgenia Levina, Gayathri Mahalingam, Anali Makoui, Peter Malith, Ana Martinez, Jessica McIntyre, Bharath Natarajan, José Luis Oqueli, Enrique Perez, Irena Petrovic, Shukria Nizami, Sigrid Nord-Champie, Mark Pfeifer, Nazifa Rahimi Sidiq, Ramachander Rao Sriram, Maribel Raudales, Ashwin Ravikumar, Karin Rivas, Alberto Sato, Saket Srivastava, Balaji Subramanian, Cenia Tamo, Anjali Tyagi, Tanja Vurunic, Lisa Warner, and Valerie Weiler.

Special thanks for assistance in synthesizing data and editing text go to Jane Harvey, Paula Andrea Lopez, and Carter Winkle.

Colleagues from the Florida Center for Survivors of Torture in Clearwater, Florida, were most helpful in introducing me to fascinating respondents. Thank you, Janet Blair, Cynthia Hewiett, Rev. John Kivuva Mwiya, and Larisa Zaks.

Other friends who identified respondents and arranged interviews for me include Fred Lamar, Rachel Maddux, Barbara Smith-Palinkas, and Helen Stevens.

Preface

"But that's not cheating!" Both my young Colombian houseguests blurted out this reaction in unison. I had just related what I considered to be an appalling cheating incident in an undergraduate course that I was teaching. The wayward students in question had falsified a document, submitting it as their own work for a group grade. Days later a Bosnian respondent remarked, "I approve of cheating." It reinforces learning, he explained. "Oh yes, we really know how to cheat," a Salvadoran student chuckled, proceeding to fill me in on a long series of cheating strategies ranging from the ingenious to the downright foolish. "There is no one who would not cheat," seriously declared yet another respondent, this time from Ukraine.

My (apparently culturally derived) righteous indignation is aroused every time the subject of cheating is broached. For me it is a moral issue and a very personal one. I cheated once—only once—as a seventh grader longing for a perfect score on a geography quiz that required students to list all the African countries inhabited by the tsetse fly. I got caught, of course, and have never gotten over the shame. What bothered me, aside from my fall from grace, was that I didn't "have" to cheat. In other words, I was at the top of my class academically. Cheating, I firmly believed (at least until researching this book), was only for people who did not have the intellectual resources to succeed.

Today I am learning that "having to cheat" is a matter of interpretation. During my adolescent brush with cheating, my goal was to get an A+ on a quiz because I was accustomed to excelling and was not prepared to let a tsetse fly tarnish my flawless record. It was not a matter of failing to score among the top 5 percent of the entire population of graduating seniors in my country on a national exam that would determine whether or not I would have the chance to gain admission to one of the seven existing universities in my country. It did not occur to me to cheat in order to make sure I would get a job (not even a good job) when I graduated. Whether or not I would be able to put food on the table for my family when I grew up was not the kind of consequence I "had" to confront. Nor was I going to shame my family if my grades were mediocre. "If you want to be a ditch digger," my father used to say, "go ahead and be a ditch digger." "Just make sure you're a darned good one," he would add. The Indian friend with whom I shared this anecdote thought my father's position was scandalous. "My father would rather die than have a ditch digger for a son or daughter," she gasped. "Why did he not encourage you to become a doctor or a lawyer?"

Would I have been more prone to cheat if my parents watched my grades like a hawk? Would I have done it if the quiz were an annual exam that determined whether or not I would advance to Grade 8? Might I have cheated if I knew I would not be given partial credit for the countries I did correctly identify? Would I have cheated if the test had been oral rather than written? What if it were unannounced? Closed book? What if I could not play the odds via multiple-choice, fill-in-the-blank, matching, and true/false items but was expected to provide the sum and substance about all I knew about the tsetse fly in a short essay or presentation? What if all the other kids' parents were offering the teacher "incentives" in return for passing grades, but my parents could not afford to? What if there were no extra-credit points? To turn the tables, what if the other students in the class were depending on me, the smartest kid in the class, to deliver them from the aforementioned snares? And what if cheating had become so socially acceptable because of the pressure of these circumstances that it seemed more like an innocent prank rather than a moral failing?

There but for the grace of a U.S. education go I. But wait! Barely have the words appeared on my computer screen before I remember an article I read on the Internet. In a survey of U.S. high school and university students reported in 2004 (McCabeam), a full 76 percent of public school students revealed that they had cheated on a test at least once, and 61 percent admitted to plagiarizing. In another study reported by McCabeam (2004), who admitted to having cheated the most? *Answer:* business majors, male students, students with low GPAs, athletes, and members of fraternities and sororities. Why? Most report that they lacked sufficient time to study, that they succumbed to pressure from parents to do well in school, that they regarded the assignments on which they cheated as meaningless, that their teachers compelled them to cheat because the instructors had such poor pedagogical skills, that cheating off the Internet is too easy to resist, that students who do not cheat will be socially out of sync with classmates who do cheat, or that competition for jobs or entrance to prestigious degree programs is increasing.

So who are we to judge? One of the objectives of this book rests on just this question, namely to identify the circumstances that give rise to practices that may be considered common and acceptable in one country but strange and undesirable in another. An added dimension to this objective is emotional—to accept, to some extent, that this behavior is neither right nor wrong but in accordance with the environment in which it occurs.

Other objectives of the volume include:

- To anticipate that there will be differences between the way refugee and immigrant learners regard learning and the way North Americans perceive the process and practice of education.
- To inform educators and others who work with refugees and immigrants about the specific schooling traditions, practices, circumstances, and expectations that follow these individuals to their new homes in North America.

■ To enable North American teachers and other school personnel not only to better understand the backgrounds of their students but to more effectively address these learners' needs and help them to succeed academically and adjust culturally.

The degree to which the information contained in this book may support these objectives is limited by two main factors. The first is the extent to which readers translate the factual data about schools in various countries into insights and insights into action. In other words, while awareness itself of background differences is beneficial, finding a concrete way to enhance a student's learning and adjustment can be much more powerful. The second limitation lies in the inability of a resource guide such as this, with its coverage of 18 different countries, to offer an in-depth treatment of each country's educational, cultural, and linguistic systems. As much as possible, I have identified the dominant trends, pivotal events, and essential factors that emerged in my research. To the best of my ability, I did not impose my own interpretation on the data but let my sources speak through the text. However, when generalization became unavoidable, I did exercise caution and used "red flags" with terms such as *in general, tends to,* and *many people.*

The content of this book is based on data derived from a variety of sources: informants originating from the countries represented in the text, long-term visitors to the countries covered in the book, teachers of students whose countries are described, service providers who are in regular contact with refugees and immigrants, official government documents emanating from the United States as well as ministries of education abroad, reports and articles published by well-known and highly respected national and international organizations and agencies, journal articles, books, transcripts of National Public Radio features, magazines, newspapers, and Internet websites. The reader is directed to the Select Bibliography at the back of the book for a more complete and specific list of the sources and will note that the chapters themselves contain a minimum of in-text citations.

The countries chosen for presentation herein by and large represent those from which most of today's U.S. immigrants, refugees, asylum seekers, and undocumented residents were born (see Table 1). Several countries from the list were addressed in an earlier University of Michigan Press publication, *Understanding Your International Students: An Educational, Cultural, and Linguistic Guide,* edited by me and published in 2003. The previous volume focused almost exclusively on students of university-level English for Academic Purposes and the countries from which they originate—namely, Brazil, Colombia, Côte d'Ivoire, Egypt, Japan, Korea, Mexico, Morocco, People's Republic of China, Russia, Saudi Arabia, and Taiwan. Because certain areas of the United States have a high concentration of immigrants and refugees from Cuba, Haiti, Poland, and Vietnam enrolled in community college ESL programs, those countries were included as well. Abbreviated chapters on Kuwait, Thailand, Turkey, United Arab Emirates, and Venezuela have been posted on the University of Michigan website (*www.press.umich.edu/esl*).

The primary difference between the previous volume and this one is that the former focuses essentially, though not exclusively, on non-immigrant residents. While greater numbers of international students are findings jobs in North America and requesting that their status be changed to permanent residents, the vast majority return to their home countries. Thus, their residence may range from a few months to a several years. Immigrants, on the other hand, leave their homes looking for a new life. It is almost always a permanent change. Refugees flee their homes and the imminent danger that surrounds them, often spending many years in refugee camps in neighboring countries while waiting for the violence that drove them away to subside or for host countries to process their requests for resettlement to a new country. Many refugees dream of returning to their home countries even after many years of residence in their adopted land. Asylees or asylum seekers, unlike refugees, do not request protection and a safe haven until after they have arrived in the new country. Often they are desperate to escape threats and persecution at home and either do not know about or cannot afford to wait out the long and laborious legal process through which refugees must otherwise proceed. Undocumented residents deliberately avoid any legal procedures to gain the right to live in the United States for fear that they will be deported and thus condemned to a hard and short life of poverty, sickness, violence, and often repression.

The result is a wave of newcomers the size of which is unprecedented in the history of the United States, and it is not expected to subside any time soon. The U.S. Census Bureau has projected that the total population of the country will rise to 400,000,000 within the next 50 years largely because of immigration. The Census Bureau reports that some 1,300,000 legal and illegal immigrants each year take up residence in the United States. Of the 288,000,000 people living in the United States today, roughly 11.5 percent are foreign-born. Indeed, the number of newcomers since 1970 who have made the States their new home now exceeds the total number of immigrants ever to have settled in the United States prior to that year (Camarota and McArdle 2003). Where they settle has changed, too (see Table 2). Minnesota has this past year surpassed Florida in refugee resettlement, and many midwestern states, long bastions of European homogeneity out "in the middle of nowhere," now have a new look and sound. Mary Pipher offers an exquisite description of the cultural and ethnic transition of her Lincoln, Nebraska community in her book *The Middle of Everywhere.*

Earlier it was stated that the fundamental difference between the previous volume *(Understanding Your International Students)* and the present one *(Understanding Your Refugee and Immigrant Students)* lay in the populations that each book describes, namely international students versus refugees and immigrants. This critical distinction influenced the organization as well as the content of the current work. For example, because poverty plays such a key role in the lives of many refugees, data concerning per capita income, percentage of the population living below the poverty line, literacy rate, and life expectancy were added to the initial description of each country. Also now included in the discussion of the historical background of each country is a brief summary of the immigration patterns of its people, particularly with respect to their migration to the United States.

To the deep culture section of each chapter a list of proverbs and a folk tale from the country under review were introduced since both forms of folklore are used by members of virtually every culture to communicate the worldview of the community and to inculcate into each successive generation the basic values of the group. No attempt was made to interpret these items. As simple as they may appear, they are charged with a complex blend of undertones and associations best left to the reader to discover through reflection and discussion with representatives of the culture whose folklore is under the microscope.

Like the previous volume, *Understanding Your Refugee and Immigrant Students* contains a personal perspective (called Personal Snapshot in the earlier work). This brief section allows the voice of an individual with first-hand experience in the target country to be heard. Thus, contributors include refugees, immigrants, and their relatives as well as U.S. teachers, former Peace Corps volunteers, and visitors to the countries under review. Some of the insights came directly from face-to-face or e-mail interviews while others were drawn from Internet sources such as blogs.

Finally, as far as changes between the two volumes are concerned, the reader may note that the section headings have been modified slightly. For example, the section called Personal Snapshot in the preceding book is now simply Personal Perspective, the Cultural Close-Up is now Deep Culture Perspective, and A Closer Look and Protocol are now merged to form Surface Culture Perspective. The general type of information contained within each section remains unchanged, but the new headings more effectively capture the distinct focus of the section content.

A comparison of the content of each chapter, however, will reveal that specific topics, such as sexuality or conversational style, may not be consistently addressed in each chapter of the book. During the research process, when mention of particular cultural phenomena emerged frequently or with unusual vigor, they were integrated into the text. When information about certain cultural issues was difficult to access or when the data collected were ambiguous, sparse, or inappropriate, the decision was often made to forego discussion of such issues.

No single book can address every question and concern relevant to immigration, its impact on education, and its effect on those who cross borders—physical and cultural. Teachers of all disciplines, school administrators, policymakers, curriculum developers, physical and mental health care providers, safety professionals, clerical staff, and many others at all levels of the educational system are now confronted regularly by the realities of immigration. But they do so with a severely limited reservoir of resources, training, and knowledge to see them through.

State-funded and federally funded programs have begun to assist with the adjustments that are required if schools are to effectively respond to the needs of immigrant and refugee students. Sadly, most are inadequate despite the intentions of project directors, whose efforts are too often thwarted by the sheer breadth of the task at hand. Teaching people who have been uprooted from family, friends, and familiar surroundings, traditions, and values introduces unique challenges that were not commonly found in the mainstream North American classroom of a decade or so ago. General cultural adjustment is only one fragment of the kaleidoscope of today's classroom. Symptoms of post-traumatic stress disorder is another; language difficulties another. The gap between schooling practices "back home" and those in North America adds an extra dimension of complexity to the situation.

Understanding Your Refugee and Immigrant Students provides an excellent starting point for anyone interested in helping to narrow this gap. Readers who use this book as a reference to quickly inform themselves about the background of a specific group of newcomers or those who work systematically through the text, underlining or highlighting passages that strike them as particularly compelling or jotting comments and questions in the margins, will in the process identify issues and topics that will inevitably find their way into discussions with friends, family, coworkers, supervisors, or perhaps even with the refugees and immigrants with whom they interact. Sharing insights with others often moves individuals to a higher level of understanding and motivates them to seek further discoveries. Some readers may wish to use this volume in a more structured and purposeful way. Faculty in teacher education programs at the university level and social studies teachers at the middle and high school levels, for example, may consider the following options as assignments for their students:

- *Mini-ethnographic Interviews*: use selected chapters from the text to prepare for mini-ethnographic interviews of classmates or others in the community who may be refugees or immigrants
- *Compare/Contrast*: compare a single variable across countries (e.g., literacy rates around the world or classroom-based non-verbal communication in five countries), by region (e.g., immigration patterns among Latin Americans), or between the United States and another country (e.g., expectations of parents in the United States or Canada versus Ukraine)
- *Country Reports*: assign student presentations summarizing individual countries using a multi-media format
- *Values Clarification*: identify the cultural values that underlie a set of classroom practices in the country of origin that diverge from those in the host country

- *Reflections*: reflect on thoughts and feelings one might have if one were to trade places with a refugee or immigrant from a particular country

- *Losses and Gains*: identify material, cultural, and personal losses and gains one might experience as a result of being a refugee or immigrant from a particular country

- *Problem/Solution*: ask a representative from a specific country to respond to the Potential Adjustment Challenges scenario at the end of the selected chapter and compare that person's response with the one given in the book

- *Proverbs*: find the English equivalents of the proverbs provided in each chapter; speculate about the values and messages reflected in the proverbs that have no English equivalents

- *Newcomers' Guide*: using the same section headings seen in the text, create a guidebook called *Understanding Your New School* to introduce refugee and immigrant students and/or their parents to the cultural practices and expectations of your institution.

In a word, *Understanding Your Refugee and Immigrant Students* can serve as more than a reference guide. Though it is packed with hundreds of interesting cultural tidbits, its ability to inform is just one of several functions it can serve.

When I set out to research this book, I knew I would be fascinated by what I would discover. I did not realize how humbling an experience it would be, however. Stuck in my mind was a fanciful Neil Diamond-esque "they're comin' to America" image of immigrants, full of excitement and promise. Despite what I had read in the newspaper and seen on television about the impact of war, poverty, repression, ethnic cleansing, and the like on human beings in other countries, it was not until I filled my hours, head, and heart with the details of the day-to-day lives of these people that my perspective began to change. At first I was amazed at and deeply grateful for my good fortune. *How charmed is my life compared to those of so many others in the world!* Next, I experienced crushing guilt. *Why is it that I'm so blessed, but others are not? And what am I supposed to do about it?* Then came awe. *How strong these people are! How brave! How resilient.* And finally, faith. *If we, as humans, are engineered in basically the same way, then their strength is my strength, their courage is my courage, and their resilience is my resilience.*

It is my hope that those who read this book will make the vicarious journey from homeland to adopted country and gain a deeper appreciation for how schools back home affect classrooms here.

—Jeffra Flaitz, 2006

Table 1. Country of Birth and Number of Immigrants, [Refugees/Asylees, and] Undocumented Persons Entering the U.S.: Fiscal Years [1990] and 2000

Country	Immigrants 1990–2004	Refugees/Asylees 1991–2004	Undocumented
Afghanistan	26,961	13,160	
Bosnia-Herzegovina	104,862	101,834	
Brazil	92,308	277	
Colombia	224,213	2,566	
Côte d'Ivoire	5,953	399	
Croatia	14,548	9,362	
Cuba	277,273	215,917	
Dominican Republic	483,748	279	
Ecuador	124,891	348	
Egypt	69,763	1,325	
El Salvador	418,098	4,912	
Ethiopia	81,191	23,390	
Guatemala	197,618	3,523	
Haiti	275,789	11,876	
Honduras	102,030	1,482	158,000
India	675,854	7,742	70,000
Indonesia	27,963	413	n/a
Iran	178,785	36,479	15,000
Iraq	58,640	32,022	n/a
Japan	98,813	45	14,000
Korea	277,665	40	55,000
Laos	58,751	38,584	n/a
Liberia	27,685	8,746	11,000
Mexico	3,647,466	790	4,808,000
Morocco	36,875	36	6,000
Nicaragua	148,195	23,423	21,000
People's Republic of China	665,911	10,799	115,000
Peru	165,805	3,765	61,000
Philippines	776,995	1,190	85,000
Poland	239,489	7,687	467
Russia	196,586	74,560	46,000
Saudi Arabia	12,080	1,109	n/a
Somalia	34,466	29,202	n/a
Sudan	22,601	11,382	1,000
Taiwan	159,419	n/a	n/a
Thailand	73,290	24,380	n/a
Turkey	42,293	680	6,000
Ukraine	208,810	139,800	n/a
Vietnam	592,725	228,546	n/a

Sources

Office of Homeland Security, "Immigration by Region and Selected Country of Last Residence: Fiscal Years 1820–2004."

Office of Homeland Security, "Refugees and Asylees Granted Lawful Permanent Resident Status and Selected Country of Birth: Fiscal Years 1946–2004."

Office of Homeland Security, U.S. Immigration and Naturalization Service, Office of Policy and Planning, "Estimates of the Unauthorized Immigrant Population Residing in the United States: 1990 to 2000."

Table 2. U.S. State Residency of the Foreign Born in 2000

Country		State 1	State 2	State 3	State 4	State 5	State 6	State 7
Mexico	9,161,419	CA 3,889,695	TX 1,870,787	IL 609,0068	AZ 435,001	GA 196,011	CO 192,427	FL 189,819
China/Hong Kong/Taiwan	1,492,532	CA 556,283	NY 292,717	NJ 71,035	TX 67,366	MA 53,495	IL 50,383	WA 35,876
Philippines	1,394,675	CA 670,560	HI 104,862	NY 74,061	NJ 70,670	IL 67,840	WA 46,382	TX 45,665
India	1,018,393	CA 197,918	NY 117,889	NJ 117,687	IL 86,242	TX 78,172	MI 39,470	PA 38,767
Vietnam	986,198	CA 408,581	TX 104,356	WA 41,636	FL 33,260	GA 32,811	MA 31,805	VA 31,479
Former USSR	890,530	NY 233,724	CA 181,800	IL 56,274	NJ 47,687	PA 44,998	WA 43,846	MA 38,561
Cuba	878,085	FL 652,660	NJ 52,525	CA 40,644	NY 37,749	TX 15,581	IL 9,547	NV 7,206
Korea	857,387	CA 269,346	NY 91,568	NJ 50,092	VA 39,346	IL 37,787	WA 36,811	TX 34,469
Canada	843,880	CA 135,135	FL 100,922	NY 58,548	MI 53,704	WA 48,666	TX 40,247	MA 38,043
El Salvador	824,692	CA 365,356	TX 98,247	NY 69,191	VA 55,923	MD 37,980	NJ 25,547	FL 24,685
Germany	712,175	CA 92,481	NY 67,544	FL 64,409	TX 40,041	NJ 34,154	IL 33,882	PA 24,230
Dom. Rep.	710,985	NY 415,026	NJ 106,120	FL 69,449	MA 41,551	RI 16,172	PA 9,078	CT 6,974
UK	674,211	CA 131,648	FL 63,029	NY 61,627	TX 34,385	NJ 31,206	MA 25,658	VA 21,049
Jamaica	513,228	NY 214,993	FL 127,591	NJ 30,100	CT 28,757	MD 20,804	MA 13,749	GA 11,845
Colombia	500,413	FL 157,3007	NY 112,484	NJ 79,902	CA 29,105	TX 18,567	MA 14,628	CT 13,222
Poland	480,492	IL 139,729	NY 97,643	NJ 59,182	CA 29,861	FL 27,764	CA 24,628	MI 16,296
Italy	473,756	NY 147,372	NJ 58,669	CA 39,932	FL 31,088	MA 30,208	PA 28,752	CT 26,443
Guatemala	468,583	CA 205,885	FL 35,499	NY 26,722	IL 22,355	TX 21,540	NJ 16,841	VA 15,095
Haiti	408,731	FL 166,778	NY 123,737	MA 33,640	NJ 29,620	IL 7,602	CT 7,019	PA 5,508
Japan	345,566	CA 111,453	NY 33,383	HI 19,840	WA 14,912	IL 13,833	TX 13,174	FL 11,295
Iran	282,326	CA 160,456	NY 18,261	TX 13,557	MD 11,734	VA 10,979	FL 8,927	IL 5,392
Ecuador	281,137	NY 127,451	NJ 43,224	FL 27,326	CA 24,340	CT 10,127	IL 9,288	MA 4,711
Peru	268,896	FL 49,919	NJ 49,444	VA 43,436	NY 40,190	VA 16,661	TX 11,612	MD 63,396
Fmr Yugoslavia	274,602	NY 50,801	IL 35,258	CA 28,421	MI 17,017	OH 15,568	NJ 15,372	FL 12,569
Honduras	253,615	FL 50,599	CA 42,614	NY 37,530	TX 31,430	NJ 17,779	LA 9,317	VA 7,802
Nicaragua	232,039	FL 98,021	CA 70,001	NY 11,525	TX 11,180	LA 5,918	LA 4,176	NJ 3,565
Portugal	221,282	MA 65,382	NJ 35,778	FL 35,273	FL 23,357	NY 16,596	NY 14,821	FL 5,398
Pakistan	218,777	NY 44,636	TX 30,640	NJ 28,714	IL 21,893	NJ 19,257	NJ 15,950	FL 8,832
Brazil	211,260	FL 43,082	MA 38,566	NY 23,577	NY 20,857	NJ 20,519	NJ 10,726	TX 7,175
Guyana	200,837	NY 130,154	FL 17,034	NJ 14,402	CA 6,547	MD 4,877	MD 4,012	TX 3,569
Laos	196,079	CA 63,574	MN 26,281	WI 15,762	TX 10,452	NC 6,456	WA 5,891	MI 5,707
Trinidad and Tobago	194,083	NY 97,073	FL 27,989	NJ 12,738	MD 12,466	CA 7,489	TX 5,418	MA 5,388
Thailand	168,158	CA 64,889	MN 10,229	WA 8,419	NY 7,807	IL 6,809	TX 6,557	WI 6,205
Greece	163,645	NY 35,980	NJ 18,360	IL 17,708	MA 13,938	CA 13,820	FL 9,636	PA 8,693

Source: Camarota and McArdle. *Where Immigrants Live.*

Contents

El Salvador

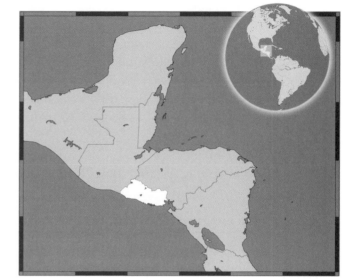

■ EL SALVADOR *Upclose*

Capital: San Salvador

Population: 6,822,378 (June 2006)

Size: 21,040 sq. km. (8,124 sq. mi.) (slightly smaller than Massachusetts)

Location: in Central America between Guatemala to the northwest and Honduras to the northeast and bordered by the Pacific Ocean on the west

Climate: tropical on the coast with rainy season from May to October and dry season from November to April, but temperate in higher regions

Terrain: mountainous with narrow coastal region and central plains

Monetary Unit: U.S. dollar

Religion: 83% Roman Catholic, with a presence of nearly 1 million Protestant evangelicals

Language(s): Spanish, Nahua (an Amerindian language)

Literacy Rate: total population 80.2%; men 82.8%; women 77.7% (2003)

Ethnicity: mestizo (mixed Ameridian-Spanish or assimilated Amerindian) 90%, Amerindian 1%, white 9%

Per Capita Income: US$1,943 (2006)

Population Distribution: 60% urban, 40% rural (2003)

Population below Poverty Line: 36.1% (2004)

Life Expectancy: total population 70.92 years; men 67.31 years; women 74.7 years (2006)

Government: republic

PUBLIC HOLIDAYS		
	January 1	New Year's Day
	week before Easter*	Holy Week
	May 1	Labor Day
	June 22	Teachers' Day
	August 3, 4, 5, 6	*Semana de Agosto* (Feast of San Salvador)
	September 15	Independence Day
	October 12	Columbus Day
	November 2	*Día de los Muertos* (All Souls' Day)
	December 25	Christmas
	December 31	New Year's Eve
		variable dates

■ Personal Perspective

When I came to the United States, I found studying to be very easy. I was happy about that because in El Salvador school is very demanding. Here, for example, tests cover a whole range of items, from easy to difficult, but at home all the questions were the hardest ones imaginable, so you study for the hardest ones. You don't have a choice. If you fail, you fail. There are no second chances, no summer school.

—Salvadoran university student in the United States

■ Historical Perspective

IMMIGRATION TO THE UNITED STATES

Large-scale Salvadoran immigration to the United States, legal and illegal, began in the early 1980s as those caught in the midst of a violent civil war sought refuge abroad. In addition to death squads that roamed the country arbitrarily murdering some 70,000 citizens, social and political repression and major economic failings on a national scale caused great suffering and sacrifice on the part of the people of El Salvador. Between 1979 and 1991, more than one-fifth of the population (approximately 1.5 million)—mostly young, high school–educated men—fled the country.

Today approximately one Salvadoran in 1,000 leaves the country, primarily to find work abroad. Most Salvadoran immigrants in the United States occupy blue-collar positions, but nearly 25 percent of El Salvador's immigrants aged 25 or older have attended college. Studies report that approximately 25 percent of Salvadoran families in the States have an annual income of US$50,000 or more. In fact, 81 percent of male Salvadoran immigrants are employed. While some 50 percent earn less than US$30,000 per year, most families are able to earn enough *migradollars* to send home. An estimated US$2.5 billion are reinvested in El Salvador this way. The practice not only helps support remaining family members but is considered a type of development aid for El Salvador as it constitutes more than 17 percent of the country's gross domestic product.

According to the 2000 U.S. Census, almost 825,000 Salvadoran immigrants were living in the United States. This number, however, provides only part of the picture as many who registered during the last census did not indicate their specific country of origin. Some estimates place the actual number of Salvadorans at two million. Many, however, are undocumented. The states reporting the largest numbers of immigrants from El Salvador according to 2003 data include, in numeric order, California, Texas, New York, Virginia, Maryland, New Jersey, and Florida.

HISTORICAL SYNOPSIS

In 1821 El Salvador won its independence from Spain, afterward belonging to the Central American Federation until 1839. A succession of military governments administered the nation for more than a century. Their reputation for brutality and repression and the dramatically widening socioeconomic gulf between rich and poor led to a left-wing insurgency in the late 1970s to which the military government responded with a severe crackdown on dissidents and benign indifference to the formation of paramilitary death squads. Throughout the 1970s and 1980s the Salvadoran government was supported by the U.S. government through the investment of some US$4 billion in aid and military training. The civil war that erupted during this period lasted 12 years and ended with peace accords in 1992.

Though improvements are under way, the country is still plagued with serious economic and social problems largely brought about by the enormous gap and resulting inequalities between rich and poor. To complicate matters, El Salvador's population is disproportionately large in comparison to its land mass and constitutes the smallest nation in Central America. Malnutrition and disease proliferate in the countryside, and medical attention, whether one lives in an urban or rural area, is reported to be poor. It is estimated that 85 percent of El Salvador's water is undrinkable and that the number of deaths resulting from consuming contaminated water surpasses the death toll from the country's civil war.

The 1992 peace accords brought democracy to El Salvador as well as modernization of education and industry. Despite the promise of a brighter future, the plight of many Salvadorans remains a critical issue. The loss of adult men to the war or to emigration has created a generation of young people whose families are either led by a single mother (25 percent of households) or whose parents are working abroad, leaving them in the care of grandparents or other struggling relatives. For approximately 8 percent of those under the age of 18, both parents are living abroad. The incidence of gang activity, school dropouts, and teen pregnancy has skyrocketed as a result. A reported 60 percent of Salvadoran children today are born out of wedlock, and many children end up living on the street without the structure or emotional and financial support of even a single-parent family. Other Salvadoran youth whose parents have emigrated enjoy many of the amenities so coveted by their peers in the United States. Being on the receiving end of CD and DVD players, fashionable clothing, and even cars leaves some young people feeling that hard work and discipline are irrelevant to their lives. Their school performance suffers as a result, and it is not unusual for these young people to become cynical and apathetic, believing as they sometimes do that they have no control over their futures. Finally, because the country's military governments have failed repeatedly to recognize the severe poverty and desperation of the majority of Salvadorans, the memory of widespread death, torture, fear, and paranoia has not been extinguished.

■ Deep Culture Perspective

DEEP CULTURE BELIEFS

- Salvadoran culture is more collectivist than individualistic. Interdependence of friends, coworkers, and family allows individuals to receive the support of the group with the expectation of reciprocity as needed in the future. A nurturing and cooperative attitude toward one another is strongly encouraged, although individuals from wealthier families may promote a greater degree of competitiveness.

- Women are generally assigned traditional roles. Girls are expected to marry, look after children, and obey their husbands, none of which requires an education, according to both parents and daughters. Girls are expected to be chaste on their wedding night, but the value of chastity for young men is not equally important. While *machismo* is commonly understood to be part of Salvadoran culture, the female version is less obvious but still prevalent. *Machisma* or *matriarquia* characterizes a woman who at home controls the family by vehemently scolding its members, especially the husband. A *mandona,* or one who orders another person about, may bully a husband into doing household chores and fetching items from the store.

- Men are not only the family's wage earners, but they occupy most positions of authority and power in virtually every aspect of Salvadoran culture, although this is slowly changing. Sometimes men look down on women, and domestic abuse is not uncommon nor is sexual harassment at work or in public. Fathers and mothers alike are complicit in fostering the values and behaviors of *machismo* in their sons. Boys are encouraged to attend school and to use their formal training to support their future families. They are allowed to be more independent than girls.

- Salvadorans have a reputation for hard work to the extent that laziness is thought to be sinful. Regardless of one's occupation, if a person is holding down a job, he (less often she) is considered worthy of the respect of others.

- Salvadorans tend to respect rules, regulations, and other forms of control. Many are averse to risk and change.

- Humility is a virtue that most Salvadorans value in themselves and others as is self-discipline in the face of adversity. Bavolek (1997) reports that the top five values of Salvadorans are family unity, religion, respect for elders, hard work, and education.

- El Salvador is called "the land of the smile" in recognition of its friendly and outgoing people.

PROVERBS

- A closed mouth gathers no flies.
- The one who does not cry does not suckle.
- He who goes to bed with a baby wakes up wet.
- The sleeping shrimp gets carried away by the current.
- He who wants blue sky has to work for it.
- Better one bird in the hand than a hundred in the air.

FOLK TALE

According to Mayan legend, a beautiful young woman gave birth to a son who was the offspring of an illicit love affair. The woman's father, ashamed and furious, cast an evil spell on both mother and child. For his part, the boy was cursed to live his whole life the size of a child. Moreover, his feet were turned backward as a reflection of the twisted love between his mother and father. Indeed, as he got older, he became quite ugly. He was the size of a ten-year-old, had a shiny fat belly, and his toenails were long and pointed. He wandered from village to village wearing nothing more than a hat, so that people, and especially young girls, were afraid of him. El Cipitío was rarely seen, however. At night he would creep into homes and scrounge for burned bread crusts left in the ashes.

El Cipitío had a tendency to fall in love easily. He would appear to the girl of his fancy when she was all alone, declare his love, and beg her to marry him. One day he approached Rufina in this way. Rufina's mother calmed her daughter's fear and gave her a secret that she could use to get rid of El Cipitío. The next day Rufina told El Cipitío that he must demonstrate his love for her by traveling to the ocean and bringing back a wave. El Cipitío was filled with joy and happily left for the sea but never returned.

Administrative Perspective

OFFICIAL EDUCATIONAL POLICY

In 1995 El Salvador's Ministry of Education (MINED) launched a ten-year plan to reform secondary education. The plan calls for making education available to a greater number of adolescents, raising educational standards, and improving school administration. These objectives are part of MINED's four overarching goals, namely to prepare Salvadoran youth for participation in the global marketplace, engender responsible citizenship to promote peace, develop greater appreciation for diversity, and provide the training necessary to overcome generations of poverty. While these measures are aimed at reducing Salvadoran youth's interest in gang activity and violence, the rising rate of teen pregnancy, and the overall disaffection of young people, El Salvador's leaders hope these reforms will also improve the country's economic well being.

The curricular changes under way include requiring students to spend 40 hours per week in class as compared with the 27-hour seat-time requirement before the plan was implemented. New methodologies are also being introduced to replace the previous emphasis on memorization and mechanical learning strategies, and new courses on the environment, population, health, equity, values, human rights, and consumerism are being not just added to the conventional curriculum but integrated into it so that courses in physics, algebra, or geography, for example, become more practical by addressing the social, economic, and political contexts that give them meaning.

EDUCATION AT A GLANCE

See the Education at a Glance table on page 7.

Level/Age	Hours/Calendar	Language of Instruction	Compulsory Attendance	Exams	Grading System	Curriculum	Cost	Enrollment
Parvularia (pre-school) ages 4–5	Variable	Spanish	No	None	None	Language development and social skills		42% of total pre-school-age children are enrolled
Kinder (kindergarten) age 6	Jan. 15 to Oct. 31 (public schools)	Spanish	No	None	None	Pre-reading skills taught in some private pre-schools		No data available
Basica (primary) Grades 1–9 ages 7–15	Late Aug. to early June (private schools) Public schools: 7:00 AM–noon with 20-minute midmorning break Private schools: 7:00 AM–3:00 PM with midmorning and lunch break	Spanish, but English in bilingual schools. Sometimes the same curriculum is offered in English in the morning and Spanish in the afternoon.	Yes, up to age 14	Fill-in-the-blank, essay, definitions, summaries, paraphrasing. Some oral testing; recitation of memorized lists of terms or definitions Students must pass all final course exams in order to advance to next grade (one out of every two children nationwide has repeated at least one grade). University entrance exam introduced in early 1990s, but little academic competition for admission.	0–10 scale 6–10 pass 0–5 fail No letter grades are assigned.	Mathematics, local and national language, science, music, social studies/history; reading; art	Free for public school students, but school fees come to approximately US$275 per year. Tuition at binational or bilingual private schools; the most expensive private schools, may reach US$2,500 per year plus a US$3,000 initial sign-up fee.	80.9% of primary school-age children are enrolled. 71% of primary school students are girls. 80.7% of primary school-age male students are enrolled. 70.7% of primary school students reach 5th grade. 23% of the Salvadoran adult population has no formal education; 21% has 1–3 years; 23% has 4–6 years. The average Salvadoran adult has 5.2 years of schooling.
Bachillerato General Grades 10–11 ages 15–17 *Bachillerato Vocacional* Grades 10–12 ages 15–18			No			*Bachillerato General* Students take language and literature, mathematics, natural sciences, social and civic studies, foreign language, information systems, adolescent psychology, plus optional activities. *Bachillerato Vocacional* Students take specialized courses for the job market.		39.3% of secondary school-age children are enrolled. 36.7% of secondary school-age girls are enrolled; 37% of eligible males are enrolled. 14% of the adult Salvadoran population has 7–9 years of education; 12% has 10–12 years.
University ages 17+ 1st stage (technical): 2–4 yrs 2nd stage (bachelor's): 5 yrs 3rd stage (master's): 2 yrs after bachelor's 4th stage (doctorate): 7 yrs	Same as above with classes held during the day and evening	Spanish	No	Written thesis required at end of the 5th year of the undergraduate degree.		No general education requirements. Students proceed directly to specializations. No electives.	Public universities can cost as little as US$36 per year, but more typically tuition costs between US$400 and US$2,000 per year.	18% of secondary school graduates are enrolled in universities. 7% of the Salvadoran population has 13+ years of education.

■ Surface Culture Perspective

CLASSROOMS

- There are enormous differences between public and private schools and between urban and rural schools in El Salvador, particularly in terms of facilities. Ninety percent of El Salvador's secondary schools exist in urban areas, and 98 percent of private schools are city based. In addition, urban schools in general receive disproportionately favorable amounts of government funding. The San Salvador school district, for example, receives nearly 50 percent of the government's educational allocation. Some 45 percent of secondary school students attend private schools. Public schools and classrooms tend to be in chronic disrepair with worse conditions prevalent in rural settings. Very few schools have air conditioning. Rural schools may consist of little more than sheets of corrugated metal propped up on two-by-fours over a dirt floor.

- Basic supplies such as blackboards and chalk—particularly those that are up-to-date—may be scarce. Students are given a list of school supplies that they must purchase to begin the school year. Schools do not supply books, paper, pencils, erasers, rulers, or any other student materials. These can be costly, especially for families with a large number of children in school.

- Decorations such as flags, posters, and portraits of Salvadoran leaders are generally not present in classrooms.

- School campuses may vary as far as layout is concerned. Most are one-, two-, or three-story structures without corridors, cafeterias, assembly halls, health rooms, computer labs, gyms, or libraries. There is usually an open space where students congregate for recess or school assemblies, and small kiosks where students may purchase snacks may be on or near campus. Some schools have a small *capilla* or chapel on campus. Many private schools (even some small universities) operate out of private homes.

- Official reports estimate the teacher-student ratio at the primary level to be 1:25. At the secondary level, the ratio is 1:29. However, actual figures are much higher due to problems with educational data collection and reporting in El Salvador.

TEACHERS' STATUS

- Salvadorans hold teachers in the same high esteem as they do doctors, priests, and other professionals. English teachers, in particular, are well respected.

- Primary and secondary school teachers receive three years of university or technical institute preparation before they begin their careers in education.

- Teachers in El Salvador work under difficult circumstances and receive very low pay, necessitating many to take on additional assignments in private schools or to teach more than one shift at their home schools. As a result, some teachers may be in the classroom for up to 12 hours per day from 7:00 AM to 7:00 PM.
- The mean monthly salary for teachers in 2002 was approximately US$380.
- A law introduced in 1995 aims to improve the quality of education by rewarding teachers who pursue advanced degrees and demonstrate excellence in the classroom. According to this law, pay increases for teachers are to be earned as a result of their credentials and performance rather than length of tenure in the school system.
- Many teachers suffered persecution and death if they chose to join a teachers' union during the country's civil war. The decline in the number of teachers led to the informal establishment of a volunteer teaching system.

TEACHER-STUDENT RELATIONSHIP

- According to Salvadoran students and their parents, teachers hold among the highest positions possible in a community.
- Neither children nor parents are likely to challenge a teacher's decision. The teacher may be very direct in advising parents how to treat children at home and reprimanding parents when their children misbehave or do not try hard enough in school. Classes are cancelled on parent-teacher conference days; the event is too important to relegate to an evening time slot.
- The relationship between teacher and student is similar to that in North America. At the beginning, interactions tend to be more formal, but later, depending on the teacher, the relationship may become friendlier, yet still be respectful. In terms of strictness, however, Salvadoran teachers are considered to be less lenient than U.S. teachers in the event of misbehavior and more serious in their expectations of students.
- Teachers expect students to be attentive and quiet during the lesson. Students are seated in rows rather than in clusters or pairs in order to discourage socializing during class.

TEACHING PRACTICES

- Traditional teaching practices still prevail in El Salvador, meaning that teachers tend to be authoritarian and discourage active student participation. The teacher has full control over the content, pace, and structure of the class.
- One of the most common teaching strategies in El Salvador is dictation. Teachers read from a text while students record the lecture verbatim in their copybooks, or teachers write notes on the blackboard for students

to copy carefully. Rote memorization of the notes followed by recitation, either individually or in chorus, is standard practice. Teachers may also base their lectures on the textbook rather than read from it verbatim. This allows them to clarify concepts and terms so that the students benefit more from the material.

- The students' comprehension of the homework is determined the day after it is assigned by posing questions about the text that correspond to the level of difficulty and mastery expected of the students. If the students have difficulty with the questions, the teacher proceeds to explain and elaborate upon the concepts to reinforce and prepare the students for upcoming exams.

TEACHERS' DRESS

- Some private schools require teachers to wear uniforms. At a private religious school for girls, for example, the teachers may wear ankle-length skirts and high-collared blouses.
- Younger teachers today can wear their regular street clothes to class. Their attire may include jeans.

DISCIPLINE AND CLASS MANAGEMENT

- It is not unusual for more traditional teachers to use mild corporal punishment to respond to inappropriate student behavior. They may, for example, strike a student's hand with a wooden ruler. More modern teachers may simply send the misbehaving student to the principal's office. Another common practice is to move the student's desk out of the classroom and oblige him or her to sit there until class is finished. Sometimes teachers will report offensive behavior to parents via the student's daily pocket agenda. Such notes are expected to be read and signed by the parents and returned to the teacher. Teachers may also use the student's agenda to report a low grade on an assignment.
- Infractions that will usually result in punishment include talking in class while the teacher is lecturing, throwing objects, or hitting other students.
- Most schools have a weekly activity called *Lunes Cívico*. Every Monday the students arrange themselves by grade and class in the school courtyard, sing the national anthem, and recite the pledge of allegiance. Each week different students are selected to carry the El Salvador flag and, in some schools, those from other Central American countries. A tribute to one of these countries may follow and may include singing the national anthem of the selected country and/or performing dances or reciting historical or cultural facts about that chosen nation.

STUDENTS' CIRCUMSTANCES

- Schools in the countryside can be located too far from a child's home to make attendance possible. Rural secondary schools are not as prevalent as primary schools.
- Primary education is free, but such items as mandatory school uniforms, monthly school fees, and basic supplies can cost up to US$275 per year, a sum that is often beyond the means of rural families.
- When children from poor families reach adolescence, their attendance at school may be regarded as too great a sacrifice to continue. Consequently, many students drop out to help at home with childcare or fieldwork or by selling a range of inexpensive items such as tortillas or cigarettes on the street.
- Students often live in abject conditions and come from dirty neighborhoods and overcrowded homes constructed from cinderblock and corrugated metal over a cement floor. Hot water is a luxury that most families cannot enjoy; 30 percent of urban and 78 percent of rural households do not have running water at all. Air pollution in the cities has become a major problem.
- Appliances such as telephones, stoves, microwaves, and washing machines are rare, although many homes have a television. Programs broadcast from the United States are popular. Many Salvadorans own cell phones.
- After immigrating to the United States, most Salvadorans are resigned to living in substandard housing in unsafe neighborhoods while working multiple, low-paying menial jobs. Their absence from home often leaves children essentially unsupervised and feeling insecure.
- In all likelihood, Salvadoran immigrants who entered the United States in the 1980s suffered extreme hardship, terror, and danger both at home and in their exodus, especially if they were escorted here by *coyotes,* or border smugglers. They arrived traumatized and with little formal education or English language skills. They may pass deeply rooted feelings of anxiety to their children.

STUDENT-STUDENT RELATIONSHIP

- Students tend to form strong friendships in school because cohorts of learners move together through the school system, rather than being assigned to different classes from one year to the next. Cliques of two or three students are not uncommon.
- It is not unusual for a student to have many of his or her relatives attending the same school. Students frequently gravitate to family during recess and may get together after class to socialize and study.
- Public schools, until recently, were segregated by gender. Many private religious schools continue this practice.

- Many Salvadoran students will help each other during tests. For example, they may pass notes to each other bearing answers to certain items or may enable a friend seated at an adjacent desk to copy from his or her own test paper.
- Couples who are discovered holding hands, kissing, or engaging in any other romantic or sexual behavior at school will be suspended.

STUDENTS' LEARNING PRACTICES

- Students study independently when the subject matter is theory oriented, but they may nevertheless gather together in one place to study to keep each other company.
- Students will form pairs or groups when they have to solve problems or work on a project. Often one person in the group may understand an item better than the others and can explain and clarify it for the others. At another time, a different person will offer an insight or solution that the others may not have yet discovered. In this manner, each member of the group gives his or her best and the students complement each other and reach a level of excellence that might not have been possible had they worked individually.
- As tests can mean the difference between repeating a grade and advancing on to the next, students may engage in various kinds of "cheating" to enhance their test performance. Writing answers on the palms or forearms is a common strategy as is hiding a small "cheat sheet" under one's clothing. Needless to say, students who are caught cheating will either be given a zero for the assessment or a note will be sent home to the parents.

STUDENTS' DRESS

- Even in poorer communities, schools usually require students to wear a uniform. Those unable to afford uniforms may not be allowed to attend classes. A school uniform can cost a parent a week's salary. Shoes tend to be more expensive than the shirts, trousers, or skirts that may constitute the dress code.
- School uniforms are distinctive for each school in terms of color combination but generally consist of a pleated skirt and white, short-sleeved blouse for girls and dark or khaki trousers and white shirt for boys. Both boys and girls are normally required to wear black or brown loafers. Uniforms are usually made from inexpensive fabric.
- Boys' hair must be neatly trimmed and relatively short. Neither boys nor girls may sport body piercing or tattoos. Students cannot wear hats in school. Regardless of the cost or quality of the uniform, students must keep them absolutely clean and free of wrinkles. Shirts cannot be worn untucked.

GIFTS FOR THE TEACHER

- Candy, desk ornaments, picture frames, inexpensive jewelry, and flowers are appropriate gifts for teachers. (White flowers, however, are only given in the event of death.) Individual students and their parents usually give the teacher a gift for Teachers' Day, Christmas, or for his or her birthday. A birthday cake may also be presented to the teacher and shared with the class in some cases.
- Students pay tribute to their teachers on Teachers' Day by holding an assembly in the school courtyard. They will often line up according to class and grade, listen to the principal give a short speech honoring the teachers, and perform some kind of rehearsed dance. Students sometimes also prepare parties in their individual classrooms, bringing food from home and gifts for the teacher.

NONVERBAL COMMUNICATION

- Salvadorans are taught that it is impolite to point one's finger at another person. In the case of summoning a friend, they stretch out the right arm with the palm down and wiggle their fingers.
- Expressive facial communication and hand gestures often accompany speech.
- It is considered vulgar to yawn in public.
- Salvadorans may simply nod or shake hands when they meet but may grasp the other's hand less firmly and hold on to it longer than their North American counterparts. A man must wait for a woman to initiate a handshake.
- It is appropriate for couples to walk hand-in-hand in public.
- As a rule, Salvadorans avoid and do not approve of loud public discourse.
- Being on time for a meeting or for class may not seem to be a serious commitment to a Salvadoran. Students are rarely absent from class, however, unless they have a very good reason.

FORMS OF ADDRESS

- People in positions of authority expect others to address them by title alone—e.g., Doctor for physicians, *Profesor/a* for teachers at all levels of education, *Ingeniero/a* for engineers, *Arquitecto/a* for architects, and *Abogado* for attorneys.
- People who are elderly or strangers are usually addressed using *Señor/a* or *Señorita* plus family name.
- Salvadorans often inherit one last name from their father (e.g., Lopez) and one from their mother (e.g., Alvarado), with the father's name occurring first, as in Paula Lopez Alvarado. However, one does not use both names when addressing the individual; thus, Paula Lopez Alvarado would be called Paula Lopez.

APPROPRIATE TOPICS

- Asking about another's family is appropriate for conversation as is discussion of Salvadoran culture, history, and geography.
- It is best to avoid discussing national or local politics or religion with Salvadorans unless a level of trust has been built between interlocutors. It is reported that teachers at some schools in El Salvador have been advised to confine class discussion to uncontroversial topics to reduce the possibility of conflict in the classroom.

OUTSIDE OF CLASS

- The volume and pace of school work for Salvadoran students, especially for those attending urban schools, tends to be heavier and faster compared with their North American counterparts. Instructors assign a good deal of homework every day to allow students to learn outside the classroom as well as during the lesson.
- The type of homework assigned depends on the course but may include exercises, projects, research, or other activities that strengthen and complement the students' knowledge base and their readiness for exams.
- Students from affluent families frequently take private lessons after school. They may study piano or dance, get additional English language tutoring, or join a tennis or soccer team.

Potential Adjustment Challenges

PROBLEMS/SOLUTIONS

Problem

The father of one of my Salvadoran students doesn't have a job, but he seems to be in good health and is relatively young. Wouldn't he set a better example for his kids if he worked?

Solution

Salvadorans who emigrated during or shortly after the country's civil war may have been witness to atrocities, such as the murder of family members. They are likely to fall victim to Post-Traumatic Stress Disorder (PTSD). The sound of helicopters, for example, may traumatize a person who associates the sound (or any sudden loud noise) with war and terror. The effects of PTSD are often so debilitating as to prevent individuals from holding down a job.

Problem

I have a young boy in my class who recently joined his parents who immigrated to the United States from El Salvador five years ago. He seems totally disinterested in learning, even laying his head on his desk when I work with him during pull-out sessions.

Solution

It is not unusual for Salvadoran children to be left behind when their fathers or both parents emigrate to the United States, an event that is particularly difficult for young children to comprehend. Many make the journey themselves once their parents' circumstances have stabilized, which can be many years after the initial departure. Sometimes they join fathers who have divorced their wives and remarried in the States, thus complicating the adjustment process. Depression and "acting out" can occur as a result of the clash between the child's expectations of a happy family life and greater material comfort on one hand and the reality of life as an immigrant on the other.

Problem

I thought Salvadoran immigrants were poverty-stricken and war-weary, but I have a student from El Salvador who talks about his maid back home and the club where he and his siblings went to swim and play tennis.

Solution

Salvadoran urban dwellers may not have experienced the horrors of civil war in the same direct fashion as those living in the country. There is a great deal of economic and social class disparity between Salvadorans as well, and so teachers should not expect the backgrounds of their Salvadoran students to be similar.

Guatemala

 GUATEMALA *Upclose*

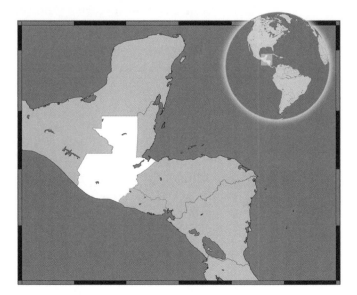

Capital: Guatemala City

Population: 12,293,545 (June 2006)

Size: 108,890 sq. km. (42,043 sq. mi.) (slightly smaller than Tennessee)

Location: in Central America, bordered on the west by the Pacific Ocean, on the east by the Caribbean Sea (Gulf of Honduras), on the southwest by El Salvador, on the southeast by Honduras, on the north and northwest by Mexico, and on the northeast by Belize

Climate: hot and humid in low-lying areas and cooler and drier in mountainous regions

Terrain: narrow coastal plains, mountains, and a rolling plateau

Monetary Unit: quetzal (7.61 per U.S. dollar) (June 2006)

Religion: Roman Catholic, Protestant, indigenous Mayan beliefs

Language(s): Spanish 60%, Amerindian languages 40% (23 officially recognized Amerindian languages, including Quiche, Cakchiquel, Kekchi, Mam, Garifuna, and Xinca)

Literacy Rate: total population 70.6%; men 78%; women 63.3% (2003)

Ethnicity: mestizo (mixed Amerindian and European, also called *Ladino*) 55%, Amerindian or predominantly Amerindian 43%, whites and others 2%

Per Capita Income: US$1,629 (2006)

Population Distribution: 46% urban, 54% rural (2003)

Population below Poverty Line: 75% (2004)

Life Expectancy: total population 65.2 years; men 64.3 years; women 66.1 years (2006)

Government: constitutional democratic republic

PUBLIC HOLIDAYS			
January 1	New Year's Day	October 20	Revolution Day
Thursday before Easter*	Holy Thursday	November 2	All Souls' Day
Friday before Easter*	Good Friday	December 25	Christmas
Saturday before Easter*	Easter Saturday		
May 1	Labor Day		
June 30	Army Day		
August 15	Assumption Day		
September 15	Independence Day		*variable dates*

Personal Perspective

I'll admit it. I thought Mayans were an extinct people. Imagine my embarrassment when I learned that Tohil, my Guatemalan student, was Mayan. For months I couldn't get a word out of him in either English or Spanish. I considered him defiant, in fact, until I heard another ESL teacher talking about her Mayan students and the fact that they speak their own language and had little exposure to Spanish in Guatemala.

—ESL teacher

Historical Perspective

IMMIGRATION TO THE UNITED STATES

Guatemalans suffered greatly during their country's 36-year guerrilla war (1960–1996), which claimed the lives of nearly 200,000 people, most of them Mayan Indians. Another million Guatemalans were forced to flee their homes and villages, finding refuge within the country, while about 150,000 found their way to refugee camps over the border in Mexico. In 1996 a peace accord was signed, and conditions in the country began to normalize. However, hundreds of thousands of people still live in extreme poverty as a result of the war. Roughly 45,000 widows today head up single-parent households; some 100,000 to 250,000 children lost both parents during the war, leaving them to fend for themselves on the streets with few prospects for a normal life.

The outflow of refugees from Guatemala continues today. A reported 21,000 Guatemalans per year leave their country in search of greater prosperity and safety. In 2002, more than 16,000 Guatemalans immigrated to the United States. Another 10,000 entered the country as refugees, and an estimated 144,000 entered illegally, bringing the total number of Guatemalans living in the United States to nearly 500,000. The majority are of Mayan ancestry and do not speak Spanish as their first language. Those coming to the States in the early 1980s were largely middle- and upper-class individuals, such as intellectuals and students as well as labor organizers and activists. Mayan farmers followed when the Gautemalan government adopted a "scorched earth" policy from 1981–1983 that decimated their homes and fields and produced hundreds of thousands of casualties. In 1998 Hurricane Mitch caused such widespread physical and economic destruction that another large wave of immigration gathered, bringing the number of Guatemalan immigrants in the city of Chicago alone to an estimated 50,000 to 80,000 by the year 2000. Most other Guatemalan immigrants have settled in the following states (in numeric order): California, Florida, New York, Illinois, Texas, New Jersey, and Virginia, according to 2003 data. Many of those who arrived in the 1980s with professional status were able to enter the professional workforce here, but the Mayan farmers often occupy low-level positions in factories and restaurants.

HISTORICAL SYNOPSIS

When the Spaniards arrived in 1523 to colonize the area now known as Guatemala, they found what remained of a vibrant and powerful Mayan civilization that had survived for a thousand years but had then mysteriously collapsed. The native Mayans were easily conquered and their land appropriated and allocated to Spanish landlords. When in 1821 Guatemala won its independence from Spain, the Mayans lost control of the little land they still held and became indentured servants to Guatemalans with Spanish blood, so that the fortunes of the latter grew impressively.

A string of military regimes and civilian governments wielded short-term control over the country during the 20th century. Members of the political left and right sparred continuously, but little attention was paid to the plight of the Mayan farmers. However, reformers such as Juan José Arévalo and, later, Jacobo Arbenz Guzmán advocated for the reappropriation to the Mayans of land that had been taken over by large foreign enterprises such as the United Fruit Company. Before these reforms could be implemented, the United States intervened, claiming a Communist threat in the region, and assisted with the overthrow and exile of Arbenz Guzmán. The repressive military governments that followed incited Guatemalans to civil war in 1960, a war that was to last 36 years, during which time the division between rich and poor expanded dramatically. The war ended in 1996 with peace accords, followed in 1999 by free elections. Today more than 60 percent of the land in Guatemala is still owned by fewer than 2 percent of the population.

■ Deep Culture Perspective

DEEP CULTURE BELIEFS

- The Guatemalan family is often an extended family conventionally made up of grandparents, parents, and unmarried children. Sometimes a married son or daughter lives with the extended family as well.
- Although progress can be seen in the cities, Guatemalan men and women do not enjoy equal status, particularly within the home where the culture of *machismo* dominates. Boys are allowed more freedom than girls. A Guatemalan girl may be married at age 14 and may give birth to a dozen children, several of whom will not live through infancy.

- Family life is cherished by Guatemalans. Family members live in close proximity to one another so that large gatherings of relatives are convenient and frequent. Indeed, invitations are never extended to an individual; the entire family is included. Individuals rarely live alone.
- Elders are deeply respected and relied upon for their guidance. The metaphor of a mirror is often used to represent the role of elders since young people see themselves and their potential by watching their older relatives carefully.
- For young Mayan couples that are too poor to afford a formal church wedding or who do not live in the vicinity of a church, common-law ceremonies are sometimes celebrated.
- Since sexuality is rarely discussed even between mothers and daughters, many girls who engage in premarital sex know little or nothing about birth control, and even if they become pregnant they may not know how they conceived. The life of a woman who bears a child out of wedlock is destined to be harsh. Marriage later on to a man of good standing is improbable, and families tend to resent the shame brought on them by the unwed mother. Married Mayan women may be afraid to use contraception even when it is available because of their husbands' *machista* attitude toward them despite the known dangers of repeated pregnancies in an environment in which malnutrition is common and medical attention scarce.
- Superstitious beliefs are not uncommon among Guatemalans, especially among Mayans. Superstitions that revolve around pregnancy and childbirth include staying away from people or animals who are in the process of dying for fear that the fright will remain with the child and affect him or her for life, stuffing the mother's ears with cotton during childbirth to avoid exposure to the voices of evil spirits, and refraining from looking directly at a newborn for fear of passing on the evil eye and a lifetime of sickness or ill fortune. *Ladinos* (Guatemalans of Hispanic lineage) generally adopt Western values, speak Spanish, and welcome change, while the *indigenas* (Mayans) tend to hold to traditional ways of life and speaking.

PROVERBS

- Every person is the age of his heart.
- The deepest waters make the least noise.
- It's not the fault of the parrot but of the one who teaches him to talk.

FOLK TALE

Once upon a time there lived a yellow cricket. He loved to sing and had a beautiful voice. Every evening at dusk he would leave his home in the cieba tree to make his way to the wheat fields where he would sing all night with his friends about the village people with whom he lived and their work in the fields. As he moved from the tree to the wheat fields, he would sing to the women who knew by his song that it was time for their men to return home. The yellow cricket sang to the returning farmers, too, and they knew that the cricket's day was just beginning. Because of the rhythm of his activities, there was no need for clocks in the village.

At the end of one particular night, the yellow cricket was praised heartily by his cricket friends who declared that he had so fine a voice that it was wasted on the poor village. They urged him to take his song to the sea and to tell the ocean about the village, the planting and harvesting of wheat, and about the essential job of crickets, which was to remind the wheat through their evensong that it was the staff of life for the villagers and therefore had much value and importance.

Although he was afraid of the long journey and what the sea might think of his song, the cricket decided to follow the advice of his friends. To that end, he stopped singing in the evening in order to protect his voice from the cold and damp and to conserve his strength, which he would need for the long trip to the sea.

On the day that he left the village, the cricket heard the villagers cry, "Safe journey, yellow cricket! We will miss you." They were sad to see the cricket depart, but they believed that he had a great mission that he could not neglect, and they were proud that the sea would soon learn about them and their lives.

Finally the little cricket arrived at the seaside. He perched on a rock overlooking the great expanse of blue-green water and began to sing a beautiful song about the dreams of the villagers. The women, he chirruped, yearned to dive to the bottom of the ocean. The men imagined themselves climbing up to the mountaintops. The yellow cricket's song was truly magnificent, but the mighty waves of the sea were so loud that the cricket's song couldn't be heard no matter how much he raised his voice. He was hurt to realize that the sea didn't seem to care about his efforts and continued its roar.

Soon the cricket could sing no more. He had once and for all ruined his voice and would never sing again. He returned to the village, but without his melodious song, the men and women began to rely on the monotonous ticking of their new clocks, and the wheat forgot the former splendor of its calling.

Administrative Perspective

OFFICIAL EDUCATIONAL POLICY

Following the 1996 peace accords, a number of reforms in the interest of the Mayan people were instituted, including a new Design for Educational Reform crafted by several commissions made up of a broad spectrum of representatives from Guatemalan society. The 20-year plan aims to make quality education more accessible to all sectors of the Guatemalan population. Specifically, it calls for full government subsidies to pay for the school expenses of children for the first three years of their education, more serious attention to gender issues, and the creation of more effective and widespread bilingual curricula. Acknowledging the disproportionate needs of Guatemalans living in war-ravaged areas as opposed to the cities, a significant share of the reforms is aimed at rural education. In addition to offering support for bilingual programs, the government intends to create dual-shift schools to accommodate a larger number of students and reduce class size. Administrative oversight functions are to undergo reform as well, allowing more authority and input from local schools and communities.

EDUCATION AT A GLANCE

See the Education at a Glance table on page 22.

GUATEMALA

Level/Age	Hours/Calendar	Language of Instruction	Compulsory Attendance	Exams	Grading System	Curriculum	Cost	Enrollment
Primary Grades 1–6 ages 7–13	Jan.–Nov. 7:30 AM to 2:00 or 3:00 PM	Spanish Mayan dialects (may be used at the primary level as a large percentage of Guatemalan students do not speak Spanish)	Yes	Students receive a Certificate of Completion.	100-point scale 91–100 excellent 80–90 very good 51–79 good 0–50 fail	Math, Spanish, reading, social studies, natural sciences, industrial arts, music, plastic arts, physical education, computer science (where possible), English (required from 4th grade)	Free, but students must pay for supplies, uniform, shoes, monthly fees (which increase as child advances to higher grades). Private schools are tuition collecting.	Grade 1 intake 60.7% (of which 46.8% is female) but in 2000, 43% of 1st grade students repeated the year or dropped out of school. Approximately 50% of primary students reach Grade 5.
Basic secondary Grades 7–9 ages 13–16			Yes, to age 14	Students receive Diploma de Estudios.	Same as above. Minimum score of 51 to receive the bach. from public school; private schools require a minimum score of 61 to award the degree.	Math, Spanish, literature, social studies, biology, English, industrial arts, plastic arts, music, physical education, computer science (where possible), accounting	Same as above	26.2% of all secondary school-age students are enrolled; 46.9% of secondary enrollment is female.
Diversified secondary Grades 10–11 ages 16–18 Technical secondary Grades 10–12 ages 15–19			No	From diversified secondary schools students receive a Bachillerato in Science and Letters, needed for entrance to university plus an exam; from technical secondary schools, students receive a Perito Comercial, Industrial, Agrícola, or Técnico, or a teacher training qualification.	Same as above. Bachillerato requires 51% from public schools and 61% from private schools.	Math, Spanish, literature, social studies, economics, biology, psychology, statistics, chemistry, physics, music, physical education, computer sciences (where possible), industrial arts, plastic arts, and English Specializations available in computer science, health science, primary urban education, primary rural education, kindergarten education, music education, physical education, hotel and tourism, auto mechanics, electronics, refrigeration and air conditioning, construction, merchandising and advertising, (bilingual) executive secretary		
University ages 19+ 1st stage Diplomado or Técnico 2–3.5 years 2nd stage Licenciatura 4–5 years (6 for medicine) 3rd stage Maestría 1–2 years Doctorado 2 years	Same as above		No	For Licenciatura, Maestría, and Doctorado, students defend a thesis.	Same as above	Degree programs in all fields at undergraduate and graduate levels depending on the university.	University of San Carlos of Guatemala is tuition-free, but private tuition-collecting universities have dramatically multiplied.	Total enrollment 8.5%

22

Surface Culture Perspective

CLASSROOMS

- The quality of facilities available for education in Guatemala varies greatly depending on whether the school is located in the city or in the country. Urban schools, especially private schools patronized by the wealthy, are usually better equipped with desks, chalkboards, and lavatories, but rural schools may lack walls, let alone amenities such as books. To conserve paper, students may use the dirt floor to solve math problems or draw figures.

- Classrooms tend to be small in comparison to those found in North America. The number of students working in one classroom, however, can be twice as great, reaching 60 students per classroom, although the official reported teacher-student ratio at primary level is 1:33 and 1:13 at secondary level. To accommodate such large groups, desks may be replaced by cinder blocks on which children perch during lessons.

- Books, notebooks, pencils, erasers, and uniforms must be purchased by a student's parents, an expense that often exceeds the family's resources as more than 20 percent of Guatemala's people live on approximately US$1 per day. Some schools have sets of books that are loaned to the students, but they are frequently out-of-date or not age- or level-appropriate.

- Rural schools are often many miles away from a student's home. The distance affects enrollment and attendance. Girls, in particular, are less likely to be allowed to make the long trek due to safety considerations. Many rural schools only offer instruction for the first two or three grades. Secondary schools in the rural areas are less common than primary schools.

TEACHERS' STATUS

- Guatemala's teachers at the primary and secondary levels may receive inadequate preparation for teaching. Special teacher-training high schools offer teacher preparation courses for those hoping to teach in primary schools, but in reality only 25 percent of teachers at the primary and secondary levels receive teaching certificates. Those intending to teach at the secondary level attend universities where they receive training for three years before being certified. To teach at a university an individual must have a *Licenciatura* degree.

- Compensation for Guatemala's teachers is meager and inconsistent, giving rise to frequent strikes. Not only have teachers demanded of the government a 60 percent raise in salary with paychecks distributed on a more frequent basis (i.e., monthly as opposed to quarterly), they have lobbied for improvements for students as well in the form of more school meal programs; educational supplies including books, desks, and chairs; long-overdue building renovations; and more funding for bilingual education. If the requested pay increase were to be approved, Guatemalan teachers would make the equivalent of US$450 per month rather than US$280.

TEACHER-STUDENT RELATIONSHIP

- Gender discrimination may find its way into the classroom not only through textbook and curriculum content but in the differential manner in which teachers treat students.
- Students speak to their teachers with respect and consider them friends and counselors.
- Teachers tend to support their students with their confidence and help when necessary.
- Parents treat the teacher with respect as is befitting the person who is charged with the education of their children. Parents expect teachers to not only teach their children academic subjects but to give them moral instruction as well. Many parents discharge to teachers the heavy responsibility of advising children who have strayed and who have problems with drugs, gangs, sex, and alcoholism.

TEACHING PRACTICES

- The prevailing methodology in most Guatemalan schools is lecture accompanied by verbatim dictation.
- At the primary school level, the curriculum is delivered by a single teacher possessing a high school diploma while the remainder of the curriculum—i.e., physical education, music, industrial arts, and home economics—is taught by different teachers. Secondary level teachers are university graduates, although, because of the shortage of qualified teachers, they may not have the required disciplinary training in the courses they are subsequently assigned to teach.
- To the extent that it is possible, teachers supplement their teaching by the use of audio-visuals, computers (which are not available in most public schools), or through lectures and seminars presented by visiting experts.
- Secondary level teachers, much more so than their primary counterparts, assign more research and group projects.

TEACHERS' DRESS

- Guatemalans take pride in their appearance. Teachers will take care that their clothing is clean and conservative.

DISCIPLINE AND CLASS MANAGEMENT

- Guatemalan teachers are expected to assert their authority in the classroom. They may adopt a severe and threatening attitude toward students, be prone to shouting, and regularly demand that students leave the class and report to the principal's office.
- While admonishing a student in class may be a normal practice, teachers may confront the unruly student privately to obtain a better effect. Parents may also be called in to exert influence over the student.

STUDENTS' CIRCUMSTANCES

- Parents in rural areas tend to be torn between sending their children to school and keeping them at home to help with the maintenance of the household or with the production of arts and crafts that may be sold at market. Many look to education to improve the lot of their children, especially their daughters, in a changing world where women's participation in the workforce has become a necessity. Nevertheless, they may prefer their children receive the kind of training that develops skill and knowledge for farming rather than training that is less practical.

STUDENT-STUDENT RELATIONSHIP

- Students develop warm friendships with one another as they progress through the school grades together, although they tend not to study in groups after class.

STUDENTS' LEARNING PRACTICES

- In the typical Guatemalan classroom students are not encouraged to actively participate. Thus, if they don't understand a concept in class, they will not feel comfortable asking for clarification.
- Students at both the primary and secondary level enjoy working in groups as it gives them the sense of taking an active part in their education.
- Use of the Internet and audio-visual aids tend to motivate students in Guatemalan schools.

STUDENTS' DRESS

- Most schools have a dress code that includes wearing a uniform to school. The type of uniform varies from school to school, but typically includes a skirt or jumper plus blouse for girls and long trousers and shirt for boys. Schools also tend to place restrictions on the kinds of shoes students must wear. Generally speaking, sneakers or tennis shoes are not allowed.

GIFTS FOR THE TEACHER

- In general, Guatemalan students are not accustomed to giving gifts to their teachers except to celebrate Teachers' Day on June 25. The types of gifts depend on the ability of parents to acquire them, but typically expensive items are not sought. In fact, the gift can be a rose, chocolates, fruits, or knick-knacks for the office, although in wealthier communities the teacher may receive a sound system for Teachers' Day.

NONVERBAL COMMUNICATION

- When trying to get another person's attention in public, Guatemalans refrain from shouting the individual's name but instead will use a hissing sound much like the "psssst" used by North Americans to summon another person in a quiet place such as a library.
- Guatemalans tend to avoid using loud voices in public. In fact, they may be described as soft-spoken.
- Compared with their North American counterparts, Guatemalans may seem formal and invariably polite.
- Punctuality is a valued behavior among most Guatemalans, especially those that live in the city.
- Shaking hands firmly upon meeting is more appropriate among *Ladinos* than it is among the less demonstrative Mayan population. When the latter shake hands, there is only very brief contact and light pressure.

FORMS OF ADDRESS

- Students address the teacher as *Señor, Señora,* or *Señorita,* often with the title followed by the teacher's last name. At the university level, it is more common for students to call the teacher *Professor* or *Profesora.*

APPROPRIATE TOPICS

- Soccer is a popular conversation topic as the game has an avid following in Guatemala.
- When talking with a *Ladino,* it is important to know the person well before you broach the topic of the mistreatment of the Mayans and the socioeconomic gap between *Ladinos* and Mayans.
- Topics such as illegal drugs, homosexuality/sexuality, international adoption, human rights violations, politics in general, and criticism of the Catholic Church are not eagerly welcomed in conversation.

OUTSIDE OF CLASS

- It is not uncommon for poor children to spend three to four hours per day helping with housework. Girls, however, are three times as likely to do chores as boys.

- As much as 28 percent of Guatemalan children age 7 to 14 work in addition to, but mostly instead of, going to school. Many girls work as maids in the homes of middle- and upper-class families, beginning their service as early as 10 years of age. They are sometimes threatened, beaten, harassed, and sexually abused. Moreover, they rarely receive days off for illness or pleasure. Two-thirds of these girls stay in school. Others find work in one of the 250 *maquilas,* U.S. or South Korean factories that produce almost US$500,000 per year in clothing that is pieced together by some 80,000 Guatemalan workers (mostly women) before being exported duty-free to the United States. Those who are employed by the *maquilas* often work more than ten hours per day under unsafe and unhealthy conditions and for poverty wages. Guatemalan children, mostly boys, may also work as garbage collectors, in construction, on coffee plantations, and in fireworks factories where safety risks are extremely high and accidents (even death) are frequent. Working children spend approximately 58 hours per week at their jobs, leaving no time for school.

Potential Adjustment Challenges

PROBLEMS/SOLUTIONS

Problem

Last week the principal brought a new Guatemalan student to my class. I minored in Spanish as an undergraduate so was looking forward to speaking with her in her language, but she looked at me as if I were speaking Greek!

Solution

Spanish is the language of instruction in the majority of Guatemalan schools, but for most Mayan children, it is a second language, and one in which they may have difficulty. Mayan children who have not attended school before coming to the United States may not know any Spanish.

Problem

I was surprised to learn that the mother of my Guatemalan student can't tell time. Is it because she doesn't have any formal education?

Solution

If this individual lived in the countryside, chances are she could judge the time of day by the position of the sun in the sky and by using other natural signs in the environment. Her daily routine may have involved getting up before dawn to begin to make tortillas or cook rice and beans for the family's breakfast, sweeping the floor after the men have gone off to the fields to work, weaving blankets and clothing with the female members of the family, and preparing dinner for the returning menfolk. In other words, clocks and watches were probably unnecessary.

Problem

I asked my Guatemalan student if he would like to accompany my family to Catholic Mass some Sunday, but he refused abruptly. Is religious practice a private activity in Guatemala?

Solution

Your student might not be Catholic. Protestantism is on the rise in Central America, especially as an increasing number of faith groups travel there on missions to build schools and churches and spread the Gospel. Protestants in some parts of Latin America, however, are criticized for abandoning the Catholic faith, and evangelical Protestants are sometimes the victims of harassment and even torture.

Honduras

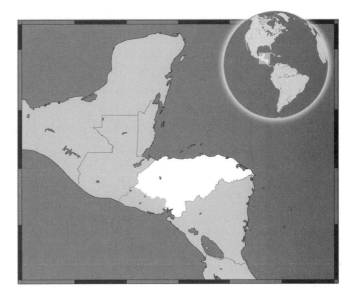

■ HONDURAS *Upclose*

Capital: Tegucigalpa

Population: 7,326,496 (June 2006)

Size: 112,090 sq. km. (43,278 sq. mi.) (slightly larger than Tennessee)

Location: in Central America between the Caribbean Sea on the east and the Pacific Ocean on the west and bordered by El Salvador, Guatemala, and Belize on the north and by Nicaragua on the south

Climate: hot and humid year-round in the north, with drier and cooler temperatures in the mountains of the interior (rainy season extends from June to November)

Terrain: mountainous interior with flat plains along the coasts

Monetary Unit: lempira (18.86 per U.S. dollar) (June 2006)

Religion: Roman Catholic 97%, Protestant 3%

Language(s): Spanish and Amerindian dialects

Literacy Rate: total population 76.2%; men 76.1%; women 76.3% (2003)

Ethnicity: mestizo (mixed Amerindian and European) 90%, Amerindian 7%, black 2%, white 1%

Per Capita Income: US$930 (2004) US$827 (2006)

Population Distribution: 46% urban, 54% rural (2003)

Population below Poverty Line: 53% (1993)

Life Expectancy: total population 68.8 years; men 67.0 years; women 70.5 years (2006)

Government: democratic constitutional republic

PUBLIC HOLIDAYS			
January 1	New Year's Day	October 21	Armed Forces Day
Thursday before Easter*	Holy Thursday	December 25	Christmas
Friday before Easter*	Good Friday		
Saturday before Easter*	Holy Saturday		
April 14	Day of the Americas		
May 1	Labor Day		
September 15	Independence Day		
October 3	Morazán Day (Soldiers Day)		
October 12	*Día de la Raza* (Columbus Day)		*variable dates*

Personal Perspective

One day in my ESL class I was sitting at a long seminar table with my teacher and classmates. The teacher was returning graded homework papers. Instead of standing up and individually presenting the papers to each of us, she slid the papers across the table in our direction. I left the class very upset that day because I felt the teacher didn't respect me. She acted as if neither I nor the paper were important. In my country, a teacher would only do such a thing if she deliberately wanted to convey a message of disrespect.

—*Honduran university graduate student in the United States*

Historical Perspective

IMMIGRATION TO THE UNITED STATES

The numbers of Honduran immigrants, refugees, and unauthorized individuals crossing the border to the United States increased dramatically after Hurricane Mitch devastated this Central American country in 1998. In fact, according to the U.S. Census Bureau, there was a five-fold increase from 1980 to 2000 (approximately 50,000), bringing the total estimated Honduran population in the United States to more than 200,000. Florida, California, New York, and Texas (in that order) received the greatest numbers of Honduran newcomers, but New Jersey, Virginia, North Carolina, Louisiana, and Illinois also attracted significant numbers of refugees.

The hurricane's destruction of coffee and banana plantations and the subsequent years of waiting for the replacement plants to bear fruit left many Honduran farmers with barely the means for subsistence. Some 55 percent of farmers in Honduras earn no more than the equivalent of US$70 in a year's time. This, in addition to the unrest in Central America, the use of the country by the United States to launch military forays into neighboring countries, and International Monetary Fund (IMF) initiatives that destabilized the rural financial structure, contributed to a steady flow of individuals and families out of Honduras to the United States. Having, in many cases, successfully escaped their initial poverty, the country's immigrants send an average of US$1.2 billion per year to their relatives in Honduras.

HISTORICAL SYNOPSIS

Before the arrival of Christopher Columbus in 1502, Honduras was populated mainly by the descendants of the ancient Mayans whose prowess in art, mathematics, and astronomy is a source of great pride among present-day Hondurans. The Spaniards, searching for gold and silver, met resistance from the local people despite the efforts of conquistadors such as Hernán Cortés. In 1537 the Hondurans rebelled against the Spaniards under the leadership of Chief Lempira, but the assassination of Lempira, in addition to many deaths resulting from the fighting as well as from disease and abuse, weakened the insurrections to follow.

It was not until the colony's gold and silver deposits gave out that the region was left in peace. In 1831 Honduras, together with Nicaragua, El Salvador, Costa Rica, and Guatemala, broke with Spain, forming the United Provinces of Central America (UPCA), and in 1838 Honduras separated from the UPCA to form its own sovereign state. Nonetheless, by the beginning of the 20th century, Honduras had once again been overtaken, economically if not politically, by foreign powers. One in particular, United Fruit, a U.S. corporation, bought up vast tracts of fertile land, established a monopoly over the banana trade, and employed large numbers of desperate Hondurans who reluctantly agreed to work long hours at very low wages and to forgo medical and vacation benefits as well as the opportunity to join labor unions. A settlement was reached in 1954 after 30,000 workers went on strike against the banana companies as well as other North American–operated industries such as those involved with mining and coffee production.

The military governed Honduras for a quarter century until 1982 when democratic elections were held. Shortly thereafter the United States established military bases in Honduras from which it launched attacks against the leftist Sandinistas of Nicaragua and welcomed other *contras* (armed counterrevolutionary forces opposed to the Sandinista government) into their protective care.

Through the 1990s Honduras struggled with other manifestations of foreign occupation. *Maquiladoras,* or apparel assembly factories owned primarily by U.S. and Asian companies, drew the poor by the thousands to labor in their workshops for meager compensation (although many considered themselves lucky to have as "good" a job as theirs in the *maquiladora*). They challenged the service and resource limits of the cities located in the free enterprise zones along the Caribbean coast, a situation that was exacerbated by the influx of destitute refugees from Hurricane Mitch in 1998. Estimates of the death toll range from 5,600 to 7,000 and the damage between US$1.7 and US$2 million. Floods and mudslides followed in 1999. As a result, Honduras today stands as the most economically underdeveloped country in Latin America, and it is one of the poorest countries in the Western Hemisphere. In addition to the natural disasters to which it is prone, the country faces widespread poverty, unemployment, crime, rampant government corruption, variable pricing of banana and coffee on world markets, and continuing dependence on U.S. trade. For this reason, Honduras is attempting to expand the range of products it can export and is hoping to attract ecotourists, much like Belize and Costa Rica have successfully done.

Deep Culture Perspective

DEEP CULTURE BELIEFS

- As in most of Latin America, family in Honduras is perhaps the most important cultural institution. The extended family—made up of grandparents, parents, and children plus one or two aunts and uncles—is common, and its members find not only security and identity within the family unit but valuable resources as well. Kin support each other through good times and bad with economic assistance and other forms of aid that may result in entree to better jobs, schools, and housing.

- Honduran family members are known to be deeply loyal to one another to the extent that outsiders may be considered just the opposite—that is, unworthy of trust. Branches of the family tree benefit from similar ties, although one family group may be significantly more prosperous than another family group and limit its interaction, if not its sharing, with the less well-off relatives.

- As members of a culture that is strongly based on the primacy of family and community over the individual, Hondurans are likely to make decisions collaboratively and bear in mind how the decision will affect others. They may also defer to church officials or the rulings of the Catholic Church to resolve problems but may otherwise not be persuaded by impersonal arguments or influenced by notions such as "progress."

- Hondurans tend to be open, relaxed, gracious, and friendly people who are proud of their lineage and eager to open their homes and hearts to strangers. They are sensitive to the feelings of others as well and, thus, will work hard to protect another's pride and sense of honor. It is important to most Hondurans to maintain a sense of harmony and peace and to enjoy life.

- Problems may be regarded as worthy of attention at a later point, so efforts to resolve them may take longer than in a North American environment. There are few "workaholics" in Honduras, that designation reserved for Salvadorans. Time, too, is not as carefully measured and is regarded as less critical in the overall scheme of interaction; thus, Hondurans can arrive up to 30 minutes late for a meeting and not seem concerned about the delay.

- More than 60 percent of Hondurans live in rural areas under conditions of dire poverty. They attempt to farm the little arable land made available to them after the large foreign agricultural corporations that grow bananas, coffee, and pineapples for export staked their claims. The availability of cultivatable farmland has further diminished as a result of the expansion of the export cattle industry.

- The middle class, made up of academics, small business operators, and civil servants, is small but growing despite the economic setback suffered after Hurricane Mitch struck the country in 1998.

- There also exists a small Honduran minority, namely those affiliated with the military, whose economic and political power captures the vast majority of the country's resources. Wealth is amassed not only through the perquisites bestowed on those in the armed forces but also via great tracts of property owned and passed down from generation to generation as well as from business transactions with foreign corporations. Social class is a clear and powerful divider in Honduras with respect to access to or exclusion from valued resources and opportunities. The main class antagonisms are found between the wealthy and the poor.

- In the rural areas of Honduras, gender roles remain fairly traditional. Women take care of the household and raise the children, and men farm or earn money to support the family in other ways but tend not to take much responsibility in the rearing of their children. However, changes have been under way in recent years in the larger towns and cities of Honduras where women are entering the workforce in greater numbers, are setting up and operating small businesses, and are even making their way into the world of politics, still a predominantly male domain. Urban men, too, have begun to appreciate the contributions of women in traditionally male-dominated occupations. Their interest in daily family issues and concerns is also on the rise.

- Religion plays a central role in the lives of most Hondurans, who tend to be practicing Catholics. It is not, however, clearly present in the workplace. Other Christian religions have taken root in Honduras over the past decades, and although their doctrines may be more limiting in terms of such practices as consuming alcohol and dancing, there is little discord between Catholic and Protestant groups nor is there persecution of members of the Evangelical movement as in some other Latin American countries. Honduran Catholics may honor a multitude of saints, praying to each for aid according to their respective type of benefaction. The Virgin Mary is the most frequently venerated saint, and her image is omnipresent in Honduran homes. Every town has a patron saint as well whose feast day is grandly and solemnly celebrated once a year. The Virgin of Suyapa is Honduras's patron saint.

- The Honduran population is primarily composed of *Indios,* people whose ancestry is a mix of Mayan and Spanish, and *Garifunas,* the descendants of African slaves. Conflict between the two groups is unusual.

PROVERBS

- ◼ Grief shared is half grief. Joy shared is double joy.
- ◼ Don't eat a mango until it's ripe.
- ◼ Where there is food for two, there is food for three.
- ◼ There is more time than life.
- ◼ It is better to have many children since maybe one of them will be useful.

FOLK TALE

One day a young Garifuna Indian mother walked out in the yard only to discover that one of the family's chickens had been snatched and eaten by a hawk. This was the second time in one week that this had happened, and it was causing alarm in the family, for they depended on the chickens for eggs, fertilizer, and meat.

The young mother charged her oldest son to watch over the chickens the next day so that she could tend to the cooking and cleaning. The boy, however, was a typical ten-year-old. Watching chickens was boring, and he longed to go fishing instead. Thinking that he would take a break from his guard duty, the boy began to gather his fishing gear, but just as he was about to leave the yard, his mother appeared. "Salvadór," she shouted, "don't you dare abandon these chickens. It's your job to make sure that the hawk doesn't steal one today."

With that Salvadór's mother returned to the house, but the boy was still determined to go fishing. Suddenly, an idea occurred to him. He quickly secured the chickens and departed for the river feeling satisfied that he could both enjoy himself and do his job. However, when he returned an hour later, he found his mother sobbing and infuriated. "Look what you've done, you selfish boy," she cried. He looked around him and saw hundreds of feathers on the ground and droplets of red blood. His great idea had not served him well. He had tied all the chickens together before he left, believing that this would prevent the hawk from stealing them. In fact, the hawk had stolen every one of the chickens and had done so all at once thanks to the boy's creative but flawed plan.

▌Administrative Perspective

OFFICIAL EDUCATIONAL POLICY

Honduras established its first national public education system in 1957. Not only were the mechanisms for free public education created, but policy, protocol, and curricula were written, and schools were built. According to the country's constitution, education for all children aged 7 to 14 is compulsory and free. Any person completing the primary level is also obligated, or at least encouraged, by the Honduran government to teach two or more illiterate adults to read and write.

Despite the earnest intentions of the government, however, it has been unable to accomplish its educational goals, and the quality of education overall in Honduras has remained at a relatively poor level. Major obstacles—economic, political, and environmental—have frustrated the implementation of the national plan. Today there are still not enough schools or qualified teachers. The availability of teaching materials is severely limited, and the cost for texts and supplies is high. Many children live too far away from a school, so illiteracy is rampant, especially in the countryside (80 percent in rural areas). Rural schools frequently combine grade levels and/or offer no more than three or four years of instruction. Teachers in these regions may have 80 children at a time in a single classroom. Sometimes children who have learned to read lose the ability over time due to the unavailability of the kinds of reading materials (newspaper, magazine, even brochures and manuals) that are taken for granted in more affluent nations.

These problems came to the attention of the international community in the aftermath of Hurricane Mitch. Shortly thereafter a new program called *Educatodos,* or Education for All, was launched with the help of the U.S. Agency for International Development (USAID). *Educatodos* targets adolescents and young adults in areas hardest hit by the hurricane and those who are most likely to immigrate illegally to the United States (i.e., males between 18 and 44 years old). These individuals may participate in distance-learning programs whose content corresponds to Grades 1–6. Instructional broadcasts over the radio are combined with the support of an on-site aide who helps students with workbook exercises and other assignments. The program also calls for later expansion to Grades 7–9 and the upgrading of the technological component to include televisions, VCRs/DVD players, and computers.

Honduras has also launched a Reconstruction Master Plan that encourages local communities to become more engaged with areas schools and schooling. A World Bank initiative to distribute textbooks, prepare teachers, write curricula, improve compensation for teachers, and design more effective assessments of student progress has been delayed due to project mismanagement but is on track for revival in the near future. Another undertaking introduced by the German government included the construction of a new building for the Ministry of Education, and the government of Spain set up literacy and pre-school programs. Assistance from a number of other donors (e.g., UNESCO and UNICEF) has been extended as well.

HONDURAS

Level/Age	Hours/Calendar	Language of Instruction	Compulsory Attendance	Exams	Grading System	Curriculum	Cost	Enrollment
Primary Grades 1–6 ages 6–13	Feb.–Nov. with 1 week holiday in June and 1 week before Easter for *Semana Santa*	Spanish (with some English used in the Bay Islands and in bilingual schools)	Yes, to age 12	Students pay a fee to take midterm and final exams (cost of paper and printing).	100-point scale 91–100 excellent 80–90 very good 60–79 good 1–59 unsatisfactory or 5-point scale pass/ fail = 3 Report cards are issued 4 times a year.	Math, natural sciences, technology and communication, social sciences, English		87.62% of primary school-age children are enrolled; 49.6% are female.
Lower secondary Grades 7–9 ages 12–15			No	Students take achievement tests at end of lower secondary to determine if they advance to grade 10.		Same as primary plus vocational-technical training	Public schools offer free tuition, but parents must cover fees for books, uniforms, and other supplies.	26.2% of secondary school-age children are enrolled.
Diversified secondary Grades 10–11 ages 15–17 Technical secondary Grades 10–12 ages 15–18	7:00 AM–noon 12:30 PM–5:30 PM		No	From the diversified secondary, students receive a *Bachillerato* required for admission to university; from the technical secondary, students receive a *Perito* or *Bachillerato* in their specialization.		In the diversified secondary, students may specialize in literary or scientific streams; in the technical secondary, various specializations are available.		1 out of every 10 primary school graduates advances to secondary level.
University ages 18/19+ 1st stage (bachelor's) 3–4 years 2nd stage (*Maestría*) 2–3 years 3rd stage (*Doctorado* in dentistry or medicine) 6–7 years		Spanish	No	At the 1st stage, students are awarded a *Bachillerato universitario,* a *Licenciatura,* or a professional qualification.	100-point scale pass/ fail = 60	All students must take a general orientation course before embarking on their studies; no electives.	Tuition free at public universities, but students pay registration and testing fees.	Total enrollment 14.7%.

Surface Culture Perspective

CLASSROOMS

- Most Honduran schools are small and overcrowded. Some 40 to 80 students may be crammed into one of the two classrooms that constitute the physical plant. Bathrooms may be outdoor latrines, and fans, even if they are available, may not be functional because of the instability of the electrical system. Sometimes set days of the week are designated as nonelectricity days.

- Schools were a popular refuge for those whose homes had been destroyed by Hurricane Mitch. Both during and after the storm, these structures were the most solid and secure and so attracted groups of families who had no other place to take shelter. Housing thus took precedence over schooling. School buildings were occupied for months on end by storm refugees, effectively disrupting education for tens of thousands of Honduran school children. During this period, the schools suffered physical stresses for which they were not designed, and school supplies disappeared as well.

- Upon entering an urban classroom, one may see rows of desks designed for two students each, a blackboard, the Honduran flag, a map of Honduras, a portrait of either the President of Honduras or of one of the country's liberators or founders—for example, Francisco Morazán, Dionisio de Herrera, or Padre Trino. Schools are typically built in a square with the center portion used for assemblies and exercise breaks. Attached to the inside perimeter of the school is a covered walk. Windows do not have glass panes; screens may or may not be installed. Public schools rarely have a fleet of buses to transport students to and from school. Instead, students either walk, ride a bicycle, or take a public bus. Media labs are uncommon, and science labs, though they may exist, may have limited or outdated equipment. Replacement parts for devices such as overhead and movie projectors are virtually impossible to obtain.

- Even in public schools, students must pay a modest tuition, which does not include the cost of textbooks. Tuition covers the cost of paper and printing of exams. Books may be older editions, expensive, and in limited supply. Approximately 6 percent of the Honduran government's revenue is designated for the country's only university. While university tuition is only US$20 per semester, students are taxed an additional administrative fee of approximately US$388 to graduate.

TEACHERS' STATUS

- To teach at the primary school level, students receive three years of training after successfully completing the lower secondary level of their education. They then graduate with a *Maestro de Educacíon Primaria* certificate. Prospective secondary school teachers attend the National

Pedagogical University or the National Autonomous University to obtain the *Licenciatura.*

- Due to low salaries (approximately US$150 per month), inadequate teacher preparation, poor working conditions, and mismanagement of the local and national education systems, Honduran teachers frequently strike for better wages and look for better employment, leaving their teaching positions as soon as possible. Qualified teachers are always in short supply, so frequently young women with no more than a few years of high school and no school diploma will take on the task of educating children, especially in rural areas.

- Honduran teachers often teach two shifts per day to increase their salaries and to help the school alleviate the persistent problem of overcrowding by offering morning instruction for one group of learners and afternoon instruction for another. These teachers may also be at one school location in the morning and move to another school for the afternoon session.

TEACHER-STUDENT RELATIONSHIP

- The most beloved teachers are those who are considered to be approachable, accessible, and friendly. Students respect teachers who plan their lessons carefully and give feedback on homework assignments.

- There is little parental involvement in school activities and schoolwork. Many feel that they are already sufficiently overwhelmed with the pressures and demands of their daily lives.

TEACHING PRACTICES

- Honduran students tend to expect their teachers to be fonts of knowledge from which they may drink deeply. Students do not perceive themselves to be responsible for their own learning, so they adopt an attitude of "teacher gives and student takes."

- Lecture is the most common method of instruction, although at the university level it may be followed by small- or large-group discussion.

- The hallmark of a good teacher in Honduras is the attempt to marry instructional content with the day-to-day needs of the students who usually will earn their livings in the community in which they were schooled.

TEACHERS' DRESS

- Female teachers—indeed Honduran women in general—do not wear shorts in public and often will not wear slacks to school. It is more common and acceptable to see them in dresses or skirts and blouses.

- Male teachers frequently wear trousers and a *guayabera,* the tailored, often embroidered, decorative shirt that is worn outside the pants.

DISCIPLINE AND CLASS MANAGEMENT

• Classrooms are not considered places for levity (no "Fun Fridays" or storytelling time), and teachers tend to be strict. Honduran students, nonetheless, are said to be disruptive during lessons, especially as they get older and gang activity exerts more pressure on young people. Teachers may respond by subtracting points from the student's grade, using corporal punishment (e.g., pulling the student's ears, slapping the hands with a ruler), sending the mischief-maker to the principal's office, contacting the parents, or having the student write "I will not…" 100 times on the blackboard. In severe cases, the child will be expelled from school.

STUDENTS' CIRCUMSTANCES

• In rural areas, students may have to rise between 3:00 AM to 5:00 AM in order to complete their household chores and walk the long distance to school. After the morning session has ended, many children return home to resume their chores.
• Given the need for practical skills that will lead directly to financial support of the family, parents sometimes do not appreciate the value of school or homework for their children. Parents either may not be interested in helping children with assignments or may be unable to do so because of their limited academic knowledge.

STUDENT-STUDENT RELATIONSHIP

• Normally, students attend the same school from start to finish of their education. Only in rare cases would a student change schools.
• Honduran students frequently help each other pass tests by alerting their friends to the content of a test if they have had the opportunity to take the exam before others. Sometimes a student will manage to steal a test and share it with his/her classmates. It is not uncommon to obtain test items by offering a monetary incentive to the individual charged with photocopying responsibilities. Such activities are reportedly more common in private schools than in the public schools. A student who is caught cheating will receive a "0" on the exam or assignment, but there may be little concern on the part of the student. This may explain why some students think of cheating as an amusing adventure.

STUDENTS' LEARNING PRACTICES

• In situations where no textbooks are available, students copy down everything the teacher writes on the blackboard and virtually all of his or her lecture.
• Students read much less as part of their homework assignments than they may in North America. They tend to memorize their notes and textbooks with minimal deep understanding or interpretation.

STUDENTS' DRESS

- In private school, students wear uniforms usually consisting of black pants or skirt, a knit shirt bearing the school's logo, and black shoes.
- Girls are expected to dress modestly. Make-up and nail polish are generally not permitted, blouses must be buttoned to the neck, and the hems of skirts must not fall above the knee.
- Many students, especially in rural areas, cannot afford to buy school uniforms and/or shoes so must forgo an education.

GIFTS FOR THE TEACHER

- On Teachers' Day in Honduras (September 17), students present their teachers with flowers, chocolates, or fruit. At the end of the school year, it is acceptable for teachers to receive from their students plants, candy, flowers, or small decorative items such as picture frames.
- Occasionally a teacher will be invited to the home of a student. It is good form for the teacher to arrive with a small gift for the family. Sometimes the invitation or a gift from the parents is followed by a request that the teacher serve as an after-school tutor for the child.

EXAMS

- There are fewer tests given in Honduran schools than in most of North America, and they tend to be more difficult (e.g., items may be taken from the footnotes of a textbook) and rigorously graded and entail higher stakes as well.
- Test task types normally include matching, multiple choice, and essay writing. The answer to a math problem is only one part of the item; students must show the steps they used to solve the problem, and this, too, is graded.

NONVERBAL COMMUNICATION

- Honduran women give each other one kiss on the cheek when they greet. The same is done for the meeting of a woman and a man. Older women may take each other's forearms or give each other a pat on the arm or shoulder. Men shake hands with each other, sometimes grasping the shoulder of the other or holding the arm of their interlocutor throughout the conversation. It is customary when entering a room at a social event to shake hands with every person present. This handshake may be limp in comparison with the typical North American handshake, but the distance between conversation partners is closer. Girls may promenade holding each other's hands, and young couples, too, may hold hands or even kiss in public.

- Hondurans pride themselves on their politeness, so passing another on the street without offering a greeting (e.g., *buenos días*) would be considered discourteous.
- To be polite and accommodating, some Hondurans offer the answer that they believe the other wants to hear rather than offend that person by delivering a negative response. In fact, "no" may be replaced by "maybe" or "we'll see."
- A number of gestures used by Hondurans are unfamiliar to their North American neighbors. If a person places a finger below his or her eye, it suggests caution. Putting one hand on the opposite elbow is a reference to stinginess. Disapproval may be communicated nonverbally by wagging the index finger sideways. To show solidarity or approval, Hondurans may clasp their hands together. A person who is being scolded will cast his or her eyes to the floor.

FORMS OF ADDRESS

- While Honduran teachers will usually call their students by first name, students would never address their teachers in the same fashion, nor would the students' parents. Instead, students use the title *Profesor* or *Profesora* (or *profe* for short), and parents address the teacher as *Señor* or *Señora*. University students may call their teachers in the social sciences and humanities *Licenciado* or *Licenciada* if the teacher has obtained a bachelor's degree, but *Ingeniero* or *Ingeniera* is used for engineering professors. Calling a university professor *Doctor* is considered too formal, and thus is rare. *Maestro* may be used when addressing construction workers, painters, etc. Individuals in the community who are well known and highly respected are frequently called by the title *Don* and *Doña,* as in *Don Pedro* or *Doña Flor.*
- Hondurans typically have three names. The first name is chosen for them at birth, but it is followed by the father's family name and then by the mother's family name. Thus, baby Gloria who is born to Pedro Chacón and Maria Flores officially becomes Gloria Chacón Flores. When she marries Raul Ponte, she drops her mother's family name (Flores) and adopts her husband's family name (Ponte). Now she is Gloria Chacón del Ponte.
- The term *mojado,* which means wet in Spanish, applies to Honduran men that have made their way to the United States, albeit illegally. This term is not pejorative. Indeed, to "go *mojado*" is seen as a sort of labor of love and is used with pride. Individuals take great risks to cross the border, but if they succeed in finding work, they can support both themselves and their families back home.

APPROPRIATE TOPICS

- Discussion of the culture of Honduras or its history and geography are quite acceptable. Hondurans will appreciate positive remarks about the food, hotels, and landmarks of their cities and communities. However, topics that may be embarrassing to Hondurans, especially in conversation with a foreign visitor, are avoided. The country's political turmoil or poverty, for example, would be considered somewhat awkward as a discussion topic in class, as would abortion, (homo)sexuality, religion, and euthanasia.

- In Honduras, the terms "America" and "Americans" apply to their world region and identities in addition to those of people from the United States. They may feel offended when foreign visitors use these terms to distinguish between the United States and Central America.

OUTSIDE OF CLASS

- Students in urban areas may be assigned 2 to 2.5 hours of homework per night, but in rural areas teachers may refrain from making assignments in consideration of the responsibilities that students may have at home. Sometimes children are taken out of school to help supplement the family's income by selling newspapers or other items on the street, to give parents a hand in the fields, or to care for younger siblings.

- In more affluent schools, extracurricular activities sometimes include band, sports, science fairs, and drama festivals, but such things are not widespread. *Fútbol* (soccer), the national sport, is the only exception. Teams are formed for all ages and levels, although girls rarely participate. Many Hondurans enjoy playing baseball as well, and basketball has begun to attract an increasing number of enthusiasts. Again, girls tend not to engage in sports to the extent that boys do; they often become fine dancers, skilled not only in the popular dances of the day but in traditional styles of dancing as well. There are plenty of opportunities to dance since holidays and often weekends are celebrated with music played by a band in the heart of the village. Among the games that Honduran children enjoy is *cantarito,* a variation on kick the can, and *enchute,* which involves catching a cup with the end of a stick.

▎Potential Adjustment Challenges

PROBLEMS/SOLUTIONS

Problem

I sent a packet of worksheets home with my Honduran student so that her parents could help her practice her English, but she never brings them back to me. Why might that be?

Solution

Although city dwellers may have a modicum of basic proficiency in English, it is unlikely that children from the countryside have parents whose English is strong enough to assist them with homework. One possibility is that your student and her family may come from the countryside.

Problem

I feel bad about assigning homework that requires students to access information from the Internet because I'm not sure my Honduran student has a computer at home. If not, could the parents just drive my student to the public library where I know there are lots of computers?

Solution

Many Honduran immigrants are struggling to make ends meet, and they may be sending money home at the same time. Chances are, therefore, that purchasing a computer and paying for Internet access would be considered a luxury that the family would forgo, leaving their children without the same technological support at home that their mainstream peers may take for granted. In fact, there may be little reading material in the household of a poor immigrant family. Tampa, Florida residents may recall the true story of a young Honduran boy who sold food on Sunday mornings to make money for his family. They were poor and didn't own reference books or a computer. His parents did not own a car nor were they licensed to drive. In addition, they were too occupied with their own multiple jobs and family responsibilities to accompany their son to the library, so the boy had to ride his bicycle to the library in order to complete some of his homework assignments. On one such expedition, the child was struck by a car driven by a drunk driver and was killed.

Problem

I was told that yesterday Jeannette, one of my U.S. students, offered Clara, her Honduran classmate, half of her peanut butter and jelly sandwich because Clara said she hadn't eaten breakfast, forgot her lunch, and was starving. However, Clara refused Jeannette's sandwich. Why did she hint around that she wanted Jeannette to share her food?

Solution

Snacks or sandwiches made with peanut butter may be refused by Hondurans because this particular food item is not known or eaten in Honduras.

Nicaragua

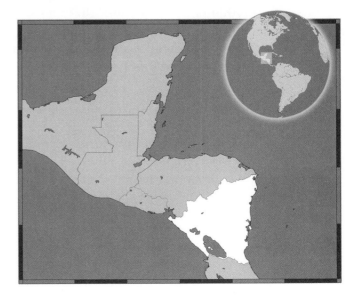

■ NICARAGUA *Upclose*

Capital: Managua

Population: 5,570,129 (June 2006)

Size: 129,494 sq. km. (49,998 sq. mi.) (approximately the size of New York)

Location: in Central America bordered on the west by the Pacific Ocean, on the east by the Caribbean Sea, on the north by Honduras, and on the south by Costa Rica

Climate: hot and humid in the lowlands with cooler temperatures in higher elevations

Terrain: coastal flatlands in the east and west; mountains further inland

Monetary Unit: gold córdoba (7.61 per U.S. dollar) (June 2006)

Religion: Roman Catholic 85%, Protestant 15%

Language(s): Spanish (official), English and indigenous languages along the Atlantic coast

Literacy Rate: total population 67.5%; men 67.2%; women 67.8% (2003)

Ethnicity: mestizo (mixed Amerindian and European) 69%, white 17%, black 9%, Amerindian 5%

Per Capita Income: $326 (2006)

Population Distribution: 57% urban, 43% rural (2003)

Population below Poverty Line: 50% (2001)

Life Expectancy: total population 70.33 years; men 68.3 years; women 72.5 years (2006)

Government: republic

PUBLIC HOLIDAYS

January 1	New Year's Day	December 8	Feast of the Immaculate Conception
Thursday before Easter*	Holy Thursday	December 25	Christmas Day
Friday before Easter*	Good Friday		
May 1	Labor Day		
May 30	Mother's Day		
July 29	Liberation Day		
August 1	Santo Domingo Day		
September 14	Battle of San Jacinto		
September 15	Independence Day		
November 2	All Souls' Day		*variable dates*

Personal Perspective

Everything in the U.S. seems big to me. Even my school here seems more like a city. At home, I'm used to knowing everybody, and everybody knowing me because the community is just the right size. Here I'm a stranger, but it seems like everybody else is, too!

—*ESL student in the United States*

Historical Perspective

HISTORICAL SYNOPSIS

Before the arrival of the first Spanish conquistadors in 1522, the area now known as Nicaragua was settled by groups of Amerindians—namely, the Mískotos, Sumos, Ramas, Nicaraos, Chorotegas, and Lencas—who lived along either the Pacific or the Caribbean coast. One of the leaders of the region was Chief Nicarao, from whom the country eventually got its name. These indigenous residents repelled the Spaniards' first attempts at conquest, but in 1524 they were unable to drive out the invaders and soon succumbed to Spanish rule, which lasted until 1821 when Nicaragua joined the United Provinces of Central America to declare its independence from Spain. By 1838, Nicaragua was a sovereign nation.

U.S. involvement in Nicaraguan politics initially developed out of an interest in creating a shortcut through Nicaragua from the Atlantic to the Pacific Ocean. Soon thereafter a private U.S. citizen (also a physician, lawyer, and soldier of fortune), William Walker, became involved in Nicaragua's civil war in 1855, declaring himself president and governing the country for one year before he was ousted by Nicaraguans when his plans for the annexation of other Latin American countries were revealed. (Walker was later executed by the Honduran government.) The United States was again caught up in Nicaraguan political affairs in 1912 when it sent U.S. Marines to Nicaragua during that country's second civil war. Although the war came to an end, U.S. troops remained until they were forcibly turned out in 1933 under the military leadership of General Augusto César Sandino. General Anastasio Somoza García, known as a ruthless dictator, succeeded Sandino after the latter's assassination, but members of the Sandinista National Liberation Front eventually ousted Somoza, introducing much needed economic and social reforms and nationalizing industry and some private property. The U.S. position on the Sandinistas was one of opposition, and it allied itself with the anti-Sandinista movement, supporting the *contras* with weapons and troops. A Marxist leader, Daniel Ortega Saavedra, was elected president of Nicaragua in 1984, but by 1990 the United States, through the heavy financial subsidizing of the National Opposition Union, had maneuvered a conservative candidate into a position of power, and along with widespread disillusionment over the failures of the *Sandinistas,* Arnoldo Alemán Lacayo was elected president.

Despite improvements in Nicaragua's economy, the country remains plagued by poverty and a stark disparity between classes. In fact, it ranks first in the world in terms of the percentage of household income held by the top 10 percent of the total population. In other words, 10 percent of Nicaraguans receive more than 48 percent of the country's income. It also ranks first in the world for mortality from avalanches, landslides, and floods and ranks first, second, third, or fourth in the world for a long list of health-based mortalities. Nicaragua, however, has so far been spared from the AIDS epidemic; the country holds the fourth lowest rank worldwide in AIDS mortality. Peace, too, has returned to the country. In fact, fighters turned in their weapons in a nationwide cash-for-guns exchange, and in Managua a peace monument has been erected out of the AK-47s that were surrendered.

Deep Culture Perspective

DEEP CULTURE BELIEFS

- The extended family is the most common household unit in Nicaragua. Grandparents and sometimes married aunts and uncles and their families may live under one roof. Such relationships are more than logistically convenient or necessary and function as a source of support throughout the lifetime of an individual.
- The kinship system called *compadrazgo* compensates for the general lack of financial or social power of individuals in Nicaraguan society. Godparents, called either *compadre* (co-father) or *comadre* (co-mother), can provide much needed work-related connections, may help a godchild out financially, and often counsel and care for a godchild as much as a parent would.
- There are also many single-parent households headed mostly by women who were widowed during the war. Nicaraguan women, in general, are beginning to assert their right to be heard and to participate actively in the world of work outside the home. In a traditional household, however, men are typically in charge and prefer to be the sole breadwinners unless economic conditions force the wives to work as well. As Nicaraguan men are loath to assume responsibility on the domestic front, a woman who works outside the home typically experiences no relief from her household duties. The conservative government that came to power in 1990, with the strong support of the Catholic Church, attempted to pass legislation restricting women's rights and delimiting their activity to the home, but the response of Nicaragua's women was to take to the streets in protest.

- The Vatican opposed many of the socialist reforms introduced by President Daniel Ortega and the *Sandinistas* in the 1980s, but Nicaraguan priests and other religious leaders tended to side with the Marxists, as they appeared to be more directly involved in lifting Nicaraguans out of poverty. Their outspokenness and work with the *Sandinistas* was many times answered by government harassment and even assassination. Today, despite its controversial policies on women's roles, the Catholic Church holds a prominent position in Nicaraguan culture, and the Vatican has significant influence over the Nicaraguan government's policies on a variety of social issues. Moreover, it is not uncommon to find prominent religious leaders holding prestigious positions in the Nicaraguan government. Although Nicaraguan Amerindians come from a culture rich in traditional beliefs, most now are followers of Christianity. Evangelical non-Catholic churches (Baptist, Moravian, Assembly of God) abound in Nicaragua, though most notably in the eastern part of the country.

- Many Nicaraguans believe in "black magic" and attribute much of their misfortune to the deliberate sabotage of their lives by others using spells and potions. Such beliefs will sometimes lead them to conduct cleansing rituals or to take more drastic action such as moving out of a house or village. Pain and illness may also be treated, and even resolved, through calling on supernatural spirits.

- Most Nicaraguans live an agrarian life. They either farm their own land or work the fields of more affluent land owners. While corn, beans, and rice are staples of the Nicaraguan diet, other crops such as cotton, sugar, oranges, bananas, and coffee are produced primarily for export. Pine, mahogany, and cedar trees are often felled to support the lucrative, but environmentally controversial, lumber industry as well. Although by law children under the age of 14 are not allowed to work, families are often compelled to put their underage children to work either in the fields or on the street.

- Nicaraguans tend to be gregarious and avidly social and friendly people. They enjoy conversation and gatherings of most kinds, especially if they have the opportunity to interact. They spend much of their free time visiting with relatives.

PROVERBS

- It takes two to make a quarrel but only one to end it.
- A shrimp that sleeps will be taken away by the tide.
- Have patience, fleas, for the night is long!
- You make a road by walking on it.

FOLK TALE

Once upon a time there lived a king who owned many precious things, among which was a beautiful ring. Three of the king's servants stole it and hid it in the stomach of a very large fish that lived in the lake on the palace grounds. The king, believing that he had misplaced the ring, assembled the soothsayers of the kingdom. "Be my guest in my palace for three days," he said, "but know that if you cannot tell me where to find my ring before the time is up, I will order my henchmen to chop off your heads!" Not one of the soothsayers volunteered. However, there appeared at the palace a ragged old man named Mr. Cricket. Dying of hunger, he stood before the king and announced that he would find the ring. Immediately a wonderful feast, clean and beautiful clothes, and a staff of accommodating servants were placed at the old man's disposal.

That night when he went to bed, Mr. Cricket commented aloud to himself about Day One, "Ahhh... I have already seen the first, so I have two more to go." Overhearing his words, one of the thieves determined that the old man knew her identity. On the second night, Mr. Cricket again lay down, sighing aloud, "Ahhh... Now I have seen two. Only one more remains." The second thief overheard these words and trembled at the thought that the "soothsayer" now knew her identity. On the third night, Mr. Cricket was truly happy and had no fear of the death that would come to him the next day when the king discovered that he had deceived him. Falling into bed, the old man said with deep satisfaction, "Ahhh... now I have seen all three." When the third thief heard these words, he and the other two guilty servants fell on their knees before the old man to confess, revealed the location of the stolen ring, and begged not to be exposed.

The next day, Mr. Cricket told the king to look for the ring in the stomach of the large fish that lived in the lake next to the palace. Although the king was delighted to have his ring back, he doubted the powers of the old man and decided to give him an additional test. When the old man turned away, the king scooped up a cricket from the ground and placed it in his pocket. "Tell me, wise soothsayer, what do I have in my pocket here?" The old man had no idea. Scratching his chin and shaking his head, he sadly pronounced, "Oh Mr. Cricket, what a bind you are in." Not realizing that the old man's name was Mr. Cricket, the king was amazed and bestowed on Mr. Cricket a great number of precious gifts, which the old man graciously accepted before leaving the palace and settling in a new home far away.

Administrative Perspective

OFFICIAL EDUCATIONAL POLICY

Guaranteed compulsory education was not a legal right for Nicaraguan children until after the Somoza dictatorship ended in 1979. Before that time, only a privileged few in Nicaragua had access to education. In 1980, however, the *Sandinistas* launched a successful campaign to increase literacy. The National Literacy Crusade not only increased the literacy rate of poor Nicaraguans but also brought primary school enrollment up to more than one million.

In 2001, a new governmental initiative called the SGPRS, or Strengthened Growth and Poverty Reduction Strategy, was introduced with the overarching goal of reducing extreme poverty by one-half by the year 2015. Education figures into the plan strongly. It focuses on increasing school enrollments and retention, increasing the number and quality of rural schools, and developing and implementing a viable national education plan. Those in charge of the plan also hope to continue the process of decentralization of education in Nicaragua, bringing more power to and encouraging more input from local schools and parents. Distance education for non–school age learners is also a priority. The plan thus far has in some cases exceeded expectations—for example, in the area of school reconstruction and the raising of teachers' salaries by 28 percent. Due perhaps to these successes as well as the obvious need for educational reform, the World Bank made Nicaragua one of the beneficiaries of a new Education For All (EFA) program, an initiative designed to increase enrollment and raise the standard of instruction, especially for children aged 13 or younger.

EDUCATION AT A GLANCE

See the Education at a Glance table on page 50.

NICARAGUA

Level/Age	Hours/Calendar	Language of Instruction	Compulsory Attendance	Exams	Grading System	Curriculum	Cost	Enrollment
Primary Grades 1–6 ages 6–12	Mar.–Dec. with the month of July reserved for a midyear vacation. (Classes are not held during *Semana Santa* or Holy Week.) 7:00 AM–noon or 1:00 PM Overcrowded schools may offer a morning shift followed by an afternoon shift (noon or 1:00 PM–5:00 or 6:00 PM). School children never eat lunch at school. No cafeterias. Snack bars sell donuts, pizza, Coke®, etc.	Spanish (Some bilingual schools exist where English, German, or French are combined with Spanish.)	Yes	4 end-of-term exams (worth 75% of final grade) plus 1 final exam (worth 25% of final grade) Final exams tend to include most recent material covered, though they technically are to be comprehensive. Exam item types: true/false + explanation, multiple choice + explanation, sentence completion, short answers (definitions, explanations, classifications, etc.) Primary school-leaving credential: *Diploma de Educación Primaria*	90%–100% outstanding 80%–89% very good 70%–79% good 60%–69% average 0–49% fail Points awarded for accuracy. Neatness can constitute up to 40% of an overall grade.	Reading, writing, grammar, spelling, vocabulary, handwriting, math, art, music, social studies, physical education, Spanish language	Free, but with "voluntary fees" of US$1–2 per month Costs at private schools may go beyond tuition to personal possessions such as computers, cars, credit cards, clothing, and other manifestations of material competition among students.	Total enrollment 80.75% of which 49.4% is female. Poor urban children complete an average of 3 years of school; 1.6 years for rural children. It takes an average of 10.3 years to complete the full 6-year primary school cycle—nearly 500,000 school-age children are not enrolled. Only 29% complete primary school.
Basic secondary Grades 7–9 ages 12–15			Yes, to age 13	Basic secondary school-leaving credential: *Diploma de Curso Básico*	No points deducted for repetition, failure to cite sources, express opinions, or support assertions with evidence.	Spanish, foreign language, math, geography, natural sciences, civics, physical education, practical training		Total enrollment 35.5% of which 53.4% is female, but in diversified secondary females represent 67% of the total enrollment.
Diversified secondary Grades 10–11 ages 15–17			No	Diversified secondary school-leaving credential: *Bachillerato* in humanities or sciences (this plus the national entrance exam is necessary for admission to university).		Spanish, foreign language, math, chemistry, biology, economics, civics, physical education		Estimates claim that some 322,000 under the age of 17 are working rather than attending school.
Technical secondary Grades 10–12 ages 15–18				Technical secondary school-leaving credential: *Técnico Medio*				
University ages 19+ *Licenciatura* 4–5 years Professional qualification 2–5 years (e.g., accounting 2 years, engineering and medicine 6 years) *Maestría* 2 years beyond the *Licenciatura*		Spanish	No	Students prepare a thesis for *Maestría*.	Highest: 100% Pass/fail: 70% Lowest: 0%	Degree programs in all fields at undergraduate level and graduate level depending on the university	US$800 per year for public universities; up to US$8,000 for private universities	Total enrollment 11.5%

Surface Culture Perspective

CLASSROOMS

- Most public schools in Nicaragua, whether located in the city or in the countryside, are in severe disrepair and have few basic facilities, such as desks and books. Private schools tend to be in better condition and are better equipped.
- Schools are typically laid out in a large square with a courtyard or playground in the middle. A wall surrounds the school, and a gate offers entry to the school; entry to the classrooms is gained only from the courtyard. There are rarely windows in classrooms that look out onto the street. The buildings are usually constructed of cinderblock rather than brick or wood. Some schools have bars on the windows.
- In schools that have desks, students sit in rows, their desks close to each other but separated, rather than pushed together. A blackboard is typically found at the front of the class, though it may be in such poor condition that whatever is written on it is difficult to read. Some schools may have a handpainted mural or inspirational quote painted on the back wall (e.g., *El respeto a los demás comienza con el respeto a tí mismo* or "Respect for others begins with respect for oneself"). A drawing of the Virgin Mary or a crucifix on the wall is not an unusual image in a Nicaraguan classroom.
- There are normally more children enrolled in a given school than there is room to accommodate them, so schools often offer at least two shifts of instruction. The morning shift typically runs from 7:00 AM to noon, with the second shift beginning just after lunch.
- Even in high school and university, it is the teacher, not the students, who move from classroom to classroom.

TEACHERS' STATUS

- Nicaraguan teachers tend to be so poorly compensated that they will often take to the street *en masse* to protest. Hunger strikes are also not uncommon. Sometimes such strikes result in the delay of the beginning of the school year or the prolonged cancellation of classes. Teachers claim that their 2005 salaries barely met the standard living index (US$126/month) and that they are forced to take on extra jobs to provide for their families.
- To teach at the pre-primary or primary school level, by law teachers are to have completed a five-year secondary-level training program following successful completion of primary school. Three of the first five years of training are general, and the last two, delivered at a teachers' college or *Escuela Normal,* are focused on the prospective teacher's specialization. Upon graduation, the individual receives a *Diploma de Maestro de Educación Primaria.*

- Those hoping to receive the *Título de Profesor de Educación Media* and to teach at the secondary level must complete four years of study at the university and receive a *Licenciatura*.

TEACHER-STUDENT RELATIONSHIP

- Teachers tend to expect students to try to leave the classroom, assemblies, or to generally escape required gatherings to join their friends. For this reason, many teachers are obliged to patrol the school grounds, checking bathrooms, for example, during class periods, to make sure that no student is where he or she does not belong at a particular time. In most schools, students are not allowed to leave the classroom without permission.
- While female teachers tend to be more nurturing and friendlier than male teachers, the relationship between teacher and students can be strained as teachers strive to maintain order and students attempt to circumvent rules. Teachers consider themselves responsible for the socialization of learners and will frequently send a message about social boundaries and obligations via the conduct grade that accompanies the academic grade a student receives at the end of the term.
- At the university level, the relationship between teacher and students is much less restrictive. It is not unusual for some teachers to socialize after class with the students. Some may be compelled to offer better grades to students with whom they have become friendly.

TEACHING PRACTICES

- There is little give-and-take in a typical Nicaraguan classroom. Instead, the teacher lectures while the students transfer as much as possible to their notebooks. Many teachers regularly check these notebooks to ensure that students have been paying attention. Students whose notebooks fall short of the teacher's expectations must bring their parents to school for a conference with the teacher. The parents of academically weak students are also called upon to pick up their child's report card themselves rather than receiving it from the student when grades are released.
- Although teachers may assign homework, they do not always check its accuracy. They generally do not assign credit when homework is done appropriately; however, if it is not done or done poorly, teachers tend to subtract points from the student's grade.
- Teachers who are considered to be effective are credited with giving clear explanations and abundant examples on the blackboard. Teachers with many years of experience are usually appreciated as are those who give two to three hours of homework per night.

TEACHERS' DRESS

- Male teachers usually wear short-sleeved shirts and trousers. Female teachers may wear fashionable but modest attire. The dress code depends, too, on the type of school (public, private, religious) in which one works. Shorts for either men or women are reserved for the beach or vacation resorts but are not worn on the street or to work. In general, Nicaraguans are careful about their appearance and will appear at work in clean and pressed clothing.

DISCIPLINE AND CLASS MANAGEMENT

- Although sometimes a student's antics can amuse an instructor and prompt him or her to laugh aloud, in general, Nicaraguan teachers are very strict. Misbehavior is often punished by sending the offending student to the principal's office, but some teachers will answer misconduct via lowered grades. Occasionally students will be expelled after a number of warnings have been issued and disregarded.
- Troublemakers usually try to sit at the back of the class, but as their misbehavior increases, teachers will bring them to the desks at the front of the classroom. They may also shame students who misbehave or are academically slow or lazy by saying such things as "You're going to end up as the janitor at this school."
- Teachers assign two types of grades at the end of the year—a grade for academic performance and a grade for conduct. The conduct grade is given in primary and secondary school.

STUDENTS' CIRCUMSTANCES

- Although education is free and compulsory till the age of 13, many school-aged children are unable to complete more than a few years of schooling. Parents may need their children to help at home in the fields or look after siblings, or they may send their children to the streets to sell candy, tortillas, or water.
- Some students are so poor that they do not have money to buy paper and pencils, let alone textbooks. When this is the case, many students will listen carefully to the teacher and try to memorize everything he or she has said.
- Not all Nicaraguan students are native or even proficient speakers of Spanish. Those living along the Caribbean coast may receive instruction in their native language and take classes in Spanish as a second language.

STUDENT-STUDENT RELATIONSHIP

- Nicaraguan students are used to knowing the names and backgrounds of virtually everyone at their school. Even at university, when students pass on campus they will greet each other and recognize the class or home town of the other.
- Students in Nicaragua are often adept at helping each other cheat on exams, with outstanding and weak students engaging in the practice equally. They may devise elaborate or ingenious techniques such as inserting a tightly rolled-up cheat sheet into the barrel of a pen, creating gestures representing different answers, or writing the answers on the soles of one's shoes. Additionally, students sometimes create a distraction so that the teacher is preoccupied while other students consult one another for answers. They may also loan each other their copybooks and do each other's homework if a friend is falling behind in school.

STUDENTS' LEARNING PRACTICES

- Whereas North American students are often expected to be original in their work and thinking in school, Nicaraguan students dedicate their energies to noting and memorizing as much as possible of what the teacher has said or covered in class, knowing that this will constitute the content of the next exam.
- Students' opinions are usually not solicited in class, and routine chatter is discouraged. Students who talk during the lesson are usually reprimanded.

STUDENTS' DRESS

- Most schools—whether private or public, urban or rural—require students to wear a uniform. Very poor schools may be a rare exception; in fact, many children cannot attend school because their families cannot afford to buy uniforms. Generally speaking, school children cannot sport tattoos, and girls cannot wear earrings or make-up. Their hair must be pulled up or back, and in addition to their skirt falling no higher than the knee, they are required to wear knee-high socks. All students must come to school with their uniforms clean and their shoes polished.

GIFTS FOR THE TEACHER

- Depending on whether or not the teacher is popular with the students, gifts may be presented to the teacher on Teachers' Day, Mothers Day, or the teacher's birthday, although gift-giving is only authorized by the school administration on Teachers' Day. Not all students will give a teacher a gift on Teachers' Day, and an instructor will not be offended if some students bring nothing for him or her. There are no big parties, but the instructor may choose to take the students on a field trip on Teachers' Day rather than holding class.

- Appropriate gifts for the teacher include perfume or a purse for female teachers or a briefcase for a male teacher.
- At the end of the school year, a handful of female students normally collects money for a gift for the teacher and plans a small class party with cake or pizza.

NONVERBAL COMMUNICATION

- Touching and close physical proximity are the norm during conversations with acquaintances, although men and women may not display as much of this physical warmth toward one another as they would with friends of the same gender. Directly meeting another person's eye gaze is considered somewhat aggressive when speaking, however.
- When meeting someone for the first time, it is appropriate to shake hands with either a man or a woman. Once a friendship is established, however, a hug or kiss on the cheek is expected.
- Nicaraguans may point with their lips rather than with the index finger.
- Sticking the thumb between the middle and index finger (called "the fig") is obscene and sexual in Nicaragua. North Americans who tease children in this way by making the gesture and suggesting that they have captured the child's nose will cause great offense to the parents or other adults.
- North Americans may find that Nicaraguans are less direct in expressing themselves. Sensitive to the feelings of others, they may avoid conflict and disagreement, avoiding such situations by being circumspect in the expression of their opinions. With those considered to have a higher status, Nicaraguans may be loath to say "no" or "I don't know."
- Time is not as carefully measured and monitored among Nicaraguans as it is among their North American peers. Thus, they may appear for appointments and other scheduled activities up to one hour late. This does not mean that Nicaraguans are not hardworking or careful about their work. Some cite the hot climate as an element that naturally slows individuals down.
- When arriving at the home of a friend, it is customary to be offered (and to accept) a refreshing drink. If food is prepared, the guest will offer lavish praise and show his or her appreciation of the host's hospitality.
- It is considered polite to rise when an older person enters a room and to pay special attention to him or her. In general, respect for the elderly is sacrosanct in Nicaragua.

Forms of Address

- Typically, Nicaraguans have two first names plus the family name of their mother plus their father's family name. Luis Enrique Rodriguez Perez, thus, may be called Luis Enrique by his friends. His father would be Señor Rodriguez Toledo. His mother, formally Señorita Perez Alvarado, would have dropped her mother's name (Alvarado), replaced it with her husband's family name (Rodriguez), but retained her father's name preceded by *de* as in Señora Rodriguez de Perez.
- Nicaraguans, like most Spanish speaking people, will make use of the distinction between the formal and informal pronoun "you." Thus, *Usted* is used when speaking to older people, those in positions of higher authority, or strangers while *tú* is used for communication with family, children, and friends.
- The title *Don* (masc.) or *Donna* (fem.) may be placed before an individual's first name to show respect. *Don Fernando* or *Donna Flor* both convey special deference.
- Nicknames are common among family members and friends in Nicaragua. To North Americans, these names may sometimes suggest insensitivity or racism, as when a woman is called *gorda* (fat) or *flaca* (skinny) or a man is called *negro* (black), *chino* (Chinese), or *turk* (Turk), but these names are not intended to convey any more than affection.

Appropriate Topics

- Teachers generally do not proclaim their political position or try to influence their students in terms of politics. Whether or not, for example, they are *Sandinistas* is considered a private choice. Politics can be an inappropriate topic in many public forums since there are often sharp divisions between people on sociopolitical issues, but among close friends, friendly arguments over politics are not uncommon.
- It is common for adult Nicaraguans to question each other about their marital status, number of children, and birthplace when they are first introduced. These inquiries are thought to be manifestations of interest and friendliness, not an invasion of privacy.
- Nicaraguans are often delighted to talk about their country's history, geography, culture, and cuisine.

Outside of Class

- Baseball is perhaps the most popular pastime in Nicaragua, where members of major baseball teams are regarded as superstars and play in large baseball stadiums, such as the one in Managua that seats 40,000 people. Boys and men play it throughout their lives, and women are avid fans and spectators. Even the poorest village will often have a baseball diamond, although children may be forced to use a stick for a bat and a rolled-up sock for a ball. A proud nation cheered Nicaragua's ranking of fourth in the world at the 1996 Olympics.

- In addition to baseball, Nicaraguan children enjoy soccer and basketball. Girls, especially, frequently play volleyball and basketball. Checkers, marbles, hide-and-seek, skipping rope, hopscotch, and *trompo* (a game played with a top and string) are popular as well.

- Most Nicaraguans are too poor to go on family vacations, but those who are able visit the Caribbean or Pacific coastal resorts or make camping trips into the mountains.

- Nicaraguan children are accustomed to large amounts of daily homework in each course they take. The assignment may involve conducting some outside research on a topic, reading from the textbook, or answering the questions at the end of a textbook chapter.

Potential Adjustment Challenges

PROBLEMS/SOLUTIONS

Problem

I have a Nicaraguan student who rarely gets his homework assignments in to me on time. Is he taking advantage of my good nature?

Solution

Nicaraguans may not respond to deadlines as readily as their North American classmates. In no way is this behavior indicative of how the student feels about the teacher. It is simply a reflection of a more relaxed orientation to time.

Problem

The father of my only Nicaraguan student is a doctor, and the family lives in a very nice part of town, and yet I'm told that they're refugees. I thought Nicaraguan refugees were poor farmers.

Solution

Although there is an extreme disparity between rich and poor in Nicaragua, members of both economic classes have made their way to North America either as refugees or immigrants. As a result, teachers should not assume that all their Nicaraguan students will have similar experiences or needs.

Problem

I have a Nicaraguan student who is studying at my university on a full scholarship. He is very bright, but he has admitted to me that he hasn't yet seriously attempted any of his classwork, and it's already mid-semester! Is it common for Nicaraguans to take such a casual approach to their education?

Solution

Nicaraguans deeply value education and are willing to work hard to achieve academic success. However, university students may at first look upon their time in college as a gift of freedom and may skip classes in order to socialize with friends. Some are easily influenced by less serious peers and get redirected from the academic path set by their parents.

Ecuador

■ ECUADOR *Upclose*

Capital: Quito

Population: 13,547,510 (June 2006)

Size: 283,560 sq. km. (109,483 sq. mi.) (slightly smaller than Nevada)

Location: on the Pacific coast of South America, between Peru and Colombia (the Galápagos Islands were annexed as an Ecuadorian territory in 1832)

Climate: tropical in the lowland Amazonian jungle and along the coast and cooler at higher elevations inland

Terrain: consists of *la costa,* or coastal plain, the Andean central highlands *(la sierra),* and the flat-to-somewhat-rolling eastern rainforest lowlands *(el oriente)*

Monetary Unit: U.S. dollar

Religion: 95% Roman Catholic, with considerable conversion to Protestantism (especially evangelical and Pentecostal churches) since the late 1960s

Language(s): Spanish (official and predominant language of Ecuador), with additional Amerindian languages, most notably Quechua

Literacy Rate: total population 92.5%; men 94%; women 91% (2003)

Ethnicity: mestizo (mixed Amerindian and European) 65%, Amerindian 25%, Spanish and others 7%, black 3%

Per Capita Income: US$1,044 (2006)

Population Distribution: 62% urban, 38% rural (2003)

Population below Poverty Line: 41% (2006)

Life Expectancy: total population 76 years; men 73.1 years; women 79 years (2006)

Government: republic

PUBLIC HOLIDAYS				
	January 1	New Year's Day	July 24	Simon Bolivar Day
	Thursday before Easter	Maundy Thursday	August 10	Independence Day
	Friday before Easter	Good Friday	November 2	Memorial Day/All Soul's Day
	May 1	Labor Day	December 25	Christmas Day
	May 24	Anniversary of the	December 31	New Year's Eve
		Battle of Pichincha		
	May 26	Corpus Christi		

▉ Personal Perspective

What were the challenges I faced when I first came to the U.S. as a student? Mainly the language. My family was wasn't that well off, so I didn't get to go to one of the many bilingual or binational schools. That would have made my transition easier. But I did go to a private school, and I found school here in the United States to be too easy. That's why the challenge was more cultural. It's hard to leave your friends and make new ones, especially when you're at an age when your friends mean the world to you. Ecuadorian children arrive here more innocent about dating and sexual issues than their American classmates, so the adjustment is difficult.
—*Ecuadorian undergraduate university student in the United States*

▉ Historical Perspective

IMMIGRATION TO THE UNITED STATES

Like many struggling economies in the world, Ecuador has grown ever more reliant upon monies sent home by resettled Ecuadorians in countries such as the United States and Spain. It is reported that in 2000 a total of US$1.3 billion was sent back to Ecuador by immigrants who had made their homes in the United States and Spain. The U.S. Census of 2000 accounted for nearly 260,000 Ecuadorians living in the United States. The primary reason for the mass departure is increasing poverty; although in 1995, 34 percent of Ecuadorians lived at or below the poverty level, by 2002 that number had increased to 60 percent. Salaries as low as US$10 a month, unemployment, the rising cost of living, and inflation that reached 95 percent in 2000 when Ecuador adopted the U.S. dollar as its currency—all combined to compel some 7–10 percent of Ecuadorans to leave their country in search of a better life and a reported 45 percent to claim an interest in emigrating.

Low salaries make the financial costs associated with immigration seem all the more staggering, with fees from US$10,000 to US$13,000 per individual (children being the most expensive to transport). The debt incurred for what is not always safe passage must be paid off in interest-bearing installments to those providing smugglers' services, which are estimated to generate some US$20 billion in annual profits. In addition to issues associated with poverty, Ecuadorians are said to leave their country in search of *un espejismo,* or a mirage of how they dream life will be in their newly adopted home.

Whereas Ecuadorian migration to the United States was once concentrated in New York City, today states such as New Jersey, California, Connecticut, Florida, Illinois, and Texas also have large Ecuadorian immigrant communities. Earlier groups often consisted largely of young men from the rural areas of Ecuador who arrived with work permits. Those who have arrived since 9/11/2001 come as often from the cities as from the countryside, and they may come from the professional or middle class rather than from the peasantry. Most who come are women, and working papers are much harder to obtain either legally or through the payment of exorbitant fees to illegal visa brokers. These impediments have led significant numbers of Ecuadorians to migrate to Spain, where they constitute the largest and fastest growing immigrant population in Spain. Despite an improvement in living conditions, most Ecuadorian immigrants work unpleasant, monotonous, and physically demanding (and even dangerous) jobs in factories, construction sites, and restaurants, living frugally and spending as little of their earnings as possible in order to help their families back home.

HISTORICAL SYNOPSIS

Emerging from the collapse of what was known as *el Gran Colombia* in 1830, the Republic of Ecuador separated from Colombia and Venezuela to form its own nation. In 1832, the Galápagos Islands were annexed as an Ecuadorian territory. (In 1835, Charles Darwin made his first visit there for research.) Conflicts with bordering neighbors have brought about numerous territorial losses; in particular, relations with Peru have been fraught with conflict or war for the past two centuries. Following the unstable political conditions of the 19th century and the economic distress and political unrest that followed World War I, Ecuador had 22 chiefs of state in the period between 1925 and 1948. Following 13 years of relative stability, President José M. Velasco Ibarra was overthrown by a military *coup d'état,* which then brought about 20 years of military rule.

Modern Ecuador has since had constitutionally elected governments; yet that is not to say that transitions between governments have been smooth or that in the majority of cases presidents have been able to serve out their full terms. Still, despite its chronicle of political and military upheavals in the early 20th century, Ecuador has remained relatively peaceful in recent years. Its inflation, however, is among the highest in the region. This led the government to replace the national currency with the U.S. dollar in 2000 in an attempt to curb inflation and to stabilize the country's financial systems. Ecuador mints currency in the same denominations as the United States, though they are not accepted as legal tender in the United States.

Deep Culture Perspective

DEEP CULTURE BELIEFS

• An emphasis on family as a venerated institution is shared by both Hispanic and Amerindian traditions in Ecuador. Extended families are the norm in household living arrangements, with married couples often residing with the parents and unmarried children of one of the spouses after marriage. Aging parents will frequently remain in the family homestead with the youngest son and his family acting as caregivers.

- The unchallenged head of household in Ecuador is the man. Though perhaps a loving parent, he is not prone to take a committed role in the routine operation of the family.

- Women's roles within the family remain centered around the management of the household and the raising of children. Even today with more opportunities for a professional career, particularly in cities, women are expected to remain subordinate to their husbands in most matters.

- There tends to be a double standard with regard to marital fidelity issues in urban Ecuador, with men not surprisingly landing on the permissive side of extramarital relationships. Among the rural indigenous populations, however, there is a strong moral code that demands faithfulness on the part of both men and women.

- Kinship is recognized beyond the nuclear family. In rural areas where most marriages take place within small communities, generations of intermarriages created a network of kinship ties throughout the district. Because one's ties were so broad in scope, an individual might actively choose which kinships to recognize and cultivate in order to better serve immediate family needs.

- Extension of kinship, often referred to as "fictive kinship," through the Hispanic and Native Amerindian traditions of *compadres,* is quite common in Ecuador. These loyal friendships are so highly regarded that arguments or criticisms that would be tolerated among relatives would be unimaginable with one's *compadres.* People may choose *compadres* of equal or greater social status.

- Godparent selection is a common and important custom for baptism, confirmation, and marriage. The godparents assume financial obligations to the child or couple. Because ties with *compadres* may cut across class and ethnic boundaries, those with a lower social class or having fewer financial resources often ask influential or wealthy whites to serve as godparents.

- The dichotomy between conservative and progressive exists in Ecuador within both its social and cultural constructs. Women are free to pursue any line of occupation; yet one's social class, more than one's gender, may be the factor that predicts success. Those women who do succeed in occupying positions beyond that of secretary, for example, will likely still encounter flirting and sexual innuendo as part of office culture in Ecuador. This is perhaps attributable to the alleged belief among Ecuadorian men that women would be insulted if men refrained from making comments about the woman's appearance.

- There has historically been evidence suggesting that Ecuador is a somewhat racist society where the lightness or darkness of one's skin reflects the position within the social order. This is perhaps a colonial legacy, but as an expression in Ecuador asserts, "more money is located in lighter hands; less money in darker."

- An invitation to go out generally carries with it the assumption that the inviter will pay for the invitées.
- Within the Ecuadorian workplace, favoritism often plays a role in hiring and privilege-granting practices. Who one knows rather than what one knows is an axiom shared by many cultures. Generally, Ecuadorians expect and anticipate getting help from friends in positions of power. That said, those in power who help others would insist that the recipient of their aid or generosity meet their end of the bargain and may not hesitate to dismiss a friend who failed to meet this expectation.
- The Catholic religion in Ecuador has incorporated into it aspects of the spiritual traditions of native cultures that worshipped astrological features such as the stars, sun, and moon.

PROVERBS

- It is one thing to cackle and another to lay an egg.
- Anger of the mind is poison to the soul.
- When one helps another, both gain in strength.

FOLK TALE

There once was a king whose son was deathly ill. After many attempts to cure the young man, the king prayed to the gods asking for help. A voice finally came back, accompanied by the appearance of a golden cup. The voice advised the king to send one of his subjects to a magic lake that lay at the end of the earth and to fill the cup with water from the lake. Many attempted the task in hope of a fine reward from the king, but no one was able to find the magic lake. Two wily brothers planned to obtain water from a nearby lake and so attempted to deceive the king, but the golden cup would not hold the water, and the brothers were imprisoned for their trickery.

Their sister, however, was a good-hearted and sincere creature and begged her parents to allow her to go off in search of the magic lake at the end of the earth. Accompanied by her pet llama, she spent the first night of her journey in a state of bliss, but on the second night a cougar threatened to devour the girl and her pet, so she urged the llama to return to the safety of her family's farm.

Afraid that she would be attacked by the cougar, the next night the girl buried her pouch of food beneath a tree and climbed high into the branches. At dawn she was awoken by the tittering of birds, who thanked her for the corn she had left for them and promised to help her find the magic lake. Each bird gave her a feather out of which she made a fan. She was told that any request she made would be fulfilled by the fan, and it would protect her from harm as well.

Eventually, the girl found the magic lake and began to gather water for the sick prince. Time after time, however, monsters would rise out of the water or swoop down on her from the sky to threaten her. She had only to hold the fan in front of her face to send these menacing creatures into a deep sleep. In this way, she was able to collect the magic water and deliver it to the king. The prince recovered fully from his illness, the king rewarded the girl with the release of her brothers and a large farm for her parents, and she and the prince fell in love and married. Her kindness, concern for others, and willingness to sacrifice her own well-being became legendary throughout the land.

■ Administrative Perspective

OFFICIAL EDUCATIONAL POLICY

It may be said that there is a certain contradiction in Ecuador's educational policies. The constitution requires that 30 percent of gross revenue be committed to education; yet the government's stated goal is to dedicate 11 percent of the budget to the education needs of its citizens. Major expansion in the educational opportunities afforded Ecuadorians occurred throughout the 1960s and 1970s. These efforts to increase enrollments were met with associated problems such as keeping up with school construction, procuring adequate teaching materials, and hiring trained and qualified instructors. In secondary and higher education, many of the teachers engaged during this period lacked full accreditation, especially within rural regions. In the 1980s, the Ministry of Education and Culture focused its attention on literacy programs in rural, non-Spanish speaking communities and have had some success, though literacy rates among Ecuador's indigenous populations are estimated to be below 72 percent.

Nevertheless, both enrollment and literacy rates as viewed across the entire populace are above 90 percent, with average years of schooling for Ecuadorians at 6.4 years. Only about 50 percent of the student population will enter into secondary education. And while inequalities in access to education between urban and rural populations continue to be considerable, the education gender gap has been eliminated, with females currently outpacing their male counterparts.

EDUCATION AT A GLANCE

See the Education at a Glance table on page 65.

ECUADOR

Level/Age	Hours/Calendar	Language of Instruction	Compulsory Attendance	Exams	Grading System	Curriculum	Cost	Enrollment
Pre-school ages 4–5	7:30 AM to 1:30 PM	Spanish	No	None	No data available	Manners, colors, numbers, shapes, hygiene	No data available	No data available
Primary Grades 1–6 ages 6–12	Private schools may set own school hours, and elective courses may be offered between 1:30 and 3:00 PM	French, German, or English at the bilingual/binational schools	Yes, though only about 50% finish	Upon successful completion of primary level, students receive a *Certificado de Sufficiencia en los Estudios Primarios.* Most important tests administered every three months. A final exam in every subject is administered at the end of the school year. Students who do not pass a subject may sit for a make-up exam one month before the start of the next school year.	20-point scale 19–20 excellent 16–18 very good 14–15 good 12–13 average 0–11 unsatisfactory	Reading, writing, mathematics, geography, regional or local history, social studies, Spanish language	Public schools are free. Costs for private schools vary from US$80 per month to US$500 per month. Parents of both private and public school students must purchase books and supplies.	Grade 1 intake 82%, with 77% reaching 5th grade; total enrollment is 99% of which 49.1% is female. Average years of schooling for an Ecuadorian adult is 6.4 years. Only 50% finish Grade 6.
Basic secondary Grades 7–9 ages 12–15	May to Jan. on the coast Oct. to July in Quito and the highlands Recesses are often called so that teachers may attend faculty meetings.		Yes, to age 15	Upon successful completion of basic secondary level, students receive a *Diploma.* Throughout secondary level, quarterly tests are administered for which students must receive 40 out of 60 in order to advance to the next level. Most important tests administered every three months. A final exam in every subject is administered at the end of the school year. Students who do not pass a subject may sit for a make-up exam one month before the start of the next school year.		Global geography, national and world history, social studies, algebra, statistics, physics, chemistry, biology, Spanish, English		Total enrollment is 48% of which 49.7% is female.
Diversified secondary Grades 10–13 ages 15–18 Vocational *Instituto Técnico* ages 18–20			No	Upon successful completion of diversified secondary, students receive a *Bachillerato* that is required for university admission. Most important tests administered every three months. A final exam in every subject is administered at the end of the school year. Students who do not pass a subject may sit for a make-up exam one month before the start of the next school year.		Students specialize in one of three tracks—humanities, sciences, or technology—or they may take specialized courses that prepare them for technical schools or teacher training.		Only 50% finish Grade 12.
University ages 19+	Oct. to July		No	Mid-term and end-of-year exams	100-point or 10-point scale pass/fail= 55% or 6/7 achievement of a score of 6 out of a total possible 7 points	Students are required to declare their major before beginning coursework and cannot change after they have begun to take classes. Bachelor's, master's, and doctoral degrees in education, humanities, natural sciences, business, law, medicine, etc.	Annual tuition costs vary according to discipline and level of study.	No data available

Surface Culture Perspective

CLASSROOMS

- Schools in many poorer communities have few resources that can be dedicated to schools. Many schools have only one or two classrooms led by one or two teachers for all primary grades. One-third of all schools in Ecuador have only one teacher.
- The physical resources for schools are generally very poor. Some classrooms may have dirt floors protected only by roofs made of canvas. Accesses to clean water and toilet facilities are also common problems.
- Many schools lack texts and teaching materials.
- The average teacher-student ratio is 1:23 at the primary level and 1:17 at the secondary level. These are official statistics, however. Anecdotal reports claim class size varies significantly from 30 to 60.

TEACHERS' STATUS

- According to UNESCO, 87 percent of primary school teachers and 72 percent of high school teachers in Ecuador have received teacher preparation and training.
- Those primary school teachers who have received training typically have participated in two-year post-*Bachillerato* courses at the *Institutos Pedagógicos* where they obtain the title of *Profesor en Educación Primaria*. Others who have attended four- to five-year courses through a university may earn their *Licenciado en Educatión Primaria* as part of their full university degree in primary education.
- Secondary school teachers are generally expected to have been trained in four-year university programs leading to a *Licenciado de Educación Media*.
- There have been high turnover rates among teachers due in large part to the reduction in teacher salaries (which fall between US$160 and US$350 per month for public school teachers) as well as the poor conditions of the facilities in which instructors are expected to work.
- Over the past 15 years, an average of at least one month of each academic year has been lost due to teacher strikes. Teacher strikes affect poor rural areas as well, where approximately nine school days are lost monthly. The overall absentee rate for teachers in Ecuador is reported to be 14 percent annually, arguably an impediment to learning.

TEACHER-STUDENT RELATIONSHIP

- The relationship between teacher and student may vary depending upon whether the school is public or private. Relationships are generally closer at private schools. Students may join teachers in strikes protesting low wages and poor working conditions.

- Private school teachers, much more so than their public school counterparts, are discouraged from using corporal punishment with students. Thus, rather than hitting students' hands with a ruler to discipline them, private school teachers frequently find ways to motivate learners to behave.

TEACHING PRACTICES

- In public schools teachers often encourage students to memorize subject matter. Private school teachers supplement memorization with projects, experiments, and a variety of interactive activities.
- Whether in private or public schools, teachers tend to "pile on" homework.

TEACHERS' DRESS

- Clothing worn by teachers tends to be somewhat conservative, though women's skirts are often above the knee and form-fitting. Men in high or supervisory positions wear suits, while those with less authority wear trousers, shirts, and ties. It would be inappropriate for teachers to wear casual sportswear or sneakers when in the classroom.

DISCIPLINE AND CLASS MANAGEMENT

- Conflicts with students are generally addressed in private and with discretion. Ecuadorians seldom are direct in communicating dissatisfaction with performance and have an expectation that one's tone should always remain polite.
- Demonstrative praise is given when Ecuadorian teachers are pleased with the work of a student's performance. Less enthusiastic praise or more restrained acclamation may be a sign of displeasure of performance.

STUDENTS' CIRCUMSTANCES

- Wealth can make a significant difference in the future of an Ecuadorian student as the country is one of economic extremes. Parents with a low income generally cannot afford to send their children to private schools, which are publicly acknowledged to be better equipped, staffed, funded, and monitored. More affluent parents not only are able to send their children to private school, but can choose the school. In other words, they are not restricted by the neighborhood in which they live but by their financial resources.

STUDENT-STUDENT RELATIONSHIP

- Ecuadorian students are usually very close to one another. They may stay overnight at a classmate's house not just to study but to have fun. Young people spend a good deal of time together attending parties, going to movies, playing sports, etc.
- It is common for students to form study groups as most tend to prefer collective rather than individual activity.

STUDENTS' LEARNING PRACTICES

- Students in Ecuador seem to thrive in lively, talkative, and unrepressed environments. Classrooms that to an outsider seem chaotic may, from the Ecuadorian perspective, be seen as encouraging of interaction and exploration of students' own interests. Students typically exhibit a great desire both to learn and to be in school.

STUDENTS' DRESS

- Children in primary and secondary schools wear uniforms, while university students wear what they wish.
- School uniforms normally consist of a white cotton shirt plus skirt for girls and pants for boys. Each school has its own distinctive uniform.

GIFTS FOR THE TEACHER

- Students are generally not in the habit of giving gifts to teachers, but on occasion they will give the teacher a small gift or perhaps money collected from their classmates, as a Christmas present.
- When presented with a gift by an Ecuadorian student, it is expected that the teacher will act openly appreciative.
- A wrapped gift would generally not be opened upon acceptance.
- If a teacher is invited to the home of a student, flowers, pastries, or chocolates are an appropriate gift. One should avoid lilies and marigolds—flowers culturally associated with funerals.
- In contexts other than that of teacher-student, if one is invited to the home of an associate teacher, fine wines and liquors make good gifts, but foreign beer is avoided. A gift for any children in the household is also appreciated.

NONVERBAL COMMUNICATION

- Ecuadorians may not have as strict a sense of what it means to be on time or tardy in the way that their North American counterparts do. Supervisors, or those who view themselves as important, may see their lateness as an entitlement appropriate to their status. Arriving late at one's office, however, is not acceptable. Punctuality is valued, as is the willingness to work beyond the scope of a project or task.

- Greetings are very important in Ecuadorian culture, so one should expect loud and warm greetings from one's students. These greetings may be accompanied by physical closeness. A kiss on the right cheek is considered acceptable during an initial contact between parents and a female teacher in formal settings, and men usually offer a right-handed handshake with the left hand patting the other man's right shoulder. Through one's distance and firmness of handshake one can establish boundaries if reticent about kissing as a greeting. Firmness of a handshake, however, is a measure of sincerity.

- Ecuadorians from differing backgrounds and ethnicities may react differently to physicality among strangers and acquaintances. Indigenous peoples or those from more working class backgrounds may be shy about offering their hands or expressing themselves physically. Mestizos and whites may be more apt to kiss or hug a new social contact.

- Making eye contact is important when speaking or as an acknowledgment when a person enters the room. One may, however, encounter difficulty achieving eye contact with indigenous peoples from Ecuador as they have a tradition of averting their eyes as a way of showing respect to those whom they presume to be more educated, wealthy, or a visitor in their home or village.

- Touching and hugging is common among friends in Ecuador, particularly in the highlands. On the coast, women—and on occasion men—walk down public streets holding hands and generally have more physical contact with each other. Ecuadorian couples feel comfortable engaging in public displays of affection so long as it is limited to hand-holding or a man's arm around his girlfriend or wife.

- Gestures and facial expressions are integral to communication in Ecuador, yet there are few specific gestures used by Ecuadorians while speaking. Those from the coast tend to gesticulate more than those from the highland regions. An interesting gesture faux pas to avoid is that of indicating the height of a person using an extended flat hand. This gesture is specifically used to indicate the height of an animal or object, not a person. To indicate the height of people, one bends the hand at the first knuckle with the fingers straight.

- People from the coast are generally less reserved than those from the highlands, though regardless of region, in all situations politeness is held in high regard. In general, Ecuadorians do not raise their voices when angry. A more clipped tone may, however, indicate an irritation below the surface.

- In Ecuador, requests for information or assistance are always begun with a greeting. Exchanging a bit of small talk before getting down to the business at hand is also considered polite.

Forms of Address

- As is common with most Hispanic cultures, there are both formal and informal ways of addressing people. Use of the formal *Usted* is seen in office settings. When one makes initial contact with someone in Ecuador, it is best to address him or her by title followed by the person's last name. Persons who are, or feel they are, of a higher rank often set the level of formality with those who may be socially beneath them. The informal *tú* is used among friends or following an invitation by others to be addressed as tú.
- The informal contraction of *vosotros* or *vos* may also be used when referring to a person directly. It does not imply a plural and is often interchanged with *tú*. *Vosotros,* in its full form, is not used in Ecuador.
- As is the tradition with many Hispanic cultures, Ecuadorians use two surnames—the first from their father, followed by their mother's. The father's surname is generally used when addressing someone. When a woman marries, she typically adds and goes by her husband's surname.
- Ecuadorians generally use status indicators when referring to someone who is a medical doctor or who holds a Ph.D. with the titles *Doctor* or *Doctora. Licenciado/a* is the title used for those who have earned their bachelor's degree, which would replace *Señor/Señora/Señorita* when appropriate.
- One typically employs formal usage with people such as taxi drivers or security guards, though Ecuadorians often use the informal with their own maids or service providers to assert social class distinction. Visitors to Ecuador are advised to use polite and formal forms of address as a general rule.

Appropriate Topics

- Ecuadorians generally have a genuine interest in the details of others' lives and appreciate the same consideration. Conversation topics often include family, work history, and home origin. One's marital or relationship status is often revealed early on when first encountering someone in order to communicate whether or not one is romantically available; this is especially true of fair-skinned individuals as in Ecuador they may consider themselves to be more desirable socially and, thus, want to set boundaries with new acquaintances from the start.
- Generally, sex is not a topic of polite conversation, though personal issues such as one's weight, age, or salary are fair game. In fact, an unwillingness to share details will likely be regarded with suspicion and be considered offensive.
- Challenges from outsiders as to how things are done or perceived in Ecuador may be met with a protectionist reaction. Issues such as politics, gay rights, or human rights for indigenous peoples may be best left alone unless broached by the Ecuadorian him- or herself.

- While humor in conversation is generally appropriate in conversation, the topic areas may stray into uncomfortable territory for many North Americans. Ecuadorian humor has a tendency toward the stereotyping of peoples from different regions, ethnicities, and gender. Cynicism toward public figures is manifest in the Ecuadorian New Year's Eve tradition of making effigies of their political leaders and burning them at midnight.
- In urban regions, the topic of religion is generally not problematic since most Ecuadorians are Catholic. Rural communities, however, have seen an influx of Protestant missionaries during the last 30 years, and so one may encounter varying degrees of comfort with regard to religion as a topic of discussion. Atheism is viewed by most Ecuadorians with caution, so that if one is an atheist, the conventional wisdom is to say that one believes in God while trying to avoid a conversation that leads to a discussion about the church one attends.
- A popular topic with most Ecuadorians seems to be if the 2001 currency conversion to the U.S. dollar has or has not changed their country's economy.

OUTSIDE OF CLASS

- Salsa dancing is a popular pastime in Ecuador, as is the sport of *fútbol* (i.e., soccer).
- Many Ecuadorians are followers of television soap operas, or *novelas,* which are typically broadcast in the evenings.

Potential Adjustment Challenges

PROBLEMS/SOLUTIONS

Problem

I have been working with the mothers of some of my Ecuadorian students on a proposal to create a newcomer program for our incoming immigrant and refugee students. I invited them to join me for a light dinner after school to continue to plan the proposal, and I was surprised when they allowed me to pay for all four of us without even offering to take care of the tip. Were they perhaps unable to pay and too embarrassed to say so?

Solution

Chances are they were following an Ecuadorian tradition—when you invite another person for a drink or a meal, you are automatically offering to pay.

Problem

Camila, my student from Ecuador, failed her first spelling test with a score of 20. At first her face told me that she was elated, but she then she pointed at the F and asked, "Why F, teacher? I get 20." How are we miscommunicating?

Solution

A 19 or 20 on a test is the highest grade possible in the Ecuadorian school system. It is considered excellent; 16–18 is very good; 14–15 is good; 12–13 is average; and 11–0 is unsatisfactory.

Problem

I have a student from Ecuador who missed school for almost the entire month of January because his parents had taken him to South America for Christmas vacation. Don't the parents realize that their child is going to have a hard time making up for lost time once they return?

Solution

Christmas falls during summer in the southern hemisphere, and for students who attend schools that run from May to January, this is also the time of their long-awaited summer break. No doubt, your student's family wants to take advantage of the rare opportunity to spend time with relatives and friends in Ecuador during their holidays.

Peru

■ PERU *Upclose*

Capital: Lima

Population: 28,302,603 (June 2006)

Size: 1,285,220 sq. km. (496,226 sq. mi.) (slightly smaller than Alaska)

Location: in western South America, bordering the Pacific Ocean, between Chile and Ecuador (also borders Colombia and Brazil to the east)

Climate: generally tropical in the east and dry desert in the west, with conditions varying from temperate to frigid in the Andes

Terrain: narrow plain along the western coast running parallel with the Andes mountains with highland jungles in the southeast and lowland jungles in the northeast along the Amazon Basin

Monetary Unit: nuevo sol (3.26 per U.S. dollar) (June 2006)

Religion: Roman Catholic 90%

Language(s): Predominantly Spanish with Quechua, the native Peruvian language, spoken outside urban centers; Aymará, as well as a number of minor Amazonian languages, are spoken as well

Literacy Rate: total population 87.7%; men 93.5%; women 82.1% (2004)

Ethnicity: Amerindian 45%; mestizo (mixed Amerindian and white) 37%; white 15%; black, Japanese, Chinese, and other 3%; Quechua and the Aymará make up the majority of Peru's population

Per Capita Income: US$1,870 (2006)

Population Distribution: 74% urban, 26% rural (2003)

Population below Poverty Line: 54% (2003)

Life Expectancy: total population 69.8 years; men 68.1 years; women 71.7 years (2006)

Government: constitutional republic

PUBLIC HOLIDAYS			
January 1	New Year's Day	October 8	Battle of Angamos
January 18	Anniversary of the Founding of Lima	October 18, 19, and 28	*Señor de los Milagros* (Our Lord of Miracles)
Thursday before Easter	Holy Thursday	November 1	All Saints' Day
Friday before Easter	Holy Friday	December 8	Feast of the Immaculate Conception
May 1	Labor Day		
June 29	St. Peter and St. Paul Day		
July 28 and 29	Independence Day celebrations	December 25	Christmas
August 30	St. Rosa of Lima		

▧ Personal Perspective

When I left my country for the United States in 1989, it was both exhilarating and heartbreaking for my family and me. I was a doctor in Peru, which, though considered a good job, did not come with the financial rewards one commonly associates with such a profession. Times were difficult both socially and economically in Peru at that time, and I wanted to be able to help provide for the family. I struck out on my own on a tourist visa, leaving behind my elderly parents, whom I wasn't sure I would ever see again.

At first I worked cleaning apartments and ironing shirts in a factory. Eventually, I found a job in a medical office that agreed to sponsor me for citizenship. Because I had already stayed beyond my tourist visa, however, I was unable to leave and reenter the United States to visit my family in Peru. My father died during this time.

Although I am now practicing medicine in the States, first I had to repeat the examinations, residencies, and fellowships that I had already successfully completed in Peru. I am able now to visit my family several times a year and help support them financially.

—medical doctor originally from Peru

▧ Historical Perspective

IMMIGRATION TO THE UNITED STATES

While Peruvians have been migrating to the United States since the 1800s, the largest resettlements of Peruvians have occurred since the 1950s and 1960s. Immigrants arriving during this period tended to be financially affluent, socially well positioned, and professionally trained. However, peasants and middle-class Peruvians supplanted their upper-class compatriots during the second large wave of Peruvian immigration to the United States in the 1970s. By the 1980s, sheep herders and more members of the urban middle class had begun to join the exodus out of Peru to the United States, many settling in New York, New Jersey, California, Florida, Illinois, and Washington, DC. The fourth wave of Peruvian immigrants constitutes the largest thus far. It began in the 1990s. Some 63 percent of those immigrating from Peru arrived in the 1990s. Many were well educated; more than 35 percent possessed a high school diploma, and more than 45 percent had some university education. In comparison, not even 2 percent of Peruvians in Peru possess a university diploma.

Most Peruvian immigration can be attributed to political and economic instability. Kidnappings, bombings, and other hostilities associated with revolutionary groups such as *Sendero Luminoso,* or Shining Path, in the 1980s motivated many Peruvians to seek safety, but after the decline of terrorism in Peru and the economic reforms of President Alberto Fujimori, unemployment replaced terror as the impetus for immigration. Peru's unemployment rate in 2000 stood at 40 percent, and opportunities have increasingly been limited to men and nonindigenous individuals. Peruvian immigration to the United States has grown at a rate of 87 percent since 1990.

HISTORICAL SYNOPSIS

Several prominent Andean civilizations, most notably the Inca Empire *(Tawantinsuyo),* developed and thrived in ancient Peru. The Spanish *conquistadores* invaded Peru in 1532 and by the following year had subsequently captured the capital city of Cuzco, where the last Inca king, Atahualpa, was executed, thus beginning the process of Spanish hegemony. The year 1821 brought about Peruvian declarations of independence from Spain, which, following numerous attempts to regain its former colonies, were ultimately recognized in 1879. Since 1980, modern Peru has been a democratic constitutional republic. Elected President in 1990, Alberto Fujimori inherited a country on the brink of collapse, suffering from hyperinflation, mismanagement, and guerrilla warfare. After only a year, Fujimori brought relative stability to the economy and took dictatorial, yet effective, measures to fight the guerrilla factions such as the Shining Path and *Tupac Amaru.* His hard-line tactics in dealing with rebel groups eventually appeared to influence his governing policies and dealings with those who held differing political views. Fujimori began the removal of government officials, including Supreme Court justices and judges, who delayed his political agenda, which included the reinterpreting of a constitutional amendment prohibiting a president from holding a third five-year term in office. Arguing that the amendment had been approved while serving his first term (and therefore was not in force until his second), Fujimori won his third term in 2000, though there were widespread allegations of fraud and corruption. He soon resigned under threat of congressional investigation while traveling in Japan, where he remains in exile today. New elections were ultimately held, and in June 2001, Alejandro Toledo was elected president. Toledo has since lost the enthusiastic proletariat support he once enjoyed as a result of unfulfilled political promises and the country's economic downturn. Many Peruvians, in fact, would support the return to power of Fujimori. They point to such factors as Toledo's broken promises, the reorganization of terrorist groups, the higher cost of living, and the failure of the government to raise the minimum wage for the past three years.

Deep Culture Perspective

DEEP CULTURE BELIEFS

- The Peruvian family may generally be said to have a high degree of both nuclear and intergenerational family unity, with extended families often occupying the same dwelling. Immigrant Peruvians are frequently relied upon by remaining family members back home for financial assistance.
- Somewhat counterintuitively, the average size of Peruvian families in urban regions is greater than those in rural areas where one might expect large agricultural families to predominate. This may be due in part to a trending migration into the cities by highlanders in search of better employment opportunities.
- Though changing, families are patricentric with the male head of household considered the authority. Women have traditionally controlled and managed internal household affairs. However, due to economic stresses and social changes, women have increasingly sought salaried work outside the home to meet familial needs. This is especially true in poorer rural areas where occurrences of abandonment or migration to the cities by males in search of work are increasingly on the rise. Single-parent households in both urban and rural communities are almost exclusively headed by women.
- Religion is at the center of many Peruvian customs. Respect for religion is a trait held even by those who are not devout or who may indeed be agnostic.
- Having household servants is quite common in urban middle- and upper-class Peruvian homes. These mostly female servants (called *la empleada* or *la muchacha*) are typically young highland migrant women who have sought domestic positions when first arriving in urban cities such as Lima. Though low paying and not without hardships, these jobs are often seen by the women as useful in providing a framework for learning city life, along with providing room and board for some, and an opportunity to attend night school.
- In the metropolitan capital city of Lima, 47 percent of the population lives in squatter settlements, the *pueblos jovenes* (young towns), or *barriadas* (shanty towns), built in the foothills of the Andes by rural migrating Peruvians seeking a better life. These settlements typically started as empty desert land laid claim by means of makeshift structures of cardboard and reed mats *(esteras)*. As they could afford, residents structurally upgraded their homes, and gradually many of the communities took on the appearance of a city. This process continues to be repeated to this day, though there is little assurance that municipal services such as electricity, water, and sewage will be extended to new

developments. San Martín de Porres is an example of a successful transition from a *pueblo joven* established in the early 1950s to what is today a successful working-class region that belies its origins as a squatters' settlement.

- Among the urban poor within the *barriadas,* the men often travel long distances by bus to construction work sites in the cities where they are not likely to be provided with protective equipment, such as hard hats, gloves, or boots. Modern buildings are erected more with intensive labor than machinery due to the surplus of men desperate for work. The women may also have domestic duties in the homes of others in the city, in addition to their duties of water hauling, daily meal preparation, handcrafts, and child care.

- An unfortunate stereotype of the Andean rural poor being inefficient and lazy workers could not be further from the truth. Andean peasants lead laborious lives, caring for their animals, and often traversing great distances to their small farms *(chacras)* while making their way on foot up steep mountainous trails carrying loads of produce, firewood, and tools on their backs. Social support networks are generally well developed in peasant societies, with members of its community caring for those who may have suffered a poor harvest or some other form of hardship.

- Native Andean llamas and alpacas are commonly found in the central and southern Andes, where they are still widely used for wool, meat, and for transportation of goods.

- Human labor, too, plays an important role in the transfer of commodities or merchandise for market, especially in rural areas. In addition to carrying heavy and awkward burdens on their backs, peasant women and girls spin wool that is later to be hand-woven into clothing, blankets, and other handicrafts.

- The ancient kinship system of patrilineages (sometimes called *castas*) survives in many Quechua communities. In such communities, wives belong to the lineage of their father, and thus their own children to the father's side as well. This system is at odds with Peruvian law and its bilateral Hispanic system that includes the mother's name and lineage as part of the extended family.

- Homes in middle- and upper-class city neighborhoods are well cared for, often with patios and yards surrounded by security walls with electrical devices to keep out thieves. Many neighborhoods collectively fund unarmed security patrols for their communities as a deterrent to crime.

- Though Lima is a metropolitan city of approximately 6.5 million, in the afternoons one can often hear sounds of the *d'Onofrio* ice cream vendors on bicycles, and the occasional knife grinder's bell announcing his presence in the *barrio.*

PROVERBS

- Little by little, one walks far.
- It is better to prevent than to cure.
- No one says his own buttermilk is sour.
- He who has no godparent will not get baptized.
- In life, the son is scornful of the father. In business, the father is scornful of the son.
- Never kill a nesting bird.
- The continuous drip polishes the stone.
- The sleeping lobster is carried away by the stream.
- You go out for wool but come back shorn.
- You cannot catch a trout without getting your feet wet.

FOLK TALE

Many, many years ago there was a married couple, Manco Capac and Mama Ocllo. They were the son and daughter of the Sun God, having been created by him on an island in Lake Titicaca. Their mission was to find the perfect spot for the creation of a new and powerful empire. The Sun God gave Manco Capac a golden staff, which was to be thrust into the earth once he and Mama Ocllo discovered where they were to create their empire. The two walked and walked many kilometers until they reached a hill overlooking Cuzco. There, Manco Capac's staff sank easily into the earth, where he then proclaimed Cuzco to be the navel of the world, the land of the Inca.

Administrative Perspective

OFFICIAL EDUCATIONAL POLICY

Education is regarded to be the key to progress and personal advancement for both urban and rural citizenry, and efforts have been made by the Ministry of Education to improve not only the quality of its compulsory education system but also the equality with which state resources are expended. The public primary school enrollment reported by the Ministry is approximately 92 percent, yet critics claim that the quality of education still suffers, due in no small part to the lack of funding and often poorly trained and financially unmotivated teachers available. These statistics, it is also argued, may not take into account drop-out rates or children who are truant or who skip class in order to work to contribute toward their family's income. Secondary schools fare far worse with enrollment rates at 66 percent.

Official school curricula require 900 hours of classroom instruction per year; yet in Peru's urban schools, fewer than 500 hours are typically provided, and rural schools provide only about 300 hours of instruction. Those who can afford it send their children to private schools or institutions where the educational standards are of a quality comparable to those of other countries.

Within rural communities, one of the most important steps toward economic self-sufficiency and social mobility out of the presumed hardships of the indigenous caste is the presence of a village school and teacher. Primary schools are the chief resources for acquiring a basic ability to use written and spoken Spanish. While Peru's constitution recognizes Quechua as an official language, in order to participate in and have access to state services, one must, for the most part, be able to communicate in Spanish. Historically there has been racial and ethnic discrimination against Peru's native peoples by the urban majority, and even today, there are signs of perhaps unconscious perpetuation through unofficial school policies that encourage the discarding of native languages and attire and through the societal lampooning of native cultural practices, or equating indigenous culture with stupidity, poverty, and drunkenness while extolling the virtues of the Spanish-speaking, white-collar, urban standard of living.

EDUCATION AT A GLANCE

See the Education at a Glance table on page 80.

PERU

Level/Age	Hours/Calendar	Language of Instruction	Compulsory Attendance	Exams	Grading System	Curriculum	Cost	Enrollment
Primary *jardin* (ages 5–6) *Educación primaria* Grades 1–6 ages 6–11	Apr.-Dec. with a 3-week break in July for Independence celebrations. (Some schools may begin in mid-March to compensate for loss of school days from numerous workers' strikes.) Students in *jardin* begin at 9:00 AM and finish at noon or 1:00 PM. Others begin at 8:00 AM and finish at 2:00 PM.	Spanish, Quechua, and Aymara are decreed by government as languages of instruction, but Spanish predominates, especially in urban areas. In the many private schools operated	Yes, both *jardin* and *primaria*	Mixed format including fill-in-the-blank, short definitions, short answers, matching, true/false, and some multiple choice Students are not required to write long essays except as part of literature classes. Many quizzes are oral.	A, B, C, D There is no F, but student will be required to repeat level. Students receive a report card every three months.	Math, religion, natural sciences, art, physical education, Spanish language and literature, foreign language	Free, except for nominal sums collected from parents at the beginning of the school year to pay for basic supplies and food (sometimes even water and electricity). The government provides very little support beyond the teachers' salaries and some textbooks and supplies.	Total enrollment 104.5% of which 49% is female 11% of girls in primary level are not in school. 88% of primary-level students reach Grade 5. 80% of primary-level students advance to secondary level.
Secondary *Ciclo general* Grades 7–9 ages 12–14 *Académico* or *Técnico* Grades 10–12 ages 14–17	Apr.-Dec. with a 3-week break in July for Independence celebrations In warm months, school day runs from 7:30 AM–2:00 PM with a breakfast hour in the AM or lunch break at noon. In colder months, school day extends from 8:00 or 8:30 AM to 2:30 or 3:00 PM. Some schools operate two shifts per day (7:15 AM to 12:30 PM and 12:40 PM –6:00 PM).	by U.S. interests, the language of instruction may be English for part of the day.	Yes, until age 16	Same as above From academic secondary, students receive a *Certificado de Educación Segundaria Común Completa*; from technical secondary, students receive a *Diploma de Aptitud Professional*; an entrance exam is required for admission to university.	20-point scale pass/fail = 11 points	General studies for first two years, after which students choose between academic and technical tracks	Government schools are free, while private schools can be expensive by Peruvian standards.	Total enrollment is 66% of which 47.9% is female The average Peruvian adult has completed 7.6 years of schooling.
University ages 18 +	Apr.-Dec. with variable hours for classes	Spanish	No	Frequent quizzes (multiple choice, true/ false, short answer) on reading assignments plus final exams	Same as above	General studies and specialized courses	US$200 to US$800 per semester in private universities or around US$40 per semester in public universities	29% of secondary level graduates attend university.

Surface Culture Perspective

CLASSROOMS

- Students typically sit at two-person student tables arranged four columns across and five rows deep, while instructors' desks are often placed in the front right corner of the classroom. Blackboards and bulletin boards continue to be commonplace.
- Though class size is decreasing due to a surplus of teachers and lower student enrollments, classrooms of 40 to 50 students, especially in the urban public schools, is not uncommon. Private school class size hovers around 25–30, and sections are often designated for accelerated versus mainstream students.
- Classroom amenities vary greatly in Peru, especially when contrasting government-funded public schools with private schools. In general, and as might be expected, the private school facilities are superior to those in public schools, and are, in fact, often equivalent to those one might find in any developed nation.
- In 2001, the government launched *Project Huascarán* whose aim was to provide Internet access to 690 schools throughout Peru by the end of 2003 in an attempt to narrow the gap between public and private education. Still, technology in classrooms is more likely found to be more and abundant and more fully maintained and upgraded in private schools.
- Most private schools in Peru are affiliated with religious institutions and often subscribe to a single-sex student environment. Private schools are expensive from the perspective of most Peruvians, with tuitions as high as US$8,000 annually.
- Rural schools are often not well constructed, and there have been reported incidents of collapse.

TEACHERS' STATUS

- Within the government funded schools of Peru, teachers are among the lowest-paid public employees, earning a monthly salary of approximately US$230 a month. There are social and job security retirement benefits available for tenured teachers (those with formal, full-time positions in the public school sector) who make up 75 percent of the teaching community.
- Unless a teacher has a special connection in the government or is at the very top of his or her graduating class, most will be sent for their first assignments to the countryside for up to five years. Often, students in the remote rural areas speak only Quechua or Aymara, so communication between teacher and students can be very difficult as most teachers do not speak the indigenous languages.
- Teachers are well respected in Peru, especially at the district level where they often hold leadership positions in their communities. In rural areas, where they may be the only person with a university education,

teachers often wield an extraordinary level of influence, acting as mediator, counselor, and spokesperson for the village.

- While both men and women actively pursue teaching positions for reasons of altruism and social or personal advancement, teaching opportunities for women have been especially important in many of the rural areas for their role in advancing women's sociopolitical roles that had once been closed to them in a nation steeped in Andean sociocultural tradition.

- The success of a school may depend on the motivation and vision of its director (or principal). As the government provides only minimal support for schools, it is essential that the director strongly advocate for the school in the business community and motivate parents to do the same.

TEACHER-STUDENT RELATIONSHIP

- Teacher and students relations in Peru tend to be very friendly. Of course, as noted earlier, class sizes may be as many as 50 students, so it is very difficult for genuine friendships to be formed. At the elementary level, students regard their teachers are nurturers and may even give the teacher a kiss upon arriving at school. By secondary school, however, teachers may still be friendly but not necessarily affectionate.

- Parents tend to be very involved in the life of the school. Parents from each class will elect a president, secretary, and treasurer who will advocate in any number of ways for the class. For example, they may solicit donations of computers and other supplies or may organize volunteers for various functions (such as cooking food for school lunches or collecting funds to supplement the basic provisions—usually rice and lentils—sent by the government).

TEACHING PRACTICES

- Generally, teachers have in the past been trained to focus students on correctness and conformity in their classrooms. This strict focus on correctness often results in students' fear of risk-taking and in arriving at the conclusion that it may be better to provide no answer than to be wrong.

- Many teachers will conduct class with an open gradebook in their hands. They will ask questions and note which student answered first, giving that student a point if the answer is correct.

- Many teachers are unmotivated to adapt their teaching materials or behaviors to meet the sociocultural needs of their students, but others will balance traditional methods with more interactive practices that engage the students in active learning.

- There is a significant difference in teaching method between teachers in private versus public schools. Whereas public school teachers may encourage students to focus on the regurgitation of information, private school teachers are more likely to develop and reward analysis and discovery.

- Though officially rejected, some teachers may still hold the view of "teacher as God" and "student as ignorant."
- At the secondary school level, students are rarely required to write a long research paper. At the university, however, this practice is more common.

TEACHERS' DRESS

- Clothing worn by teachers tends to be somewhat formal, with women's skirts or dresses at a modest length. Shorts would not be worn no matter the temperature, and wearing sandals rather than shoes may garner criticism from coworkers.
- In private schools, teachers may be required to wear uniforms.

DISCIPLINE AND CLASS MANAGEMENT

- It may be that in the past there were fewer behavioral problems with students in Peru. Perhaps due partially to the difficult economic situation, this appears to be changing.
- Typically, teachers have little time to discipline students due to their large class sizes, so that speaking with a child's parent or giving a poor or failing grade may be the only repercussion for student misconduct.

STUDENTS' CIRCUMSTANCES

- Parents do not typically help their children with homework; yet, it is not unusual for primary students in more affluent schools to have notebook ticklers of homework assignments that require parent sign-off to obtain credit.
- In remote schools, most students have only a rudimentary proficiency in Spanish. This increases their cognitive load as instruction usually is given in Spanish and prevents parents from assisting with homework.
- Some extracurricular activities such as dances and trips are supported through parent involvement.
- In poor neighborhoods even the city students may come to school without having eaten breakfast or slept sufficiently. They often have chores do to at home, especially if the family is large. As a consequence, they may lack energy in class and eventually drop out to help bring income into the family.

STUDENT-STUDENT RELATIONSHIP

- Friendships are an important element of classroom dynamics in Peru. Students socialize in groups, meeting in parks, on the plaza, at restaurants, and even at bus stops. The latter is a popular location for students from all-boys or all-girls schools to meet one another.

- Some competitiveness in schoolwork exists in the Peruvian classroom, with a handful of students vying for first place in achievement. The remaining students, however, may be apathetic to the rivalries of their more able peers.
- It is not uncommon for students to study for exams together. Many will also meet after school to complete homework assignments together, dividing up the items and then sharing answers.

STUDENTS' LEARNING PRACTICES

- Teamwork is the mantra of many Peruvians who can appreciate working toward obtaining the best possible results through a combined effort. However, in more affluent schools students may compete with each other for top positions. They vie for points that are recorded every time a student answers a question first and correctly. Every class recognizes its top three point-earning students.
- Fear of failure and concepts of financial gain or loss are sometimes used as motivating factors in improving performance.
- In traditional Quechua cultures, the trait of risk-taking is acceptable and encouraged, though the practices of the national education system appear to have quashed this arguably beneficial quality. Students from these cultures may be shy, nervous, reserved, perhaps unwilling to participate and may benefit from programs that support their self-esteem and self-assurance.

STUDENTS' DRESS

- Uniforms are worn by roughly 80 percent of primary and secondary school students, though some schools now allow students to wear street clothes. Where the cost of the uniform has become controversial (sometimes to the point where students drop out of school rather than spend the money on a new uniform every year), the dress code has become more relaxed. School uniforms may change from year to year in more prosperous neighborhoods.

GIFTS FOR THE TEACHER

- In general, gifts are not exchanged between students and teachers. Popular teachers may receive simple gifts from individual students on their birthdays, and the whole class will contribute toward a gift for their teacher on Teachers' Day (June 6).
- Teachers' Day celebrations generally involve the cancellation of classes and performances in the school courtyard by each class in front of the rest of the school. Each teacher is presented with a gift from the class (e.g., picture frames, knick-knacks for the teacher's desk, perfume, inexpensive jewelry).

- When visiting a family, foreigners may bring chocolates or flowers, but yellow flowers are avoided as they carry the message "I hate you." Red roses bear with them the connotation of romance.
- A gift with any reference to the number 13 is inappropriate as are handkerchiefs (which denote sadness) and knives (denoting the end of a relationship).

NONVERBAL COMMUNICATION

- Eye contact when speaking and a firm handshake are seen as a sign of honesty, a trait well appreciated in Peru.
- In addition to greeting one another by shaking hands, Peruvian women and people of the opposite sex will kiss each other once on the cheek. Unless men are familial, they would generally never kiss.
- Public displays of affection are generally frowned upon; so too are public displays of anger.
- Casual touching of people in conversation is not a cause for concern yet not appropriate for a first meeting.
- Peruvians have a "North American" sensibility when it comes to personal space. Standing too close may be considered offensive by some.
- Winking is a sign of intimacy.
- It is not unusual for Peruvians to walk arm-in-arm when walking. This is true for both males and females.
- "I'm thinking" is demonstrated through gesture by tapping one's head. Tapping the temple can mean "this person is crazy," and tapping the forehead may mean "this person is stupid."
- Peruvians may point with their lips. It is considered quite rude to point a finger at another person.
- Crossing one's legs with an ankle resting on the knee of the opposite leg is considered improper. Crossing them at the knees does not raise any eyebrows.

FORMS OF ADDRESS

- Educational achievement is highly respected. Teachers are typically addressed as *Profesor* or *Profesora* at the high school level and *Doctor* or *Doctora* at the university level. At the primary level, teachers are usually called *Señor* or *Señorita*. Parents may call teachers by title plus first name, as in *Profesora Carmen*.
- As is the tradition in many Hispanic cultures, Peruvians (with the exception of some Andean cultures) have two surnames—the first from their father, the second from the mother. The father's surname is generally used when addressing someone. When a woman marries, she most typically adds and goes by her husband's surname.

APPROPRIATE TOPICS

- Peruvians generally welcome conversations about their historic and rich culture as well as learning about the cultures of others. They are also fond of talking about politics.
- With regard to personal issues such as age, weight, marital status, and religion, Peruvians are fairly open and candid. In an introductory conversation, a Peruvian may inquire as to whether or not one is Catholic. An answer in the affirmative results in immediate acceptance; non-Catholics, who through a follow-up query identify a belief in God, are also generally welcomed. Nonbelievers may be cautiously received.
- Peruvians have an excellent sense of humor, which can at times be self-deprecating. Yet humor critical of the country or its citizens by outsiders, or humor of a particularly personal nature, would be far less warmly welcomed.

OUTSIDE OF CLASS

- Students in Peru rarely have responsibilities outside the realm of their homework activities, which are often described as "not light, but also not heavy."
- In the upper and middle classes, for a student to have a part-time job while in school or university would be highly unusual.
- Many secondary schools have a band that makes public performances and competes with other bands for city or district awards. Other types of after-school clubs are less common, but children of more affluent parents may be tutored in English or other exam subjects, or they may take classes in karate, tennis, art, etc.

▨ Potential Adjustment Challenges

PROBLEMS/SOLUTIONS

Problem

The parents of my student from Peru are planning to take her out of school when she turns 16. She's a good student, so I don't understand why her parents would want to limit her opportunity to attend college and start a career.

Solution

Peruvians from remote villages sometimes believe that education is a waste of time for girls. Their proper place is thought to be in the home, and a girl of 16 ought to be looking for someone who will take care of her in the future. The idea of a young woman striking out in the professional workforce and delaying marriage and family until her mid- or late-twenties contradicts what they believe to be a safe and appropriate life for their daughters.

Problem

I know that my new student from Peru speaks Quechua and Spanish, but I cannot get her to teach me even a few words in Quechua. She's not a shy person, so I'm not sure why she's so reluctant to speak Quechua.

Solution

Quechua-speaking Peruvians have been indirectly taught that their language is somehow inferior to Spanish, although almost 25 percent of the population are native speakers of Quechua. Spanish-speaking Peruvians are invariably more affluent than Quechua speakers, so there are economic facets of the problem. In other words, Spanish is a prestige language, while Quechua is not.

Problem

I have been struggling to help a Peruvian student in my university decide on a major, but he can't seem to identify any one area that really attracts him nor do the various tests of his abilities, interest, and personality seem to sway him one way or another. I'm getting tired of his regular visits to my office to hash over this issue.

Solution

Peruvian universities in general offer fewer degree programs than those in the United States, so the choices are perhaps not as overwhelming as they may be in the United States. Furthermore, family input usually helps an individual make up his or her mind, but if family members don't have a good idea of what options are available, they may be of little assistance.

Dominican Republic

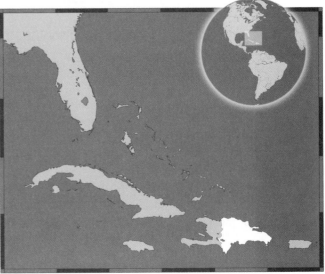

■ DOMINICAN REPUBLIC *Upclose*

Capital: Santo Domingo

Population: 9,183,984 (June 2006)

Size: 48,730 sq. km. (18,815 sq. mi.) (the size of New Hampshire and Vermont combined)

Location: eastern two-thirds of the island of Hispaniola bordered by Haiti to the west, the Caribbean Sea to the south, and the Atlantic Ocean to the north

Climate: tropical maritime with variation in rainfall, but not temperature, from season to season

Terrain: rugged highlands and mountains with fertile valleys in between

Monetary Unit: peso (7.62 per U.S. dollar) (June 2006)

Religion: Roman Catholic 95%

Language(s): Spanish

Literacy Rate: total population 84.7%; men 84.6%; women 84.8% (2003)

Ethnicity: white 16%, black 11%, mixed 73%

Per Capita Income: US$2,094 (2006)

Population Distribution: 59% urban, 41% rural (2003)

Population below Poverty Line: 25% (2006)

Life Expectancy: total population 71.7 years; men 70.2; women 73.3 years (2006)

Government: representative democracy

PUBLIC HOLIDAYS		
	January 1	New Year's Day
	January 6	Epiphany
	January 21	Our Lady of Altagracia Day
	January 26	Juan Pablo Duarte's birthday
	February 27	Independence Day
	Friday before Easter	Good Friday
	May 1	Labor Day
	May 26	Corpus Christi
	August 16	Restoration Day
	September 24	Our Lady of Las Mercedes Day
	November 6	Constitution Day
	December 25	Christmas Day

Personal Perspective

My friend Rafael left his little mountain village in search of a better life, but before he could barely begin, a freak kitchen accident left him burned, scarred, and immobilized. He didn't give in to what many saw as his fate, that is to give up and die, and today, after several operations, many kindnesses, and sheer determination, Rafael is functional and happy.

In many ways, Rafael represents the many paradoxes of the Dominican Republic. There is joy and suffering, hope and desperation, rich and poor, compassion and cruelty. Institutional violence, too, persists in the larger Dominican society today in the form of stark class divisions, discrimination, elitism, abject poverty, and numerous violations of basic human rights including inadequate education, health care, housing, and nutrition. Many poor people, nevertheless, have hope that they can somehow maneuver their way to better education and economic security, and I have frequently been witness to incredible dedication to family, joyfulness of spirit, solidarity, love of others, and service through sacrifice. The challenge for the people of the Dominican Republic as they navigate their way through the processes of globalization is going to be to retain their unique spirit and identity amidst the various forces of development that often inadvertently undermine it.

—ESL teacher who lived
as a child in the Dominican Republic

Historical Perspective

IMMIGRATION TO THE UNITED STATES

The reason for the migration of large numbers of Dominicans is neither flight from a repressive government (as with the Republic's neighbor, Cuba) nor the constant fear of social chaos and governmental brutality (as with Haiti). In the decade spanning 1990 to 2000, Dominican immigrants arriving in the United States were escaping a steep economic decline in their home country. In fact, Dominican immigration to the United States virtually doubled in this ten-year span with 70 percent settling in New York City. Contrary to popular assumptions, these immigrants did not represent the Dominican Republic's poor. Although some Dominicans make the journey to the United States in boats unfit for the dangerous crossing, it is its working-class population, those economically solvent enough to afford the cost of starting over in a new country, who constitute the largest percentage of immigrants to the United States from the Dominican Republic. Ten percent of Dominican immigrants have a college education, and 42 percent are high school graduates with 48 percent beginning, but failing to complete, high school. Often unable to resume their former professions, well-educated Dominican immigrants work blue-collar or service jobs and supplement their income by driving cabs, selling lottery tickets, babysitting, or renting out rooms in their apartments. Some start their own small businesses as well.

HISTORICAL SYNOPSIS

The island of Hispaniola, which the Dominican Republic today shares with Haiti, was claimed for Spain by Christopher Columbus in 1492. The indigenous population of Tainos and Caribs welcomed Columbus, but they were forced into slave labor when the Spanish discovered gold on the island. In fact, the indigenous population was virtually eliminated by the Spanish. When Columbus arrived on Hispaniola, there were a million Tainos, but only 50 years later, a mere 500 remained. For this reason, African slaves were brought to the island to replace the indigenous workers. French colonizers also eventually obtained a foothold on the western part of the island, and after feuding with Spain over the territory, won it in 1697 via the signing of the Treaty of Ryswick. After winning its independence from France in 1804, Haiti overtook the Dominican Republic, which, in turn, declared its independence from Haiti in 1821, but did not gain full independence until 1844. In this way, the small island of Hispaniola was influenced by the people of two distinct cultures and languages. To this day, Dominicans and Haitians maintain an adversarial attitude toward one another.

Until 1966 the Dominican Republic was governed by a series of regimes and dictatorships. The United States intervened in 1916, occupying the nation for eight years and equipping the Dominican Republic with its first professionally trained military. By 1930 its leader, Rafael Trujillo, came to power, acquired enormous wealth at the expense of those he ruled, and was assassinated in 1961. Trujillo was followed by Joaquin Balaguer, who was elected president in 1963, went into exile, and then returned to serve as president of the Dominican Republic from 1966 to 1978, with democratic elections continuing to take place in the country thereafter. The economy of the Dominican Republic is now one of the fastest growing in the Western Hemisphere.

▋Deep Culture Perspective

DEEP CULTURE BELIEFS

- The Dominican family has been described as a "bulwark" in the sense that it has served as the primary source of strength, stability, and identity throughout the country's uneven political and social history. Family loyalty runs so deep in the Dominican Republic that it extends beyond the home, permeating virtually every aspect of daily life and surviving such trends as mass migration to the city and abroad. Economically disadvantaged distant relatives expect and receive assistance from their wealthier kin in the form of a tract of land to temporarily farm or pay for hire. Sometimes they will even ask a more affluent relative to informally adopt one of their children in order to improve the well-being of the child. The quid pro quo is that the adopted child will do much of the housework and his/her family will receive a constant stream of assistance. Great shame is attached to family members who do not offer support to their less well-off kin. Nonetheless, close relatives who are in a position to reciprocate may obtain more favors.

- Part of the kinship system is a social bond called *compadrazgo.* Members of the *compadrazgo,* or *compadres,* may or may not be related by blood, but their role is firmly entrenched in the family structure. *Compadres* are similar to godparents in the United States, at least to the extent that they are selected at the godchild's baptism. However, the *compadres* form and sustain a stronger bond not only with the child but with the child's parents as well. They hold one another in high esteem and address one another with the formal *Usted* (you) rather than *tú,* the informal variation of the pronoun. A falling out with *compadres* may constitute a serious development in the life of the family, depending on the individuals.

- Polygamy and common-law marriages are both somewhat acceptable forms of partnership between rural men and women in the Dominican Republic in addition to legal monogamous marriage, religious and civil. Members of the middle and upper classes tend to opt for the latter, but older or poorer Dominicans may choose free unions due to the financial and administrative impediments to divorce and to marriage in this predominantly Roman Catholic country. Men are generally not chastised if they have children by more than one woman or if they have more than one romantic interest at a time as long as they are able to provide equivalent care for the full range of family members. Even after the dissolution of a legally unrecognized marriage, the father is expected to support his offspring if they have been legally adopted by him. His female partner is given the house in which the couple resided during their union. Common-law unions are becoming less popular, however, as Dominican women gain more social, political, and economic rights and power.

- The gender roles of Dominicans are generally well defined. Boys are allowed more freedom to explore, experiment, and misbehave while girls are watched and groomed more carefully, encouraged to maintain a ladylike demeanor, and protected from the sexual advances of boys. In that vein, girls are expected to be virgins upon marriage, although this is not the case for boys. Once a couple establishes its household, the man's role is to serve as its head, and the woman's to bear and raise children and look after the household. Sometimes, however, these roles are reversed, especially if the man has deserted the family. Gender of the parent can also affect the manner in which he or she relates to the children. In general, the relationship between mother and child is close and nurturing while the father's relationship with the child, especially in the countryside, tends to be based on authority and respect, and his involvement in routine family matters may be quite limited.

- Under the law, Dominican men and women are equal, as are all its citizens. Women make up the majority of university students, and inroads in terms of equal pay for equal work are beginning to be made. More women can be seen on the political stage, especially at the community level, and an estimated 90 percent of provincial governors are women.

- Although slavery brought large numbers of Africans to the Dominican Republic, this part of the country's ethnic legacy is largely downplayed. Despite the intermarriage of Spaniards, Africans, and indigenous peoples over the centuries, many Dominicans gravitate toward a Spanish cultural identity in terms of standards of beauty. They may favor the lighter skin and facial features of their European colonizers. (Indeed, a Dominican driver's license will indicate which of eight skin tones the driver has.) The influence of the civil rights and Black Power movements in the United States played a role in counteracting that particular bias. Skin color, nevertheless, does not prevent a Dominican from attaining education, wealth, or social standing. The lack of these attributes, however, often limits an individual's opportunities for advancement.

- The Dominican Republic's Catholic population tends to observe its faith via such practices as regular attendance at mass, baptism of its children, and celebration of holy days. People turn to church rituals in particular and religion in general to address problems and seek comfort and guidance. Rural residents tend to be more observant than city dwellers, and young people have begun to step away from the regular religious practices of their elders.

- The Dominican Republic's social class structure has six layers, namely the ruling class, political class, professional class, working class, lower class, and the destitute. The gap between rich and poor is wide; 10 percent of the population enjoys 42 percent of the per capita gross national product while at the bottom of the hierarchy, the Dominican Republic's poorest 50 percent claims only 20 percent. One's position on the social ladder is significant not only for the stature it brings to individuals and their families but also in terms of access to resources such as quality education, private health care, and luxury recreational facilities. In neither marriage nor friendship do members of one class tend to cross over to another, although more fortunate Dominicans do not scorn those from another class but treat them with kindness and concern. Friendship may lead to the expectation of special favors, which may be another reason why there is little mixing of classes.

PROVERBS

- He that is born to be hanged shall never be drowned.
- He that was born under a three-penny planet shall never be worth two pennies.
- For whatever you are destined to do, that path will fall in place in front of you.

FOLK TALE

Once upon a time there was a rich man who had a pure and beautiful daughter. She spent many hours in prayer, and so, hearing that her father would be making a journey to Santo Domingo, requested that he bring her back a picture of Our Lady of Altagracia. After finishing his business in town, the man asked about for the portrait but could find no one who recognized the name of the saint. Toward the end of his stay, the man was invited to spend the night with an old friend who listened with interest to the man's story of his child's request and inability to fulfill it. They were sitting outside discussing the man's predicament when a ragged old gentleman with a long white beard approached them. Reaching into his battered bag, the old man pulled out an object, and holding it before the father and his host, said, "This is what you are looking for." Indeed, it was a portrait of the Virgin of Altagracia. Delighted, the father rejoiced, and the host invited the old man to stay the night. When dawn arrived the old man was nowhere to be seen, and, indeed, he never appeared again. Once he returned to his home, the father placed the portrait on the mantle, and his daughter said her prayers before the image. The next morning, however, the picture was gone. After searching the entire house, they finally found the portrait outside. This experience would be repeated every night and every morning. Finally, convinced that the portrait of the Virgin of Altagracia was imbued with miraculous power, the man and his daughter took it to the church, where it rests until this very day.

Administrative Perspective

OFFICIAL EDUCATIONAL POLICY

After the departure of Trujillo in the mid-1960s, one of the top priorities for the Dominican government was education. School curricula at the time failed to address the practical needs of learners and generally did not serve regional needs or national plans for development. Better pre-service training of more teachers and administrators was placed on the agenda as was improvement in the student assessment system.

Not only was revision of the curriculum called for but the need to increase enrollment and to construct more schools was also given serious attention. Low enrollment at both the primary and secondary levels was so widespread that within 20 years of governmental efforts to address the problem primary school enrollment was twice the size it had previously been, and secondary school enrollment was four times greater. Before the reforms, some 17 percent of primary schools in rural areas lacked all six grades, making advancement to the secondary level all but impossible. The quality of instruction was low as well, and textbooks, supplies, and school uniforms were prohibitively expensive for the poor.

Expansion of the educational system, however, imposed a cost that exceeded the resources of the country. Rural areas tended to be neglected in favor of urban areas. Schools remained unbuilt, unfinished, or in disrepair, and availability of teaching supplies (desks, chairs, books) was severely limited. Moreover, the government could barely afford to pay its teachers. That, in combination with the lack of prestige associated with teaching and the belief that teaching was not an appropriate career for men, resulted in a serious teacher shortage.

Efforts to improve education in the Dominican Republic have also focused on providing more books, book bags, and school supplies to public school students; on increasing the quality and dissemination of information and programs about nutrition and health; on strengthening the teaching of English by using methods adopted from bilingual schools; on raising the quality of teacher training and in-service professional development; on implementing a series of national exams at all levels; and on introducing more information technology to the public schools and to low-income communities. In the latter case, trucks containing computer stations moved from one community to another, allowing individuals to temporarily access the Internet or complete word-processing tasks.

Funding from private sources and from a variety of organizations such as USAID and the World Bank support the Ten-Year Plan for Educational Reform in the Dominican Republic, whose efforts were previously described, but political power struggles, corruption, and lack of efficient coordination and management at the community level have left the plan and its many well-intentioned initiatives unfulfilled.

EDUCATION AT A GLANCE

See the Education at a Glance table on page 95.

Dominican Republic

Level/Age	Hours/Calendar	Language of Instruction	Compulsory Attendance	Exams	Grading System	Curriculum	Cost	Enrollment
Pre-school ages 3–6	Aug.–June	Spanish	No	N/A	N/A	No data available	No data available	No data available
Primary Grades 1–6 ages 7–14	Morning shift 8:00 AM–noon; afternoon shift 2:00 PM–5:30 PM; evening shift 6:30 PM–9:30 PM	Spanish (English in private bilingual schools)	Yes	Students are awarded *Certificado de Sufficiencis en Los Estudios Primarios.*	100-point system; pass/fail 70%	Math, Spanish, English, science, history, and physical education	Free	93% of primary school-age children are enrolled; 48% are female (16% of primary school-age girls are not enrolled). 75% of primary school students reach Grade 5. Grade 1 intake is 63% overall. The average Dominican adult receives 4.9 years of schooling.
Secondary Grades 7–12 ages 14–19			Yes, to age 17	In traditional cycle, students receive *Bachillerato* in their specialization; in new or reform cycle, students receive *Bachillerato en Ciencias y Letras*; in technical education, students receive the title of *Perito.* Primary school teachers receive training at the secondary level and graduate with title of *Maestro Normal.*	100-point system A 90–100 B 80–89 C 70–79 D 0–69	In intermediate/second cycle, students follow an academic, technical/vocational, or teacher training track; in the reform cycle there is more choice of specializations.	Free but 33% enroll in private schools.	40.2% of secondary school-age children are enrolled; 55% are female.
University ages 20+		Spanish	No	*Técnico, Professor,* or *Certificado de Estudios Superiores* (secondary teaching certificate), *Licenciatura* (first stage degree), *Especialista, Maestra, Doctor* (second stage degree)	100-point system; pass/fail 70%	Four-year degree programs in most fields. Engineering and architecture require six years. Doctorates awarded in law, medicine, veterinary medicine, and dentistry.	No data available	Total enrollment 23%

Surface Culture Perspective

CLASSROOMS

- Although schools and classroom facilities vary depending on whether they are located in an urban or rural area, the average Dominican school would be a building whose classrooms have plenty of large windows to allow for the movement of breezes to cool the space. No fans or air conditioners are found in classrooms, but some administrative offices may have them if resources allow. In the city, classrooms may directly face the street, so ambient noise and comments from passersby can be a constant distraction. In the mountains and countryside, especially in the southwest, where schools may be in disrepair, unfinished, or simply nonexistent, classes may be conducted on a patio-like area covered with a roof but having no walls. Urban classrooms typically have a closet where supplies, when available, are stored. Teachers share materials with one another. Sometimes only one tape recorder or overhead projector is available for the entire school. Teachers may also carry their own chalk and erasers due to the frequent disappearance of certain supplies. A chalkboard, usually with a green surface, is placed at the front of the classroom. Some universities equip graduate classrooms with whiteboards and air conditioning. Although the infrastructure of public universities as a whole is better than that of the primary and secondary public schools, it is not uncommon for equipment to be broken or stolen. Students frequently organize strikes and protests in response to the deficits in their learning environments.
- In more modern schools, students sit at a desk-type chair like those found in many U.S. schools, but in other schools that have not been remodeled, each student sits on a chair in front of a small table. In a few areas, they may sit at long, picnic table–type desks with approximately three students to a bench that lacks back support. The teacher's desk is located in the front of the classroom atop a platform that allows for better visual control of the students. The whole classroom is filled with desks, in contrast to many U.S. classrooms that have plenty of empty space for a variety of activities.
- Classroom decoration, when it is present at all, is limited to educational posters displaying the alphabet or colors at the primary level. Patriotic symbols such as flags and portraits of national heroes are common in classrooms, and some may also have religious images such as a crucifix, the Virgin Mary, or the Sacred Heart. Walls are generally painted beige-brown, green, or conservative colors.
- Students are expected to obtain their own books either by purchasing or borrowing them. However, books are expensive and difficult to come by. Schools generally do not have their own libraries, and public libraries are not common, either. Sometimes teachers, parents, and students attempt to collect books for a classroom library.

- Computing technology is limited in both urban and rural areas, but rural and public schools suffer the greatest disadvantage. The situation is complicated by frequent and sustained power outages as well as by the expense of setting up labs with updated hardware and sufficient software, not to mention rapid Internet access. To compensate for these restrictions, students can go to the equivalent of cybercafes to buy time on a computer to complete homework assignments or conduct research for school. The expense prevents many students from choosing this option. Nowadays more and more students are able to purchase their own personal computers for home use.
- The official teacher-student ratio is reported to be 1:41 at the primary level and 1:31 at the secondary level.
- Most public schools do not have cafeterias where students may eat, but the government has recently introduced a program that provides breakfast for students in the primary grades and subsidies of approximately US$10 per month for rural families with two or more children in school. Since classes run from 8:00 AM to 1:00 PM, students return home for a hot lunch. If there are afternoon activities, students will return to school at 2:00 PM or 3:00 PM. In some schools an afternoon shift of classes is offered, in which case students begin their school day at 2:00 PM and are dismissed at 6:00 PM. In rare cases an evening schedule is also available, running from 6:00 PM to 10:00 PM, and Saturday classes from 2:00 PM to 6:00 PM may also be offered. The rationale behind the split schedule was initially to allow young people to assist their parents with fieldwork during harvest time. However, returning from the fields to school became a difficult and unpopular practice.
- Students either return home to eat or bring food with them to school. Bathrooms tend to be little more than latrines. Electricity may not be available, or there may be frequent power failures.
- Private schools offer many more amenities than do public schools and are often on par with peer institutions in North America.

TEACHERS' STATUS

- Pre-service training to become a primary school teacher is obtained at the secondary level following Grade 10. The title *Maestro Normal* is earned after two years of study.
- Pre-service training to become a secondary school teacher can be obtained via a program lasting two to three years and terminating with the award of the title of *Técnico, Profesor,* or *Certificado de Estudios Superiores.* A second option is to enter a four-year program to prepare upper secondary school teachers. Graduates earn the title *Licenciado.*
- Dominican teachers earn approximately US$180–$200 per month. Regular paychecks are not to be expected as a result of budgetary constraints or administrative mismanagement.

TEACHER-STUDENT RELATIONSHIP

• The relationship between teachers and students is basically formal; they tend to keep their distance from one another. As teachers tend to be strict and poised to take disciplinary measures, students may fear them and, therefore, obey them. The relationship tends to be more antagonistic than trusting.

• Some students complain that disregarding a teacher's directives, no matter how wrong they may be, is like an egg about to be crushed by a rock. On the other hand, teachers who are friendly and accommodating could be mistaken for being weak and unable or unwilling to control the class and thus lose the respect of the students.

• In higher education and private schools, the relationship may be warmer, but distance is kept either way. In exceptional cases, teacher and student can become true friends. At any rate, there is little time for students and teachers to interact outside of class.

• Office hours are not required, unless a project under way or exam time is approaching. Students normally ask teachers for clarification or help during the class session. They may also hire their teachers to serve as private tutors.

TEACHING PRACTICES

• Dominican teachers generally lecture and expect students to record both the lecture and the information from the blackboard in their notebooks. This practice has even been observed at the kindergarten level. Lectures are sometimes supplemented by exercises and quizzes.

• Many teachers teach to the national exams, which all students must take. They may obtain copies of previous exams and use these as the basis for the curriculum, often excluding the students' other academic needs and interests.

• Reading assignments may be made by the teachers, but frequently students rely on the lecture notes. Since the cost of textbooks is high, it is sometimes difficult to obtain the books even if students have the funds to pay for them, and tests are based on information provided in class. When readings are assigned, the teacher generally asks questions of the students the next day. She or he may also give pop quizzes.

• Most teachers are not encouraged to reflect on their teaching methods and evaluate their effectiveness. Instead, they expect students to learn and succeed by their own devices.

TEACHERS' DRESS

• Teachers' dress is neither formal nor casual. Female teachers may wear a blouse and skirt or pants. Male teachers usually wear a long- or short-sleeved shirt and pants. T-shirts or polo shirts may be worn during physical education classes.

- Dominicans in general like to be well groomed and coiffed despite the heat or humidity.

DISCIPLINE AND CLASS MANAGEMENT

- Discipline problems are more common at the primary and secondary school levels than in universities and colleges. Strategies range from giving oral reprimands to being sent to the principal's office where the student is reprimanded by the principal, who may also send a note home to the parents asking them to meet for a discussion of the child's behavior or to sign the note and return it to school with the child. Serious violations can be punished by suspension or dismissal. Corporal punishment is used less now than in the past but can include striking a student with a belt, ruler, stick, or the back of one's hand.
- At the university level, students may be sent to an internal disciplinary court where their cases may be heard and action taken.
- Class attendance is not compulsory, but there is an established limit of absences allowed by the university. It is up to the professor to enforce the absentee policy or not.

STUDENTS' CIRCUMSTANCES

- A private school practice is to bring teachers and parents together at the beginning of the school year and throughout the term to discuss their mutual expectations and the children's progress. Parents meet the teachers again at the close of the school year when the final grade reports are distributed directly to parents rather than sending them home with the students. In public schools, such meetings do not take place. In the ideal scenario, the parents are expected to track the academic progress of their children by checking the monthly grade reports and helping children with homework assignments when necessary. Typically, however, parents view the teacher as the only person responsible for their children's academic development and may blame the teacher when the child does not succeed.
- Dominican immigrant children in the United States are twice as likely as Mexican immigrant children to have parents with high school diplomas and three times as likely to have parents with college degrees.

STUDENT-STUDENT RELATIONSHIP

- Unless strictly monitored and disciplined, Dominican students are energetic in class and may enjoy chatting in class, making comments to other students across the room, giggling, and generally making considerable noise.

- Dominican students can be observed to be both cooperative and competitive. The competitive dimension manifests itself between groups rather than between individuals, but cooperation is more important in protecting themselves and one another from the severity of the teacher. Thus, students will meet to study together and work on assignments. Some even prepare crib sheets in groups. Being part of a group is an important aspect in a Dominican student's life.

STUDENTS' LEARNING PRACTICES

- Dominican students may attempt to carry out academic tasks without asking for clarification or assistance from the teacher. Instead, they may turn to their classmates for help.
- While students in public schools may spend much of their class time taking notes and listening quietly to the teacher's lecture, the private schools often engage students in more dynamic learning, and teaching practices tend to be more similar to those found in many North American classrooms. Thus, some teachers strive to incorporate into their classes elements of role play for vocabulary learning and discovery methods for other types of learning tasks.

STUDENTS' DRESS

- All students in the Dominican Republic are expected to wear uniforms, which they are required to buy unless they are very poor and receive assistance for uniforms and books from the government. The official school uniform mandated by the government consists of a blue short-sleeved knit shirt plus khaki pants for boys and skirts for girls. The skirt must be long enough to cover the girl's knees. No large or flashy jewelry is allowed. Students must also wear white, black, or dark brown socks and dark brown or black dress shoes. For physical education classes, the uniform consists of a white t-shirt and navy colored shorts that fall midway above the knee plus sport shoes and socks.
- Students in private schools are not required to wear the state-mandated uniform but must observe the dress code of their school. Generally private schools require short-sleeved polo shirts with the school's colors and seal and long pants (sometimes jeans), plus dark socks and shoes.
- Although children may play barefoot in the streets, they keep their school uniforms sparkling clean.
- Universities and colleges do not require students to wear a uniform, but a dress code is generally observed to maintain decency and good behavior and to avoid social disruption.

GIFTS FOR THE TEACHER

- Gifts for the teachers are generally given at Christmas and at the end of the school year when parents pick up their child's final grade report. Gifts for the teachers are not intended as bribes for better grades but as tokens of appreciation.
- No cash gifts or expensive objects are given, but items for the teacher's personal use are acceptable. Bags for female teachers and handkerchiefs for male teachers are the most common. A decorative accessory for the teacher's living room is common as well.

NONVERBAL COMMUNICATION

- Punctuality is a variable value among Dominicans. They may pay more attention to the clock if they have an appointment for an employment interview or other professional business. Otherwise, they may arrive several minutes to well past the appointed time. In some cases, they may not show at all. Punctuality on the part of foreigners, however, is expected.
- When introduced for the first time, adults will shake hands and may continue to do so at subsequent meetings. Dominican women may also give each other a cheek-to-cheek kiss in the air. This is common in female-male encounters as well. Failure to shake hands or kiss is considered extremely impolite. Even when entering a public space such as a store, bus, waiting room, classroom, or clinic, Dominicans will greet the individual or group already assembled, and they, in turn, will respond with a similar greeting.
- When invited to the home of a Dominican, guests expect to be offered a beverage and invited to eat with the family. Turning down an offer in no way implies rudeness.
- Dominican conversation is usually punctuated by frequent hand gestures, animated facial expression, and relatively high volume, especially with friends.
- If a Dominican wrinkles his or her nose in response to a request or question, it may signal a lack of understanding or hearing clearly rather than distaste for the request. They are not likely to say "what?" to elicit repetition or clarification but perhaps "pardon?"
- It is not unusual to see Dominican friends hug and kiss each other in public and make other displays of affection, such as touching frequently while conversing. Physical affection between members of the same gender is acceptable, so men and boys may walk arm-in-arm or "hang on" each other while talking. Couples may hold hands, but most other romantic manifestations of affection are frowned upon. Public display of anger, on the other hand, is considered unacceptable unless it is mild, such as a conflict that might erupt following a casual game of dominoes.
- Eye contact is important to most Dominicans while they are engaged in conversation.

FORMS OF ADDRESS

- While Mr. and Mrs. are frequently used among Dominicans, they prefer to be addressed with the title of the educational degree that they may have obtained plus last name (e.g., *Licenciado/a* for those with degree in business or the humanities, *Ingeniero* for engineering, or *Doctor* for medicine). *Don* or *Doña* plus first name and *Señor, Señora,* and *Señorita* plus last name are also common. Thus José Pérez might be addressed as *Don José, Señor Pérez,* or *Licenciado Pérez. To* show respect, Dominicans will address strangers and older people with *Usted* (formal you) rather than *tú.*
- When Dominicans meet for the first time, they will be very interested in each other's family names and try to determine if they know each other's relatives. This enables them to locate the new acquaintance within the social structure. Having ties to a prominent family is an asset in friendship.

APPROPRIATE TOPICS

- Lively conversation about family can be expected when gathering with Dominicans for the first time. They may ask about the number of children a couple has as well as the number of siblings one has. Questions about age will normally follow and are not considered taboo in the least. Older Dominicans may even boast about their age, claiming that they are fit and attractive for their age.
- Baseball is an important pastime in the Dominican Republic, and many boys hope to become major league ball players when they grow up. Dreams of Sammy Sosa–type fame and fortune are shared by the relatives of promising athletes.
- The topic of politics is a risky one for casual acquaintances and strangers, especially if negative or contrary opinions are expressed. Many Dominicans hold prejudices against Haitians, so the relationship between the two nations and their people can make for a tense discussion topic.
- Dominicans take religion very seriously and do not appreciate jokes about it, though they tend to be jovial people who greatly enjoy humor. Individuals who do not share the same religious beliefs may end up arguing and their relationship marred by the conflict.

OUTSIDE OF CLASS

- In public school, depending on the class, homework can range from completing exercises from the textbook to writing short papers or preparing presentations for class based on the textbook content. In math or physics classes, students may be asked to solve problems for homework. Requiring students to research topics outside of class is not common, at least not on a large scale. Instead, out-of-class research consists of gathering information and perhaps paraphrasing it; this is generally done in history or geography classes. Essay writing may be a requirement in the higher grades; students in Grade 6 and below may write a short composition of no more than a page. Individual or group projects may be assigned by university professors.

- Homework for each individual class tends to be light, but assignments from six to eight classes, when put together, can become heavy. The amount and length of assignments increases at the university level.

- Students in public schools might work a full- or part-time job to help support the family, and this could diminish their academic performance. There are cases where students just drop out school so they could focus their attention only on work. If students in private schools work, these employment obligations are usually small tasks assigned in relatives' or friends' businesses; this allows flexibility so their academic performance is not affected. Outside the classroom, students might enroll in other classes also, but this is optional and depends on the possibilities as well. These other classes could be technology related (use of software, repair, and maintenance, etc.), language related (French or English classes in private institutes), or of any other nature (technical schools, arts and crafts, etc.). Some help with household duties, and some are just full-time students.

- Singing is a favorite form of entertainment and relaxation for many Dominicans, but it also prepares one for a hard task (such as doing school work) and accompanies work in the fields and kitchen. Love songs are offered via serenade to the object of one's affection, but there are also popular songs for praying and for burying a loved one.

- Dance, too, is an expression of joy for many Dominicans, and the vibrant and contagious beat of the *merengue* is the best loved.

Potential Adjustment Challenges

PROBLEMS/SOLUTIONS

Problem

I'm curious as to why my student from the Dominican Republic doesn't "hang out" with other Black students.

Solution

African-American students grow up cloaked by the issue of race, but in the Dominican Republic skin color does not determine identity or interfere with economic mobility or social interaction as it tends to in the United States, although in the Dominican Republic, people with lighter complexions may be favored in terms of standards of beauty. Dominican immigrant children may, therefore, be confused by the role that race plays in making friends and might feel anger toward those who expect them to lean one way or the other.

Problem

The parents of one of my Dominican students recently sent the child back to the Dominican Republic to live with her grandparents. Why would they want to deny their son all the benefits of a U.S. education?

Solution

Some Dominican parents may take their children out of school in North America and send them back home in an effort to prevent them from experimenting with drugs, joining gangs, and participating in other potentially harmful youth culture activity that is reported to be common in U.S. schools.

Problem

I have a Dominican student whose wardrobe is the envy of all the other students. How can someone from such a poor country afford to spend so much money on clothes?

Solution

Teachers should not assume that all Dominican children come from impoverished homes and schools. Some have attended private schools in their country that afforded them many of the same facilities and opportunities their North American peers enjoy.

Bosnia-Herzegovina

■ BOSNIA-HERZEGOVINA *Upclose*

Capital: Sarajevo

Population: 4,498,976 (June 2006)

Size: 51,129 sq. km. (19,741 sq. mi.) (slightly smaller than West Virginia)

Location: triangle-shaped country in southeastern Europe, bordered to the east and north by Croatia and to the west by Serbia and Montenegro with a 12-mile coastline on the Adriatic; divided into the Federation of Bosnia and Herzegovina and the Serbian Republic (or *Republika Srpska*)

Climate: hot in summer and cold in winter; mountainous regions have cool summers and long, harsh winters; coastal areas have milder, wetter winters

Terrain: mountainous with valleys

Monetary Unit: marka or BAM (1.553 per U.S. dollar) (June 2006)

Religion: Muslim 40%, Orthodox 31%, Roman Catholic 15%, other 14%

Language(s): Bosnian, Croatian, Serbian

Literacy Rate: total population 94.6%; men 98.4%; women 91.9% (2000)

Ethnicity: Bosniak 48%, Serb 37.1%, Croat 14.3%, other 0.6% (2000) *Note:* Bosniak has replaced Muslim as an ethnic term in part to avoid confusion with the religious term Muslim, an adherent of Islam

Per Capita Income: US$1,137 (2006)

Population Distribution: 44% urban, 56% rural (2003)

Population below Poverty Line: 25% (2004)

Life Expectancy: total population 78 years; men 74.4 years; women 81.9 years

Government: Bosnian-Croation Federal Republic and Serbian Republic

<table>
<tr><td rowspan="14" style="writing-mode: vertical-rl;">PUBLIC HOLIDAYS</td></tr>
<tr><td>January 1</td><td>New Year's Day (C)</td><td>Friday before Easter</td><td>Good Friday (C, O)</td></tr>
<tr><td>January 6</td><td>Christmas Eve (O)</td><td>Monday after Easter</td><td>Easter Monday (C, O)</td></tr>
<tr><td>January 7</td><td>Christmas Day (O)</td><td>May 1</td><td>Labor Day</td></tr>
<tr><td>January 14</td><td>New Year's Day (O)</td><td>August 15</td><td>Assumption Day (Ca)</td></tr>
<tr><td>January 21*</td><td>Eid al Adha</td><td>November 1</td><td>All Saints' Day (Ca)</td></tr>
<tr><td></td><td>(Feast of the Sacrifice) (M)</td><td>November 3*</td><td>Eid al Fitr (end of Ramadan) (M)</td></tr>
<tr><td>January 27</td><td>St. Sava's Day (O)</td><td>November 25</td><td>National Day</td></tr>
<tr><td>March 1</td><td>Independence Day</td><td>December 25</td><td>Christmas Day (C)</td></tr>
</table>

C = Christian holidays, Ca = Catholic holidays, M = Muslim holidays, O = Orthodox holidays

variable dates

Personal Perspective

The Serb and Bosnian students remained remote, learning methodically and unemotionally. I couldn't reach them, for their suffering had been too great. One boy insisted on running around the classroom, bending to pick up imaginary pieces of what? The older boys shook their heads and somehow reassured the class that this was alright and to be ignored. Weeks later, when that boy could talk to me a little, he told me he was picking up the pieces of his father. . . . Stories began to stumble out from numb minds. Dark hidden parts of the brain buried deep the sinister horrors of war which day and night continued to rage, only a jet flight away. We wept in the classroom for the suffering that was to continue for months. Survival had wiped everything away, emotions, good-byes, treasured belongings, memories, grandparents, earth that had been tilled for generations. The human spirit had been numbed, and bright light almost extinguished. These young men and women had been forced to the edge of humanity and they knew it.

—Madden-Shephard (2005)

Historical Perspective

IMMIGRATION TO THE UNITED STATES

Before the 1992–1995 civil war in Bosnia-Herzegovina, the small number of Bosnians who entered the United States were mainly Serbs and Croats. Very few entered as refugees, and most were able to settle into existing small Serbian and Croatian communities in the United States. The war killed 200,000 people (50,000 of whom were children) and produced approximately 1.3 million refugees, leading some 200,000 Bosnians to enter the United States as refugees or asylees when the fighting came to an end. Large Bosnian communities began to emerge in St. Louis and Chicago. However, unlike groups of Russian refugees arriving at approximately the same time, Bosnians initially enjoyed few pre-existing communities, organizations, services, and institutions that would facilitate their adjustment. The relative obscurity of their native language in the United States contributed to the slow and painful transition.

Most Bosnian refugees living in the United States today are Muslim. Most are from rural areas and were forced to flee their homes with virtually no time to pack, let alone to learn English and save money for resettlement first in one country and then in another. Families were often separated as they sought safety. Women and children, left alone when the men were abducted, incarcerated, beaten, and starved, could no longer wait for the return of their husbands and fathers. Many were taken to Germany or Hungary where they were granted temporary asylum and were allowed to work and set up households. Others waited in refugee camps for their opportunity to start a new life abroad. The inflow of refugees from Bosnia-Herzegovina is now slight compared to the previous decades. However, a significant number still live outside their homeland, afraid to return because of persistent persecution and reprisals. Nevertheless, they have come under pressure from some of their host countries, which have turned from encouraging voluntary repatriation to imposing forced repatriation.

HISTORICAL SYNOPSIS

Bosnia-Herzegovina has had an extremely complex ethnic and political history. After World War II, it was part of the Yugoslav Socialist Federation, which was composed of six ethnically and religiously diverse republics: Slovakia, Croatia, Bosnia and Herzegovina, Macedonia, Serbia, and Montenegro. During the Soviet era, its premier was a ruthless military officer, Marshal Josip Broz Tito, and though ethnic tensions existed, the country of Yugoslavia remained united under his command. With the collapse of communism in the early 1990s, however, the different ethnic groups sought independence on different terms, and conflict broke out. In 1991 Croatia and Slovakia declared independence. In an election, Bosnian Croats and Bosniaks (Bosnian Muslims) voted for independence against the wishes of the Bosnian Serbs, who were outraged that such a decision had not been reached through consensus. Fighting broke out between the Bosnian Serbs, backed by the Yugoslav army, and the Croatian-backed Bosnian Croats who were allied with the Bosnia-Muslims. Fighting was vicious, and a major strategy adopted by both Serbs and Muslims during the war was that of ethnic cleansing, involving atrocities such as torture, murder, massacres, and rape as a means of wiping out minority ethnic communities or humiliating them and forcing them to flee. Fighting was not only brutal but very complex. Whole communities, neighbors, and even families were ripped apart by ethnic differences, and unlikely alliances were made between the various ethnic groups in different regions for different purposes. The international community was finally shaken out of its passivity by Serbian aggression after a cease-fire between the Muslims and Croats was signed in 1994, and NATO air strikes ultimately forced the Serbs to sign the Dayton Peace Accords of 1995.

Tensions continued and finally erupted in 1998 in the Serbian province of Kosovo, where Albanian Muslims had long desired independence. The threat of the brutal Serbian crackdown on both the Kosovo Liberation Army and the civilian population and the potential for a Bosnian-like humanitarian catastrophe led to NATO's second campaign of air strikes against the Serbs. Today, Kosovo remains an autonomous region within Serbia and Montenegro, with its ultimate fate not yet decided, and Bosnia-Herzegovina is an independent democratic country made up of two regions—the Federation of Bosnia and Herzegovina and the Serbian Republic. Nevertheless, under the surface of both areas, old structures and tensions remain.

Deep Culture Perspective

DEEP CULTURE BELIEFS

- The differences between the various groups in Bosnia-Herzegovina have religion at their root, with Serbs mostly Orthodox Christian, Croats mostly Roman Catholic, and Bosniaks predominantly Muslim.
- Bosnian culture is basically male orientated. Women do not easily live independently, especially in the villages, and although many hold down responsible jobs, they still are expected to run the household. The current international presence in this country means that women's issues are receiving more attention, and in some areas men are taking more of a role in raising children, though this varies considerably. Thus, though women have status in Bosnia-Herzegovina, few women wield much economic power.
- Ethnicity, which can easily be discerned from an individual's name, is still a very important factor in any interaction. It can affect such things as level of salary within a company and acceptance in a particular community. Even in international organizations, ethnic discrimination is practiced, though there is more of a tendency to work together because of the salaries. Class, usually reflected in level of education, is also an important feature of identity.
- Families tend to embody a mixture of traditional patriarchy with more modern relationships. The high number of university-educated people has influenced society in terms of redefining gender roles. In general, the Bosnian-Herzegovian social structure reflects its European history, though there still exists some of the Slavic tradition of the extended family.

PROVERBS

- One who lies for you will also lie against you.
- A brave man is seldom hurt in the back.
- The eyes of all cheats are full of tears.
- When an ant gets wings, it loses its head.
- Two things rule the world—reward and punishment.
- Why would you use poison if you can kill with honey?

FOLK TALE

Once there lived a young maiden who went with her sisters one warm summer day to take a cool dip in a nearby lake. As the girls were enjoying their luxurious respite from the midsummer heat, the young maiden suddenly realized that a small snake had taken up residence in her sleeve.

She screamed with fright, shaking her arm and running frantically along the shore trying to dislodge the creature. Finally, she stopped flailing her arms when the snake began to speak. "Dear lady," he said gently. "I cannot leave your sleeve until you consent to marry my king." Although she herself was somewhat ambivalent, her sisters rejoiced at the plan, thinking that a sister married to royalty would certainly bring them fine husbands and fortune.

Finally, the maiden agreed to marry the king, but her parents were violently opposed to the plan. When a brigade of royally dispatched snakes arrived at the family's home that night to escort the young girl to her betrothed, the parents quickly grabbed a snow-white sheep, wrapped it in cloth, and presented it to the entourage in place of their daughter. The brigade was almost fooled but for the bleating of the lamb. "We must have your daughter now. We will not be deceived." Reluctant still, the parents next placed a downy white goose on a string and presented the fowl to the snakes with tears in their eyes and blubbering, "Good-bye, fair daughter." But as they were leaving the homestead, a partridge swooped down and whispered to the leader of the retinue, "Don't be fooled. Your bride is but a goose!"

No longer able to continue the charade, the parents sadly bade farewell to their daughter, who was taken to the bottom of the lake and married to the snake king. The couple lived happily for many years, and their three children gave them great pleasure and pride. However, the queen missed her family keenly, begging her husband constantly to let her go to pay them a visit. Regardless of her promises and pleadings, the king refused to allow her to leave.

He loved her deeply, however, and regretted that his wife's continuing sorrow was his own doing, so he gave her his permission to leave the lake and visit her family. The queen and her children were instructed to use a secret incantation to reenter the lake at the end of their earthly visit, and off they went to be reunited with the queen's family. After several enjoyable days, the children became more comfortable with their grandparents and blurted out the magic incantation. Without a moment's hesitation, the father ran to the lake and chanted the spell, and when the snake king surfaced, he cut him to pieces. All this transpired without the knowledge of the queen, who assembled her children and returned to the lake shore to rejoin her husband in their underwater home. With eyes closed, she carefully enunciated the special chant but was aghast to behold a crimson red wave soaking her feet. The reality of her husband's fate washed over her as well, and, in grief, she walked across the sand and transformed herself and her children into trees.

Administrative Perspective

OFFICIAL EDUCATIONAL POLICY

The very different political structures of the two entities that make up the Bosnia-Herzegovina Federation and the Serbian Republic are reflected in the way that education is governed. In the Serbian Republic there is a Ministry of Education, and educational policy is centrally decided and administered. In the Federation it is very much decentralized. Each canton, or administrative region, has power over its own education policy and administration and can, in turn, defer that power to the municipalities themselves, which is often done if a municipal's ethnic makeup is different from that of the majority of the canton.

Education is, to a large extent, a battleground of ethnic rivalry since control of it is deemed very important in developing national and group identities. Sometimes education is used to promote racial hatred and intolerance, with the various groups using textbooks that blame the other side for its aggression and war crimes. In some cases, children from different ethnic groups enter the same school building through different doors, go to different classrooms, and are taught by different teachers. These schools are often called the "two schools under one roof" system. However, the Council of Europe is trying to bring an end to these practices and in 2002 gained the agreement of the Federation and Serbian Republic to implement a core curriculum to facilitate both student mobility from one region to another and also the reentry of returnees.

EDUCATION AT A GLANCE

See the Education at a Glance table on page 111.

BOSNIA-HERZEGOVINA

Level/Age	Hours/Calendar	Language of Instruction	Compulsory Attendance	Exams	Grading System	Curriculum	Cost	Enrollment
Primary Grades 1–8 ages 7–15	Classes from Oct. to July broken into two semesters. Mon.–Fri. two shifts per day. 8:00 AM –1:00 PM 1:30 PM – 6:30 PM. 45-minute classes with a 5-min. break between classes	Serbo-Croatian	Yes, to age 15	Short-answer, problem solving, definitions, no multiple choice; essays only in literature courses. Mostly oral exams; student is called to the front of the classroom to answer questions for approximately 10 minutes. No final exams; no formal exam schedule; students are examined once or twice per semester and at any time during the school year with no forewarning.	5-point scale with 5 being the highest. End-of-year points for conduct added to final grade. Failure in one school subject requires the student to attend summer school. If the student fails the summer school exam, he or she must repeat the level.	Different curricula and textbooks are used in schools in the different territories.	Free, but students pay for books and supplies	Primary: 90%
Secondary Grades 9–12 ages 15–19. Attendance for 4 years required for university entrance			No	Students successfully completing the secondary level receive a general secondary school-leaving certificate. Those graduating from technical secondary schools receive a diploma.		Students take approximately 16 classes at a time. Two branches: general and technical/vocational. Both include an element of vocational training. Technical schools have a more professional orientation.		Secondary: 56%
University ages 19+. *Više Škole* 2-year diploma course; universities 1st degree, 2–3 years; 2nd stage 4–6 years; master's 2 years	Classes from Oct. to July broken into two semesters. Mon.–Fri.		No	Successful performance on a university entrance exam is required for admission. A student may decide when to take the exams for his/her level. Exams are offered in Sept., Nov, Jan, Mar, and June. Most exams are oral.	5–10 scale, with 6 as minimum passing grade	Non-university *Više Škole* offer professional qualifications in various scientific and artistic fields; 2nd stage university programs offer the opportunity to specialize in these fields; master's level involves defense of a thesis; Ph.D. level involves public defense of a thesis after independent research.	The top-scoring 180 students do not pay tuition, but their attendance is monitored. Tuition-paying students are not required to attend class, and their attendance is not monitored.	No data available

▉ Surface Culture Perspective

CLASSROOMS

- During the civil war, some 60 percent of schools, libraries, and gyms were commandeered as military supply and training sites, looted, or burned down, leading to a shortage of books and equipment. Sometimes, they were taken over by refugees, and students and their teachers would retreat to the hallways and corridors for classes. Today, many schools lack electricity, telecommunications, a proper water supply, and heating systems. Teaching tools are equally inadequate.
- Because of the politicization of education, attempts to deliver improved instruction in Bosnia-Herzegovina have been hampered. Many schools were destroyed or damaged during the war and have not yet been rebuilt or repaired.
- Education is almost entirely dependent on funds from the central government, and because of the stagnation in the economy, money for schools is lacking. This is not a new phenomenon; even before the collapse of communism, money for books and equipment was running out. The reconstruction efforts in Bosnia-Herzegovina have resulted in the restoration of most primary schools, but secondary schools and institutions of higher education remain in severe disrepair, and some have been condemned.
- In Serbian regions especially, schools are often very overcrowded with up to 2,700 children in an elementary school. As there are not enough classrooms to accommodate such numbers, schools often must operate in shifts (different groups of learners morning and afternoon). The student-teacher ratio in the Federation is 20 to 1, while in the Serbian Republic it is 18 to 1.

TEACHERS' STATUS

- Primary-level teachers traditionally receive two years of post-secondary training. Secondary-level teachers are university graduates with a four-year pedagogic degree.
- Teachers are rarely trained or skilled in modern teaching methods and may be described in reports as incompetent. Only 25 percent of teachers are said to be qualified to teach the level and grade to which they are assigned.
- Teachers' salaries are very low and sometimes irregular. The average salary is approximately US$230 per month. Unsurprisingly, many teachers lack motivation to invest time in preparing for class or in improving their skills, and strikes for better pay and working conditions are not uncommon.

- Teachers typically work 42 hours per week, 25 of which are spent in the classroom.
- Few university students aspire to a career in education; thus, Bosnia-Herzegovina has for many years experienced a severe teacher shortage, more so in the rural areas than in the urban areas. Some teachers are still living as refugees outside the borders of Bosnia-Herzegovina and are waiting for assurances of safety before returning to their homes and jobs.

TEACHER-STUDENT RELATIONSHIP

- Teachers tend to be highly respected in Bosnia-Herzegovina. This is especially so since they are perceived as holding enormous power over students by being in control of their grades.
- Students sometimes complain of poor relations with teachers, especially in the Serbian Republic.
- Many teachers are at a loss with how to deal with the vestiges of shock and trauma experienced by their students during the war. They express frustration at the ethnic strife that still lingers in their communities and affects students' attitudes and performance.
- During the first four years of schooling, students are taught all subjects by a single teacher. However, beginning in Grade 5, different subjects are taught by different teachers.

TEACHING PRACTICES

- Although traditional expectations of memorization and verbatim recitation still hold sway in much of the country's education system, some seminars are available to help teachers become aware of and use more modern, interactive teaching methods.
- Most teachers have internalized the notion that learning is listening and teaching is talking. They see learning as essentially a process of absorption of information.
- More recently trained teachers will engage students in discussion in class, inviting their questions and providing explanation and clarification as a regular part of the class.

TEACHERS' DRESS

- In urban areas, dressing casually for work is acceptable. In more rural areas, standards of dress are higher, and great importance is given to appearance. During the summer, women dress with more freedom than during the winter, when practicality becomes more of a factor.
- Importance is placed on the cleanliness of shoes.

DISCIPLINE AND CLASS MANAGEMENT

- The parents of students who misbehave will likely find out about their child's school comportment during monthly parent-teacher conferences. At these meetings, the teacher shares information with the parents about the child's grades and attendance, and parents usually discipline their child at home to avoid further embarrassment.
- Corporal punishment is legally permissible and practiced in many schools.
- A student's name and grades are read aloud before the assembly of teachers and parents at general parent-teacher meetings. As this can be a humiliating experience for parents, it can be considered a form of discipline on the part of the student.

STUDENTS' CIRCUMSTANCES

- Secondary-level enrollment stands at only 56 percent, compared to 90 percent at the primary level, often because children from poor and minority families are compelled to leave school to support the family.
- Students with special needs are barely acknowledged or accommodated in Bosnia-Herzegovinian schools.
- Changes in education have not yet caught up with the change in the society from a socialist state to a democracy with a free labor market, which means that young people are not being taught the skills necessary for them to find jobs in the increasingly important service sector. As a consequence, young people are leaving the country, which, in turn, creates its own labor shortage.

STUDENT-STUDENT RELATIONSHIP

- Camaraderie between students is an important part of school life, with student-student relationships being far more important than teacher-student relationships.
- The hatred that brewed between Bosnian Muslims and Bosnian Serbs during the war is still palpable in classrooms when the two groups come together. Frequently, they occupy different classrooms to avoid conflict.
- Group success is important, though the success of the individual is also esteemed.
- All grades are made public.

STUDENTS' LEARNING PRACTICES

- Bosnian students, in general, are not hesitant to ask questions of the teacher in class. In fact, quiet chitchatting while the teacher is lecturing is not uncommon and is somewhat tolerated.

- Every class has a student monitor who is responsible for assisting the teacher by, for example, bringing maps to class, reporting student absences, and cleaning the blackboard.
- Students take notes of the teacher's lectures and information written on the board, filling copybooks that they later use to study. Teachers do not collect or check the copybooks.
- At the end of the school year, students in some schools will burn their books or rip them apart as a kind of celebration of the end of a long and difficult period.
- Parents may use their connections to persuade a teacher to give their child a better grade than he or she deserves.
- Strong students frequently allow classmates to copy their homework from their notebooks. Although most willingly offer their assistance in this way, they are sometimes compelled to do so as a result of being pressured by a bully.
- Students consider cheating on exams and homework socially acceptable and even find that the many strategies they use (e.g., crib sheets) enhance their learning of the subject content.

STUDENTS' DRESS

- Students wear uniforms up to Grade 7, after which street attire is appropriate for school. However, skirts must conform to certain length standards (e.g., no miniskirts), and girls are prohibited from wearing tank tops.

GIFTS FOR THE TEACHER

- There is no Teachers' Day celebrated in Bosnia-Herzegovina, although students may present a gift to the teacher for his or her birthday (this is generally the case at the primary school level).

NONVERBAL COMMUNICATION

- Personal space tends to be closer than in North America, especially among friends. Physical distance tends to reflect perceived social distance and is greater between new acquaintances.
- It is important to shake hands when meeting someone for the first time, though a man should wait for a woman to proffer a hand. Friends hug and kiss more readily, and close friends of the same sex holding hands or linking arms while walking along a street is not uncommon.
- Maintaining eye contact is more important to people in Bosnia-Herzegovina than to North Americans, as it affirms honesty and good faith. However, if more than one speaker is talking at the same time, a frequent phenomenon when groups are gathered, it may be difficult for an outsider to determine with whom he or she should maintain

eye contact. Certainly, eye contact is important when raising a toast or clinking glasses.

- A smile or pleasant facial expression is important for making a good impression and for ensuring smooth interaction.
- People are generally extremely hospitable to the extent that they may answer a question by giving the response they feel the listener wants, rather than what is actually true. Also, people will make great efforts to obtain information for a visitor and to be helpful.
- Heated discussions that are nonetheless friendly may occur between people who know each other well but are inappropriate for new acquaintances.
- Punctuality can be a thorny issue with people from Bosnia-Herzegovina as they have a tendency to leave things to the last minute. Deadlines can also be problematic unless expectations are clearly set.
- Gestures that can be offensive to people from Bosnia-Herzegovina include beckoning someone with up-turned hand or with only the index finger, the North American "OK" sign made by forming a circle with the thumb and index finger, and the "horn" sign made by simultaneously extending the index finger and pinkie. Also, yawning, stretching, and cracking one's knuckles are considered rude.
- Raising the first three fingers of the hand was used by the Serbs to indicate victory during the country's civil war. It should be avoided at all costs in the Bosniak and Croat communities.

FORMS OF ADDRESS

- Primary school students are called by their first names, but in secondary school teachers call their students by family name unless they are on unusually friendly terms. At the university, professors refer to their students as "young colleague."
- Students at the primary level call their teachers *učitelj* (masc.) or *učiteljica* (fem.). By high school, students begin to address their teachers as *nastavnik* (meaning mentor, teacher, or instructor), and by college they refer to their teachers as "professor."
- On first acquaintance, it is polite to address people as Mr., Mrs., or Miss plus family or first name—the practice varies between regions and communities.
- Many family names in Bosnia-Herzegovina end with *ic*. For example, Sulemanagic is clearly a Bosniak or Muslim name.

APPROPRIATE TOPICS

- Given the traumatic events of the recent past, it is clearly advisable to keep away from discussions about the events of the 1992–95 war, both military and political. Sometimes, talking about family and work, otherwise safe topics, can evoke painful memories, though some people may find a certain catharsis in such conversations.

- The hospitable nature of the people of Bosnia-Herzegovina can make them curious about a new acquaintance, and it is not uncommon for them to ask questions such as, "Are you married," "Do you have children," or "What's your job?"
- Because people find so much enjoyment in each other's company and group activities are particularly valued, conversation is a favorite pastime. It is not uncommon for discussions of obscure, often historical topics to last for hours.
- Maintaining the appearance of masculine dominance is important for some men in Bosnia-Herzegovina, making comments or topics that threaten that image unwelcome.
- Some culture groups within Bosnia-Herzegovina may feel obliged to give an object to a person who expresses great admiration for it; therefore, compliments are not made indiscriminately.

OUTSIDE OF CLASS

- In Soviet times, schools offered students many extracurricular activities. In some schools such activities continue to a greater or lesser extent. They include choir, music, folk and drama groups, and sports clubs and teams, all of which could compete in interschool, regional, and even national competitions.
- During children's week in early October, cultural, educational, and recreational events are organized. Often, however, there is neither the space for such events nor the money to pay teachers to organize them. Older students may spend much of their free time sitting in cafes.

Potential Adjustment Challenges

PROBLEMS/SOLUTIONS

Problem

I have been surprised at the openly derogatory and sarcastic comments that my Bosnian student makes about other ethnic groups in his country. I can't understand such intolerance in such a young person.

Solution

People from the former Yugoslavia suffered from ethnic violence, cruelty, intolerance, prejudice, and hatred for so many years that letting go of their anger and fear is far from easy or automatic, even though many have escaped the terror to make new lives in North America and relative peace has come to their part of the world. Ethnic intolerance had, in many cases, become culturally endemic. This is perhaps why some Bosnian students have difficulties in adjusting to the multi-ethnic and multi-cultural nature of life in the North American schools. The roots of ethnic strife and strategies for creating a more harmonious society are now being addressed via the introduction of peace studies throughout the Bosnia-Herzegovina public school curriculum.

Problem

I recently learned that one of my Bosnian students has not been able to complete his homework because he doesn't have access to the Internet at home. I've been giving him F's and dirty looks. Why didn't he just tell me?

Solution

Some Bosnian learners may be reluctant to ask for help for a variety of reasons. For example, because at one time ordinary citizens may have been abused or betrayed by authorities (even teachers and neighbors), they may be loath to reveal their personal problems because they do not trust anyone who appears to be in a position of authority. It is possible that they may misinterpret your intentions.

Problem

One of my Bosnian students is extremely withdrawn. She never raises her hand to speak and barely ekes out a response when I call on her. Why is she so shy?

Solution

This student may not be as much shy as she is a victim of PTSD—Post-Traumatic Stress Disorder. Most children who lived in Bosnia-Herzegovina during the civil war witnessed unspeakable atrocities, which may have included watching their parents and loved ones being tortured, raped, or murdered by strangers and even neighbors. Symptoms of PTSD are, therefore, to be expected.

Croatia

■ CROATIA *Upclose*

Capital: Zagreb

Population: 4,494,749 (June 2006)

Size: 56,542 sq. km. (21,831 sq. mi.) (slightly smaller than West Virginia)

Location: southeastern Europe, bordered by the Adriatic Sea on the east/southeast, between Bosnia-Herzegovina to the south, Serbia and Montenegro to the east, Hungary to the northeast, and Slovenia to the northwest; a chain of nearly 1,000 islands parallels the coast

Climate: Mediterranean along the coast with mild winters and dry summers; continental in the northern plains with cold winters and hot summers; alpine in the central mountainous region

Terrain: low mountains along the Adriatic coast, flatlands along the border with Hungary, and an interior of mountains and forests

Monetary Unit: kuna (5.77 per U.S. dollar) (June 2006)

Religion: Roman Catholic 87.8%, Orthodox 4.4%, Muslim 1.3%, Protestant 0.3%, others and unknown 6.2%

Language(s): Croatian 96%, other 4% (including Italian, Hungarian, Czech, Slovak, and German)

Literacy Rate: total population 98.5%; men 99.4%; women 97.8% (2003)

Ethnicity: Croat 89.6%, Serb 4.5%, Bosniak 0.5%, Hungarian 0.4%, Slovene 0.3%, Czech 0.2%, Roma 0.2%, Albanian 0.1%, Montenegrin 0.1%, others 4.1%

Per Capita Income: US$4,430 (2006)

Population Distribution: 59% urban; 41% rural (2003)

Population below Poverty Line: 11% (2003)

Life Expectancy: total population 74.7 years; men 71.0 years; women 78.5 years (2006)

Government: presidential/parliamentary democracy

PUBLIC HOLIDAYS				
	January 1	New Year's Day	August 5	Thanksgiving Day
	January 6	Epiphany	August 15	Assumption of Mary
	Friday before Easter	Good Friday	October 8	Independence Day
	Monday after Easter	Easter Monday	November 1	All Saints Day
	May 1	Labor Day	November 3–5*	End of Ramadan
	June 22	Anti-Fascism Day	December 25	Christmas
	June 25	Statehood Day (National Day)	December 26	Saint Stephen's Day

variable dates

Note: Orthodox, Muslim, and Jewish Croatians may take the following days for vacation, although they are not considered public holidays for the rest of the population: Ramadan Bairam (Muslim), Kurban Bairam (Muslim), Rosh Hashanah (Jewish), Yom Kippur (Jewish), and Old Christmas (Orthodox).

▪ Personal Perspective

Well, it happened some years ago, just after the war in Croatia. Teaching was a particularly difficult job at the time because some students had lost one/both parents. We were really trying hard to create an optimistic and enthusiastic atmosphere in the classroom. It happened while I was having a lesson on Present Simple vs Present Continuous (asking about jobs, careers, etc.). It was a class of fourteen-year-olds. I asked a boy in the first row. *T: What do you do? S: I'm a student. T: Very well, and what does your father do? S: Er...er...I don't know. T: What do you mean, you don't know? S: Well, he died last year. I hope he's in heaven but I don't know what he's doing right now.* The class bursts into laughter and I feel terrible. *T: Oh, I'm so sorry, dear, I didn't know.*

Now I know I should have dropped the subject, but no, I went on all confused. *T: Well. maybe your mate can help you. Petar, what does your father do? PETAR: My father's dead, too.* (Oh, no, not again!) *T: I'm really sorry. Let's drop the subject, you can ask me anything you want.* I don't know how I managed to survive. Poor kids, I was so sorry. There's one thing I'm positive about—since then I've never asked any of my students: "What does your father do?" I learnt my lesson well!

—Tranfiae (2004)

▪ Historical Perspective

IMMIGRATION TO THE UNITED STATES

Several waves of Croatian immigrants have settled in the United States beginning in the early 1880s. The first were fishermen and fruit growers who gravitated mainly to the Mississippi Delta and the California coast. The second large-scale arrival occurred at the turn of the century. Peasants and unskilled laborers fled poverty conditions in Croatia to seek a better life as blue-collar workers in the large industrial cities of Pittsburgh, Chicago, and Detroit. After World War II, additional Croatian political refugees fled the Communist government led by Marshal Tito. Then, in 1991, Croatia broke away from the Socialist Federal Republic of Yugoslavia, and a brutal four-year civil war between the Croatian army and Yugoslavia-backed Croatian Serbs ensued in which assassinations, torture, arbitrary arrests, and ethnic cleansing were perpetrated by both Croats and Serbs. Some 300,000 Croatian Serbs fled Croatia at this time to find refuge in neighboring countries that had made up the former Yugoslavia. The approximately 225,000 who made their way to the United States settled primarily in Missouri, Florida, Illinois, Michigan, Arizona, New York, and Texas. Although both the U.S. and Croatian governments have provided the means for refugees to return home, many Croatian Serbs fear persistent ethnically motivated intimidation and discrimination and more than 330,000 Croats have not been repatriated.

HISTORICAL SYNOPSIS

Croatia today is a multiethnic nation but initially was settled by Slavic groups migrating from Ukraine. The territory was subsumed under the Hungarians in 1091, the Hapsburgs in the mid-1400s, and by the Austro-Hungarian Empire up until the end of World War I when in 1918 it united with neighboring territories to become the Kingdom of Serbs, Croats, and Slovenes. In 1929 the Kingdom was renamed Yugoslavia, which in turn became the Socialist Federal Republic of Yugoslavia after World War II under Marshall Tito. Croatia was then one of six relatively autonomous republics of Yugoslavia. Tito's death, the disintegration of the Soviet bloc in the 1980s, and the Croatian republic's growing economic strength led Croatia to declare its independence from Yugoslavia in 1991, but internal ethnic strife between the Croats and the Serbs turned into civil war within one month of Croatian independence. Croatian Serbs, resisting the establishment of a Croat state, declared their independence from Croatia and received military support from the communist Yugoslav People's Army to retain control over Serb-dominant sections of Croatia. They met fierce resistance from the Croatian army. Several cease-fires were called and broken over the next several years as a campaign of ethnic cleansing by Serbs (98 percent of Croats in the Serbian areas were forcibly removed) and destruction of Croat towns was undertaken, and atrocities were committed by both Croats and Serbs throughout the conflict. More than 150,000 Serbs were either driven out of Croatia or fled the country for fear of their lives. It took several years for the world to take notice and for the UN to intervene in the genocide. The UN troops concentrated on protecting the Serbian population, demoted to a "national minority" rather than a "constituent nation" after independence from Yugoslavia, making return of Croatian refugees all the more unlikely.

Finally, the Dayton Peace Accords were signed by Croatia in 1995 and were seriously implemented (as far as return of refugees, national conciliation, and democratization are concerned) beginning in 2000 under the coalition government of Prime Minister Racan and subsequent administrations. Today, Croats and Serbs continue to be suspicious of each other, and numerous conflict resolution plans have had to be introduced to teach the citizens of Croatia to respect ethnic diversity if not to live in harmony. Croatians living in Serbia suffer institutional and social discrimination not unlike the Serbs living in Croatia.

As for language use within this multi-ethnic nation, Croatian is the country's official language and is spoken by the majority of people. Most Croatians also speak at least one foreign language, such as German, French, Italian, Czech, or Hungarian. Most younger people speak some English. Croatian belongs to the South Slavic branch of the Slavic language group, which also includes Serbian, Bosnian, Slovene, Macedonian, and Bulgarian. The structures and vocabularies of Serbian, Croatian, and Bosnian are so similar that speakers of any one of them can easily understand one another; consequently, outside of Croatia, the three languages are usually referred to as one, called Serbo-Croatian.

Until the 19th century, Croatian was written in the Latin or Glagolithic scripts. Glagolithic is a unique script whose origins are disputed, though it appears to have arisen sometime before the Middle Ages. The Bas-ka Tablet from 1100 CE is the oldest example of this writing, while The Annals, from 1177, mention that when Pope Alexander visited Zadar, he was greeted with enthusiasm and the singing of the people in the Croatian language. Today, written Croatian uses the Latin script.

Deep Culture Perspective

DEEP CULTURE BELIEFS

- Typical Croatian families live several generations to a home, either a modern apartment building in the city, a carved and decorated wooden house in the countryside, or a white-washed stone or concrete structure along the coast. Their members derive a strong sense of security and unity from the tight bonds they form with one another. Households are usually led by the eldest male, and often include grandparents and other relatives from both sides of the family, especially in rural areas. A child's godparents may live with the family as well, as their responsibility is great and their role cherished in Croatian families. Children are often strictly disciplined not only by their parents but by their godparents. Smaller, nuclear families are becoming more the norm in the cities, and women are beginning to share equal authority with men over the home, but in the countryside the extended family structure helps ensure that land will be passed down from one generation to the next and plenty of children will be on hand to farm the family's property. Croatian folklore abounds with songs and poems about the family. Their love for and loyalty to each other is played out in reality as well. Family members often receive preferential treatment at work, for example, and may learn of and apply and interview for employment vacancies before any official posting is made.
- Ritual is important to many Croatians especially with regard to birth, death, and marriage. Religion often plays a role in ceremonies related to these events, so church weddings, for example, are common as well as quite large, typically involving entire villages if the celebration takes place in the countryside. In addition to a church service, life-cycle ceremonies often include a lavish feast.
- Croatian women are guaranteed equality with men as far as hiring and promotion in the workplace are concerned and as such make up nearly 50 percent of the labor force. They pursue professions in medicine and engineering to a greater extent than do women in the United States and are frequently lawyers and architects as well as teachers. Also generously protected by the constitution is a woman's right to

maternity leave and personal leave to look after sick children. Despite these entitlements, salaries for Croatian women still lag behind those of their male counterparts in parallel positions.

• The Tito regime quashed religious expression in general and the practice of Catholicism in particular, but following Croatia's declaration of independence it experienced a strong resurgence. Catholicism had been ensconced in Croat culture since the Middle Ages to the extent that the Croatian language was used during the Mass supplanting the Vatican proscribed language, Latin. Similar to Catholics in many parts of the world, Croats venerate the Virgin Mary, whom they call *Gospa* and the Queen of Peace, and make pilgrimages to the site where she is said to have appeared. Croatian Serbs generally adhere to Eastern Orthodox Christianity. While the two religions share many commonalities, the Orthodox Church does not acknowledge the authority of the Vatican. Its priests are also allowed to marry, and its adherents revere a number of icons rather than the Virgin Mary. Croatia's Protestants are largely Lutherans or those belonging to the Christian Reformed Church. Jews represent only a small portion of Croats since their ancestors' expulsion to Nazi concentration camps during World War II or immigration to Israel. Croatia's Muslim population is small as well but has coexisted with other religious groups in the country since the 10th century.

PROVERBS

■ The person who is singing is not a bad thing thinking.

■ A sparrow in the hand is better then a pigeon on the branch.

■ He who gets up early is doubly lucky.

■ A splinter doesn't land far from the trunk.

■ Where people are promising much to you, bring a small bag.

■ There is no such thing as a quiet child nor a young grandmother.

■ What you can do today do not postpone until tomorrow.

■ Those who study will know; those who save will have.

■ He who digs a trap for others will end up in it himself.

FOLK TALE

Once upon a time there was an old mill that people were afraid to approach for they believed it to be haunted by a she-wolf. One day, however, a soldier entered the mill in order to find a place to sleep. After building a fire in the main chamber, he climbed to another level and bored a hold in the floor so that he could keep an eye on the chamber below. Soon, the she-wolf entered the mill and approached the fire. "Skin off! Skin off! Skin off!" she repeated until her skin fell on the ground like a thick coat and revealed a beautiful young maiden. She hung her skin on a peg, curled up before the fire, and fell asleep.

Eventually, the soldier descended into the room, and nailed the skin to the mill wheel. When the maiden awoke, she screamed at the presence of the interloper and repeated, "Skin on! Skin on! Skin on!" But as the skin was nailed to the mill wheel, she could not reclaim it. The soldier seized the opportunity to take the maiden away and marry her.

Several years later the woman's eldest son reported that he had heard she was a she-wolf. His father had confirmed the tale, telling his son that his mother's wolf skin was nailed to the mill wheel. "Well," said the mother, "if I am a she-wolf, where is my skin?" Her son, eager to prove he was correct, cried, "It's at the old mill nailed to the wheel!" "I see," calmly replied the woman. "Thank you for this delightful revelation." After that day, the woman was never seen again.

Administrative Perspective

OFFICIAL EDUCATIONAL POLICY

Upon declaring its independence, Croatia found itself in a position to revise the educational system and is now undergoing the slow process of reform. A major portion of the undertaking involves the depoliticization of education, as the institution had for many years been influenced more by ideology than by the science of pedagogy. In many cases, curricular revision has had to take a back seat to more urgent challenges such as the rebuilding of schools following their destruction during the post-independence war, often call the Homeland War by Croats. Nevertheless, a number of major initiatives were placed on the agenda (though not fully implemented) including the elimination of courses and materials that adopted a Communist perspective (e.g., planned economy vs. free enterprise, Communism vs. humanism); the reintroduction of catechism as an elective; reduction of the course load and mandatory hours of instruction; opening of schools that allow students to study in their native language; creation of optional and alternative instructional programs and private schools (e.g., non-secular schools); and rewriting, publishing, and distribution of textbooks. The latter took place in the republics of the former Yugoslavia as well, but the accounts of the war and the interpretation of the history of the region vary from nation to nation.

Another significant introduction to the Croatian educational system is the National Program of Education for Human Rights. This government program is wide ranging, affecting primary and secondary schools as well as adult and vocational education and permeating all subject areas as well as after-school programs. The plan aims to address and resolve the interethnic conflict that nearly destroyed Croatia after independence. The objective is to cultivate cross-cultural understanding and to instill peace and respect for human rights through the teaching of the principles of democratic citizenship. Teachers are seen as the key to the success of this initiative; thus, serious work has been done to coordinate and support teachers through meetings, electronic networks and databases and provision of pedagogical resources and through modeling training practices such as teamwork, critical thinking, problem solving, and group projects.

EDUCATION AT A GLANCE

See the Education at a Glance table on page 126.

CROATIA

Level/Age	Hours/Calendar	Language of Instruction	Compulsory Attendance	Exams	Grading System	Curriculum	Cost	Enrollment
Pre-school ages up to 6	No data available	Serbo-Croatian	Yes, but it is not universally enforced.	No data available	No data available	Preparation for 1st grade based on principles of humanism		32% of children attend pre-school.
Primary Grades 1–8 ages 6–14	Oct.-June; long vacation June 15–Sept. 30 8:00 AM–3:00 PM		Yes	Short answer, definitions, no multiple choice Frequent impromptu oral exams of selected students	1–5 point scale 5 excellent 4 very good 3 good 2 satisfactory 1 unsatisfactory	Classes with single teacher until 4th grade, then specialized classes introduced; teachers choose from 6 parallel curriculum course books.	Free	Total enrollment 79% of which 48.5% is female.
Secondary Grades 9–12 ages 14–18	Same as above		Yes, until age 15	Students sit for the *Matura*, the final exam taken at the end of secondary school. A passing score authorizes entry into a university. Students in the vocational track sit for a separate exam and receive a vocational qualification upon successful completion.		Secondary schools consist of general, linguistic, classical, and scientific grammar schools; vocational schools, which include a period of practical instruction; and art schools, which include music, dance, visual arts, and design.		Total enrollment 79% of which 49.7% is female.
University ages 19+ Diploma, 4–6 years; master's and Ph.D.			No	For both master's and Ph.D. students defend a thesis.	Same as above	Universities offer either university studies that qualify students for high-level professional artistic or scientific work or professional studies.	US$0–$1,028 per year	Total enrollment is 28.3%.

Surface Culture Perspective

CLASSROOMS

- Modern schools in Croatia are equipped with instructional technology such as VCRs, computers, and video cameras. Virtually every school has a library on campus as well. Surveys suggest that while teachers may have access to various types of technological equipment for teaching, many do not know how to use them or fail to use them due to lack of time in the curriculum.
- Classrooms tend to be large with 25–30 students per class. Each student sits with another classmate at one table. There are generally three rows of tables in each classroom. Some classrooms are equipped with the kinds of student desks with which U.S. students are familiar.
- Many classrooms are decorated with students' work. For example, teachers may place student artwork or outstanding essays on the bulletin board, though this is done as much to motivate other students to perform at a higher level than to acknowledge certain students. Some classrooms display the national flag and/or the framed picture of an important person from national history.
- Textbooks are not free of charge, and parents must buy them for their children, which has become an expense that many families can barely afford. The Ministry of Education has to approve the textbooks in order for them to be used. Every school in the country uses the same kind of books and follows the same national curriculum. For example, every 8th grade in every school uses the same textbook for history, biology, math, and so forth.

TEACHERS' STATUS

- Prospective primary and secondary school teachers prepare for four years and a yearlong internship before obtaining a teaching certificate. Secondary school teachers receive the title of professor upon graduation. Neither pre-service nor in-service teacher training is considered adequate by outside evaluation bodies, although the majority of teachers possess the required official qualifications. Even at the vocational level, instruction has been criticized for being overly academic rather than practical. One of the predicaments with pre-service education is that it forces prospective teachers to specialize in only one or two areas.
- While there is not a teaching shortage in Croatia, salaries for teachers are low. The average monthly teacher's salary is US$350, while the national average for all occupations is US$400. This discrepancy, plus the shifting demands placed on teachers since independence, has led to strikes, protests, a decline in the status of teachers, and a general sense of professional insecurity. Moreover, fewer and fewer high school graduates are pursuing careers in education due to low wages and prestige as well as lack of monetary incentive to upgrade teaching skills once one's career is launched.

- The Croatian system of education is still highly centralized; therefore, teachers have little opportunity to influence the national curriculum. The system is also inadequately funded, the budget inequitably distributed, and coordination among the various levels and types of administrators poor.

TEACHER-STUDENT RELATIONSHIP

- Despite the declining attractiveness of a career in education, teachers are still well respected by students and parents, who generally have a formal relationship.
- Students in Croatia do not formally evaluate their teachers, even at the university level.
- Teachers are expected to discipline students by teaching them how to behave in school settings.
- Every class of students is assigned a lead teacher who delivers instruction in at least one subject to this particular class. Every week for one class period the lead teacher also meets with the class to discuss school-related problems that the students might be experiencing. They go with their lead teacher on field trips and on a major end-of-school-year excursion for three to seven days, the destination of which is selected by the lead teacher and the class.

TEACHING PRACTICES

- Lecturing is the most common method of teaching in Croatian schools. As the teacher is considered the content expert, classes tend to be teacher centered with little or no opportunity given to students to express opinions, engage in problem-solving activities, participate in class or small-group discussion, or ask questions of the teacher. Nevertheless, in a recent survey of Croatian teachers' self-perceived teaching methods, more than 50 percent of the respondents reported that they frequently used group work, practical tasks, and interdisciplinary assignments. Dramatization, group discussion, and outside-of-class projects were less often reported to be used.
- The national curriculum and textbooks lead teachers to concentrate on facts over skills. Testing, too, tends to focus students' energy on what is sometimes called "factology." Teachers thus will reward students for producing the "right" answers rather than for taking initiative, thinking creatively, solving problems, analyzing, and being flexible and resourceful. Students are also recognized for being obedient. As a result, Croatian workers are found by their employers to have strong reading and writing skills but underdeveloped skills in self-management, analysis, and teamwork. Computer literacy and foreign language skills are also considered somewhat low in comparison with the needs of the workplace.

TEACHERS' DRESS

- Female teachers, like most Croatian women, especially those in big cities such as Zagreb, tend to be fashion-conscious and enjoy following the latest European trends in attire. Male teachers are less focused on current fashions, but they may be concerned, nonetheless, with appearing professional and neat. Summer weather conditions create no departure from this inclination. Regardless of the season, teachers usually dress formally.

DISCIPLINE AND CLASS MANAGEMENT

- Every school has a clear code of conduct, which teachers do not hesitate to enforce. There is no eating or drinking in class; students may be punished for talking while the teacher is presenting a lesson; and students may only speak after raising their hands, receiving permission from the teacher, and standing up. When the teacher enters the classroom, the students must stand, greet the teacher in chorus, and remain standing until the teachers says, "You may sit down."
- Teachers often maintain discipline by giving students something to do (keeping them busy) at all times. For example, if one student finishes a task before the others, the teacher will assign him/her another assignment to do until everybody else is done.
- It is said that Croatians are a proud people who are not accustomed to direct and public criticism, so they can become easily offended when singled out and reprimanded in front of others.

STUDENTS' CIRCUMSTANCES

- Students are pressured by teachers and parents to do well in primary school because grade point average is very important for admission to the high school of one's choice. Teachers organize meetings with parents at least twice a semester to discuss the children's progress. In general, parent-teacher meetings take place four to five times per year.
- Students who are averse to studying for exams or who suspect that they may not perform as well as their parents expect may attempt to cheat. Although cheating it is not allowed, of course, students may be knowledgeable about a variety of ways to circumvent the system.
- Parents, and particularly mothers, often help students with homework. An educational survey (Bras-Car 2000) conducted by the Education For All (EFA) Forum reported that students whose fathers assisted them with homework achieved less than did students whose mothers came to their aid. The study also suggested mothers praise and reward their children more often for academic achievement, but they also administer more warnings and reprimands about school work than do fathers.

STUDENT-STUDENT RELATIONSHIP

• The relationship between and among students is very close. Many form strong bonds that may last a lifetime, and adults may attempt to locate and reunite with former classmates by conducting Internet searches.
• A teacher's written notes on a student's homework assignments and exams are not considered private. Students readily share them with their classmates, and they are aware of the grades that each has received.

STUDENTS' LEARNING PRACTICES

• Students study by memorizing facts and important information from the textbook and/or lecture notes.
• Students sometimes report that they enjoy more discovery- and discussion-oriented learning tasks but ultimately recognize the importance of memorization to obtain good grades.
• Many Croatian students respond positively, in terms of their motivation, academic achievement, and the breadth of learning strategies used, to demanding teachers. In general, girls tend to be more motivated to study than boys.

STUDENTS' DRESS

• Croatian students do not wear school uniforms. Girls, in particular, are fond of wearing the latest fashions from Europe and the United States.

GIFTS FOR THE TEACHER

• Students may give their teachers gifts such as flowers, jewelry, a vase, or a set of glasses at the end of the school year and when they are ready to graduate. Female teachers receive gifts from students on International Women's Day (March 8) as well.
• Christmas gifts are less commonly given in Croatia than in the United States due to the spiritual, rather than commercial, nature of the holiday. Instead, gift giving is reserved for St. Nicholas Day (December 6). Children are often told that the gifts were brought by the Baby Jesus, although during the Communist-era Father Frost was said to have brought gifts on New Year's Day. Children lay out a pair of polished boots to receive the gifts much as Christian children in the United States may hang stockings.

NONVERBAL COMMUNICATION

- When meeting each other for the first time or greeting each other on a regular basis, Croatians generally shake hands regardless of gender. Friends may sometimes kiss each other on both cheeks. There is usually not contact during conversation, although speakers may lean forward when they interact. Maintenance of personal space is not as strictly monitored as it might be in North America. Women may be seen holding hands as they walk together.
- Expressive hand and arm gestures are commonly used among Croatians engaged in conversation, and they normally maintain eye contact as well. Diverting one's eyes can suggest a lack of interest in the conversation partner. Unless provoked into anger, Croatians are not likely to point at others using the index finger or wave a pointed index finger in the air as this is considered rude. Also considered inappropriate is a hand gesture made by bending the middle and ring fingers toward the palm and extending the index and little finger. This gesture conveys anger or spite. Raising the thumb, index, and middle fingers together is used by nationalist Serbs; it is unwise to use it in the company of nationalist Croats.
- Some Croatians may take the initiative to visit another person without waiting for an invitation.
- Croatians tend to prefer using a strong and confident voice and manner when speaking to others. Those who are most soft-spoken may be seen as weak and vulnerable. Crying in public may produce the same impression. Croatians frequently take a dim view of emotional outbursts in general.
- The expression "Relax, we still have time" is commonly used in the workplace since deadlines, and time in general, tend to be more elastic than in North America. Activity may suddenly speed up as a deadline approaches so that it can be met.
- Croatians tend to be great lovers of dark humor, irony, and cynicism even if it is at the expense of a friend. They may poke fun at each other, chiding each other about past mistakes, bad decisions, bad luck, drinking episodes, and region of origin.

FORMS OF ADDRESS

- Students address male teachers with *Nastavnik* and female teachers with *Nastavnica* in primary school. Secondary school teachers are addressed with *Professor* (masculine form) or *Profesorka* (feminine form).
- Until Croatians are clearly well acquainted, they will not address each other using first names. Instead, they use last names or *Gospodin* (Mr.), *Gospodga* (Mrs.), or *Gospodicna* (Miss) plus last name.
- In many parts of Croatia, people greet each other by saying *"Bok,"* meaning God.

APPROPRIATE TOPICS

- Family is a frequent topic in conversation as is work, food, health, the environment, sports (especially soccer), celebrities, and world events. When discussing family, it may not be appropriate to divulge information about problems and misfortune. Croatians have direct and recent experience with tragedy, often involving the abuse or murder of immediate family members. They are likely to find accounts of routine family turmoil relatively trivial in comparison to their own troubles and will often be loath to reveal their own heartbreak and difficulty with adjusting to loss.

- Questions about the recent war may invite a highly emotional response as most Croatians experienced its horrors first-hand and are still suffering from it as individuals and as a society. The differences and similarities among Croats, Serbs, and Bosnians is also a complex and emotionally charged topic of conversation.

- It is not appropriate to discuss salaries, the cost of items, or the amount of money one does or does not have. Religion, too, is strictly avoided in public conversation.

OUTSIDE OF CLASS

- Teachers assign, and students expect, a good deal of homework in every subject every night. Homework usually consists of practice exercises reinforcing the content of the day's lessons.

- After school, many Croatian students do their homework, watch television, play computer games, or get together in the neighborhood with friends. After-school tutoring in music, art, dance, foreign language, and sports is popular as well.

- On weekends and holidays many Croatians enjoy hiking in the country's forests and climbing its many hills and mountains. Hunting for boar, pheasants, rabbits, and even bears is popular among men while women gather truffles and other edible mushrooms and berries. The Adriatic coast is another popular recreation area as are the numerous thermal springs and mud baths.

Potential Adjustment Challenges

PROBLEMS/SOLUTIONS

Problem

In a discussion with my Croatian students, I marveled at their special talent for learning English, especially coming from a country where they had little exposure to the language. Judging by their reactions, I knew I had said something wrong, but I have no idea what.

Solution

By suggesting that the credit for your students' progress lay in their personal abilities, you revealed your lack of awareness about the quality of foreign language education in Croatia, which has historically been very high. The curriculum has been stable over many years, and teachers are well trained. Indeed, the requirement that they hold a bachelor's degree in order to obtain a teaching position is strictly observed. What's more, Croatians enjoy widespread exposure to English through subtitled television programs.

Problem

I have a Croatian student who barely participates in small group activity, but who on the whole seems comfortable in class and is progressing well. Should I be concerned?

Solution

If you want your student to get more from small group activity, you may need to talk to him or her directly about the benefits of such interaction. Be aware, however, that Croatians are more accustomed to studying in a large group, and small group or pair work is not common. In general, organizing instruction to meet the individual needs of learners is a new concept in Croatia.

Ukraine

■ UKRAINE *Upclose*

Capital: Kiev

Population: 46,710,816 (June 2006)

Size: 603,700 sq. km. (233,090 sq. mi.) (slightly smaller than Texas)

Location: Eastern Europe, bordered on the west by Moldova, Romania, Hungary, Slovakia, and Poland, on the north by Belarus, on the east by Russia; and on the south by the Black Sea

Climate: temperate-continental with Mediterranean conditions far to the south on the Crimean Peninsula

Terrain: steppes (fertile plains) cover most of the country, with the Carpathian Mountains in the west and more mountainous areas on the Crimean Peninsula

Monetary Unit: hryvnia (5.00 per U.S dollar) (June 2006)

Religion: Ukrainian Orthodox (Kiev Patriarchate) 19%; Orthodox (undeclared jurisdiction) 16%; Ukrainian Orthodox (Moscow Patriarchate) 9%; Ukrainian Greek Catholic 6%; Ukrainian Autocephalous Orthodox 1.7%; Protestant, Jewish, or without denomination 38%

Language(s): Ukrainian, Russian, Romanian, Polish, Hungarian

Literacy Rate: total population 99.7%; men 99.8%; women 99.6% (2003)

Ethnicity: Ukrainian 77.8%, Russian 17.3%, Belarusian 0.6%, Moldovan 0.5%, Crimean Tatar 0.5%, Bulgarian 0.4%, Hungarian 0.3%, Romanian 0.3%, Polish 0.3%, Jewish 0.2%, other 1.8%

Per Capita Income: US$749 (June 2006)

Population Distribution: 67% urban, 33% rural (2003)

Population below Poverty Line: 29% (2003)

Life Expectancy: total population 69.9 years; men 64.7 years; women 75.6 years (2006)

Government: republic

PUBLIC HOLIDAYS			
January 1	New Year's Day	May 30	Holy Trinity
January 7	Orthodox Christmas Day	June 28	Constitution Day
January 14	Orthodox New Year	August 24	Independence Day
March 8	Women's Day	October (first Sunday)*	Teachers' Day
Friday before Easter	Good Friday		
Monday after Easter	Easter Monday		
May 1	Labor Day		
May 9	Victory Day		

*variable dates

■ Personal Perspective

More broken promises. The government says it will increase our pay as teachers, but instead of the 50 hryvnias we were promised, the actual raise was only nine hryvnias. Yes, nine pitiful hryvnias to reward me for my long service in education. And they wonder why there are so many teaching vacancies! Employment may skyrocket, but nobody seems to be willing to teach for free. I think the Ministry should canvass the schools to find out how many teachers, especially male teachers, have quit recently. They would find that a lot of new teachers abandon ship even before they've taught five years. How can school reforms be implemented if the teachers have walked away? The government really needs to think about this.

—Ukrainian teacher

■ Historical Perspective

IMMIGRATION TO THE UNITED STATES

Immigration experts identify four distinct waves of Ukrainian immigration to the United States. The first wave spanned the years 1870 to 1899 and was driven by working-class Ukrainians seeking jobs in agriculture or their own land to farm in Virginia, New Jersey, New York, North Dakota, Wisconsin, and Texas. Others gravitated to the coal mines of Pennsylvania and West Virginia.

The second wave, from 1900 to 1914, consisted of the poorest members of the Ukrainian population at the time. Although many settled in larger industrial cities such as Chicago, Buffalo, Pittsburgh, Baltimore, Detroit, and Cleveland, others went to work in the Pennsylvania mines as scabs during miners' strikes.

The third wave from 1920 to 1939 brought Ukrainian political refugees from the professional classes, who were seeking refuge from the newly formed Soviet Union as well as the politically orchestrated famine of 1932–1933 and Stalin's massive executions between 1937 and 1938.

The fourth wave began in 1991 with Ukraine's independence from Russia and extends to 2001. During this decade some 56,000 Ukrainians legally entered the country as immigrants. However, the number expands to nearly 135,000 and perhaps more if Ukrainians who have overstayed their temporary visa limitations are considered. The median age of entrants has gone from 40 years of age to 25.5 years of age, and they are more prone today to settle on the West Coast of the United States where the competition for good jobs is less intense. Highly educated immigrants nonetheless are frequently unsuccessful in their attempts to regain their status in the professions they practiced in Ukraine due to their lack of English language proficiency and unfamiliarity with job-seeking resources and protocols.

HISTORICAL SYNOPSIS

Ukraine was part of Kievan Rus, the first Slavic nation and the largest and most powerful state in 10th- and 11th-century Europe. Invasions and internal conflicts led to a series of takeovers by foreign powers, including Lithuania and Poland. Eventually Russia gained control over Ukraine and in 1920 forcibly brought into the Soviet Union after which more than eight million Ukrainians died as the result of two artificial famines. Another eight million perished at the hands of the Germans and Soviets during World War II. The year 1991 marked the start of Ukraine's independence from Russia and a difficult period of nation building in which crime, corruption, mafia activity, and lingering political resentments have posed significant obstacles to reform. It is important to note that as citizens of a newly independent state that is no longer a region of the former Soviet Union, Ukrainians insist that the article "the" preceding the name of the country (Ukraine) be dropped.

The following statistics give a sense of how Ukraine fares today in a number of areas. The country ranks first in the world in nuclear reactors under construction, nuclear waste generated, and carbon dioxide pollution from fossil fuels. It ranks second in the world for total number of movie theaters (after the United States) and third in the use of tobacco among young people. In terms of public spending per primary school pupil, Ukraine ranks fourth in the world, but it also holds the same rank for people who claim themselves to be "not very or not at all happy." The country has the fifth highest male literacy rate in the world.

▊Deep Culture Perspective

DEEP CULTURE BELIEFS

- Because Ukraine is bordered by so many countries, its people have adopted many of the cultural values, traditions, and beliefs of its neighbors. It is said that from the east, Ukrainians have inherited a contemplative nature and a fondness for the abstract. From the west, they have borrowed rationalism and individualism. Ukrainians tend to value the expression of emotion, and thus are sometimes considered sentimental. Their Cossack ancestors were fearless—but also somewhat impulsive—defenders of the land and the peasants who lived on it. Their heroic legacy is a source of pride to Ukrainians.
- Many outsiders view Ukrainians as patient, introverted, and perhaps even detached as a result of the continuous struggles they have faced over their long history as a people. One behavior that is common in the rural areas, that of answering a question with another question, has been suggested to reflect the alleged guardedness of the Ukrainian

national character. Regardless of the hardships they may have historically experienced, Ukrainians are not submissive and appear optimistic about the future, even though they may not express their feelings about it with vociferous enthusiasm.

- Family is extremely important to most Ukrainians. They will sacrifice their own interests for the good of the family, and their children are lovingly nurtured through childhood and often into maturity. Some attribute the closeness of family ties in Ukraine to the country's long experience with invasions that forced people to form strong family bonds in order to successfully fend off marauders. Today's typical Ukrainian family is smaller due to a rise in the cost of living and unemployment and the cramped nature of Soviet era apartments. Divorce, too, is much more common than in the past.

- The popular Ukrainian adage "the husband holds the household by one corner and leaves the remaining three corners for his wife" reveals the strength of women within the Ukrainian family. Another expression describes the man as the head of the family but the woman as the neck, so that the head turns whichever way the neck goes. Regardless of the illusion of a man as the leader of his family, the woman is clearly not only involved but instrumental in all aspects of family decision-making.

- Under the law, Ukrainian women share equal rights with men and make up the larger half of the workforce. However, their jobs are often physically demanding and low paying; men tend to occupy professional and influential positions to a much greater extent than do women. Nevertheless, many women teach at universities; create and manage businesses; and work as engineers, doctors, and attorneys. They are simultaneously expected to do the bulk of the housekeeping (i.e., cooking, cleaning, shopping, and child rearing). Contrary to their authoritative role within the family, at work women may experience discrimination.

- Ukrainians may have a deep fondness for the countryside and nature. Its vast and fertile steppes make Ukraine the so-called "breadbasket of Europe" for its cultivation of wheat.

- Tourists to Ukraine unerringly cite its people's hospitality as one of the highlights of their visit.

- One important aspect of Russian influence on Ukrainian society is language. Since the early 20th century when the former Soviet Union assumed control over Ukraine until the country's independence in 1991, Russian was the official language; Ukrainian was spoken at home. Today most Ukrainians speak both Russian and Ukrainian as a result of prior national policy as well as intermarriage and the natural mingling of the two communities of speakers.

- Ukrainians may not only be patriotic but also are nationalistic. Their newly won independence from centuries of foreign rule has given them license to assert themselves as a pro-U.S. national force and a unique culture.

- Socializing with family and friends is one of the most popular pastimes among Ukrainians. Whether they meet at cafes or at an individual's home, they may spend hours sharing gossip, talking politics, and drinking hot tea.
- Since independence in 1991 the standard of living in Ukraine has declined (by 80 percent, according to some sources) while the cost of living has risen. Even the average life expectancy of men has fallen from 65 years of age to 58 years, and the accident at the nuclear power plant in Chernobyl in 1986 is blamed for a much greater incidence of thyroid cancer in children. Modern household appliances such as refrigerators may be more available now than before independence, but few people can afford to buy them, especially since unemployment has dramatically increased. In fact, family income is so insufficient today that many city dwellers grow vegetables to supplement their diet. More than 50 percent of the average Ukrainian's income is spent on food. Housing, too, tends to be inadequate. A typical Ukrainian apartment is one-seventh the size of the household space to which the average U.S. family is accustomed. At the same time, independence also brought ownership of private property so that some enterprising individuals have been able to erect more spacious and comfortable homes.

PROVERBS

- The church is near, but the way is icy. The tavern is far, but I will walk carefully.
- Your head is not only for putting a hat on.
- Every disadvantage has its advantage.
- Only when you have eaten a lemon do you appreciate what sugar is.
- No matter how hard you try, the bull will never give milk.
- He who is not at home is guilty.
- God blesses those who rise early.

FOLK TALE

Once upon a time, there was a great brown bear who considered himself to be superior to all the other animals living in the forest. One day he was taking a nap under a shady tree when a sudden noise startled him and woke him up. He saw a little squirrel jumping happily across the floor of the forest and scampering up its many trees. After a while, the bear grew weary of watching the frenetic squirrel, so he returned to his nap.

In the meantime, the little squirrel enjoyed her game of flying through the branches of the tree under which the big bear snoozed. But, when one of those branches broke, the poor little squirrel crashed to the ground, falling smack in the middle of the bear's big paws. The bear looked hungrily at the little squirrel and opened his great jaws, but the squirrel began to plead for her life. "If you let me go," she cried, "maybe one day I can help you, too." This amused the bear since he couldn't imagine how such a little creature could ever come to the rescue of such a mighty beast as he. Laughing condescendingly, he tossed the squirrel to the ground and wiped the tears of laughter from his eyes. The little squirrel happily scampered away.

After a while the bear rose, stretched, and lumbered off into the forest. As he was searching for berries, he spotted a piece of meat on the ground and leapt on it hungrily. But suddenly a large trap closed tight on his leg and pulled him up so that he was hanging upside down from a tree. He howled loudly. Hearing his cries, the little squirrel ran to his rescue. Quickly she began to gnaw on the rope until at last the bear was free. "You are wiser than I am, little squirrel," said the bear gratefully. "Now I understand that someone small and weak can do as much as someone who is big and strong."

Administrative Perspective

OFFICIAL EDUCATIONAL POLICY

Educational reform in Ukraine is dominated by an effort to disengage from the country's Soviet past, specifically with its totalitarian perspective on pedagogy. Whereas the Soviets focused on uniformity, today's Ukrainian leadership hopes to develop individuality among learners and to nurture the unique talents and interests of individuals. They now promote the study of disciplines that had earlier been discouraged (e.g., art, law, ecology, health) as well as the creation of innovative curricula and experimental programs.

On a more mundane level, independence introduced the Ukrainian language back into the educational system where Russian had for decades served as the language of instruction. This move has been problematic since many teachers are not native, or sometimes even proficient, speakers of Ukranian, and have had to retrain themselves in order to preserve their jobs. In addition, textbooks in Ukrainian and containing new interpretations of Ukrainian history are still in production such that some students continue to study from outdated texts.

EDUCATION AT A GLANCE

See the Education at a Glance table on page 140.

UKRAINE

Level/Age	Hours/Calendar	Language of Instruction	Compulsory Attendance	Exams	Grading System	Curriculum	Cost	Enrollment
Primary Grades 1–4 ages 6–10		Ukrainian	Yes	Exams are administered at the end of every quarter. A comprehensive final exam can be either written or oral. Questions for the oral exam are placed face down on the teacher's desk for students to draw from.	2–5 point scale 5 excellent 4 good 3 satisfactory 2 unsatisfactory A new 12-point scale has recently been introduced.	Languages and literature (mandatory foreign language classes begin in Grade 2), math, health and physical culture, technologies, arts, and the human being and the world	During Soviet times, no tuition was charged for education. Today the cost is minimal, but in the era immediately following independence, teachers and administrators were offered bribes to provide a quality education or passing grades for students. This practice, though still common, is being discouraged.	90% of females, 91% of males 99% progress to secondary level.
Lower secondary Grades 5–9 ages 10–15	Sept. to around June 20 with a break to study for end-of-year exams (quarter system) Classes last 45 minutes running from 8:00 AM to 2:00 or 2:30 PM with 15-minute breaks between classes and a half-hour break for lunch.		Yes (up to age 15)	Same as above Students receive lower secondary-leaving certificate.		Languages and literature, social science, mathematics, natural science, aesthetic culture, health and physical culture, technologies		Total enrollment 89%. Females 90.7%
Upper secondary grades 10–11/12 ages 15–17/18 Vocational 4–5 years ages 15–20			No	Same as above From general and special schools, students receive matriculation school certificate (required for university entrance). From vocational schools, they receive matriculation school certificate plus professional school-leaving diploma or vocational school-leaving certificate.		Same as above New textbooks now downplay the previously heavy emphasis on factual learning and instead focus on developing a constellation of key social, motivational, and functional competencies.		No data available
University ages 19+ 4 years for the bachelor's degree, 6 years for medical degree, 5–6 years for the master's degree	Sept. 1 to end of July with a month-long break in January Semester system		No	Students take 3–5 exams at the end of each semester. Students who do not pass cannot advance to the next semester. Master's students take a final examination and defend their thesis. Ph.D. I students publicly defend the thesis, whereas Ph.D. II students must publish theirs.	Numbered grades are not assigned. Instead, evaluations of excellent, good, and satisfactory are given.	Academic programs are in transition from purely academic content to the more practical professional needs of students. The shift includes a change in teaching methods (from lectures to more seminars) plus mandatory English classes 5 days/week.	Public universities charge no official tuition, but the few vacancies in elite fields, such as business, finance, computer science, and linguistics, generally must be obtained through bribes. Tuition in private universities ranges from US$2,000 to US$7,000 per year.	Total enrollment 43.3%. 93% of university sophomores graduate, compared to only 53% of their U.S. counterparts.

Surface Culture Perspective

CLASSROOMS

- Many schools are made from cement block. A central entrance leads to a corridor with tiled-floor classrooms on both sides. Rooms (which parents may pay to have painted at the end of the school year) tend to have high ceilings and very large windows, so there is usually good light, preferably from the left, so that a student's writing hand will not cast a shadow on the paper. Most classrooms are fitted with florescent lights as well.

- On the walls of a typical classroom in Ukraine there is a blackboard (which is sometimes actually brown and may be folded into sections), maps, a national flag, and a clock, but the walls may still seem bare compared to those in U.S. schools. Before the collapse of the Soviet Union, a picture of Lenin would also be displayed in every classroom. Chalk tends to be flaky, so chalk trays and erasers need to be cleaned daily. At the back of most classrooms is a bookcase and perhaps a closet for the students' coats. Along the windowsills there may also be flowers and plants that are carefully tended by the teacher and students. The room is maintained by the students after class as custodians only clean the stairwells, corridors, and outdoor walkways. Thus, students scrub walls, floors, and windows. They and their parents may be responsible for maintaining the school's landscaping as well.

- Students sit in pairs at tables. Each student has before him/her a small stand that holds the textbook open to the appropriate page. At the primary level there may be 30–35 students in a classroom, whereas at the middle school level the class size may range from 35–40. In Grade 1, students nap for a portion of the school day in small wooden beds that resemble a chest of drawers.

- Two children wearing red ribbons sit at a special table designated for the teacher's aides.

- The school day often begins with a recitation of the Ukrainian pledge of allegiance.

- Books, paper, pens, and other basic schools supplies are not provided by the school, so students must purchase these items, which tend to be expensive.

- Textbooks may not be as recent and plentiful as in North America, and they tend to be thinner and have smaller print and fewer pictures. If there is an insufficient number of books in a class set, students may either go to the library or borrow the teacher's book after class.

TEACHERS' STATUS

- Primary school teachers receive training and accreditation from special pedagogical institutions. Their secondary school counterparts study in institutions of higher education in separate departments and colleges (called "faculties") within the university (e.g., a prospective math teacher may study in the Faculty of Mathematics and Natural Sciences while a future history teacher will study in the Faculty of Social Sciences). As in the United States, university professors do not receive any pre-service training in pedagogy.

- In addition to the hours they spend in class and preparing their lessons, Ukrainian teachers are expected to carry out administrative, clerical, or even maintenance tasks to compensate for the lack of staff who might otherwise assume such responsibilities.

- Remuneration for teaching is often insufficient to support the expenses of a teacher and his/her family regardless of whether the individual teaches at the primary or university level. Adding insult to injury, some teachers report that their students can make more money on the black market than the teachers can make in a month. Although teachers, too, may engage in black market activity to supplement their income, others sometimes accept bribes from students or their families in exchange for better grades. More often, they give private lessons after school or work a second job. This allows them less time for preparation and can affect their performance in class, and because of their limited financial resources, many find it difficult to keep up with innovations in their fields.

TEACHER-STUDENT RELATIONSHIP

- A wide margin is maintained between most teachers and their students in Ukraine. Students often claim that they fear their teachers for not only are they very strict but are said to have a tendency to exact punishment on their students for relatively minor infractions. It is not uncommon for the teacher to send notes home to the parents calling for a face-to face meeting where sometimes the parents themselves are reprimanded for their child's behavior or academic shortcomings. The relationship between teacher and student is even more strict at the primary level than it is at higher levels.

- Students stand when the teacher enters the room and also when they are called upon to speak in class.

- It is not unusual for students or their parents to offer a teacher (or even an administrator) money in return for a good grade on a student's final exam, and teachers will not be offended by such an exchange.

TEACHING PRACTICES

- Many teachers rely on the traditional methods in which they were schooled. Thus, they may lecture or read directly from a book while students concentrate on transferring as much of the information as possible to their notebooks as photocopies are rarely distributed. Later, students will memorize the contents of the notebook to prepare for tests. Misplacing one's notebook can constitute a major crisis. Some jest that these notebooks are as holy as the Bible.

- Teachers normally collect homework or notebooks at the outset of the class period and will return them the next day with annotations made in red ink. Students are expected to correct and resubmit the homework. Teachers may pay special attention to the specific errors made by individual students so that they can quiz them on these items in class. This may involve calling the student to the front of the class to answer questions.
- Rather than the learner-centered approach often adopted by younger North American educators, Ukrainian teachers prefer a more subject-oriented approach, with the personal and social development of students assuming a lesser role. They ask relatively few questions during the lesson. Peer evaluation and other student-student activities are less common in Ukraine than in North America, as are the development of creativity and critical-thinking skills.
- Ukrainian teachers generally do not require their students to engage in collaborative process writing. Penmanship is another matter; it is a skill that students practice regularly and intensely. For Ukrainians good penmanship is a matter of pride.

TEACHERS' DRESS

- Ukrainian teachers, like their compatriots throughout the country, are fashion conscious. Personal appearance is thought to reflect one's professional and economic stature, or at least one's aspirations toward such stature.
- Male teachers often wear dark trousers with a white shirt and dark jacket. Until recently, women did not wear pants to school and usually kept necklines high and arms covered.

DISCIPLINE AND CLASS MANAGEMENT

- Teachers frequently reprimand disruptive or lazy students in front of their peers to produce more appropriate behavior.
- Rather than administering physical punishment, teachers more often ask an unruly student to leave the classroom for the remainder of the period.

STUDENTS' CIRCUMSTANCES

- In a climate of reduced spending on education, schools turn to parents to supplement the institution's limited resources. Sometimes the quid pro quo is the admission of a parent's child to the school. While some may consider this practice bribery, which is illegal in Ukraine, very often administrators have no other choice but to favor families who are either more affluent than others or who have useful connections in order to maintain the school's infrastructure.

- Parents are frequently called upon to maintain the school's physical plant. They repair broken items; upgrade and even rebuild dilapidated structures; plant trees and shrubbery; paint; wallpaper; decorate; and even obtain desks, chairs, and bookcases through their connections.
- In addition to the essential notebook in which all students keep their class notes, Ukrainian students also carry a day planner in which they write down the instructions for homework assignments and record their grades. At the lower levels, teachers record these grades in their students' day planners, but at the higher levels the teacher may call out the grade for each student who, in turn, writes it in his or her planner. In some cases, every evening parents indicate via their signature that they have seen their children's grades and homework assignments.

STUDENT-STUDENT RELATIONSHIP

- Cohorts of students are formed at the primary school level and may be maintained up until graduation. Relationships, therefore, tend to be very close.
- Students often assemble after class not necessarily to study together but to allow their friends to copy from one another's notebooks.
- Strategies for "cheating" on exams are frequently developed and shared with classmates. Writing information on the thighs or palms is a popular practice as is hiding a densely annotated piece of paper under the skirt or shirt sleeve. Sometimes students will make codified inscriptions on exam booklets to assist the next student who receives the same test packet.

STUDENTS' LEARNING PRACTICES

- Until very recently, the prevailing attitude toward learning among students was that it was serious business and would have a clear impact on the quality of their lives in the future. For this reason, they were encouraged to study hard and were conscientious about completing homework. However, some of today's students are suffering the after-effects of cultural and political independence, which is to say that the transition to democracy has created serious social and economic instability that deprives students of the kind of material and moral support as well as motivation needed for academic success. As a result, the former work ethic has diminished along with overall academic performance. This has generally not prevented Ukrainian teachers from urging their students to meet the high standards of the past using the "greater good" of the country as a motivating factor.

STUDENTS' DRESS

- At the primary level, students wear uniforms, but at the higher levels the requirement has been eliminated. Students during the Soviet era wore uniforms consisting of a long-sleeved knee-length black or brown dress for girls and, for boys, a white shirt, jacket, and dark pants. Girls were not allowed to wear cosmetics or nail polish, and their hair was to have been pulled up in a ponytail or pigtails.

- Today girls especially not only tend to be extremely fashion conscious but may make a grand show of their apparel and accessories, as these now serve as status symbols. The reason is that these items are very hard to come by in modern Ukraine; their acquisition is usually the result of connections or access to rare hard currency.

Gifts for the Teacher

- On Teachers' Day, the first Sunday in October, students celebrate by bringing bouquets of flowers and boxes of chocolates to their teachers. They also decorate the classrooms and the doors and windows of the school with all manner of ribbons, paper chains, and garlands.
- Visitors who are invited for dinner to the home of a Ukrainian might take flowers, candy, or alcohol. For special occasions, items such as ties, cigarette lighters, stationery, and costume jewelry are appreciated. Westerners might be advised to bring items that are difficult to find on the open market.

Nonverbal Communication

- Ukrainians, even children, seldom sit on the floor, nor will they point to another person with the index finger. This is considered boorish.
- People remove their shoes when they enter a household. There is often a pile of shoes just inside the door.
- Ukrainians will shake hands when they are introduced for the first time, but Ukrainian women seldom do so with each other. Friends may rest a hand on the other's shoulder or give a hug or kiss on the cheek as well.
- If one person accidentally bumps into another or steps on the other's toes, an apology is not necessarily expected. Assistance crossing the street or after a fall may not be immediately forthcoming either.
- While reserved in public, Ukrainians often engage in boisterous conversation with friends at home and are generous and warm hosts. In public, they may stand closer to each other during conversation than do people in the United States and speak at a lower volume, but constant eye contact may be considered rude. People who talk and laugh loudly in public and smile broadly are likely to be foreigners.
- Ukrainians tend to be moderately punctual, depending on their status. Those with higher status are granted more leeway with regard to time. Deadlines are respected, but outsiders may believe work toward the goal starts much too late.
- Compared with North America, there is less interpersonal privacy among Ukrainians. They may read items lying on another person's desk or appearing on another's computer screen. Listening to another's cell phone conversations or allowing others to listen to one's own conversations may not be off-limits, either.

FORMS OF ADDRESS

- Students address their teachers using the first name plus patronymic, a kind of middle name based on the father's first name—an example would be *Mykola* (first name) *Petrovych* (daughter of Petro) *Savchenko* (family name). Teachers call students by their first names.
- Addressing friends and colleagues by first name only is becoming more popular in Ukraine, particularly among young to middle-aged people.

APPROPRIATE TOPICS

- Although among themselves, Ukrainians may enjoy a vigorous debate about national politics, they may not welcome critical remarks about their country made by outsiders nor would they appreciate having Ukraine's problems, past or present, the center of a classroom discussion. They are proud of their country's accomplishments and natural beauty.
- Jokes, witticisms, and anecdotes with a surprising twist at the end are deeply enjoyed by most Ukrainians.
- It is more acceptable in Ukraine than in the United States to ask one another for special favors, and such practices are reciprocal.

OUTSIDE OF CLASS

- Homework typically consists of reading texts or memorizing long passages from the text.
- Since the typical Ukrainian curriculum is dominated by heavy subject matter, activities involving sports or music are not officially organized and offered to students. If interested, students will participate in such activities on their own time.
- While Ukrainian teenagers may have responsibilities at home in addition to focusing on their homework, they do not as a rule have paid jobs until after they graduate.
- In their spare time, Ukrainian students enjoy playing or watching soccer, going to movies, or watching television. The cost of plays, concerts, and ballets in recent years has become prohibitive, however.

■ Potential Adjustment Challenges

PROBLEMS/SOLUTIONS

Problem

A graduate student who is interviewing my ESL students for an anthropology project reported that my student from Ukraine believes me to be wasting precious class time with such things as language learning games, asking students to guess rules, and filling out Venn diagrams and other type of charts. I'm astonished. Why would she say such a thing?

Solution

Ukrainian students in North American classrooms may view the teacher as being too permissive and accommodating. In Ukraine, students have no choice over the kind of tasks or volume of material they are expected to master. Thus, they may complain that their new teacher is too concerned with not tiring students out. As a result, they may find the North American classroom to fall short in terms of content, pace, and challenge.

Problem

I studied a little Russian in college and wanted to practice with my student from Ukraine. She balked, although I know she speaks Russian.

Solution

Ukraine was dominated by the Russians during the Soviet era, and the Russian language was a required subject in Ukrainian schools, despite its unpopularity. From the Ukrainians' perspective, Russian language and culture was "forced down the throats" of a proud and unique people, a practice that was deeply resented in Ukraine.

Problem

"No one would <u>not</u> cheat," claimed one of my Ukrainian students of her peers back home. Does this mean that cheating is accepted in Ukraine?

Solution

It's not exactly accepted, but perhaps expected. There is fierce competition for scarce privilege in Ukraine, leading to behavior that Ukrainians find dishonest but necessary. It is important to point out that there are harsh consequences for students who cheat.

Afghanistan

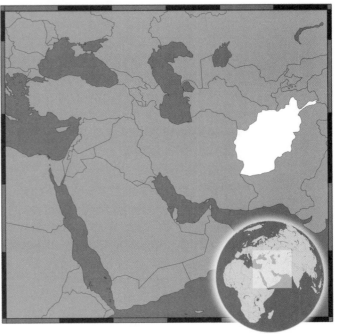

■ AFGHANISTAN *Upclose*

Capital: Kabul

Population: 31,056,997 (June 2006)

Size: 647,497 sq. km. (249,813 sq. mi.) (approximately the size of Texas)

Location: in southwest Asia, landlocked by Pakistan to the east and south, Iran to the west, Turkmenistan to the northwest, Uzbekistan and Tajikistan to the north, and China to the northeast

Climate: arid to semiarid, with extremes of temperature between day and night as well as summer and winter, summer winds of up to 100 mph (160 kph) and irregular rains in winter

Terrain: mountainous with flatlands in the north and southwest

Monetary Unit: Afghani (49.7 per U.S. dollar) (June 2006)

Religion: official religion is Islam (80% Sunni, 19% Shi'a, and 1% other sects)

Language(s): Dari and Pashto (official languages); in the north Turkmen and Uzbeki are also widely spoken

Literacy Rate: total population 36%; men 51%; women 21% (1999)

Ethnicity: 22 ethnic groups including the majority Pashtuns (53%); Tajikis (21%); Hazars (8.7%); Aimaks, Uzbekis, Turkmens, Nuristanis, and Qisilbashes (17.3%)

Per Capita Income: US$800 (2004)

Population Distribution: 23% urban, 77% rural (2003)

Population below Poverty Line: 53% (2003)

Life Expectancy: total population 43.3 years; men 43.2 years; women 43.5 years (2006)

Government: parliamentary Islamic State with a newly established constitution

PUBLIC HOLIDAYS		
	January 21*	*Eid al Adha* (Feast of the Sacrifice)
	February 9*	*Ashura* (martyrdom of Prophet Mohamed's grandson)
	March 21*	*Noruz* (Persian New Year or vernal spring equinox)
	April 18	Liberation Day
	April 21*	*Roze-Maulud* (birth of the Prophet Mohamed)
	April 28	Victory Day
	May 1	Labor Day
	August 19	National Day
	October 4*	start of Ramadan
	November 3*	*Eid-al Fitr* (end of Ramadan)
		variable dates

Personal Perspective

When I did my primary studies in Kabul, the educational system was in better condition. No school would have hired teachers lacking an advanced academic education, and the Ministry of Education gave strong financial support to schools even in the most remote parts of the country. But when war erupted among the *mujahadeen,* the situation in the city became so risky that my family needed to leave in order to survive. My mother, my siblings, and I went to Pakistan where I continued my schooling in one of the Afghani schools in Peshawar. Most of these schools are supported by NGOs (nongovernmental organizations). Our school had small classrooms with many students in each room. There was always a shortage of drinkable water. The schools couldn't afford air conditioning during the summer or heating during the winter.

Studying English in Pakistan helped put me on the path that I am now following. I am studying international relations in the United States and hope to fulfill my dream to become a human rights worker and, especially, to improve the lives of Afghani women.

—Afghani graduate student in the United States

Historical Perspective

IMMIGRATION TO THE UNITED STATES

Afghani immigration to the United States has taken place in waves. The 1979 Soviet invasion of Afghanistan led Afghani students and diplomats living in the United States to seek asylum, later followed by their relatives who entered the country as refugees through the government's family reunification program. Most came from Kabul or other larger cities but tended to be less prosperous and professional than their U.S.-based family members. Affluent ethnic Pashtuns fled Afghanistan to Pakistan and then later to the United States after the withdrawal of Soviet forces in 1989, with the number and ethnic variety of refugees increasing after the ascendancy of the Taliban in 1996 and widespread persecution of those who differed with the regime on matters of politics, race, religion, and gender. A growing number of the post-1999 refugees are widows, married women, and single women who hoped to escape the abuse and repression of the Taliban. Most suffered not only from physical and psychological abuse but also from the long-term effects of their injuries as well as from detention and malnutrition. Children, too, some of whom had been drafted as soldiers, are represented among recent refugees from Afghanistan. While some Afghani refugees today are educated professionals, recent arrivals usually do not have relatives in the United States who can assist them, may have spent several years in refugee camps, and tend to be less affluent and skilled as well as less literate. Others opt to immigrate to the United States and other Western nations after having spent years in exile in Pakistan. It is usually difficult for such refugees to find professional work in Pakistan, and settling in the West allows them to support families who remain in Pakistan or return to Afghanistan.

HISTORICAL SYNOPSIS

Afghanistan has been conquered and occupied many times in its history, by Alexander the Great in the 4th century BCE and later by various Arabic and Turkic rulers, Genghis Khan, and Tamarlene. It became an independent country in 1747 and was ruled by Pushtan Ahmad Shah Durani and his descendants for more than two centuries. In the 19th century, Afghanistan came under the influence of several European powers including the United Kingdom with whom it fought two wars. In April 1978, a left-wing coup overthrew the existing regime, which led to a period of brutal political turmoil. Then followed the 1979 invasion and subsequent occupation by the Soviet Union, which came to an end ten years later when anti-Communist forces, backed by foreign powers, ousted the Communist regime. This caused a political vacuum, and fierce fighting occurred between rival tribal leaders, or *mujahadeen,* which led to the emergence of the Taliban as a political power in 1996. For the next few years, the Taliban ruled most of the country excluding the northeast where the Northern Alliance remained in control until the attacks on the United States in September 2001 and the perceived links between the Taliban and Osama bin Laden prompted military action by a U.S.-led coalition together with the Northern Alliance that overthrew the Taliban. This was followed by the establishment of a new administration with Hamid Karzai as president, and a new constitution was signed in January 2004. This constitution gives strong powers to the executive branch of government while maintaining a moderate role for Islam and basic protection of human rights. Presidential elections were held in October 2004, confirming Karzai as president.

Afghanistan remains a very poor country with clean water and electricity accessible to only a small percentage of the population. Living standards are among the lowest in the world, but with the advent of political stability, the government along with international donors are working on the development of the infrastructure, especially housing, education, and medical care. However, land mines remain a daily danger to the population, and the illicit opium trade is a blot on the social landscape.

Deep Culture Perspective

DEEP CULTURE BELIEFS

- Afghanistan is a male-dominant society with women typically serving as homemakers. There is, however, a very big difference between city and rural people, with the latter generally far more traditional than the former. Also, because of the mountainous nature of the terrain, communication with and travel to other areas is very difficult, which tends to isolate communities.

- Friendliness and hospitality are very much features of the Afghani people, though they may be suspicious of strangers, and there are reports of racism and xenophobia. Afghans are considered to be brave and independent people, bound together by both blood and community ties. Honor and the maintaining of the honor of the family and community are still seen as very important, and there is much pride in the family. It is a very hierarchical society based on tribes, with Pashto tribes in the south and Tajik in the north. Nepotism can be a common and accepted practice.

- Afghani society is still, in general, a very religious one, though not as fundamentalist as might be assumed from the media. Islam seems to be one of the few unifying forces in the country, being the basis for both lifestyle and culture. There is no national police force in the country, and disputes are often resolved in the mosques by the local councils of community elders, called *jirgas*. Each community is in this way self-governing; as a result, the daily lives of rural people tend not to be affected by whatever force happens to be in power in Kabul.

- Education is seen as very important throughout the country, and those who are educated are normally treated with great respect. However, though comparatively few people are educated, the arts have always flourished in Afghanistan; whatever the people produce is done in such a way that makes it beautiful, whether it be grain sacks or the exterior of buildings. Most Afghans are also able to repair rather than replace their possessions and make do with very little in the way of technology.

- Partly because of continuing and widespread illiteracy in the country, there is a strong verbal tradition throughout Afghanistan. Storytelling, folklore, and oral poetry thrive, and often the stories and poems carry a message or teaching and are important in building a sense of identity and shared culture, especially in a country where there is little communication between communities and where the vast majority of the population does not have access to television or radio. Folklore is often connected to Islam, and storytellers can be both male or female, young or old, and will often add personal details to their songs and stories, which can lead to arguments over which is the right version of a tale.

PROVERBS

- ■ What you see in yourself is what you see in the world.
- ■ There are 25 uncaught sparrows for every penny.
- ■ Don't show me the palm tree; show me the dates.
- ■ Only stretch your foot to the length of your blanket.
- ■ No one says his own buttermilk is sour.

FOLK TALE

A very clever old rooster lived with some young hens on a farm. He tried to teach the hens to learn from each other so they could avoid being eaten by the wily old fox. One fine spring morning, the rooster went for a walk, and he felt so happy that he began to sing. The fox heard him and hurried toward him in the hope that he could catch him. The rooster saw the fox and flew up into a tree. The fox tried to persuade him to come down, telling him there should be no hate between the animals and that he and the rooster should enjoy the beautiful morning together. The rooster replied that he didn't know the fox, so he was surprised at the invitation. The fox tried to tell the rooster that he knew the rooster's father, but the rooster replied that his father had died the previous year. The fox responded that he had meant the rooster's mother and that he knew the whole family. The rooster expressed surprise at this, saying that he only knew that foxes and roosters were enemies and could not be friends. The fox asked if the rooster had not heard about the lion's order that all the animals must be friends, including dogs, foxes, and chickens. Then the fox noticed that the rooster was not paying attention to what he was saying but was looking off into the distance. When asked what he was looking at, the rooster described an animal like a dog. At this, the fox began to get nervous and started to leave. "Why are you going?" asked the rooster in surprise. "Weren't you just telling me about the lion's orders that all animals should be friends?" The fox replied, "I am, but I'm afraid the dog is also ignorant of the orders of the lion." He did not wait to find out.

■ Administrative Perspective

OFFICIAL EDUCATIONAL POLICY

Free and compulsory education has been enshrined in the Afghani constitution since 1931 and is present in the new constitution also. All aspects of education are controlled centrally with teachers holding civil service status. Before the conflict and military occupations that began in

1979, education had been improving. Tuition and textbooks were free, and post-secondary education was subsidized to such an extent that all students received a monthly allowance from the government. However, rural areas did not have sufficient secondary schools, and often children, especially girls, stayed at home to help in the house after the primary level. Nomadic tribes often had difficulty sending their children to school. The role of Islam in education had always been an issue of contention, with some religious leaders opposing the education of girls after age 12 (often coinciding with the onset of menses), when preparation for marriage was thought to be a higher priority.

The destruction of facilities and the displacement of people, including teachers, that began with the Soviet invasion and continued during the occupation and subsequent conflicts disrupted education enormously. Children, especially older ones, were often taught to use and maintain weapons along with studying basic religion and developing literacy, and there were as many as 25,000–30,000 child soldiers in Afghanistan. However, a literacy program introduced at the time of the Soviet invasion did achieve some success, though the literacy rate remains very low.

There is an extreme shortage of teachers in Afghanistan today, and the nature of the mountainous terrain means that establishing schools and maintaining a curriculum are extremely challenging. Many textbooks used inside and outside the country portray Russia as the enemy and the Pushtuns as models of behavior with the ruling clans somehow above the law.

EDUCATION AT A GLANCE

See the Education at a Glance table on page 154.

AFGHANISTAN

Level/Age	Hours/Calendar	Language of Instruction	Compulsory Attendance	Exams	Grading System	Curriculum	Cost	Enrollment
Primary Grades 1–6 ages 6–12	Mar. to Jan. 7- to 10-day break after midterm as well as a 3- to 4-day holiday to celebrate *Eid-al Fitr* and *Eid Ul Adha*. Classes held Saturday through Thursday.	Dari throughout the country with Pashto used in some schools in the south	Yes, to age 12	Midterm and comprehensive final exams required to advance to the next grade. Daily quizzes are frequent. Tests based on lectures, homework, and reading assignments. In the sciences, tests take the form of problem solving or multiple choice. Social science tests are short answer (definitions).	100-point scale pass/fail = 40	Revised curriculum includes life skills and "gainful" skills, which will enable students who cannot continue beyond Grade 9 to join the workforce. Inclusion of units on peace education, democracy, human rights, understanding, forgiveness, and national unity are to be part of the new curriculum as well. Other subjects: Islamic teachings, language, math, natural sciences, social science, physical education, art, computers, and "practical work"	Free	Enrollment at all levels has quadrupled since the end of the Taliban regime. The enrollment of girls has increased from 3% prior to 2003 to 30% in 2003, with 35% of primary school girls enrolled. Ratio of boys to girls is 10:1. Some 1 million primary-age girls are not enrolled.
Middle Grades 7–9 ages 13–15			No	No extended essay questions except in literature classes	Midterm exams graded on a 60-point scale.	Same as above, except that English is a required subject from Grades 7 through 12. Technical education offered at middle and lower secondary schools in commerce, applied arts, teacher training, and civil aviation as well as general education.		No data available.
Secondary Grades 10–12 ages 16–19			No	Same as above with *baccaluria* diploma awarded at the end		Same as above. Post-secondary technical education offered to 9th-grade graduates for 5 years at technical institutes.		10% of all age-appropriate children enrolled with only 3% completing secondary level.
University ages 20+ Bachelor 4 years (5 years for engineering and 7 for medicine, which is offered at master's level)		Dari	No	Entrance exam required, the results of which determine the field and institution of study. Midterm and final exams	100-point scale A = 86–100 B = 66–85 C = 50–65	Bachelor's degrees in arts, education, social science, and agriculture		Tertiary enrollments increased very slightly from 1970 to 1999. Not quite 2% of students enter university (2002).

Surface Culture Perspective

CLASSROOMS

- Many schools were looted and used as armories or hiding places by the *mujahadeen* in the period from 1991 to 1995 (i.e., after the withdrawal of Soviet occupying forces) when fighting between various factions intensified. By the time the Taliban gained power and closed schools in 1996, some 13,000 schools were completely destroyed.

- During the Soviet occupation, the typical classroom was in good condition. It included a blackboard, teacher's desk, and pairs of desks arranged in rows. Schools that survived are laid out in a square with an interior courtyard and classrooms along the perimeter facing the courtyard. While most classrooms do not have windows, they will have a door opening (but often without a door) that is covered in winter by a thick curtain to keep out the cold. Some classrooms will have coal- or wood-burning stoves for heating and fans, but not air conditioners, to cool classrooms in summer. Because the annual three-month vacation extends from January through March, students attend classes daily during the summer. There may be frequent interruptions in electrical services as the use of more fans and window air conditioners during the hotter months stresses the electrical infrastructure of communities.

- Tables, charts, and illustrations—all hand drawn and colored by the students or their relatives—may adorn the walls and be used as visual aids for teaching. No national flags or pictures of political or religious leaders are displayed, but famous quotes by poets or educators may be written on the walls.

- Teachers teach in buildings that may lack basic sanitation, heating, or running water, let alone educational supplies. In some cases, instruction is delivered out of doors under tents or trees. Afghani schools that are operated by nongovernmental organizations (NGOs) in Pakistan vary in the quality of their facilities. Some are fully equipped while others lack basic amenities such as desks.

- Afghani schools do not have cafeterias, but students who do not bring food from home may buy snacks during breaks at small privately owned kiosks on the school courtyard. Inspectors regularly check to ensure that the food is fresh and prepared under sanitary conditions. As classes generally run from 8:00 AM to 1:00 PM, most students return home after class to have a hot lunch.

- Classes of more than 50 students are not uncommon, although during the pre-Taliban days typical class size ranged from 15 to 25. The average teacher-student ratio for the primary level is 1:40 and 1:30 at the secondary level.

- While most schools may have a single computer in the main office and none in the classrooms or labs, cybercafes and libraries that provide Internet access are increasingly filling the gap in the larger cities.

TEACHERS' STATUS

- Around 100,000 teachers are certified in Afghanistan, but more than 85 percent of them have no formal teaching qualifications, some having no more than the equivalent of a 6th grade education. UNICEF is trying to address this problem by offering training, though it is difficult for UNICEF to devise programs for teachers whose education level is so low.
- The Afghani constitution declares that education must be free for all people. However, the government lacks the resources to compensate teachers for their work, and parents are generally too poor to foot teachers' salaries on their own. This dilemma has drawn the attention of the UN, which is exploring ways to rectify the situation through the international community.
- There is sometimes a perception in Afghanistan that instruction, especially to girls, is not of a very high standard.
- There are far more male than female teachers in Afghanistan. In 1990, 59 percent of teachers were female, but by 1999 that percentage had dropped to 13.5 percent.
- Teachers' salaries in Afghanistan tend to be so low that many do not enjoy even basic amenities. The average monthly salary is approximately US$50. In 2005 teachers refused to mark Teachers' Day in protest against the government's refusal to raise salaries to keep up with inflation.

TEACHER-STUDENT RELATIONSHIP

- Teachers at the primary level tend to be openly supportive and protective of their students whereas by the time students reach the high school level, they typically find teachers to be much more formal and distant. Thus, as students get older, they will be less likely to ask questions in class or express their feelings and opinions.
- Teachers are held in very high esteem in Afghanistan and are second only to parents in terms of the children's regard. Teachers of students in the lower grades will often behave much like parents, using kindness rather than fear to discipline students and openly showing physical affection. One way in which students show their respect is by remaining quiet in class. They also stand when the teacher enters and leaves the classroom or may present the teacher with a freshly picked flower if they encounter the teacher on the street or playground.
- Sometimes when students are experiencing academic difficulty, the teacher will call the parents in for a consultation. By the same token, many parents will not shy away from bringing concerns about a teacher's conduct to the principal.

TEACHING PRACTICES

- Teachers will often present and explain a subject and then expect each student to memorize, learn by rote what was presented, and recite it later in class. More modern teachers, however, will attempt to engage students in discussion or some modicum of give-and-take. Traditional teachers may read directly from a text and expect students to take verbatim notes in their copybooks. Everything that the teacher writes on the board is intended for exact duplication into the students' copybooks.

- In pre-Taliban days, teachers were required to submit detailed written lesson plans to their supervisors for each of the four classes they were assigned to teach. Yearly and monthly plans were required in addition to daily lesson plans.

- An acceptable lesson should include a warm-up (greetings, news) followed by a review in which the teacher goes around the room with an open gradebook, calling on students randomly to answer questions about the previous day's lesson and entering into the gradebook notations about their performance. Teachers may also collect homework at the beginning of the lesson and record grades on the assignment during the break between classes.

- It is not uncommon for teachers to call student volunteers to the front of the class after the lecture to summarize or reexplain key points in the lesson. This is not only a means for checking comprehension but for reteaching content and assigning points in the gradebook.

- Teachers will often ask if students need repetition or clarification of key points from the lesson and are particularly pleased when students request help.

TEACHERS' DRESS

- Under the Taliban, women throughout Afghanistan were forced to wear the *burqa,* a garment that covers the entire body and face, with netting over the eyes so that the woman could see without having her eyes visible, and teachers were no exception to this. During the reign of the Taliban, women were not allowed to work outside the home at all, regardless of whether or not they were trained as teachers. For this reason, some women used to secretly teach classes in their private homes. Today, some women have discarded the *burqa,* whereas others have kept it. In general, this issue is not seen as important a woman's issue as are poverty and lack of health care.

- Men are also expected to dress discreetly, usually wearing long pants and long-sleeved shirts or the traditional Afghan attire consisting of loose, baggy pants (or *shalwar*), a tunic (or *kameez*) to the knees or ankles, and often a turban. The ensemble is called a *shalwar kameez.*

DISCIPLINE AND CLASS MANAGEMENT

- Although corporal punishment is prohibited in Grades 1–5, it is still used in schools in Afghanistan at the higher levels. It may consist of a harsh verbal reprimand, striking the student's palm with a ruler or stick, or directing a student to stand on a chair in front of the class for several minutes. Occasionally, a student will be given a light slap on the face. That said, Afghani teachers tend to be forgiving of student mistakes, whether academic or behavioral, and will not hold grudges or be vindictive.

- Students can be punished for talking or giggling in class or for failing to turn in assigned homework. They receive grades for behavior, but frequently teachers are reluctant to officially record misbehavior since such marks can harm a student's prospects for jobs or entry into university programs.

- Teachers normally give students a warning before administering punishment. For example, a student who is out of line in class will first be reprimanded by the teacher. If the student continues to misbehave, the teacher will usually send the student into the corridor to stand and wait to be called back in to class. After perhaps five minutes, the student will be allowed to rejoin the class. However, repeated misbehavior will compel the teacher to write a note to the student's parents requesting a face-to-face meeting.

- Every class has a student captain whose job it is to wash and iron the cloth that covers the teacher's desk, bring in artificial flowers to adorn the desk, and generally organize the teacher's supplies. This student will also monitor other students, chastising those who inadvertently show disrespect to the teacher by, for example, leaning against the teacher's chair or using the teacher's desk as support while writing a note.

STUDENTS' CIRCUMSTANCES

- Girls often do not attend school beyond the age of 12 as they are either needed at home or must begin to prepare for marriage. Literacy and other studies take second place to learning how to run a home and please a husband.

- Today in big cities such as in Kabul, Mazar-e-Sharif, and Herat, most parents try to provide their daughters with a good education. Such girls are encouraged to at least have a high school education before they get married. Men from urban areas also value education in the background of prospective wives. However, a college education is not considered to be essential for women even among more intellectual families. Nevertheless, according to many Afghani families, the most respectable job for a woman to hold is that of teacher.

- Refugees who have settled in camps in Pakistan may have experienced living conditions far less comfortable than those to which they were accustomed before fleeing from Afghanistan. Houses in the refugee camps are often constructed of mud bricks, potable water is usually in short supply, and running water may be available from only one or two taps in the neighborhood. Many families keep chickens in order to supplement their diet and income. They may also sell fast food, embroider fabric, or make jewelry to sell in the market. Schools in refugee camps are generally not staffed by certified teachers, and the facilities can be crude. For example, some schools have no desks, so students must sit on a carpet during lessons.

STUDENT-STUDENT RELATIONSHIP

• Most schools are segregated by sex, especially in rural areas. At universities and private language schools today, though, boys and girls sometimes study in the same schools and classrooms.

• Students stay together as cohorts from their earliest years in school until graduation. Friendships are therefore strong. If a student is having family problems, it would not be uncommon for his or her friends to help resolve the problems by talking with the student's family members.

• Although it is not common for students to do their homework together, one student may offer to help another who is having difficulty in class. Group projects are rare, except perhaps in the sciences, but teachers may call for collaboration in the form of peer teaching when some students are progressing more slowly than other members of the class.

• Snubbing or ostracizing classmates is not tolerated. However, parents will assert their authority over a child's choice of close friends. For example, a parent may forbid a child from going to the movies or to cafes with peers who are considered to have a bad influence on the child. If the child's behavior changes, parents may visit the school and talk to his or her child's classmates to find out if any new friendships may have developed. Parents will also usually not allow their child to spend the night away from home unless it is at the home of relatives.

STUDENTS' LEARNING PRACTICES

• In less student-centered classes, learners may be expected to listen and memorize and do not take an active part in lessons and learning. However, some schools, even in rural areas, offer in-service training for teachers, who learn to conduct classes that involve greater student participation and expression of ideas and opinions.

• In some schools, class participation is part of the student's grade. One form of participation is asking the teacher to repeat or clarify parts of the lesson. Generally speaking, the most successful students are those who volunteer to come to the front of the class to summarize the content of the lesson.

• Students prefer to study on their own. Study groups are somewhat rare.

• Most Afghani students today are eager to learn. Many hope to become doctors or engineers and expect to help rebuild their country.

STUDENTS' DRESS

- Before the Soviet invasion, uniforms for girls consisted of black skirt and top, with hair tied up and back. Today, either the *burqa* or Western-style clothes are worn.

GIFTS FOR THE TEACHER

- Flowers or cards are often given to the teacher on birthdays, Teachers' Day (May 24), or to show affection or appreciation. Other small gifts may be offered as well, but teachers tend not to open them in the presence of the gift giver. Typically an announcement is made prior to Teachers' Day discouraging the students from bringing gifts, but this gesture is generally not observed by the students.
- On Teachers' Day classes are cancelled, and a party atmosphere replaces the usual strict academic tone. Students are free to wear what they like, and even a little make-up and jewelry is tolerated. The students bring food from home that they place on a long line of tables and decorate the classroom with confetti and shiny pieces of paper. They then go to the teachers' lounge (where the teachers are having a celebration of their own) and invite their favorite teachers to join them. After the teachers have eaten a little of the special dishes brought by the students, they leave so that the students can dance and eat.

NONVERBAL COMMUNICATION

- Greetings between men tend to consist of a handshake with a hug and sometimes kisses on both cheeks. Physical contact between members of the same sex is more common and more natural than in North America. However, there is very little physical contact in public throughout Afghanistan between men and women, with women often avoiding eye contact with men.
- Winking, a common gesture in North America, may cause offense in Afghanistan.
- The distance maintained by people engaged in conversation, especially if they are of the same sex, is often less than in North America, and looking closely or staring at someone is also not uncommon.
- Meetings are a common forum for creating ideas, solving problems, and generally discussing issues. However, conversations do not take such a linear direction as in North America, with a considerable amount of general talk before the point is reached.
- It is impolite to ask a direct question of someone before inquiring about his or her health.
- It is not unusual for events to occur 30 to 40 minutes after the agreed time.

FORMS OF ADDRESS

- Students and parents call teachers *mahlem sahib* (teacher sir) or *mahlem sahiba* (teacher madam).
- Teachers call students by first name plus *jan* (or dear), as in *Shukria jan.*
- In rural areas, teachers will call the mother of a student *Mother Maria jan,* meaning dear Maria's mother.

APPROPRIATE TOPICS

- Personal lives make a good introductory topic, though it could be offensive to talk about a man's wife or to ask if someone is married.
- Afghans enjoy talking about their homeland, especially their home province. They may also enjoy discussing where they have traveled.
- On first acquaintance, Afghans tend to refrain from discussing the war but may want to tell of their experiences later.
- The Afghans' love of folklore is often expressed in conversation in the form of proverbs or amusing stories.

OUTSIDE OF CLASS

- Students generally receive several hours of homework every day that may include solving problems for subjects such as mathematics, and multiple-choice, true/false, and short answers for social science subjects.
- After school, children may eat, shower, change, watch TV, do their homework, or play with their friends just until dark when they must return home. Soccer, kite flying, and kite running are popular free-time activities among boys whereas girls may go to ice cream shops or cafes to chat or may stay home and weave carpets. Visiting relatives is also a popular after-school pastime.
- Children from less affluent families may cook food at home to sell on the street. The eldest girl in a family is often responsible for all the household chores (e.g., washing clothes, doing dishes, cooking), leaving her younger siblings free to play.

Potential Adjustment Challenges

PROBLEMS/SOLUTIONS

Problem

The mother of my Afghani student, Shukria, insists that she has always been a hard worker, but I find this child very hard to manage. She seems unfocused and more interested in the social part of school than the academic part.

Solution

Afghani children are used to strict teachers who not only clearly lay down the rules and exact punishment when rules are violated, but who are severe critics of student work. This approach is thought to motivate students to work hard and achieve their best. North American teachers are often considered to be more nurturing and accommodating than their Afghani counterparts and, as a consequence, may unknowingly deny students like Shukria the security, structure, and predictability that they once found in their classrooms at home. Without this familiar context, many Afghani students can find themselves disoriented and unsure of new boundaries and expectations.

Problem

I am growing impatient with one of my Afghani students who doesn't seem to be able to express an opinion or preference. When confronted with a choice in class, he responds with some variation of "I don't know. Whatever you want."

Solution

Of course, these students have a preference, but they will not show you the disrespect of putting themselves before others. Especially at the primary and middle school levels, Afghani students are taught to be polite to the extent that they will defer to the teacher rather than satisfy their own interests.

Problem

I have a student from Afghanistan who I don't think has left campus all semester. What's going on?

Solution

Even university-age students may experience intense homesickness when they live far away from their families and friends for the first time in their lives. Lack of comfort from their familiar extended families plus new responsibilities and freedoms (even going to a shopping mall alone) can create the kind confusion and stress that some will simply choose to avoid.

Iran

■ IRAN *Upclose*

Capital: Tehran

Population: 68,688,433 (June 2006)

Size: 1,648,000 sq. km. (636,296 sq. mi.) (somewhat larger than Alaska)

Location: in the Middle East, bordered by Iraq and Turkey to the west; the Persian Gulf and the Gulf of Oman to the south; Pakistan and Afghanistan to the east; and Turkmenistan, the Caspian Sea, Azerbaijan, and Armenia to the north

Climate: mostly arid or semiarid with a subtropical climate along the Caspian coast

Terrain: rim of rugged, mountains with a high, central basin consisting of both deserts and mountains; small discontinuous plains along both coasts

Monetary Unit: Iranian rial (9,161 per U.S. dollar) (June 2006)

Religion: Shi'a Muslim 89%; Sunni Muslim 9%; Zoroastrian, Jewish, Christian, and Baha'i 2%

Language(s): Persian and Persian dialects 58%, Turkic and Turkic dialects 26%, Kurdish 9%, Luri 2%, Balochi 1%, Arabic 1%, Turkish 1%, other 2%

Literacy Rate: 79.4% total population; 85.6% men; 73% women (2003)

Ethnicity: Persian 51%, Azeri 24%, Gilaki and Mazandarani 8%, Kurd 7%, Arab 3%, Lur 2%, Baloch 2%, Turkmen 2%, other 1%

Per Capita Income: US$8,300 (2005)

Population Distribution: 67% urban, 33% rural (2003)

Population below Poverty Line: 40% (2002)

Life Expectancy: total population 70.3 years; men 68.9 years; women 71.7 years (2006)

Government: theocratic republic (Islamic Republic)

PUBLIC HOLIDAYS				
January 13*	*Eid al Adha* (Feast of the Sacrifice)		April 11*	Birthday of the Prophet and Imam Sadeq
January 31*	Islamic New Year			
February 9*	*Ashura*		June 4	Death of Imam Khomeini
February 11	Victory of the 1979 Islamic Revolution		June 5	Anniversary of the uprising against the Shah
March 20	Oil Nationalization Day			
March 21*	*Noruz* (Iranian New Year or vernal spring equinox)		August 22*	*Leilat al-Meiraj* (ascension of the Prophet)
March 28*	Death of the Prophet Mohamed and martyrdom of his grandson		September 24*	Beginning of Ramadan
			October 22*	*Eid-al-Fitr* (end of Ramadan)
April 1	Islamic Republic Day			
April 2	*Sizdah-Bedar* (Nature Day)			*variable dates

■ Personal Perspective

When I was nine years old, my family left Iran and temporarily settled in Spain before finally moving to the United States. Although my family is very open about many social and interpersonal issues, I was still very uncomfortable with and shocked by the behavior of my new classmates and teachers. I would get anxious when a boy talked to me and couldn't make eye contact with him, and when other students defended their ideas in class, I felt they were being disrespectful and felt sorry and embarrassed for the teacher. How long did it take me to overcome this discomfort? I'm now 26, and I'm still struggling with these kinds of cultural puzzles. Some people say I'm bicultural, but I don't know. In fact, I could say I don't really know where I belong.

—Iranian engineering graduate student in the United States

■ Historical Perspective

IMMIGRATION TO THE UNITED STATES

The majority of Iranian immigrants now living in the United States arrived following the 1979 Islamic revolution in Iran, but small infusions of immigrants, mostly from the upper and professional classes, had occurred during the 1950s and 1960s. In addition, by the mid-1970s, some 317,000 Iranian students and visitors were temporarily residing in the United States. These numbers rose as Iranians sought short-term sanctuary from political and religious persecution in the United States, many believing that they would wait out the revolution and eventually return to Iran. The Iran-Iraq War, which continued throughout the 1980s, however, changed the fortunes and futures of many of those visitors as they realized that they had little choice but to change their status from non-immigrant to immigrant or refugee. The numbers of immigrants intending to make the United States their new home also rose in the aftermath of the revolution. Though they may have lived prosperous lives before the revolution, the repercussions of their political views and activities frequently led many to flee Iran with little more than the clothes on their backs.

The largest Iranian communities are now found in California, New York, Virginia, Maryland, New Jersey, and Texas. An estimated 42–50 percent of Iranian immigrants reside in California. Regardless of location of settlement, Iranian immigrants tend to pursue advanced educational degrees and professional careers. More than 45 percent possess graduate degrees, and they earn roughly six times as many Ph.D.s as their non-immigrant American counterparts. In addition, the average family income for Iranian-Americans (US$55,501) exceeds the national average of US$35,000. More than 90 percent own their own homes, and more than 20 percent have started their own businesses.

HISTORICAL SYNOPSIS

Iranians are immensely proud of their long history and ancient civilization, and though this history has seen many types of rulers and regimes, historians tend to find more evidence of continuities than changes. For many centuries, Iran was the center of a sophisticated civilization, both before and after the Islamic conquest of the 7ᵗʰ century, with the Persian culture and language maintaining its identity despite changes of ruling dynasty. The most recent of these was established in 1921 when the Reza Shah Pahlavi seized power after a failed attempt at a constitutional revolution and changed the name of the country from Persia to Iran in 1935. During the period of the Shahs, there was an attempt to modernize and Westernize the country, but there were also bouts of rebellion because of the poverty and exclusion from political power felt by ordinary people. There was also fear that the Westernization process would diminish and overtake Iranian national identity and Islamic identity. Such fears culminated in the Islamic revolution of 1979, which replaced the monarch with an Islamic cleric as president, created a powerful religious elite, and transferred many private holdings to state control. The revolution introduced a period of Islamic fundamentalism influencing many aspects of the daily lives of Iranians. On November 4, 1979, a group of Iranian students stormed the U.S. embassy in Tehran, holding its occupants hostage for 444 days. A U.S. military rescue operation was unsuccessful, and it was not until U.S. President Ronald Reagan was inaugurated on January 20, 1981, and $8 billion in Iranian assets were unfrozen that the hostages were released.

In the same year, Iran began a bloody, inconclusive, and costly war with its neighbor Iraq, which lasted until 1988. Since then, there has been increasing pressure for political reform because of economic conditions, the restrictive nature of society, and the increasingly young population—more than 50 percent of Iranians are under the age of 25. In 1997 Khatami's election as president was seen as a mandate for political reform, an impression strengthened when liberals gained control of the parliament in the 2000 elections. However, attempts to bring change were consistently blocked by the conservative clergy. Elected in June 2005, President Ahmadinejad is Iran's first non-clerical president in 24 years, and he has promised to bring peace and moderation to the country. The supreme leader remains the cleric Ayatollah Khamenei.

Deep Culture Perspective

DEEP CULTURE BELIEFS

- Iranians are an intensely social people, who delight in verbal exchanges involving news, jokes, or stories.
- Hospitality, especially to outsiders, is a hallmark of Iranian culture. Iranians tend to make friends easily, are polite, and will avoid conflict if possible.
- The concept of unity is very important in both ancient Persian and modern Iranian society, with group life and activities more valued than individualism. This is reflected in the strength of family bonds and their associated privileges and obligations. The father is head of the household; his word is law, but he is also responsible for supporting the family materially, socially, and spiritually. Some conflict arises when the more liberal or religiously fundamental views of the younger generation contrast with the father's beliefs. The perceived lack of family values in Western society leads some Iranians to believe that they are superior to Westerners.
- Religion plays a crucial role in Iranian daily life, though not all Iranians are devout. The vast majority of people are Shi'a Muslims, for whom prayer times, fasting during the month of Ramadan, the giving of alms, and the role of the Imam (religious leader) are important. Other sects and religions are tolerated, though practice of these religions is necessarily discrete. Some discrimination based on religion has been reported in the areas of employment opportunities and conditions.
- The sense and realities of class structure are important in Iranian culture. The status of a family is often linked to its history and its former tribal affiliations. Prior to the revolution, status was achieved through the proximity of political connections rather than wealth, though the two were, and still are, obviously closely linked. Family elites kept political power, and marriage bound together the important families. In the 1970s, education began to be seen as a way of improving social status. Today, though family affiliations are important, education and qualifications are still seen as ways of overcoming the handicaps of social background.
- Segregation of the sexes is a feature of Iranian life, and the barriers between genders well marked. Throughout Iranian society women are to be respected, but Islamic law also often ends up restricting their lives. A visible sign of this control is the obligatory covering of all skin and hair of women in public. Occupations and social opportunities are open to women provided they do not lead to a liberalization of relations between the sexes, though clearly, attitudes and values vary greatly according to background, education, and social status. Today, more women than men are entering universities, and they are playing a part in areas of political, social, and professional life as well

as beginning to start their own businesses. However, the extent of a woman's opportunities still depends on the attitudes of her closest male relative.

PROVERBS

- Listening to good advice is the way to wealth.
- A blind man who sees is better than a sighted man who is blind.
- God provides, but He needs a nudge.
- Every tear has a smile behind it.
- Acquaintance without patience is like a candle with no light.
- He who wants a rose must respect the thorn.
- Do not cut down the tree that gives you shade.
- The world is a rose; smell it, and pass it to your friends.
- We come into this world crying while everyone around us is smiling. May we live so that when we go out of this world smiling everybody around us is weeping.
- One finger cannot lift a pebble.

FOLK TALE

Once there lived an old woodcutter who eked out a living by gathering wood in the desert and selling it in the market. One day, his daughter asked if he could buy some date cakes. To do so the old man had to sell more than the usual amount of wood, so he wandered far into the desert, returning so late that he had to sleep on the doorstep and miss dinner.

Waking early the next morning, the old woodcutter thought he could gather even more wood to sell that day at the market, but, once again, he ventured too far and was unable to return until after dark. The same thing happened on the third day. Exhausted and hungry, he sank to the ground at his doorstep and wept.

Suddenly, he heard a voice asking "What's wrong, old man?" He looked up to see a dervish standing before him, and he explained what had transpired. The dervish reminded the old man that it was Friday Eve, or the time of *Mushkil Gusha,* the Remover of Difficulties. The dervish shared some roasted chickpeas and raisins with the old man and explained that in order for the old man's good fortune to continue, every Friday Eve he must find someone in need of help, share what he has with him, and tell him the tale of *Mushkil Gusha.*

That day the man sold his wood at the market, and he and his daughter enjoyed some delicious date cakes. The next day she was noticed by the princess, who invited the daughter to serve as her handmaiden. This brought comfort and financial security to the old man and his daughter. He no longer gathered wood, and he soon forgot about the dervish's instructions.

All was well until the princess accused the daughter of stealing a necklace. To punish the girl, the old man was arrested and put in stocks in the town square. As passersby jeered at him, the old man cried out loud his remorse for not having carried out the dervish's orders. Then, a small beggar boy approached and gave the old man some chickpeas and raisins. The old man recounted his tale and told of his regret.

The next day the princess found her necklace, which she had carelessly left hanging on a tree branch while she went for a swim, and realized, of course, that the woodcutter's daughter had not taken it. By the end of the day, the woodcutter was back at home and the daughter back in the palace. Every Friday Eve after that the woodcutter made sure he found someone in need, shared what he had, and told the tale of *Mushkil Gusha*.

Administrative Perspective

OFFICIAL EDUCATIONAL POLICY

There has been much reform recently in the Iranian education system spurred mainly by the post-revolutionary social and demographic changes, notably the large number of school-age children. Throughout the country there is a need and a desire to improve all aspects of education. All schools are single sex, with any contact between the genders discouraged in and out of schools. Whereas at the elementary level teachers and students tend to be of the same sex, at higher levels, male teachers can teach at girls' schools, though there are no female teachers at boys' schools. Even staff rooms are segregated by gender. There is a suggestion that boys' schools are better equipped and maintained than girls' schools. Nevertheless, authorities are actively encouraging the attendance of girls at various types of school. The rate of primary education increased to almost 98 percent in 2000, though the rate for both sexes decreases further up the education chain, more so for girls than boys.

After the 1979 revolution, the authorities desecularized the elementary and secondary school systems by controlling and regulating books, courses, teachers, and the behavior and dress of students. Changes in higher education were more sweeping, with a purge of academic staff and students who were not considered to be sufficiently Islamic. At the high school level, a number of courses with heavy Islamic content have also been added to the curriculum, in some cases taking the place of physical education or other classes not considered to be sufficiently important. Another area of reform is the increase in the number of vocational and training schools and their orientation toward providing students with job choices, and the efforts of authorities to attract more girls to them.

EDUCATION AT A GLANCE

See the Education at a Glance table on page 170.

IRAN

Level/Age	Hours/Calendar	Language of Instruction	Compulsory Attendance	Exams	Grading System	Curriculum	Cost	Enrollment
Pre-school ages 5–6	Sep.–June 6 days per week, 24 hours per week	Farsi	No	No exam	none	Preparing students to take part in Islamic life, increasing their mental and physical power, Persian language, and skills basic numeracy	No data available	No data available
Primary Grades 1–5 ages 7–11			Yes	At the end of each year for promotion to following grade; at the end of Grade 5, students take nationwide exam.		General education curriculum	Free	97.8% of eligible population enrolled.
Middle Grades 6–8 ages 11–13		Farsi plus English as a foreign language introduced at Grade 7.	Yes	At the end of this cycle, students have to pass a regional exam to proceed to secondary cycle.	0–20-point scale: A = 17–20 B = 14–16.9 C = 12–13.9 D = 10–11.9	General education, but students' abilities and interests begin to be a factor as they prepare to decide which branch—vocational/technical or academic—they will enter in the next cycle.		90.3% of eligible population enrolled.
Secondary Grades 9–12 ages 14–17			Yes, to age 15	National exams at the end of each grade plus nationwide entrance exam for admission to associate diploma program and Konkur exam for admission to bachelor's degree program		2 main branches: academic (including literature and culture, socioeconomic, physics and math, and experiential sciences branches) and technical/vocational (including technical, business/vocational, and agricultural branches). English is introduced in Grade 7.		69.1% of eligible population enrolled.
University ages 17+ 2 years for associate diploma, 4–5 years for bachelor's degree, 2 years for master's degree, which can be thesis or non-thesis based, 3–6 years for doctorate		Farsi	No	Mid-term and end-of-year exams	Same as above; passing grades: undergraduate minimum 10, graduate minimum of 12, doctoral minimum of 14; minimum GPA of 12 at undergraduate and 14 at graduate levels	54 state-operated universities, 42 state medical schools, 289 major private universities, plus a number of new distance learning universities. Most popular fields are Humanities and Engineering; least popular is Arts.	Tuition and room and board paid by the government, except for students in private schools.	60% of enrollment is female. Although 1.5 million students pass the Konkur, places are available for only about 27% of the candidates.

Surface Culture Perspective

CLASSROOMS

• Nowhere in Iran do boys and girls study together in the same classrooms or even schools.

• Due to the large number of young people entering schools, there is a severe shortage of classrooms throughout Iran. Many existing schools are in a fairly poor state of repair. In general, classrooms tend to be fairly spartan, though some have televisions and video players. However, there has been a rapid increase in the availability and use of computers and Internet resources, especially in large cities. It is reported that 6,500 of Iran's 15,000 secondary-level schools have their own website, and some vocational and technology training courses are available at various institutions.

TEACHERS' STATUS

• Students who hope to become pre-school and primary school teachers must attend a two-year training institution after completion of 10th grade. They receive an associate diploma following this training and are qualified to teach in both rural and urban areas.

• Teachers at the middle school (guidance) level complete a similar two-year program after they have graduated from high school. Teachers in the technical and vocational schools are selected from graduates of that type of institution. In order to teach at lower secondary level, teachers need an associate degree, and to teach at higher secondary level, a bachelor's degree, both with a specialized subject.

• Because of the shortage of teachers in rural areas, special institutions have been set up in which Grade 8 graduates may train for an additional four years to become teachers. In the 1980s and early 1990s, conscripts were deployed to teach in rural areas. Such efforts have resulted in the rise of teacher qualifications from 18 percent in 1990 to more than 38 percent in 1998, with the rate of increase of female teachers keeping pace with that of their male colleagues.

• Teachers' responsibilities include preparing, proctoring, and grading the critical level-advancement and school-leaving exams during the assessment periods, as well as helping to prepare for religious and national celebrations. Teachers must also attend after-school teachers' council meetings, in which educational policies are explained and agreed to by teachers, and school- and region-wide issues are discussed. These meetings are often perceived as both burdensome and futile by teachers, and attendance can be sporadic. High school teachers are also expected to attend fairly formal meetings with parents.

- Many teachers seem to have lost interest in teaching and tend to arrive late and leave early. Teachers in Iran are very poorly and sometimes irregularly paid, which forces many to take on a second job to make ends meet. Teachers have rallied, held strikes, and protested about their conditions, accusing the government of hypocrisy, but have often been met by hostile security forces.

TEACHER-STUDENT RELATIONSHIP

- Iran's strict segregation of the sexes directly affects teacher-student relationships. Male teachers of female students may behave differently from when they work with male students. For example, male teachers do not often make full eye contact with female students, nor do they have any contact with female students outside class. The atmosphere in boys' classes tends to be lighter than in classes where the students are female and the teacher male. In rural schools especially, female students tend to be reticent about asking a male teacher a question in class.
- While in general students hold their teachers, and other authority figures, in high esteem and will do their best to behave appropriately in class, there are reports of a perception among students that teachers do not care about them and their problems. Indeed, teachers are known to advise each other against becoming too close to their pupils. The teachers' behavior often suggests to students that they feel their job is simply to teach, and the responsibility for learning lies with the students. As a consequence, many students have learned not to expect too much from their teachers.
- English is taught in schools from the 7th grade onward but often teachers lack both the skills and knowledge to teach effectively. Also, most students struggle with learning Arabic at an earlier age and, therefore, can develop a negative attitude toward learning any foreign or second language.

TEACHING PRACTICES

- Throughout Iran, schools, teachers, and local and national authorities are constantly striving to develop more modern and less teacher-based methods and materials mainly through in-service training. However, many lessons seem to consist of little more than teacher lecture with little or no student involvement or interaction.
- Although books and curricula are the same at both girls' and boys' schools, girls are often given fewer opportunities to express their own ideas or explore their own interests, especially in classes with male teachers. Similarly, male teachers in girls' classes tend not to discuss or dwell on sensitive issues, such as sexuality in Persian literature classes.
- Teachers may give the impression that they feel the classroom is designed only for delivery of the curriculum and little else. Consequently,

minimal discussion of issues outside the field of study takes place. Similarly, students report that communication with teachers is a sensitive undertaking that must be conducted within very strict boundaries that must not be crossed.

- Teachers expect students to pose questions or seek help during the breaks, but because of the teacher-centered nature and the 80- to 90-minute length of the lessons, students are often too bored and tired to do so, which can, in some cases, annoy the teacher.

TEACHERS' DRESS

- One of the most visible aspects of post-revolutionary Iranian society is the legal requirement for women to cover their hair and skin, usually with either a long coat *(manto)* and headscarf *(roosaree)* or the *chador,* a large piece of black cloth covering the head and body. Typically, more traditional Iranian women will opt for the *chador* over the *manto* and *roosaree*. When at home among family or in the presence of only other women, women may dispense with the head cover.
- The wearing of a beard among men is often equated with their desire to be like the Prophet Mohamed, who also wore a beard, though longer and fuller than those worn by modern Iranian men today. Some men choose to sport heavy moustaches. Iranians, in general, are fastidious about personal appearance and hygiene. Thus an unshaven face is more likely to mean the man is displaying his religious affiliations than that he is sloppy in his personal hygiene.
- In the same way, a tie is often associated with Western imperialism and so government employees tend to avoid wearing one, just as some businessmen and those with Western sympathies will wear one as a sign of protest.

DISCIPLINE AND CLASS MANAGEMENT

- Teachers in Iran are often heard to complain about students' behavior, and their perceived lack of motivation and discipline issues are often brought up in teachers' council meetings. It is possible that students' classroom behavior in Iran is judged more harshly by teachers than it would be in North American schools.

STUDENTS' CIRCUMSTANCES

- In Iran, parents strive to give their children—both boys and girls—the best possible education. Wealthy families may spend large amounts of money on their children's university education.
- Decisions about what to study are almost always made in consultation with parents and family elders, and often students pursue degrees in disciplines recommended by their parents rather than in those in which they have a personal interest.

- The amount of parental control of and involvement in a young person's life is often considerable, but the strength of family bonds and the love and trust children feel for their parents usually mitigates the tensions this might cause. Girls' actions and behaviors are much more controlled than boys' actions because of fears about their reputations and future prospects for marriage.
- Physical abuse by husbands and fathers is still a factor in the lives of less educated families, though it is deplored in more educated and modern circles. Often a bride's family will investigate the background of the groom to make sure there is no history of wife-beating in his family. However, such issues are not often discussed openly in Iranian society.

STUDENT-STUDENT RELATIONSHIP

- Students' relationships between and among themselves are warm and friendly. Iranian school children are naturally gregarious but always such groups are of the same gender. Segregation of the sexes is a feature of students' lives out of school as well.

STUDENTS' LEARNING PRACTICES

- Self-control and modesty in girls are considered signs of religiosity. They must not laugh too much at the teacher's jokes and must not look into the face of a male teacher.
- Teachers have remarked on the increase of noise in classes since the 1979 revolution, perhaps because of the more relaxed atmosphere in single-sex classrooms. Also, corporal punishment is now forbidden in Iranian schools, which might also account for a relaxation of tension.

STUDENTS' DRESS

- After the revolution, schools mandated the wearing of a school uniform, specifying not only the style but also the color of both dress and shoes.
- Jeans are banned in both girls' and boys' schools, and there are strict rules about the use of cosmetics by girls (e.g., girls may not wear make-up of any kind, nail polish is forbidden, and even the length of one's nails must conform to school standards).

GIFTS FOR THE TEACHER

- It is customary to bring gifts to the teacher on Teachers' Day (in early October).
- While Iranian families love entertaining outsiders, it is not customary for teachers to be invited to their pupils' homes.

NONVERBAL COMMUNICATION

- Gestures that are common in North America but considered rude or offensive in Iranian society include the "all's well" thumbs-up gesture and pointing a finger at someone. Showing the sole of the foot, slouching, and stretching one's legs in company are also rude. Iranians sitting in the passenger seat of a car will often turn around and apologize to the person sitting behind them as it is impolite to turn your back on another person.
- Yellow flowers send the message "I hate you."
- An Iranian will indicate "no" by moving his or her head up and back sharply. To indicate "yes," a slight downwards nod is given. Men often place their hands over their hearts as a gracious acknowledgment of greeting or refusal of an offering. They may put the right palm over the right eye to signify "I am at your service."
- Among members of the same gender it is common for open affection to be shown by kissing both cheeks as a greeting and by holding hands. However, these practices are not acceptable between the sexes. A foreign woman should not expect to shake hands with an Iranian man on meeting, unless, of course, a hand is proffered in greeting. A slight bow is appropriate on the part of the man, and the woman may slightly nod her head. A woman who has just been introduced to another woman will proceed rather formally, but it is common for such encounters to end with a friendly hug.
- Punctuality is important to Iranians, though flexibility is a must as often other more pressing obligations can arise. Although many Iranians joke about their tendency toward tardiness, the stereotype is not borne out by everyone.
- As a way of showing respect to their elders, young people tend not to smoke or drink alcohol in front of them. Mothers especially are revered and treated with respect.

FORMS OF ADDRESS

- Students call each other by last name, unless they are on very friendly terms with one another.
- Teachers call students by last name only. Prior to the revolution, teachers called their students by Miss, Mrs., or Mr. plus last name. Islam's influence on education today in Iran may be noted in the use of religious terms to address students, namely *isisteri* (sister) or *ibrotheri* (brother).
- Students call teachers by title (*Khanoom* or Miss, *Agha* or Mister) plus last name—*Khanoom Arani* is Miss Arani, and *Agha Arani* is Mr. Arani. The last name may be substituted by the word for teacher, *Moalem*. Thus, *Khanoom Arani* becomes *Khanoom Moalem* (Miss Teacher), and *Agha Arani* becomes *Agha Moalem* (Mr. Teacher).

- Iranians tend to be formal and do not often use first names alone. Professional title plus first or last name is appropriate. *Engineer Jehangir* (title plus first name), for example, might even be used in conversation with a friend when referring to one's spouse.

APPROPRIATE TOPICS

- Among new acquaintances safe topics of conversation revolve around hometown, work, and family, at least initially. Given the political and social restrictions in their country and the paranoia that can often linger after immigration abroad, Iranians are not always comfortable talking about politics, religion, or belief systems in general, though they may feel freer discussing these subjects with foreigners than they might with fellow Iranians.
- Discretion and indirectness are necessary tactics when initiating conversation with Iranians. Questions about health and family followed by other issues of general interest are appropriate. This is true of conversations between friends as well as new acquaintances. Personal contact is important in any relationship, including professional ones, and trust and discretion are vital.
- Like many other nationalities, Iranians are proud of their country and its history, and therefore any positive comment or observation is likely to be well received.

OUTSIDE OF CLASS

- Very few, if any, out-of-school activities are organized as much because of the gender restrictions as because teachers are often too busy with their second jobs to be available.
- Sports activities are reemerging as extracurricular activities. Sports are considered an effective distraction from the Western-type influences emerging through the Internet, movies, and music.

Potential Adjustment Challenges

PROBLEMS/SOLUTIONS

Problem

My ESL students are going to create multi-media presentations about their regions of the world. I asked Farah, my student from Iran, to focus on the Arab world. She responded, "I will focus on Iran," but in her presentation she completely ignored other Arab countries.

Solution

It is important to refrain from referring to the Iranian people as Arabs or to their culture or language as Arabic. These groups may share the same religion—Islam—but Iranians are not Arabs. The language of Iran—Persian (also called Farsi)—uses the Arabic alphabet, but Persian and Arabic are separate languages. Not only is it an error of fact to confuse these two groups, but it is critical to understand that the Persians and the Arabs have historically shared a deep animosity toward each other.

Problem

I cannot motivate my Iranian student to speak up in class, but during the break between classes she bombards me with questions. Does she do this because she's embarrassed about speaking English in front of the rest of the class?

Solution

Although individuals differ with regard to their comfort in speaking in public, it's possible that your student is simply accustomed to the practice observed in Iran of asking questions after the teacher has finished lecturing. Classes in Iran last approximately 80 to 90 minutes each, during which time the instructor holds forth without interruption. While Iranian teachers may not appreciate questions during the lecture, they will certainly expect them during the break. They might even be bewildered if no students ask questions between classes.

Problem

I have a student from Iran who is observing Ramadan. She seems tired and occasionally rests her head on her desk during class. I'm afraid she's not going to survive a month of fasting, and I wonder how fair this requirement is for children.

Solution

Fasting during Ramadan is not a 24-hour-a-day ordeal, but extends from sunrise to sunset. Your student probably gets up before dawn to eat a good meal and may be fatigued because she started her day earlier than normal. Children, the sick, the elderly, and pregnant women are not required to fast during Ramadan.

India

Capital: New Delhi

Population: 1,095,351,995 (June 2006)

Size: 3,287,590 sq. km. (1,269,346 sq. mi.) (one-third the size of the U.S.)

Location: on the subcontinent of Asia, bordered on the north by Pakistan, China, Nepal, Bangladesh, Burma, and Bhutan; by the Arabian Sea to the west; and the Bay of Bengal to the east (Sri Lanka lies off the southernmost tip of India)

Climate: tropical monsoon in the south becoming more temperate in the north with deserts in the west

Terrain: plateau in the south, high Himalaya Mountains in the north, and flat and sometimes rolling plains in the northeast along the Ganges River

Monetary unit: Indian rupee (45.85 per U.S. dollar) (June 2006)

Religion: Hindu 81.3%; Muslim 12%; Christian 2.3%; Sikh 1.9%; other groups including Buddhist, Jain, Parsi 2.5%

Language(s): Hindi (national language) spoken as a first language by 30% of Indians; English (for national, political, and commercial communication and as language of instruction in many schools); 14 additional official languages, including Bengali, Telugu, Marathi, Tamil, Urdu, Gujarati, Malayalam, Kannada, Oriya, Punjabi, Assamese, Kashmiri, Sindhi, and Sanskrit. Some 300 minor languages and 3,000 dialects are also spoken.

Literacy Rate: total population 59.5%; men 70.2%; women 48.3% (2003)

Ethnicity: Indo-Aryan 72%, Dravidian 25%, Mongoloid and other 3%

Per Capita Income: US$442 (2006)

Population Distribution: 28% urban, 72% rural (2003)

Population below Poverty Line: 25% (2002)

Life Expectancy: total population 64.7 years; men 63.9 years; women 65.6 years (2006)

Government: federal republic

PUBLIC HOLIDAYS			
January 1	New Year's Day	August 15	Independence Day
January 26	Republic Day	October 2	Birthday of Mahatma Gandhi
February 2*	*Eid-al-Adha* (Feast of the Sacrifice)	October 12	*Vilava Dasami*
February 10*	*Muharram* (Islamic New Year)		(also called *Dussera*)
March 8	Birthday of Vardhaman Mahavir	November 1*	*Diwali* (Festival of Lights)
March 25*	*Holi* (Festival of Colors)	November 3-5*	*Eid-al-Fitr* (end of Ramadan)
April 14	Birthday of Baba Saheb Ambedkar	November 26	Birthday of Guru Nanak
April 18	Birthday of Sri Rama	December 25	Christmas
May 23*	*Buddha Purnima*		*variable dates*

■ Personal Perspective

Teachers back home are looked at as scary figures who might thrash you if you don't listen to them. It is this way throughout school and college. I have never met a friendly teacher, at least not in the sense that American teachers tend to be congenial! But, actually, they need to be strict; otherwise no one would listen to them or do any homework. When I was a boy, the only thing that would make me study was a whipping from the teacher. We have a saying: "If a horse makes friends with grass, then what will he eat?" The same thing applies here.

—Indian engineering graduate student in the United States

■ Historical Perspective

IMMIGRATION TO THE UNITED STATES

Indian immigration to the United States has occurred in three phases. Middle- and upper-class students and professionals began to arrive in the 1960s. The educational and economic advantages that they had possessed on arrival led to their eventual success in the United States as individuals, and they became one of the most affluent and well-paid groups of immigrants in the United States with an annual median income exceeding all other foreign-born groups and ranking highest, as well, in the categories of household, family, and per capita income. Indians of this generation of immigrants also hold more stocks and IRAs than other immigrant populations, obtain higher levels of academic achievement, and secure more managerial and professional positions than other foreign-born groups.

When relatives of the first wave of Indian immigrants arrived, however, many of them were less accomplished and not as prepared as their predecessors to enter the professional marketplace. Instead, they found jobs in factories and restaurants, became taxi drivers, and opened small businesses. Until the 1990s, members of this wave of Indian immigration enjoyed fewer and fewer benefits in terms of income, professional status, and educational achievement. They were more likely than their forerunners to file for unemployment benefits, to lose businesses, and to fall into poverty.

The third phase of Indian immigration took place in the 1990s as the technology industry expanded. Like members of the first wave of Indian immigration, these individuals tended to be academically privileged, financially secure, and relatively young. Together these two groups account for the seeming predominance of Indian immigrants in U.S. educational institutions, hospitals and medical clinics, research laboratories, and technology companies. Indeed, their numbers in these fields are disproportionate to the actual size of the Indian population in the United

States. Reports reveal that approximately 4 percent of the physicians practicing in the United States are of Indian origin. In some cases, some 40 percent of hospital doctors and 50 percent of hospital nurses are Indian. In Ohio the ratio of Indian to non-Indian doctors is 1:6. The trend seems unlikely to abate as some 74,500 Indian students, or 13 percent of the international student population in the United States, are studying in U.S. universities. It is estimated that approximately 80 percent of the Indian students working on graduate degrees in the United States will not return to India (LaBrack 1997).

Whereas the vast majority of Indian immigrants settled in California prior to 1965, today some 70 percent of this population lives in New York, Pennsylvania, New Jersey, Texas, Michigan, Illinois, Ohio, and California, with New York City, Chicago, San Jose, Los Angeles, Long Beach, Washington, DC, and Houston leading the cities of preferred residence.

HISTORICAL SYNOPSIS

India ranks seventh in the world as far as area is concerned and second in terms of population size. Nearly 17 percent of the world's total population lives in India. The country's history goes back at least 5,000 years when it was initially populated by the members of the Indus Valley civilization, but in 1,500 BCE it was invaded by Aryan tribes, followed in the 8th century by Arab invaders and in the 12th century by the Turks and finally by merchants from Europe in the 15th century. Britain colonized India in the 19th century and continued to dominate the subcontinent until 1947 when Mohandas Karamchand Ghandi (1869–1948) led a nonviolent movement that, after many years and several imprisonments, ended in India's establishment of a sovereign state in January 1950 under the leadership of Prime Minister Jawaharlal Nehru.

India's Muslim and Hindu populations have historically been in conflict with one another, and by 1940 the violence and death that this conflict sparked convinced India's leadership of the need to create a separate Muslim state. Both Pakistan and Bangladesh thus won their independence from India, Pakistan in 1947 and Bangladesh in 1971 after two wars with India—one in the late 1960s and another in the early 1970s. Continuing violence in provinces where both Hindus and Muslims lived resulted in the death of nearly a half million people and motivated the migration of many Indian Muslims to Pakistan and thousands of Pakistani Hindus to India.

Although post-independence India began to thrive in terms of agriculture and industry, its population also dramatically expanded, along with poverty and illiteracy. Rising prices drove up inflation in the 1970s and created a recession in India, and the country's population began to experience greater and greater economic stress and political dissatisfaction. In 1975, then Prime Minister Indira Ghandi called for a state of emergency, appointing her son Sanjay as the coordinator of a sterilization program in northern India to curb the population boom. Indira Ghandi was assassinated in 1984 by her own bodyguards in retribution for her order to attack one of the most sacred Sikh shrines in Punjab as she reacted to Sikh demands for independence.

Fundamental concerns in India include the ongoing dispute with Pakistan over Kashmir, massive overpopulation, environmental degradation, extensive poverty, and ethnic and religious strife, all this despite impressive gains in economic investment and output.

■ Deep Culture Perspective

DEEP CULTURE BELIEFS

- India is a culturally and linguistically diverse country, and language is the source of much of this diversity. Because the many languages and dialects spoken in India are often not mutually intelligible, many people resort, if they can, to using English to communicate with each other. Culturally, India's diversity has developed due to its caste system, consisting of four major groups and thousands of subcastes. Religion contributes to a diverse culture as well. While most Indians are Hindu, there are significant numbers of Muslims, Buddhists, Sikhs, Christians, and followers of virtually every major religion in the world. As might be imagined, India's diversity has at times produced conflict.
- Most Indians are well versed in the cultural legacies of their civilization and can recite myths and describe the heroes and events of the past.
- The gap between city and country dwellers is striking not just in the distribution of the population (28 percent urban, 72 percent rural) but in their way of life and fundamental beliefs. While Indian cities are modern centers of business, education, culture, and politics, the rural areas are characterized by a lifestyle that is largely ancient and unchanging, despite successful efforts to raise the literacy rate, improve medical care, and upgrade the educational system. There is severe poverty in rural India as well, where the population is burgeoning and unemployment is rampant.
- The extended family is a mainstay in India. Grandparents, parents, unmarried children, and married sons with their wives and offspring often live together. Daughters join their husband's extended family when they marry. Relatives not only live together under the same roof but also enjoy mutual ownership of all property. Each member contributes to the family as best as he or she can, providing money and other resources that benefit the group and caring for those who are elderly or ill. The extended family system has begun to erode in some cases where individuals leave the home to pursue better employment and educational opportunities, often in North America. Nevertheless,

family traditions and family unity are cherished such that Indian immigrants in the United States after many years eventually create the kind of wide and mutually supportive family network that they would otherwise enjoy at home in India. One Hindu tradition that reveals the closeness of family members is the celebration of "Sisters Day" (or *Raksha Bandhan Day*) when sisters place a *rakhi* (silk talisman) on the wrist of a brother to symbolize his protection, and the brother gives the sister a gift as well.

- In a traditional Indian home, men manage the family's finances while women look after the home and children, where they wield significant power. The well-being of elders, too, is always considered, and their advice and approval sought. The oldest male generally holds the most authority and commands the most respect.

- Indians maintain a collectivistic versus an individualistic culture. Thus, decisions are made with the good of the family or group in mind, meaning that at times the individual must sacrifice his or her interests and desires for the sake of others.

- While some young Indians have begun to date Western style, most find a husband or wife through the matchmaking efforts of their parents, who regard arranging a marriage for their children to be one of the most important functions of parenthood. Parents of daughters look for sons of affluent families of the same caste to ensure the girl's well-being and to protect the family's good name and increase its connections with other well-placed members of the community. The latter is particularly valuable for those seeking special consideration in employment and in response to bureaucratic requests. With the expansion of educational opportunities for Indian women, however, arranged marriages have become a point of contention for those who reject the traditional domestic role of women. To prevent young women from abandoning the duties of home life and entertaining the notion of choosing their own spouses and lifestyles, some parents arrange to marry off their daughters while they are still quite young and indifferent to the influences of education and career. Other parents encourage their daughters to pursue an education to be better prepared for managing a household. The government, too, has responded in some cases by forbidding women of particular castes from enrolling in college or university programs. Divorce is rare in India regardless of the erosion of a marriage. In a culture that emphasizes society over the individual, divorce is thought to bring shame on the entire family.

- Some Westerners may view Indian culture as fatalistic as its members may appear to accept their station in society with little distress or attempt to change the social structure. Part of this may be attributable to the rigid caste system that prevents a person born into a lower caste from rising to a higher caste through education or wealth.

- India's caste system dates back to its early Aryan history. Virtually as well as literally divided into groups by occupation, different castes were initially created to separate the elite from the laborers. Today castes may vary from state to state. The Brahmin caste is often made up of teachers and priests, the Kshatrias are known as the warrior caste, the Vaishyas tend to be merchants, and the Sudras are what were called "untouchables" (before the term was banned in 1947). It is against the law to discriminate against members of certain castes, but the system nevertheless affects Indian politics and business. More and more young people are marrying outside their caste, something that is easier to accomplish if living abroad.

- Religion is an important part of Indian life, where its presence is seen in the routine as well as the institutional. Not only does it determine worldview and guide behavior, but its holy days are plentiful and observed even by those not formally inducted into a particular religion, somewhat as Christmas in North America is celebrated by Christians as well as followers of other faiths.

- Hinduism is India's most widespread religion. It has no particular founder, no time-honored laws, no one deity, and no formalized philosophy. However, there are three sacred texts to which Hindus turn, namely the *Rig Veda, Upanishads,* and the *Bhagavad Gita.* Shiva, Vishnu, Rama, and Krishna are among the gods and goddesses that may be worshipped by Hindus along with elements of nature and animals, such as the cow. The reason that cows are so cherished by Hindus is that each cow is seen as an independent system perfectly designed for the good of people. Placid and generous creatures, cows produce milk for nourishment, dung for fuel, and brawn for plowing fields and carrying heavy loads.

- The Sikhs, representing no more than 2 percent of India's population, practice a religion that combines tenets of both Islam and Hinduism. They worship one god and reject the caste system but observe many of the practices of the Hindus.

- Like Sikhism, Buddhism shares some of the same perspectives and practices of Hinduism. Its founder, Gautam Buddha, taught that nothing in life is impervious to change, and nothing happens by accident. He believed that our life paths are predetermined and that individuals will pass through a series of lives via reincarnation. Other tenets of Buddhism are that suffering is the plight of all human beings, that it is born out of desire, and that it can be circumvented by reducing desire, which, in turn, produces absolute enlightenment or a state of *nirvana.*

- Muslims in India hold to a belief in universal brotherhood, peace, love, and submission to God or *Allah.*

- Missionaries from Portugal, Denmark, Holland, Germany, and Great Britain brought Christianity to India, building schools as they spread the Gospel. There are approximately 30 million practicing Christians in India today.

Proverbs

- An apple changes color living with other apples.
- Call on God, but row away from the rocks.
- To hide one lie, a thousand lies are needed.
- A person who misses his chance and a monkey who misses its branch cannot be saved.
- Self praise is no praise.
- A thief is a thief whether he steals a diamond or a cucumber.
- God takes care of a blind cow.
- One who cannot dance blames the floor.
- Life is a bridge. Cross over it, but do not build a house on it.
- The cobra will bite you whether you call it "cobra" or "Mr. cobra."

Folk Tale

Once upon a time there was a very rich woman who lived in a big house and wore splendid clothes. Unfortunately, she was childless and, therefore, unhappy. Once when she complained about not being able to bear children, her friend advised her to ask one of their poor neighbors for one of their children. One neighbor had twelve children but was too poor to feed and clothe them. The rich woman's friend suggested she offer the poor mother a bag of gold for one of her children.

The next day the rich woman visited her poor neighbor. She entered the tiny house and was invited by the poor woman to sit down. Immediately, the children surrounded their mother begging for food and crying from hunger. The mother placed a portion of rice soup in twelve holes in the ground, as the family owned no bowls. After the children finished their soup, the poor mother drank what was left in the holes. Then she cried, "Please, dear God, send me another child. That way I will have another hole in the ground to eat from." The rich woman was amazed and saddened by the poor woman's plea for she saw that the mother would not give up a single child. Nevertheless, she gave the poor woman the bag of gold intended for the purchase of a child. She left the tiny house dejected but more appreciative of a mother's love.

▮ Administrative Perspective

Official Educational Policy

Education has been revered in India since its very early years. Scholarship in all areas of study flourished then as it does now. India is home to

226 universities, 428 engineering colleges and technical institutes, nearly 100 medical colleges, plus many agricultural schools and other institutions dedicated to the study of a wide range of subjects. The country excels in scientific and technological research, which has not only led to rapid modernization within India but acknowledged leadership among its peers throughout the world. India's expertise in the aerospace and nuclear energy industries, for example, is sought by many nations.

At the primary and secondary education levels as well, India has invested significant attention and resources to build and upgrade schools and curricula. In the last 50 years, the number of primary schools in India has tripled, and the number of secondary schools multiplied 18-fold. Similar increases can be noted for colleges and universities.

Illiteracy, especially among females, remains a problem in India despite the government's efforts. Approximately 60 percent of Indian women are illiterate, and a substantial percentage of Indian girls do not attend, let alone finish, school. India's National Policy on Education addresses some of these issues. Among its goals are making pre-school and primary education accessible to all children; integrating life-skills training into the curriculum; and focusing on relevance, equity, and excellence at all stages of education. Other objectives of the National Policy on Education include: reduction of the curriculum load, use of culture-specific teaching strategies and materials, decentralization of curriculum development, integration into the curriculum of information about the tenets of different religions or their value to society, creation of curricula that take a practical view of mathematics and science, provision of better and more vocational programs to prepare students for the workforce, development of a less punitive and cumbersome evaluation system, generation of plans to address through the curriculum the exigencies of globalization, and adjustment of teaching philosophies and pedagogies to treat the learner as a creator rather than a consumer of knowledge.

EDUCATION AT A GLANCE

See the Education at a Glance table on page 187.

INDIA

Level/Age	Hours/Calendar	Language of Instruction	Compulsory Attendance	Exams	Grading System	Curriculum	Cost	Enrollment
Primary Grades 1–5* ages 5 or 6–9 or 10	July–Mar. with a 1-week break for *Diwali* around the end of Oct. (or shorter *Diwali* break if vacation is allowed for Christmas) 7:00 AM–1:00 PM for Grades 1–4 (with 2 short breaks) 11:00 AM–5:00 PM for Grades 5–10 (with 2 short breaks) 200 working days per school year, beginning in different months depending on the region	Mother tongue or regional language (e.g., Bengali, Gujarati, Hindi, Punjabi, Tamil, Urdu) plus English	Yes, enforced at primary level in some, but not all, areas	Every term there are two unit tests: one midterm and one annual (final) exam. The final exam receives the greatest weight and determines whether or not the student will advance to the next grade. All exams are written and closed book, with very few multiple-choice items.	85% + = Excellent 80–85% = Superior 70–80% = Very good 60–70% = Good 50–60% = Satisfactory 40–50% = Average 35–40% = Pass Below 40% = Fail	Languages, mathematics, social sciences, science, health, physical education, and art The teaching of Hindi as a second language is required in most states.	Free, though boys may pay about US$2.00 per year in fees; girls may pay four cents. 16.5% attend tuition-collecting private schools.	82% of primary school age-children are enrolled. 67.9% of pupils reach Grade 5. The average Indian adult has 5.1 years of schooling. 43.6% of primary school students are female. 39% of primary school-age girls are not enrolled.
Middle Grades 6–8* ages 10–12			Yes			Same as above The teaching of English is compulsory from grades 6–10.		No data available
Secondary Grades 9–10 or 12* ages 13–14 or 16			Yes, to age 14	Students take public examinations at the end of Grades 10 and 12 by respective State Boards of Secondary and Higher Secondary Education.		Chemistry, biology; physics, algebra, geometry, calculus (introduced in 11th grade) history; geography, English (required) plus one of the following (Hindi, French, Spanish, German, or Sanskrit) plus the local regional language	Free to 9th grade at least; annual fee varies as noted above.	39.6% of secondary school students are female.
University ages 17+	July – Apr.	English, although private schools, rural universities, and polytechnic institutes may use the local language as the unofficial medium of instruction	No	Oral and written tests at the end of each semester. Homework assignments carry little weight as far as final grade is concerned.	65–100% = First class 50–64% = Second class 40–49% = Third class division Some universities use a marking system based on a grade point average.	Bachelor's, master's, and doctoral degrees plus certificate courses at both undergraduate and graduate levels	US$9 to US$155 per year	10.5% of eligible population is enrolled.

*The term *standard* is used in India instead of *grade* or *level*.

▪ Surface Culture Perspective

CLASSROOMS

- Facilities vary depending on whether the school is in an urban or rural setting and also on whether the urban school is private, public, or semi-private. Rural schools and urban public schools have much in common. There, education is subsidized and only the bare minimum of facilities are available. Moreover, students in such schools receive instruction in the local language rather than in English. Private schools are much better equipped, and the medium of instruction is English, but fees are high. In the semi-private schools, the curriculum and fees are controlled by the government, but the administration has some autonomy. Class size ranges from 40 to 80 students.

- In urban schools, students may sit three to five on a backless bench at tables of about four to ten feet in length. The seating arrangement is sometimes boy-girl-boy, allegedly to prevent boys from mischief. In other settings, boys and girls might be kept separate within a class and grouped according to height. In rural schools students may not have tables and benches but may sit or squat on the floor.

- The teacher's desk and chair sit on a raised platform at the front of the class.

- Maps and posters do not usually adorn the walls of classrooms, although at the primary level there may be alphabet charts and number lines displayed, and at both levels scientific charts and students' artwork may be placed on the walls. Most classrooms have a blackboard and chalk and perhaps a bulletin board where teachers may place announcements or display student work. Many schools are equipped with a health room and health clerk.

- Students and faculty assemble in lines every morning before class to sing patriotic or religious songs and recite the national pledge of allegiance. Once a week the Indian flag is raised, and the students sing the national anthem.

- Instructional technology is generally not available in schools, as electricity is either unreliable or nonexistent in many schools, especially in the countryside. Often when the electricity goes out, the teacher and students will continue the lesson seemingly unaffected by the outage. Schools are not air-conditioned, but ceiling fans may be used to cool the classrooms.

- At the college level, students try to buy their books from older students, siblings, or used bookstores. They may spend no more than US$4–10 per year for all their schoolbooks.

TEACHERS' STATUS

- Teaching as a profession is a revered job, and pre-service training for teachers is excellent, but the financial remuneration is low and depends on the school in which one teaches. Many teachers compensate by giving private lessons (also called *tuitions*). The children of educators are charged only one quarter of the fees required of other college students.

- Teachers are even more highly respected in India than parents, regardless of whether or not they are truly expert in their profession.

TEACHER-STUDENT RELATIONSHIP

- While students hold deep respect for their teachers, they may also fear them. Indian parents instruct their children to obey the teacher at all times. In fact, teachers are accorded the same authority over children as their parents for their role in helping children to achieve academic goals and honor their families.

- At the primary level, teachers may treat students as they would their own children, but once students reach the higher levels of education, this kind of nurturing and warmth diminishes, dramatically in some cases. Students, therefore, do not tend to bring their problems to their teachers.

- Incidents are sometimes reported of college professors who favor students from their own region and penalize others who are from backgrounds that the instructor scorns. Urban teachers may show an obvious preference for students from the city, while leaving rural students at a disadvantage, for example.

- Teachers and parents generally have a good rapport and try to inform each other about the student's performance at school and circumstances at home. In this way, teachers are able to play a vital role in teaching discipline.

TEACHING PRACTICES

- Most classrooms are teacher centered, with students, especially at the primary and secondary levels, relying on rote memorization as the main learning strategy. Teachers rarely use class time for craft projects (such as cutting out paper hearts) to take home to parents.

- Although students sit together at long tables, they are usually not required to engage in any group work. However, a student who completes a problem first can be asked to approach the blackboard and explain the problem to the rest of the class.

- Some teachers adopt a Socratic approach to teaching, asking spontaneous questions during the lecture. At other times, questions are used as a way to determine if a student is paying attention.

- Indian parents may consider a teacher to be caring if he or she assigns masses of homework and is strict in class.
- The government-controlled syllabus and textbooks stay the same over periods of ten or more years, so teachers may become bored with the material, lose enthusiasm for teaching, and stop preparing for class.
- In class teachers follow the prescribed textbook. They use the blackboard to write clarifications and examples, and students carefully record this information in their notebooks. Test content comes directly from the textbook, but blackboard notes can help students understand the reading assignments better.

TEACHERS' DRESS

- Female teachers usually wear *saris,* which consist of a rectangular piece of silk or cotton cloth that is five to six yards in length and wrapped carefully and gracefully around the body. Wrapping style, color, and fabric can reveal a woman's status and age, what she does for a living, where she is from, and what religion she practices. A *choli* or short, fitted blouse, is worn beneath the *sari.*
- Male teachers in the cities often wear Western shirts and pants. In the rural areas, however, they may prefer the cooler and more comfortable traditional garb called *kurtas, lungis, dhotis,* and *pyjamas.*

DISCIPLINE AND CLASS MANAGEMENT

- Teachers tend to be stricter in India than in North America. Frequently, they raise their voices at students in order to punish them in front of their peers. Students expect, and parents rely on, such public reprimands by the teacher to instill in students the rules for propriety.
- Students who disrupt the class or do not pay attention during the lesson may be asked to stand outside the classroom all day and to explain to passersby the reason that they are being punished. Teachers may send a note home to the parents if a child misbehaves in class. Students who arrive late to class could be asked to pay a fine. Severe scoldings are sometimes given for students who look out the window during class.
- Teachers may still use corporal punishment, such as slapping a student on the cheek. The objective of most disciplinary strategies is to embarrass the student in front of peers and to prevent students from getting "big heads." While some teachers resort to corporal punishment and humiliation of students, others use a combination of compassion and firmness to control their students.
- Students are not allowed to eat in class, even at the university (a violation that could warrant a week's suspension). They are expected to maintain good posture throughout class as well.

STUDENTS' CIRCUMSTANCES

- As entrance to certain schools is competitive, prospective students may have to appear for an interview with their parents who might be queried about their ability to help their children with homework and teach them English at home.
- To resolve their child's problems at school, Indian parents may go "straight to the top" as they believe that is where all major decisions are made.
- There is quite a bit of parental pressure placed on their children to succeed in school. They may try to develop a competitive spirit in their children as far as education is concerned by praising the performance of neighbor children or cousins and siblings. On the other hand, it is not uncommon for parents to brag about their children's academic successes with neighbors and relatives. Some parents reprimand their children if they fail to obtain perfect scores on tests and homework assignments, and they invest heavily in their children's education, often accruing large debts in order to support their children's schooling. After so much effort, children feel obligated to pursue careers selected for them by their parents and often sacrifice their own interests so as not to disappoint or bring shame to their parents. Indeed, most children feel that they do not have a choice of profession.
- Parents attend parent-teacher conferences with their children and sign the child's report card in the presence of the teacher. Parents may also be involved in Parent-Teacher Associations (PTAs), and are able to address a teacher's inappropriate actions or decisions via this forum. They might also make donations to the school at PTA meetings so that school facilities can be improved.

STUDENT-STUDENT RELATIONSHIP

- Students move through all grades together even at the college level and, therefore, form close friendships with other members of their cohort. At the university, freshmen learn the ropes of the school through their relationships with "seniors," any student that has completed the first year. The practice of "ragging," a rite of passage not unlike the initiation ceremonies for sorority and fraternity pledges in North America, is now banned in India. Those caught ragging can be suspended, dismissed, or jailed.
- Many Indian students describe their relationship with peers as cooperative but more competitive as they reach the higher levels, where each student tries his or her best to excel beyond the rest of the class. Students frequently study in groups and share purloined test information when available, but many prefer to study independently.

- Boys may compete against girls in class by refusing to share lecture notes. Boys in some schools try to prevent a girl from becoming the top student of the class and vice versa. Competition in sports is also common.
- Students do not develop publicly romantic relationships with the opposite sex as this is taboo.

STUDENTS' LEARNING PRACTICES

- Taking responsibility for one's own learning is not a common concept in India. Instead, students depend heavily on the teacher to provide information and then clarify material that is then carefully memorized for later testing. The development of critical thinking skills is not emphasized nor is a variety of perspectives or thinking "outside the box" encouraged. Even at the college level, students are not expected to select their own courses, with the exception of a handful of electives.

STUDENTS' DRESS

- Up until the 12th standard (grade), Indian students are required to wear uniforms. Boys wear shirts and shorts of the same color, and the girls' uniform consists of a pinafore and cotton blouse. Once they reach 9th standard, boys may wear long pants and girls a *churidhar*. Girls do not wear *saris* until they are older.
- Male Sikh students may wear a turban even during physical education class. They do not cut their hair but wrap it up in a knot at the top of the head.
- The *bindi* (or *pottu* in Tamil), is a small dot placed between the eyebrows of a woman, and represents the third eye, or the intellect. Widows are prohibited from wearing the *bindi,* but other women would not be seen in public without it. For Indian immigrants, it is a sacrifice not to wear the *bindi*.

GIFTS FOR THE TEACHER

- Students bring chocolates or some other kind of candy to school on their birthdays and share it with their teacher and classmates.
- Favorite teachers may receive an end-of-year gift from students in the form of a greeting card or perhaps fruit or candy, but the gift will not be opened in the presence of the gift giver.
- Gifts are frequently wrapped in green, yellow, or red paper, which are considered lucky colors, but black or white wrapping paper is inappropriate.

Exams

- End-of-term grades are published in the newspaper and, in the cities, may be posted on the Internet. In either case, the student's identification number is used rather than his or her name.

- Students are very test-conscious, largely because so much depends on grades and also because exams tend to be very difficult. Teachers do not offer students review questions prior to an exam but will tell them which chapters the test will cover. If items from a previous year's exam will appear on the pending exam, teachers may encourage students to read the answers so that they will have a better chance of obtaining a passing grade.

- A typical college-level test would consist of 20 two-point short-answer questions and six ten-point essay questions.

- At the end of the school year, all the students within a college will be ranked according to their performance. Out of a class of 15,000 students, those who rank from 1st to 40th place are given special recognition.

- Exams are given quarterly, at the half-year mark, and at the end of the year. Students who have been absent from class more than 75 percent of the time will not be allowed to sit for exams; as a result, class attendance is high in Indian schools. At the end of the school year, students get at least 10–15 days to prepare for final exams.

Nonverbal Communication

- Students stand to greet the teacher when he or she enters the room, must wait for the teacher to tell them to be seated, and stand again at the end of class when he or she leaves. Some professors at the college level insist that students stop and bow to them if they happen to meet in public.

- The Indian gesture to indicate "yes" is more of a head wagging from side to side (toward the shoulders) rather than the nodding up and down as seen in the United States. The latter head movement is interpreted as "no" in India. Sometimes a quick toss of the head in a backward motion is another indication of agreement.

- Indians do not greet each other by kissing, shaking hands, or touching in any way. As the soul is thought to reside in the head, it is inappropriate to touch even a child on the top of the head. Traditional Indians may one greet one another by pressing both palms together (as in prayer) just below the chin, bowing slightly, and saying *namaste*. ("I bow to the divine in you.") A traditional Indian man will never shake hands with an Indian woman.

- Although there are many sexual symbols throughout Indian culture, young people tend to be more modest than their North American counterparts, observing a strong sense of propriety that prevents them from displaying physical affection and intimacy in public.

- To indicate that one is deeply sorry for an offense, an Indian may grab his or her ears.
- It is considered impolite to pass or accept food with the left hand, which is supposed to be used for hygienic purposes and is therefore unclean. Indians may wash their hands both before and after a meal as many do not use eating utensils. Feet, too, are considered unclean, so people remove their shoes when they enter a home. Some professors insist that students take their shoes off before entering their offices. One person's feet should never touch another's; neither should they be pointed at another person.
- The North American custom of waving someone over by placing the palm up and wiggling the index finger backward and forward is considered rude in India. Instead, people turn the palm down and make a scooping motion. They will also point with their chins instead of pointing with the index finger, a gesture that is regarded as rude.
- It is considered aggressive to stand with one's hands on one's hips.
- It is rude to whistle or wink at another person.
- Indians tend to respect punctuality.
- It is polite to initially refuse offers of food or beverages, but a guest is expected to accept eventually. Complete refusal is a complete insult.

FORMS OF ADDRESS

- Teachers must be addressed as Teacher, Sir, or Madam.
- Hindu names consist of the father's initial followed by a given name. *V. Thiruselvan* would therefore be *Thiruselvan, son of V.* (perhaps Virat). His students would call him Mr. Thiruselvan. When an Indian woman marries, she takes on her husband's name as her last name and drops the father's initial. So, when *S. Kamala* (daughter of S. or Sanjay) marries *V. Thiruselvan*, she becomes Mrs. Kamala Thiruselvan.
- Muslim male names consist of a given name plus *bin* meaning "son of" plus the father's name. Djaffer bin Nasser is thus Djaffer, son of Nasser, and his students will call him Mr. Djaffer. Muslim female names consist of the woman's given name plus *binti* meaning "daughter of" plus the father's name. Kaziha binti Mohamed is thus Kaziha, daughter of Mohamed. Her students should call her Miss or Mrs. Kaziha. *Haji* (for a man) or *Hajjah* (for a woman) is a title used for those who have visited Mecca.
- Sikh names consist of the given name plus *Singh* for men or *Kaur* for women. Their students will call them Mr., Miss, Mrs., or Professor plus given name. A male teacher whose first name is Agampreet becomes Mr. Agampreet Singh, whereas a female teacher whose first name is Jaipal is Miss Jaipal Kaur.

APPROPRIATE TOPICS

- Topics that would be considered insensitive in a public conversation or one involving strangers include one's personal life, poverty in India, military expenditures, and India's foreign debt.
- Indians rarely use the word "no." Instead they may indicate it by indirect means, such as "I'll try."
- It is not necessary to say "thank you" after a meal since doing so may imply that it is a form of payment.
- Indian students may be offended if their North American teachers assume they are Hindu and speak Hindi. It is important to bear in mind that India is very diverse culturally and linguistically and that people from different areas of the country may be fiercely proud of their unique heritage.
- It is insulting to offer a Sikh person cigarettes or beef. Hindus refrain from eating beef as well, and Muslims will not eat pork.

OUTSIDE OF CLASS

- Students receive moderate to heavy homework assignments, even at the lowest levels, and it is not unusual for children to spend several hours every day on homework. Some attribute the unremarkable performance of Indian students in sports to excessive homework and school pressure that tends to drain them of energy and time so they do not get to excel in extracurricular activities.
- Homework may consist of reading and writing assignments as well as working out mathematical problems or completing worksheets. Internet or library research is still not common nor are group projects. Parents of younger children help with homework, a practice that decreases as the child progresses through the grades. Students then assume more responsibility for completing homework and studying. They may also begin taking private lessons to reinforce their academic performance.
- Some students may learn to do housework, gardening, simple cooking, cutting up vegetables, making origami figures and various crafts outside of class, but such activities compel students to sacrifice their academic studies and decrease the chances of them getting into a good college.
- When they are not studying, students enjoy field hockey, tennis, cricket, Indian games such as *kabaddi* (a combination of rugby and wrestling) and *kho-kho* (team tag), and going to movies together.
- Extracurricular school activities may include meditation and prayer; debate and speech contests; and music, drama, and dance programs. Some schools have student-written newspapers.

◼ Potential Adjustment Challenges

PROBLEMS/SOLUTIONS

Problem

You could have bowled me over with a feather today when the mother of one of my Indian students suggested that I should "beat" her child for misbehaving in class. Is this what the child expects, too?

Solution

It's possible. Indian children may be disruptive or indifferent if they perceive that there is a lack of discipline in class. They expect teachers to be severe and to scold them. Parents of such children sometimes advise teachers to use corporal punishment to reinforce their authority and correct the situation.

Problem

The parents of one of my Indian students paid me a visit today. Their objective was to persuade me to nominate their child for our school's gifted program. The problem is that while I think the child is intelligent and hard working, she isn't necessarily exceptional.

Solution

It is not unusual for Indian parents to perceive that their children's adopted educational system is inferior to the one in which they were schooled and not challenging enough, and so they may attempt to fill the gaps at home by tutoring their children in British literature and classical studies to compensate for the apparent lack of attention to these areas of knowledge. Indian students in North American primary and secondary schools may also be compelled by their parents to undergo several hours per day of academic coaching by a private tutor in addition to completing homework assignments.

Problem

Keya is one of the best students I've ever had, but she obsesses over her grades. For example, she received a 98 on a quiz yesterday, but today she was in tears as she insisted that she deserved the chance to retake the test to see if she could get a perfect score.

Solution

Indian students experience great concern over the possibility of disappointing or shaming their families. Often their parents have gone to great expense and sometimes incurred debts in order to provide a high-quality education for their children. Even good students may be stressed by the pressure to perform. This anxiety can turn into alienation or rebelliousness among less successful students.

Laos

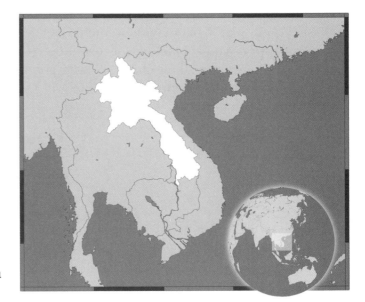

 **LAOS** *Upclose*

Capital: Vientiane

Population: 6,368,481 (June 2006)

Size: 236,800 sq. km. (91,429 sq. mi.) (somewhat larger than Utah)

Location: Southeast Asia, bordered on the west by Thailand, on the north by Burma and China, on the east by Vietnam, and on the south by Cambodia

Climate: tropical monsoon with a rainy summers and dry winters

Terrain: mountainous with high plateaus and lowlands in the west

Monetary Unit: kip (10,424 per U.S. dollar) (June 2006)

Religion: Buddhist 60%, animist and other 40% (including various Christian denominations 1.5%)

Language(s): Lao (official), French, English, and various ethnic languages

Literacy Rate: total population 66.4%; men 77.4%; women 55.5% (2002)

Ethnicity: Lao Loum 68%, Lao Theung 22%, Lao Soung (including the Hmong and the Yao) 9%, ethnic Vietnamese/Chinese 1%

Per Capita Income: US$320 (2002)

Population Distribution: 21% urban; 79% rural (2003)

Population below Poverty Line: 34% (2002)

Life Expectancy: total population 55.5 years; men 53.5 years; women 57.6 years (2006)

Government: Communist state

January 1	New Year's Day	August 13	Lao Isara
January 6	Pathet Lao Day		(Day of the free Laos)
January 20	Army Day	August 23	Liberation Day
March 8	Women's Day	October 12	Freedom from France Day
March 22	Lao People's Party Day	December 2	National Day
April 15–17	Lao New Year		
May 1	International Labor Day		
June 1	Children's Day		

PUBLIC HOLIDAYS

Personal Perspective

It is unfortunate that many Americans still refuse to understand us, the Hmong, and the struggles we endured. They must realize that we didn't come to America for economic reasons. We came to America because we had only two choices: go to a third-world country or go back to Laos and possibly face persecution. Which would you choose, especially when you had just fought with the Communists for the last ten years?

Many Americans thought we knew where we were heading for when we chose to come to America. In fact, we didn't know what America was. All we ever heard was America had giant hairy demons that ate people, which was the reason why many Hmong refused to leave their refugee camps in Thailand, so they wouldn't be fed to the hairy demons.

I don't want to go through explaining why the Hmong people relied on welfare as soon as we arrived in United States. I mean as soon as in "the very next day." Just imagine yourself in a country which you knew nothing about nor spoke its language, and you had just crossed the twilight zone into a 20th-century society from a 17th-century culture, and you had nine children plus you and your spouse. What would you do?

—Yang (2001)

Historical Perspective

IMMIGRATION TO THE UNITED STATES

Note: This chapter focuses almost exclusively on the Hmong population that has immigrated to North America. Other ethnic groups from Laos have arrived as well, but the Hmong represent by far the largest group, with some 2 million estimated to have settled in the United States since 1975.

The story of Hmong immigration is one of waves of refugees. The first group fled Laos for refugee camps in Thailand in 1975 as the Vietnam War ended. Hmong soldiers who had participated as members of the U.S. Secret Army in Laos faced the threat of death or torture at the hands of the new government, and their families lived in fear of persecution as well. Thousands died as they attempted to cross the Mekong River into Thailand or were killed by government troops before they could reach safety. There are accounts as well of babies dying from opium overdose as parents sought to quiet their children while hiding from enemy soldiers. In 1976, 750 Hmong became the first refugees admitted to the United States under the Indochina Migration and Refugee Assistance Act of 1975.

Continued arrests, abductions, and killings of former collaborators with the United States combined with a massive drought and the sacrifices related to the newly established collective farming structure led to the flight of thousands of Hmong and other Laotians from Laos from 1978 to 1982. To accommodate the 75,000 refugees (two-thirds of them Hmong highlanders) who were awaiting resettlement, 21 refugee camps were built in Thailand. In 1979 some 10,000 refugees left the camps for the United States. In 1980, approximately 27,000 were resettled in the United States. This number fell to 5,000 in 1981 and continued to decline until 1988 when more than 10,000 Hmong refugees were admitted to the United States. From 1989 to 1994, the United States welcomed more than 5,000 Hmong refugees a year. All tolled, sources report that nearly 10 percent of the Laotian population (approximately 360,000 people) left the country between 1975 and 1992. Approximately 200,000 Hmong remain in the highlands of northern Laos.

The most recent wave of Hmong immigration took place as a result of a 2003 U.S. State Department decision to admit 15,000 Hmong from the Wat Thamkrabok refugee camp in Thailand. By this time the other large refugee camps in Thailand had long been closed down, and efforts were under way to return the refugees to Laos, as they held no official status in Thailand. More than half of the Wat Thamkrabok refugees are under the age of 15 and were born in the camp. Many camp teenagers are married and have begun to produce a second generation of refugee camp residents. Unlike the first waves of refugees, the most recent are literate in Hmong and Thai and may have studied some English. They continue to settle in Minnesota, California, and Wisconsin where previous groups of Hmong had established successful communities. The 2000 U.S. Census reported that more than 186,000 Hmong now live in the United States. The Hmong community in the United States has overcome many difficulties since the 1970s. A smaller percentage is in need of welfare benefits and a larger percentage is employed and graduating from high school.

HISTORICAL SYNOPSIS

The country of Laos did not exist until the French created it as a colony in 1897. From the 14th century to the end of the 17th century, it had been part of the Lan Xang kingdom along with Cambodia, Thailand, and Vietnam. In the 18th and 19th centuries, the territory was subject to numerous invasions by its neighbors, bringing the kingdom to an end and obliging its inhabitants in 1885 to turn to Siam (now Thailand) for protection. By 1893 the French had pushed into the territory, expanding its rule over Indochina.

Laos gained its independence from France in 1953 and was governed by a monarchy, the Royal Lao Government, that had been in existence for nearly six centuries. As the Vietnam War escalated next door, the United States began to bomb Vietnamese training camps in Laos and to attack the resistance forces of the increasingly powerful Communist Pathet Lao, opponents of the monarchy. As Laos was officially a neutral country, the anti-Communist offensive in Laos became known as the U.S. Secret War.

The CIA also enlisted Hmong peasants, who had previously led peaceful agrarian lives, in its efforts to repel the Communists and prevent the extension of the Ho Chi Minh Trail into Laos. The Hmong fought heroically. By 1974 with the departure of U.S. troops from Laos, some 30,000–40,000 Hmong had perished, and the Communist Pathet Lao followed the evacuation with the creation of the Lao People's Democratic Republic, nationalization of Laos's industries, collectivization of farms, and a declaration that Hmong collaborators were to be "wiped out."

In 1986 Laos gradually began to embrace a return to private enterprise and more liberal social policies and with surprising success. Nevertheless, it remains a very poor country whose transit, communication, and electrification systems are no more than basic. Nearly 80 percent of Laotians rely on subsistence farming.

Deep Culture Perspective

DEEP CULTURE BELIEFS

- The Laotian population is dominated by the *Lao Loum* (low-country Lao), which is further subdivided into a number of ethnic groups speaking mutually intelligible varieties of the *Tai-Kadai* language family. The mid-country Lao, or *Lao Theung,* make up approximately one-quarter of the total Laotian population and are more ethnically, culturally, and linguistically different from their low- and high-country compatriots. A mere 10 percent of Laotians are *Lao Sung,* or high-country Lao. This group's ancestors came to Laos from the north (primarily Burma and China). As with the *Lao Loum* and the *Lao Theung,* the *Lao Sung* are composed of different ethnic groups, but the Hmong make up the majority of highlanders. Their society is comprised of the White Hmong, Striped Hmong, and Green (or Blue) Hmong, groups differentiated not only by the color or pattern of traditional costume but by mutually intelligible language variety.
- The Hmong identify themselves by family clan, of which there are some 15 overall. Thus, when a child is born, he or she takes the name of the father's clan. When a Hmong woman marries, she assumes the clan name of her husband. Regardless of the physical distance or personal familiarity among clan members, they view themselves as belonging to the same family and being responsible for one another economically and socially.
- Traditional Hmong live together in extended family groups that typically consist of grandparents, parents, children, and married sons and their families with the average family size ranging from 10 to 20. Family size today is decreasing; modern Hmong families may include parents, children, and the family of one married son. While establishing separate households, family members may still live very close to one another.

- Arranged marriages are common among the Hmong, and the boy's family generally pays a "bride price." Frequently, the girl is "abducted" (often willingly) by the boy and brought to his parents' household, compelling the girl's family to accept the terms of a reduced bride price. As bride price has been abandoned or minimized in many communities since the 1980s, marriages among teenagers have become more common whereas in more traditional times young men were unable to accumulate the bride price until they reached their mid-20s. They would often marry girls as young as 14 years old. Bride price also used to limit the number of wives that a man could support. Today polygamy is practiced by only 10 percent of Hmong in Laos and Thailand.

- Hmong men and women tend to adhere to roles ascribed to them by tradition. Women cook, clean, care for children, look after chickens and pigs, grind corn, husk rice, and weed fields while their husbands are responsible for tending cattle and horses, felling trees and burning brush for swidden (slash and burn) agriculture, and preparing the soil for planting. Planting, harvesting, and threshing tasks are shared by men and women. Men and elders are regarded with greater esteem than women, and wives may experience the additional burden of getting along with a demanding mother-in-law.

- Up until the 1970s, most Hmong in Laos used to move from place to place approximately every five years, or when the soil's nutrients had been exhausted. Instead of allowing fields to lie fallow for a year or more, Hmong farmers would clear a small plot of land by burning the trees and brush that grow on it and plant crops season after season until an adequate harvest could no longer be derived from the land.

- Traditional Hmong homes in the uplands of Laos are generally one-room structures with a cooking area at one end of the house and sleeping quarters at the other end. The floor is usually packed dirt, and furniture is limited to low stools, a low dining table, and low beds or benches for sleeping. One wall is normally dedicated as a shrine for the worship of ancestors, who are believed to protect the living and intercede on their behalf with ancient ancestors. Sacrifices of a chicken, rice, or wine may be combined with annual worship rituals or special occasions such as weddings to bring favorable conditions to the household and its residents.

- Animism, the belief that spirits reside in certain objects and places, is practiced by traditional Hmong. Spirits are often thought to act on people when offended by causing illness or misfortune, circumstances that may be reversed through the aid of a shaman who diagnoses the illness and administers treatments. This is normally done by appealing to the spirits to take pity on the afflicted while the shaman is in a trancelike state in which he rides to the sky spirits on a magical horse. Shamans are also thought to be able to lift curses imposed by individuals carrying a grudge. One of the benefits of the observance of animism is the Hmong's respect for animals and nature, leading them to strive to live in harmony with both.

- One of the beliefs often held by non-Christian Hmong is that at birth each individual possesses 12 souls, which may cause ill health (aches, depression, mental illness) if one or more are lost. Among the ways to lose a soul are fright caused by a sudden loud noise, fear, grief, evil spirits, and migration to another body due to unhappiness. Traditional Hmong believe that the souls of persons who die suddenly or in childbirth return as evil spirits.

- Wealth may distinguish one family from another. It may be derived from affiliation with a certain affluent clan as well as from diligence, consistently favorable weather conditions, and freedom from disease of clan members and farm animals. Opium production has been outlawed by the Laotian government, but farmers still find it to be an important cash crop whose profits may be turned into silver bars and saved for future emergencies.

- Hmong families tend to be less community centered than those in other Laotian ethnic groups. The family household takes precedence over the village and its inhabitants such that when swidden farming practices produce insufficient crop yields, single families (or small groups of families), rather than the entire village, may relocate. Within villages, several households may organize temporarily to bring in a harvest or build a house, but interfamily collaboration is more common. Nevertheless, it cannot be said that Hmong are individualistic. One's actions are always considered to have an effect on the group, and the benefits of close group membership are clear.

PROVERBS

- He who eats mushrooms must look at the stems. He who chooses a wife must look at her parents.

- When you cross a river, take off your sandals. When you immigrate to another country, take off your hat.

- Fish swim in water, birds fly in air, Hmong live on mountains.

- The mouth tastes food. The heart tastes words.

- Nine fireplaces are not as bright as the sun. Nine daughters are not worth as much as one son.

- One stick cannot cook a meal or build a fence.

- After the rainstorm, the sun is bright and the sky clears.

- It only takes one mistake to be a bad person, but it takes a lifetime to be a good person.

- Tomorrow is longer than yesterday.

- To be with a family is to be happy. To be without a family is to be lost.

FOLK TALE

Once upon a time a huge eagle, the size of 11 houses, would swoop down on a certain village and devour as many of its inhabitants as it could catch. He would appear every time a villager would grind corn or husk rice in his yard. After almost all of the village residents had been killed and consumed by the eagle, the remaining villagers gathered together to make a sacrifice to the spirits of the sky and the spirit of the region. They begged for mercy, to which the sky spirits responded that they would soon send a rescuer. As they prepared to await its arrival, the villagers took the king's daughter and hid her in a huge drum so that she would outlive the rest of them should no rescuer arrive.

When finally the rescuer arrived he could find no one in the village, for all had perished except the king's daughter whom he found when he banged on the large drum at the doorstep of the king's house. "Don't be afraid," said the rescuer. "I have come to kill the eagle." Together they began to spread grains of rice in a large bamboo tray to attract the eagle. No sooner had they done this than the eagle began to descend from above, but the man was quick with his bow and arrow and shot the eagle dead before it had time to take another life.

When the man slit the eagle's belly with his saber, he discovered that the eagle was full of human bones. Over many long days the rescuer carefully and tirelessly reconnected the bones, putting the people back together as they had been. After nine days and nights, he began to lose his concentration and reconnected the bones in a haphazard fashion. That is why, to this day, some people are left-handed and others are right-handed.

Administrative Perspective

OFFICIAL EDUCATIONAL POLICY

During colonial days, education in Laos followed the traditional French curriculum, though it was largely inaccessible to those living outside major towns. Hmong loyalty to the Royal Lao Government and the central role they played in combat on behalf of the United States was rewarded by the construction of some 300 primary schools, nine middle schools, two high schools, and a teacher preparation institute in northern Laos. The project was funded by the U.S. Agency for International Development.

After independence the Lao People's Democratic Republic (LPDR) replaced the former French curriculum with a Lao curriculum, but education was still severely underfunded and limited to cities and large towns, leaving families in the countryside no option but to send no more than one child away to a school with boarding facilities.

A campaign to increase adult literacy was taken up by the government in the early 1980s, resulting in a dramatic increase in the literacy rate among Laotians. By 1985, 92 percent of Laotian men between the ages of 15 and 45 and 76 percent of women in the same age group had acquired basic reading and writing skills. However, literacy skills tended to erode in an environment in which books, magazines, and newspapers were a rarity.

An effort to reform the education system was launched in 1986 and included plans to make the curriculum more practical, to emphasize science, to build a school in virtually every village, to train more teachers from the country's ethnic minorities, and to involve communities in implementation of educational projects. Through this plan the LPDR government hoped to ensure universal compulsory education through the end of primary school.

Lack of qualified teachers, overcrowded classrooms, limited budget allocations, and the concomitant dearth of teaching materials have hampered implementation of the reforms and resulted in dismal primary school completion rates. By some estimates, children spent an average of 12 years to finish 5 years of primary school. Secondary schools are much less prevalent in the countryside than in urban areas due in large part to the flight of Laos's professional class to Thailand after the Vietnam War. Today some 4,000 villages still have no primary school. Nevertheless, overall primary school enrollment nearly doubled from 1976 to 1992. There was much less success in enrolling *Lao Sung* children due to communication and cultural barriers. Members of ethnic minorities often do not speak the national language, Lao, and until recently may not have had a written language. *Lao Sung* girls are not encouraged to study, and they are greatly underrepresented in schools.

Those who escaped to refugee camps in Thailand have been able to take advantage of basic vocational, native literacy, and English language training programs in the camps. Children may attend English classes in the camps as well, but only about 25 percent can afford to attend the more established and better-equipped Thai schools. Some 25–35 percent of children who arrive in the United States from refugee camps have no formal educational experience.

EDUCATION AT A GLANCE

See the Education at a Glance table on page 206.

LAOS

Level/Age	Hours/Calendar	Language of Instruction	Compulsory Attendance	Exams	Grading System	Curriculum	Cost	Enrollment
Pre-primary Nursery/crèche ages 2 mos–2 years; Kindergarten ages 3–5 years		Lao	No	None	None	No data available	Most nursery schools and kindergartens are privately owned and operated; fees vary.	Due to the expense, most Laotian children cannot attend at this level.
Primary Grades 1–5 ages 6–11			Yes; 4,000 villages in mountainous region have no primary schools.	Students receive the primary school certificate upon successful completion of primary school.		Lao language, mathematics, the world around us, music, art, handicrafts, physical education		60% of Laotians have no schooling. 34% of schools offer instruction up to Grade 5. 43% of primary school students are female.
Lower secondary Grades 6–8 ages 11–14	Sept. – July long vacation July–Aug. By law, students are to receive 30 hours of instruction per week.	Lao (also French and English in some private schools)	Yes	Final exams in 5 subject areas at the end of each year. Students receive the lower secondary school diploma upon successful completion of lower secondary school.	0–10 grading scale Highest: 10 Pass/fail level: 5 Lowest: 0	Lao language, foreign language, mathematics, technology, social science, natural science, physical education, art	US$13–14 per year per child (public school)	School life expectancy for girls is 7.4 years. School life expectancy for boys is 9.3 years.
Upper secondary Grades 9–11 ages 14–17			Yes, up to age 16	Final exams in 5 subject areas at the end of each year. Students receive the upper secondary school diploma that, in addition to 5 pass grades in math and physics or chemistry, is required for admission to university; some institutions also require a national entrance exam.		Lao language, mathematics, technology, history, geography, civics, chemistry, physics, biology, physical education		School life expectancy for all children is 8.3 years (although lower for the *Lao Sung*). 37% of upper secondary students are female.
University, technical school, or higher technical college ages 17+; Bachelor's degree requires 5–7 years of study.		Lao, with English used for special evening programs	No	A degree with honors is awarded to students with an A in the final year project. Roughly 7% of those who sit for the national entrance exam are admitted to university. Exams by course (no overall exam at end of year)		Due to poor articulation between secondary school and university, bachelor degree students spend 2 years at a School of Foundation Studies (general education) before entering specialized studies. Each student must complete 8–10 weeks of practical training to graduate.	No tuition charged at public universities. Board is allocated on a quota basis. US$100–200 per semester (private English medium schools)	2% of students progress beyond secondary school. 17% of university students are female.

Surface Culture Perspective

CLASSROOMS

- Schools in the Laotian countryside are often basic and in poor repair. They may be made of bamboo and thatch over an earthen floor and sparsely furnished. Books, paper, pencils, blackboards, desks, and other teaching supplies are in short supply. Reading material of any kind outside of school, especially current newspapers, is also hard to come by. Primary schools often offer no more than two or three grade levels, and many are only open for two to three hours per day because teachers need to dedicate part of their day to farming in order to survive.

- Minimal schooling has been available in the refugee camps in Thailand. Some have been paid for by religious organizations but erected by the Hmong camp residents. Wooden tables and benches seating three students each are arranged in rows. A crude blackboard may hang on one of the walls, but there is little or no decoration of the space. Electricity may be available but is unreliable, one of the reasons why instructional technology is virtually absent. For the most part, books are the same ones used by the teachers when they were children. Camp schools offer instruction in Hmong, and classes in English are extremely popular. In fact, it is not uncommon for individuals to stand outside classroom windows to glean what they can from the lessons going on indoors. In cases where classes are filled to capacity or the fees are prohibitive, literate Hmong parents may teach their children to read at home. Most children, however, end up with very little formal education and many with none at all.

- Thai schools surrounding the refugee camps allow Hmong children to attend school up to Grade 9, and instruction is delivered in Thai. Parents who have sufficient income from family abroad or from selling vegetables or clothing in the market may be able afford the tuition at the Thai schools, but this option is not available for the vast majority of camp children.

TEACHERS' STATUS

- Prospective primary school teachers in Laos receive three years of teacher preparation following completion of the 8th grade or one year of teacher training if they have successfully completed the 11th grade. Approximately 33 percent of primary level teachers have not received any formal teacher preparation.

- To teach at the lower end of secondary education in Laos, individuals must have completed high school as well as a three-year teacher preparation program. Those who hope to teach in the upper levels of secondary school receive five years of training following high school graduation.

- The teachers in the refugee camps in Thailand are virtually all volunteers, and many are self-taught. The average salary for teachers in Laos is US$12 per month, an insufficient base that compels them to farm or moonlight in order to make ends meet. Many who are sent to the countryside not only face very low salaries but are often not paid for months on end, live in impoverished conditions, lack the resources they need to be effective, and work with students who have little genuine motivation to work hard and stay in school.

TEACHER-STUDENT RELATIONSHIP

- Hmong students and their parents often feel uncomfortable when consulted by the teacher for their ideas or opinions about pedagogical decisions such as what topics to study and which types of projects to attempt. Teachers are regarded as the only experts in such matters, while students and their parents are believed to have no authority to "interfere" in teachers' affairs. Teachers are so highly venerated, in fact, that students may not even approach them for assistance but prefer to turn to classmates before "bothering" the teacher.
- Hmong students value teachers who convey genuine concern for their students' progress, affection for their students as individuals, respect for the difficult challenges they face as learners, and sincere encouragement throughout the learning process. They believe as well that they will be less likely to learn if the bond with their teacher is not warm and strong. Students claim that teachers who assign homework are demonstrating their commitment to their students.
- Teachers will normally consult the head of the household, usually the eldest male of the family, if there is a problem with a child.

TEACHING PRACTICES

- Hmong teachers generally do not offer compliments to individual students in class, although the entire group may be praised. Referred praise may also be observed; that is, the teacher will compliment a student when speaking to a colleague or another student. Good grades are thought to be a better indicator of academic success than praise.
- Children and parents expect teachers to correct errors and to be explicit in explaining why an answer is incorrect. When students fail to grasp a concept or get low grades, the teacher will reteach the material.
- The ability to speak clearly and eloquently before others is considered a sign of a good education. Memorization and recitation of long texts is thus a common practice in classrooms, and students may be called on to perform a recitation if visitors arrive.

TEACHERS' DRESS

- Female teachers usually wear a brightly colored and intricately patterned long sarong-type skirt that falls anywhere from the ankle to the calf. A cotton shirt with short sleeves accompanies the skirt.
- Male teachers favor long pants, sometimes tied at the waist by a embroidered belt, plus a cotton dress or polo shirt.
- Both men and women wear sandals.

DISCIPLINE AND CLASS MANAGEMENT

- Corporal punishment is used both at home and at school to discourage future misbehavior, to correct a wrong, and to ensure obedience. The Lao have a saying: "If you love your cows, tie them up. If you love your children, beat them up."
- Students tend to be courteous and respectful toward their teachers and classmates. Social relationships may be more valued than academic success.
- Older children serve as role models for younger children.
- Competition is viewed in the negative light of conflict, aggression, or jealousy.
- Love and praise are generally not expressed verbally.
- Parents and teachers try to instill the virtue of self-discipline in children.
- Public punishment is administered only under exceptional circumstances since saving face is an extremely sensitive cultural issue. It is shameful both to lose face and to cause another to lose face.

STUDENTS' CIRCUMSTANCES

- Hmong immigrant children are often poorer and more culturally estranged from other refugee children, limiting the kind of resources and social integration that might otherwise promote better learning. While their living conditions will likely have improved considerably since departing the Thai refugee camps, they still often live in small, overcrowded apartments, generally have no privacy, and are frequently expected to look after younger siblings and do household chores.
- Life in the refugee camps has been described as harsh. The Hmong report frequent instances of taunting, beating, and rape by the Thai soldiers that surround the compound. There is often stench in the air from rotting garbage and open sewers, and the ground is dusty during dry months and muddy during the rainy season. Large families live cramped in shacks constructed of corrugated metal, and most have no electricity or running water. Car batteries may be used to power the rare television or computer. Aside from the profits received from sale of embroidery

or carved knives shipped to Hmong communities in the United States, most camp residents have no source of income. Camp kiosks are usually owned and operated by Thai merchants, and few Hmong have permission to leave the camp to tend the fields of Thai farmers.

- While Hmong parents place a high premium on their children's education, they themselves tend to have little to no formal schooling experience, and their literacy skills are apt to be minimal. Only 8–10 percent of Hmong parents are reported to have spent any time in school before fleeing from Laos, and, therefore, may be limited in the amount of assistance they can offer their children and in their understanding of the tasks and challenges that their children undertake in school. Nonetheless, they are reported to push both sons and daughters to excel academically. From their perspective, education renders boys more capable of supporting families; girls may be thought to be more marriageable if they have an education.

- Parental authority often erodes in households in which adults and children acculturate at dramatically different rates. Children may feel caught between the traditional world of their parents and the conflicting values of their school environment. The resulting tension can spark more frequent and intense episodes of corporal punishment.

- Hmong children are taught that hard work is one of the most important virtues. However, they may equate hard work more with physical labor than with intellectual effort. Thus, the former is seen as active and arduous while the latter is viewed as passive and easy. Poor school performance can imply that a student is also unable to apply himself or herself physically.

- Nearly 50 percent of recent arrivals from the Thamkrabok camp are 14 years of age or younger. Less than one quarter have attended Thai schools near Thamkrabok. School attendance is not required for residents of the refugee camps. Overall, some 37 percent of girls and 20 percent of boys have no formal education at all, although they may have received up to six months of English instruction as part of their cultural preparation for immigration to the United States.

STUDENT-STUDENT RELATIONSHIP

- Hmong culture is highly group oriented regardless of the setting. Hmong students, therefore, form strong bonds with classmates, enjoy working collaboratively on exercises and homework, check on each other's accuracy and achievement, and come to the aid of peers who appear to be foundering or ask for help from quicker learners. They often play the role of teacher with each other using pedagogical techniques such as correction, critique, and repetition. However, they tend to refrain from explaining and leading each other inductively with discovery strategies. When one person asks for another's assistance, it is considered rude not to offer exactly what was requested. Thus, a direct answer, rather than an explanation, is usually preferred.

- Both weak and strong students gain a sense of self-confidence from working alongside others. During exams students continue to assist one another regardless of the admonitions of U.S. teachers.
- Hmong students tend to be conscious of one another's mental and emotional state by reading their nonverbal behavior such as a quizzical look, laughing at a mistake, and looking over a classmate's shoulder.

STUDENTS' LEARNING PRACTICES

- Tests of Hmong learners have often reported them to have a preference for visual learning. That is to say, they benefit from demonstrations, the teacher's facial expression, diagrams, illustrations, overhead transparencies, videos, handouts, and many other devices that may visually reinforce aural messages. Imagery is also often used as strategy for remembering academic information. For example, the similarities between objects and scenes from home (mountains, animals, utensils, etc.) and letters or words are used to aid memory as are gestures and movement. Hmong students generally benefit from note taking, highlighting, and color coding.
- Hmong students may be field sensitive, meaning that they may approach tasks from a holistic perspective rather than analyzing the component parts. In addition, field-sensitive learners tend to be more affected by the teacher's demeanor, are extrinsically motivated and less autonomous than field-independent students, and regard learning as more personal than their field-independent counterparts.
- North American teachers have observed that many Hmong students appreciate instructions that are exact and clear. This may lead them to consult with one another after the instructor has assigned an activity, including a test, and may use more class time than expected to clarify instructions and test items both before and during an exam. "What does this question mean" and "Could you give me an example" are common queries and may indicate the Hmong students' preference for learning from observing.
- In general, Hmong children are taught to be humble and to refrain from placing themselves above or outside the group. They are, thus, reticent about speaking in class whether responding to a direct question by the teacher or volunteering an answer or opinion, even if they know the correct answer or have an interesting opinion. Responses to teachers' questions are typically prefaced by remarks such as, ""I don't know, but..." or "I don't think my answer is very good" and even "I'm embarrassed to say this, but...." In addition to avoiding the label of being a show-off, students often attempt to save face by refraining from speaking out in class and potentially making a mistake or appearing foolish to their classmates. It has been suggested that adult male students are more uneasy in this respect than are adult females.

- Hmong students can often be observed to practice their English by reading aloud. They subvocalize during independent reading sessions and frequently read aloud what they are writing during composition tasks, when called to the board, and when taking notes during a lecture. Reading aloud in pairs is also thought to be an effective learning strategy.

STUDENTS' DRESS

- Female students in Laos wear brightly colored wraparound skirts with hems that fall between the calves and ankles. Male students wear long pants, which are typically black or dark blue. Both female and male students wear short-sleeved white cotton shirts.
- The Thai school uniform typically consists of a short-sleeved white cotton shirt, blue pants or skirt, white socks, and black shoes. In some schools the boys and girls wear ties, the school pin, and special school belt.
- No uniforms are required in refugee camp schools. The children of traditional Hmong, in addition to their "street" clothes, may wear silver or brass necklaces or red or white strings around their necks, wrists, or ankles to ward off evil spirits. Bruised or red spots on a child's body may also indicate the administration of home remedies such as cupping, spooning, coining, or the application of tiger balm for colds and aches.

GIFTS FOR THE TEACHER

- Laos celebrates National Teachers' Day on October 7. On this day, students recognize the contributions and sacrifices their teachers have made for them by presenting them with practical gifts. Thus, toiletries (soap, shampoo, towels) may be more typical than candies, flowers, or knick-knacks.
- Students and their parents may sometimes give lavish compliments to the teacher in an effort to give or maintain face for the teacher.
- In extreme cases, parents may offer the teacher expensive gifts to procure special favors for their children. They do so in recognition of the role of face in manipulating the educational bureaucracy.

NONVERBAL COMMUNICATION

- Hmong typically greet each other verbally; touching while exchanging greetings, particularly shaking hands, is not common, especially between men and women. Kissing and hugging in public is considered vulgar, but female friends and some young couples may be seen holding hands.

- Laotians often press their hands or fingertips together (as in prayer) and bow slightly or incline their heads when meeting or passing in front of another person.

- It is considered bad form to touch the head of a child as the soul is thought to reside there and contact may rouse or startle the soul. Men and women are also expected to maintain a greater distance between each other when speaking. Even alluding to a romantic relationship between a man and woman may be inappropriate, and assuming that a particular man and woman are married can cause deep embarrassment.

- Direct eye contact between speakers, and especially between individuals possessing different social status, is considered impolite, so students may look down or over the teacher's shoulder when conversing.

- Many Hmong will appear reluctant to assert themselves even when responding to simple requests. Thus, expressions such as "maybe" or "I'll try" are common, and some will even say "yes" when they mean just the opposite.

- Hmong students may laugh when they make a mistake, are confused or lost, and hand in assignments. The effect can be contagious with other students joining in to help the student save face and support him or her.

- At home, most Hmong sit on mats on the floor during meals, folding their legs under them or to the side. Both males and females make sure that the soles of their feet are facing the ground or covered by the hem of a skirt. Exposing the soles of bare feet is a serious violation of etiquette.

- Tone of voice is generally low, mannerisms slight, posture erect, and overall manner reserved when interacting in public. Raucous laughter or arguing in public is taboo and will result in the loss of face.

- A Hmong woman who smokes may be considered vulgar or even immoral, but it is acceptable for men to smoke.

- When contacting the family of a Hmong student, it is important to ask to speak with the head of the household, typically the father.

- A number of behaviors that are considered unacceptable in mainstream North American culture may be either allowable in Hmong culture or completely unknown. Shutting the door of the refrigerator, sitting rather than squatting on toilets, asking before picking a neighbor's flowers, and using a tissue to blow one's nose may have to be learned by newcomers. Hmong refugees may need to be warned against putting their fingers or hands in the garbage disposal, spitting or urinating on the street, and probing their nose or ears in public. Private property and borders can be somewhat foreign concepts for some Hmong, who may be unable to appreciate the consequences of violating another's territory.

FORMS OF ADDRESS

- Initial introductions typically involve more than a greeting. Hmong individuals will ask about clan names, ages, and generations as well so that they may know how to address each other. If they belong to the same clan, they will use kinship terms (brother, sister, uncle, aunt, etc.).
- The 19 clan names are Cha or Chang, Cheng, Chu, Fang, Hang, Her, Khang, Kong, Kue, Lor or Lo, Lee or Ly, Moua, Phang, Tang, Thao, Vang, Vue, Xiong, and Yang. Popular first names for boys include Long, Pao, Teng, Thai, Tou (meaning "boy"); Toua (meaning "the first"); Lue (or "the second"); and Xang (or "the third") while for girls the most common names are May (or "girl"), Bao or Bo, Kia, May Ia, Mee, Pa, Xi, and Yi. Some names—e.g., Chue, Ka, Shua, Tong, and Yeng—can be used for either boys or girls. Double first names (e.g., KaYing Yang, Kazoua Kong-Thao, Maykao Y. Hang, and Yuepheng Xiong) have become more frequent among the Hmong diaspora, and some Hmong parents in North America have begun to give their children English, French, or Thai first names.
- In addition to the first and clan name, a Hmong man may be given an honorific (or "adult") name by his father-in-law when his wife gives birth to their first child. This new name is placed before the original first name, and the two are thus used henceforth to address the new father. Offspring will identify themselves using their father's double name as well (e.g., "I am Bao, daughter of Lue Pao").
- When Hmong women marry, they substitute their father's clan name for their husband's and frequently go by *Niam* or *Nam* (meaning "wife of") plus the husband's name. Thus, Bao Lue Pao becomes Niam Cher Long Mua, or "wife of Cher Long Mua." Mua, her husband's clan name, will supplant her own former clan name. Her husband will call her "mother of" plus the name of the couple's child so that the use of her own birth name gradually disappears.
- A typical greeting among friends is *koj tuaj los* (or "you come"), implying that one is welcome in the home of the other.
- Hmong students often address the teacher with Miss, Mrs., or Mr. plus first name. Elders, regardless of the existence of a family tie, should be addressed as "aunt" or "uncle" out of respect. Foreigners are sometimes called *Falang*, which stems from "France," home of the former French colonizers.

APPROPRIATE TOPICS

- It is considered inappropriate to compliment a parent's children. Some Hmong believe that doing so incites evil spirits to bring harm to the child and perhaps steal his or her soul.
- Political ideology tends to be a sensitive topic, and Hmong may avoid talking about the war, their flight from Laos, or conditions and treatment in the refugee camps.

- Hmong do not debate the merits of one religion over another. Spiritual beliefs are not considered a matter of choice.
- Home, family, and food are popular and acceptable conversation topics.

OUTSIDE OF CLASS

- Before fleeing to Thailand, Hmong families relied heavily on children to manage the household. Girls looked after younger siblings; cooked; cleaned; sewed and embroidered; helped their mothers care for chickens, pigs, and other small animals; and weeded crops. Boys worked with their fathers in the fields and accompanied them on hunting expeditions.
- Hmong families in North America maintain the expectation that children will help around the house, which is especially important in situations in which the parents work two jobs and must leave the household in the hands of their offspring. These responsibilities can interfere with a child's studies, but complaints are rare as family obligations are accepted as taking priority outside the classroom.

Potential Adjustment Challenges

PROBLEMS/SOLUTIONS

Problem

Sometimes when I observe the students at my school, I begin to doubt the melting pot and even the salad bowl analogy to the coming together of cultures in the United States. My mainstream and Hmong students may work together in assigned pairs and small groups in class, but they don't socialize together.

Solution

The cultural and social differences that distinguish Hmong children from their peers may be so great that they impede integration and, instead, promote alienation. This, in turn, may affect a student's self-concept as well as academic performance.

Problem

My Hmong students seem to be not only physically smaller than their mainstream peers but less developmentally advanced. I can understand the genetic roots of the former, but what contributes to the latter?

Solution

The poor diet and stress of refugee camp life can result in developmental delays in young children and depression in others. So, too, can continued poverty, lack of support from parents, and the tendency of families to move from one location to another in the middle of a school term.

Problem

I'm assuming that although Tou's parents don't speak English, he's getting plenty of exposure to his heritage language at home. Is that a reasonable assumption?

Solution

Hmong students' native language skills might not actually be very well developed due in part to the increasing presence in households of televisions and the demands of homework in English. In addition, when parents are absent, children are less likely to be entertained by folktales, poems, and other aspects of their cultural inheritance. As their English skills are also underdeveloped, the children may find themselves unable to express complex thoughts in either language.

Ethiopia

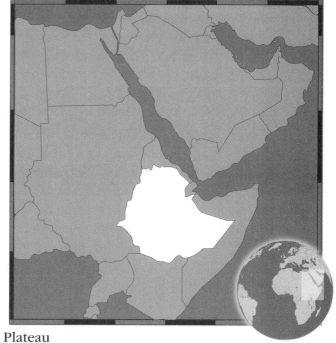

■ ETHIOPIA *Upclose*

Capital: Addis Ababa

Population: 74,777,981 (June 2006)

Size: 1,127,127 sq. km. (435,186 sq. mi.) (not quite double the size of Texas)

Location: in eastern Africa, part of the Horn of Africa, bordered by Eritrea to the north, Sudan to the west, Kenya to the south, Somalia to the east and southeast, and Djibouti to the east

Climate: tropical (hot and humid) in the lowlands, and hot and dry in desert areas that lie below the broad temperate Somali Plateau

Terrain: high Somali Plateau, mountains in the central section of the country, parted by the Great Rift Valley

Monetary Unit: birr (7.61 per U.S. dollar) (June 2006)

Religion: Muslim 45%–50%, Ethiopian Orthodox 35%–40%, animist 12%, other 3%–8%

Language(s): Amharic, Tigrinya, Oromigna, Guaragigna, Somali, Arabic, other local languages, English

Literacy Rate: total population 42.7%; men 50.3%; women 35.1% (2003)

Ethnicity: Oromo 40%, Amhara and Tigre 32%, Sidamo 9%, Shankella 6%, Somali 6%, Afar 4%, Gurage 2%, other 1%

Per Capita Income: US$91 (2006)

Population Distribution: 16% urban, 84% rural (2003)

Population below Poverty Line: 50% (2004)

Life Expectancy: total population 49.0 years; men 47.9 years; women 50.2 years (2006)

Government: federal republic

PUBLIC HOLIDAYS			
January 7	Ethiopian Christmas	May 28	Derg Downfall Day
January 19	*Timket* (Epiphany)	September 11	*Enkutatash*
January 21*	*Eid- al-Adha*		(Ethiopian New Year)
	(Feast of the Sacrifice)	September 27	*Meskel*
March 2	Adwa Victory Day		(Finding of the True Cross)
April 21	Prophet Mohammed's Birthday	November 3*	*Eid-al-Fitr*
Friday before Easter	Good Friday		(end of Ramadan)
May 1	May Day		
May 5	Patriots Victory Day		*variable dates

217

▌Personal Perspective

The first time I saw Tsegay in action, he was stepping across a desk in the back of my room with a switch in his hand to hit another boy who was talking out of turn. It was my first day at Atse Dawit School. "Hey, stop that. What do you think you're doing?" I said. "No, Madam. Is okay. He is the monitor," a student told me.

I was familiar with the monitor system of class discipline, didn't like it, and didn't want it in my classroom. I said the monitor should be elected by the class and proceeded to explain the democratic process, the duties of the monitor (no switches allowed), the responsibilities of the students to each other, to the monitor, and to their teachers. I then took nominations from the floor. They elected Ayelu Hailu, a slight twelve-year-old, the smallest boy in the class, meek and overwhelmed by his sudden elevation to high office. The students snickered when I announced the election results. He lasted four days before quitting.

The second time around, they elected Hamid, an imposing figure, six feet tall with very dark skin. But his service as monitor was a day shorter than Ayelu's. I didn't understand why he was unsuccessful until much later, when I heard him called "the black one" and *shankalla* (slave). I told the students that I was furious with them for electing two successive monitors whom they refused to respect. "Tsegay is our monitor, Madam," somebody said.

And so he was. Restored to office, he became an invaluable advisor for me, an inside operator. "Bekele is not sick, madam. He have woman." Or "Kebede hates Hamid. Better move him." When I remember my class now, Tsegay's handsome face is always in the middle of the back row, his eyes roving over the rows of students. It was the end of the year before I convinced him to give up the switch.

—Coskran (1994)

▌Historical Perspective

IMMIGRATION TO THE UNITED STATES

Ethiopian immigrants and refugees began to arrive in the United States in significant numbers in the late 1970s. They were mostly well-educated, often university-degreed, urbanites who had the economic wherewithal to flee the repressive Marxist military government of Colonel Mengistu Haile Mariam. Later a civil war, as well as Ethiopia's war with Eritrea and Sudan, produced such widespread brutality and carnage that residents of both urban and rural areas took flight, many heading for neighboring countries but many making their way to the United States. In the 20-year span from 1978 to 1998, some 37,000 Ethiopians arrived in the United

States as refugees. Between 1986 and 1998 approximately 56,000 arrived as immigrants. Today, nearly 112,000 Ethiopians make up the third largest population of sub-Saharan immigrants in the United States. They have settled primarily in California, Virginia, Washington, Maryland, Minnesota, Texas, and Georgia with large numbers in Washington, DC, as well.

After the fall of President Mariam's *Derg* (meaning "committee") regime in 1991, Oromo Ethiopians were compelled to flee due to fierce fighting among various ethnic groups. As the country faced reconstruction, the Oromo Liberation Front became increasingly dissatisfied with the proposed changes. Just one year after the new interim government was established, the Oromo Liberation Front withdrew from the governing coalition and boycotted elections, a move that resulted in social violence and political unrest. This turn of events created a large number of political refugees. All tolled, Ethiopia's brain drain has resulted in the loss of almost 75 percent of its professional class, and some 33 percent of its physicians have immigrated to the United States and Europe. In general, rural Ethiopian refugees, mostly those that arrived before 1993, are much less educated and skilled.

HISTORICAL SYNOPSIS

Ethiopia has been inhabited for some three million years. Indeed, it is home to the world's oldest human remains. It is said that Ethiopians can trace their lineage back to King Solomon and the Queen of Sheba. The Christian Kingdom of Axum changed hands several times over the course of many centuries, but not until the 7th century was Christianity challenged by Islam. By 1541 Ethiopia's emperor was compelled to turn to the Portuguese for help in putting down Muslim insurrections. Despite Portugal's subsequent attempts to establish control over Ethiopia, the country managed to remain one of only a handful of African countries to successfully resist European colonization.

Ethiopia's last and best-known emperor was Haile Selassie. At the outset of his reign, he initiated many positive reforms, such as the abolition of slavery, the institution of a national constitution, the creation of a parliament, and expansion of education and health care. Nevertheless, the Ethiopian people demanded further improvements and freedoms. Deaths from the 1973 famine, estimated to be more than 300,000, contributed to the fall of the monarchy in 1974 and the takeover by the socialist Derg in 1975 headed by Colonel Mariam.

The Derg, reputed for its cruelty and repression, imposed a Soviet-financed military campaign called the Red Terror in 1977–78 in which more than 10,000 Ethiopians in Addis Ababa lost their lives, and outside the capital entire villages were torched, schools and medical centers destroyed, and many additional Ethiopians perished. As under the Selassie regime earlier, Ethiopian citizens not only experienced violence and tyranny but also faced drought-induced starvation as well. This led to the exodus of millions across Ethiopia's borders and beyond and to the eventual success in 1991 of the Ethiopian People's Revolutionary Democratic Front (EPRDF) in overthrowing the Derg. Ethiopia's new constitution recognizes and embraces democracy and the development of private enterprise, though its population is still very poor, its institutions in need of additional reform, and its susceptibility to droughts unrelenting.

Deep Culture Perspective

DEEP CULTURE BELIEFS

- Ethiopian families tend to be tight-knit communities of several generations whose members depend on one another daily for comfort, advice, companionship, protection, and identity. The roles of husband and wife are also clearly and traditionally defined. As such, men assume a dominant role, frequently declining to do chores such as cooking, cleaning, shopping, and child rearing. While women take up these duties, they nonetheless have a strong voice in the home, manage the family's finances, and are active members of the workforce, receiving equal pay for equal work. Nevertheless, an undercurrent of gender-based discord can often be perceived in the workplace, especially if men and women compete for promotions and salary increases or if a higher-ranking woman is called upon to serve refreshments at a business meeting. Ethiopian women are often considered delicate, weak, and in need of protection. They tend to restrain their voices in public even when called upon to express an opinion. In general, parents may give freer rein to sons than to daughters.
- The socialist Derg may have established Marxist political and economic structures and practices, but it did not eliminate social class differences. Many Ethiopians are still class- and status-conscious. Prestige is gained via lineage, wealth, a position in a well-respected company, scholastic achievement, and personal contacts with influential people. Individuals who are accordingly privileged may be better able than others to obtain scarce commodities, services, and favors and to have their needs met with much greater alacrity.
- Whether one is a follower of the Ethiopian Orthodox Church or Islam, the two main religions in Ethiopia, the expression and practice of spirituality permeates all facets of Ethiopian life. There is little interfaith conflict, and traditions, rituals, and prohibitions are genuinely respected by virtually everyone for they understand that each other's core values are derived from the religion to which they adhere. Approximately 50 percent of Ethiopians are Muslim; Oromo Ethiopians (the largest ethnic group) are predominantly Sunni Muslim.
- Ethiopia's population consists of a rich mix of ethnic groups, some 85 in all, including those of sub-Saharan Bantu, Nilotic, Kushitic, Middle

Eastern, Amhara, Tigrayan, and Oromo ancestry. The latter represents the largest portion of the population, but the Amharan culture is thought to dominate due to a campaign of Amharization during the reign of Haile Selassie. Although there are more than 75 languages spoken in Ethiopia, Amharic is the official language. It is not uncommon to meet Ethiopians who speak English, French, Italian, or Arabic as well. On the whole, Ethiopians find the government's focus on ethnicity to be counterproductive and would prefer to focus on ways to make the country more prosperous and peaceful. Like gender, ethnicity may strain relationships in the workplace or in school. Favoritism based on ethnic origin can frustrate individuals and affect morale.

• Ethiopians are generally respected for being hardworking, honest, and trustworthy. They tend to take their work seriously since many have large families that depend on their income for survival. Whether they are dealing with a close friend or a stranger, Ethiopians are known to be generous and accommodating. Some describe them as reserved as well in the sense that it may be difficult to deduce their true feelings about another, especially a foreigner. Opinions are generally not directly expressed to a person with higher status or authority nor are compliments readily dispensed. By the same token, some Ethiopians may be reluctant to receive criticism.

PROVERBS

- Advise and counsel him. If he does not listen, let adversity teach him.
- What one hopes for is always better than what one has.
- A single stick may smoke, but it will not burn.
- Little by little an egg will walk.
- He who knows much does not speak much.
- The person who grew up without correction will find his mouth slipping instead of his foot.
- Where there is no shame, there is no honor.
- When the heart overflows, it comes out through the mouth.
- Confiding a secret to an unworthy person is like carrying grain in a bag with a hole in it.
- A cat may go to a monastery, but she still remains a cat.

FOLK TALE

Abegaz was a lonely man and single because there were no unmarried maidens in his village. After several years, Abegaz decided to find himself a wife. He would start with the village on the other side of the mountain. On his way, a fearsome lion let out a great roar, frightening Abegaz and his donkey so that they both ran for their lives. Exhausted, the young man eventually sat down on a rock while his donkey grazed by the trail. As Abegaz gazed at the meadow before him, his eyes fell upon a beautiful shepherd girl named Meseletch and her sheep. It was love at first sight. He introduced himself to her and then ran to find her father to ask for her hand. The request was granted, and Abegaz and Meseletch were married.

Over the years, Meseletch proved to be the perfect wife, and Abegaz became content and accustomed to the comforts that Meseletch provided. One day, though, Meseletch began to scream, although Abegaz didn't know why. He did his best to find out and calm her, but her howling continued day and night. The village healer assured Abegaz that there was a cure for her condition. "Go to the other side of the mountain," he advised, "find the mighty lion, and bring me back a single hair from his tail."

Despite his fear, Abegaz started on his way, thinking that he could no longer bear a home with a screaming wife. Soon he spotted the lion, which he watched for many hours. When the lion fell asleep, Abegaz laid a jar of milk not far from the lion and left. The next day, the milk was gone. Abegaz watched the lion again, this time from a little closer proximity, and, when the lion fell asleep, he laid some fruit and cheese at the feet of the sleeping lion. The next day, the lion greeted him with a deafening roar, to which Abegaz responded "Good morning," and offered the lion a kilo of raw meat from his hand. The lion accepted the food that day and for many days following. In fact, he and Abegaz become fast friends. Abegaz groomed the lion's mane and tail and lay down beside him to nap in the afternoon. One day he asked the lion, "Would you mind if I took a hair from your tail? It's for my wife." The lion replied, "Help yourself," so Abegaz pulled a long strand of hair from the lion's tail and quickly took it to the village healer. "Here," he said holding out the hair from the lion's tail. The healer was pleased, particularly when he learned of the friendship that had developed between Abegaz and the lion. "Now, Abegaz," said the healer shaking his head slowly. "I see that you have been a good friend to the lion, but who has been a better friend to you—the lion or your wife? Go home, Abegaz, and treat your wife better than that lion."

Administrative Perspective

OFFICIAL EDUCATIONAL POLICY

Until a system of formal education was established in Ethiopia in 1908, schooling was a privilege extended only to the Christian Amharic ruling class. However well intentioned the government's efforts were to improve and expand education for Ethiopian children in subsequent decades, the policies failed, student achievement suffered, and educational standards did not rise.

Later the Derg regime was responsible for deprivatizing education, building more schools, recruiting more and better teachers, and enrolling greater numbers of learners. More than 22 million basic reading texts were distributed throughout the country to increase literacy; this initiative was tied to an enrollment increase from 2.5 million to 4.9 million students shortly after the project was launched in 1979. In 1980 UNESCO recognized Ethiopia's successful multilingual literacy campaign with the International Reading Association Literacy Prize.

Following the overthrow of the Derg, Ethiopia's transitional government pointed out several shortcomings of the previous regime's efforts to improve education, arguing that its effect on the marketable skills of graduates had actually been inconsequential. They observed that the limited number of schools in the country and their virtual absence in the countryside left the majority of Ethiopian youngsters unable to receive an education. Moreover, they noted that many fewer female students than male students were enrolled.

Today there are two major impediments to raising the standard of public education in Ethiopia. The first is that the value of education is not always recognized. Parents may be reluctant to sacrifice the extra help at home that a child might otherwise offer, and they may fail to see how a formal education would have practical benefits for the entire family later on. The government, for its part, contributes to the low enrollment phenomenon by failing to enforce a policy of compulsory education from ages 7 to 11.

The other important obstacle that Ethiopia faces is the poor quality of the learning environment. Even as more students are enrolling in school, the resources needed to support education reforms are disappearing. Teaching supplies are in short supply, and facilities are eroding. Families are hard pressed to raise enough money for mandatory school fees. Perhaps more alarming is the decline in the availability of qualified teachers. The AIDS epidemic is partly to blame for this decline. It has claimed the lives of teachers and parents and produced thousands of orphans who must leave school to support themselves. Despite these considerable challenges, the Ethiopian government is intent on ensuring that by 2015 all children, regardless of gender, complete primary school, and that gender disparity at the secondary level will no longer be an issue.

EDUCATION AT A GLANCE

See the Education at a Glance table on page 224.

ETHIOPIA

Level/Age	Hours/Calendar	Language of Instruction	Compulsory Attendance	Exams	Grading System	Curriculum	Cost	Enrollment
Basic primary Grades 1–4 ages 6–9 General primary Grades 5–9 ages 9–13	Sep.–July with 2-week break in Feb. First shift 8:00 AM – 12:15 PM with 30-minute recess Second shift (usually for older children) 12:30 – 4:45 PM with 15-minute recess	Local or regional language until Grade 7 when instruction in English is mandatory.	Yes, from age 7 to age 11	Students receive the primary school certificate upon successful completion of school-leaving exams for this level.	100-point scale pass/fail = 50	Music, science, social studies, language arts, mathematics (with agricultural information and themes integrated throughout the curriculum in some schools)	Free	46.7% of primary school-age children are enrolled; 40.6% are female, and their school life expectancy is 3.2 years compared to 5.3 years for boys. 64% of all students reach Grade 5.
First secondary cycle Grades 9–10 ages 14–16 Second secondary cycle Grades 11–12 ages 16–18 Second technical cycle Grades 11–13 ages 16–19	Classes are 40–45 minutes long.		No	Students take a national examination at the end of the first cycle. Students take the Ethiopian General School Leaving Examination or the Ethiopian Higher Education Entrance Examination at the end of the second cycle. To pass, girls must obtain a score of 3.0 out of 4.0; boys must obtain a 3.2 out of 4.0.		Core curriculum consists of English, math, physical and life sciences, social studies, national languages, and physical education with the addition of specialized subjects depending on whether the student is enrolled in the regular or vocational/technical track.	Free	12.7% of secondary school-age children are enrolled; 39.7% are female. 84% of primary school graduates advance to secondary level.
University ages 20+ Bachelor's degree: 4–5 years Master's degree: 2 years Doctorate: 3 years beyond master's degree	Sep. – July Classes held at all hours of the day.	Only Amharic language is taught in Amharic at the university.	No	Entrance to university extremely competitive.	A, B, C, D, F pass/fail: C for undergraduates pass/fail: B for graduates	Students cannot select the area of study (e.g., business, humanities, science, social science) but can select discipline within the broader area (e.g., biology, political science, math).	Free, with the Ministry of Education covering tuition, room and board, and a small stipend, but a cost-sharing initiative has been introduced in which students must pay part of their tuition and receive no stipend.	1.6% of eligible individuals are enrolled; 25.2% are female (enrollments are presently on a steep upward trajectory).

Surface Culture Perspective

CLASSROOMS

- Schools may be no more than single classrooms built of sticks, straw, and mud with metal roofs, packed dirt floors, and no windows. These rooms are often sweltering during the day, and the sound of rain on the metal roof may make teaching virtually impossible. Toilets and drinkable water are generally unavailable. Many schools are not furnished with desks and chairs (even for the teacher); instead, children sit on the floor, on rocks, or on wood or mud benches. In better-equipped schools, children may sit three to a wooden desk and have access to a soccer field or volleyball court and perhaps a small library.

- It is not uncommon for classes of school children to cultivate small plots of vegetables adjacent to the school. These gardens are used for pedagogical purposes; in addition, the produce from these gardens can be sold at market with the profits used by the school to purchase needed supplies. While the government pays the salaries of teachers, it is often up to the community to provide all other resources and to maintain the school and grounds.

- The teacher-student ratio may range from 40:1 up to 200:1 in a single class, with the average now at 60:1 and rising. Health problems lead to absenteeism, causing class size to fluctuate broadly on a day-to-day basis. Just getting to school is problematic in many parts of Ethiopia. Children may walk for hours before reaching school, and often they are hungry and thirsty when they arrive and risk fainting in class. Girls, in particular, are vulnerable on the way to school as there have been many incidents of "hijacking" wherein young females (often no more than 10 years old) are taken by force as brides by prospective husbands whose families cannot afford the traditional bride price. Abduction of the young girls is often accompanied by rape, compelling her parents to consent to the marriage in order to protect the family's honor.

- School supplies such as books, paper, pencils, and pens are very limited. If textbooks are available, students will never write in them as they are to be recycled for future groups of learners. Often textbooks that have been ordered are delivered long after the school year has begun, and there are usually too few for the number of students. Teachers compensate by writing information on blackboards, but even these items are scarce. Sometimes a wall of the schoolroom is covered with a special paint that allows the teacher to write and erase words.

TEACHERS' STATUS

- To become a primary school teacher, high school graduates take a one-year course in one of the regional primary teacher training institutes. Prospective middle school teachers attend two years at a teacher training college, and prospective high school teachers follow a three-year course in an education college at one of the universities, receiving a bachelor's degree upon graduation. Some reports claim that less than half of Ethiopia's secondary schools teachers have degrees.

- Teachers' salaries in Ethiopia are considered very low compared to those of other civil servants in the country who also receive better vacation pay, medical insurance, and job security. During the Derg regime, the situation had become so dire that many teachers became indigent and few young people aspired to enter the teaching profession. As a result, the status of teachers declined. In addition to receiving insufficient wages, many teachers were also denied freedom of expression. Some outspoken teachers were sent to prison or simply disappeared. Today a novice teacher earns approximately US$90 per month. Performance-based pay increases have been introduced as incentive to improve teaching quality.
- Contrary to trends in many Western nations, women account for only 27 percent of the Ethiopian teaching force.
- Ethiopia has a national curriculum that all schools must follow.
- Although the official language is Amharic, new legislation gives each child the right to receive primary education in his or her mother tongue. Implementing this policy has strained the resources of the education system and resulted in the transfer of many teachers out of districts in which they do not speak the local language.

TEACHER-STUDENT RELATIONSHIP

- Teachers command the respect and affection not just of students but of the students' parents. Some claim that teachers are one step below the status of a parent in terms of the reverence they inspire. Indeed, teachers may say that they regard their students in much the same way as they do their own children and are therefore supportive and nurturing. It is considered acceptable for teachers to discipline students as they would their own offspring as well.
- When the teacher enters the classroom, students are expected to stand and greet the teacher in chorus by saying "Good morning, Teacher" or "Good afternoon, Teacher." Before class students line up by grade level to sing the national anthem. The principal and teachers form a line in front of the students.
- Apart from maintaining the school property, parents refrain from getting involved in school issues. They typically do not help their children with homework because they have no time and often because they lack the academic skills that their children are developing through formal education.
- Teachers may be challenged to motivate students in large classes where individual attention is made virtually impossible.
- Students tend not to fear asking questions in class. In fact, some schools hold weekly question-and-answer contests that set one class against another. An award is given at the end of the school year to the student with the most correct answers.

TEACHING PRACTICES

- A typical practice during class is for the teacher to write notes on the board and for students to copy the information into their notebooks. Often teachers resort to this approach if the students lack textbooks. In this sense, "the teacher is the book."
- Teachers may assign reading for homework, but students may fail to follow through since they understand that any upcoming test will comprise only what the teacher has presented in class.
- Although some teachers may assign and collect homework, often they will direct the students to exchange notebooks and correct each other's work in class. When teachers grade papers, they may take off points for poor handwriting and spelling (traditionally ½ point for every spelling error). Students will often be asked to resubmit homework papers that are marred by excessive erasures or scratch-outs.
- Characteristics considered desirable in a teacher include the ability to give illustrations and examples, involvement in extracurricular activities, use of a variety of teaching methodologies, correction of students when they make mistakes, willingness to explain and review subject matter until it is understood by the students, offering of encouragement to participate in class and ask questions, and ability to relate academic knowledge to local needs and conditions.

TEACHERS' DRESS

- Western dress is common throughout Ethiopia. However, Ethiopians tend to take pride in their outward appearance and therefore refrain from wearing shorts, jeans, or weekend clothes to work. Women may wear slacks and only cover their heads if they are deeply observant of Islam. Traditional attire may be worn at work at holiday time.

DISCIPLINE AND CLASS MANAGEMENT

- Ethiopian students tend to be well behaved. However, teachers are empowered by parents to administer strict discipline, often in the form of corporal punishment, which is thought to lead to more responsible and respectful behavior on the part of the children. Students may experience corporal punishment of the following varieties for such violations as chewing gum in class: to stand facing the corner for a long time, to perform sit-ups, to have the palm slapped with a ruler, to send students to the principal's office. More grievous offenses such as fighting, destroying school property, stealing, and bullying the teacher for assigning low grades are punished by calling the student's parents. In some schools, a committee of parents may adjudicate certain discipline problems before turning them over to the parents.

STUDENTS' CIRCUMSTANCES

- In urban areas parents are likely to place a high value on their children's education, and the children may experience considerable pressure from their families to excel. At times the stress can result in harassment of teachers with students blaming instructors for "ruining their lives" if they receive a low grade, even if little effort has been exerted.
- The countryside presents different attitudes and circumstances. Most rural families are very poor. Their villages are not electrified, there is no sewer system, and water quality is poor. As a result, diseases such as malaria, tuberculosis, worms, and eye diseases are common, but medical services are often nonexistent. It is typical for students to walk many miles to and from school each day, if there is even a school within walking distance. Harvest times may disrupt a child's education as every family member is needed to bring in the crops. Drop-out rates are very high, leading parents to question the usefulness of schooling and the wisdom of releasing children from household chores for the sake of a formal education.

STUDENT-STUDENT RELATIONSHIP

- Students living in same neighborhood often gather in the evenings to do homework and study together.

STUDENTS' LEARNING PRACTICES

- Foreign teachers report that Ethiopian students are in general hard working, bright, eager to learn, and tenacious. They may as readily ask visitors for notebooks and pens as for candy. The student's notebook, by the way, is considered precious personal property. Not only is it relatively expensive and difficult to acquire but it contains everything that the student will need to pass exams.
- The school system and teacher do not often allow students to make their own decisions, so choices regarding writing topics or class projects are not offered. In general, Ethiopian students are not encouraged to be independent learners. They are skilled at verbatim memorization, however.
- Students may prefer practical lessons that place academic knowledge (e.g., geometry, physics) at the center of day-to-day problem solving in their homes and villages. In general, students say they benefit most from learning by doing, teacher demonstrations, recitation, and teacher answers and examples in response to student questions. When the teacher is absent, students may teach each other, but this is not a practice that they readily recognize as valuable.
- Students who have access to and are able to attend school up to the end of high school take the Ethiopian School Leaving Certificate

Examination (ESLCE). Until 2003 any hope of gaining admission to a university depended on the student's performance on this exam. As one student said, "The ESLCE is your life." A good score is usually obtained by studying hard, but bribing teachers is an observed practice among wealthier students, and copying from one another during exams is frequently overlooked by test proctors. In 2004, the Ethiopian Higher Education Entrance Examination replaced the ESLCE for admission to university.

STUDENTS' DRESS

- The ideal in Ethiopian schools is for all children to wear uniforms, typically a white blouse and dark skirt or jumper for girls and dark pants and white shirt for boys. However, the cost of uniforms is often beyond the means of rural families, especially those with several children. Frequently, if a child has a clean and well-fitting uniform for school, his or her street clothes may be old, worn, and too small.

NONVERBAL COMMUNICATION

- When Ethiopian friends meet they will kiss each other three times on the cheeks (four or five times in the case of a long separation). Women will hug and kiss women, men will do the same with each other, and sometimes women will kiss men. Strangers smile broadly and shake hands warmly upon being introduced, but first contact between an adult and a child may involve kissing the child and picking him or her up. Eye contact is normally maintained during conversation except between men and women or between teacher and student.
- Kissing and shaking hands when greeting is accompanied by numerous variations on the question "How are you?" Ethiopians will invariably communicate their respect for and interest in others by inquiring about family members and circumstances.
- Holding hands in public, while moderately common among young couples, is much more acceptable for friends of the same gender. In general, the physical proximity maintained between interlocutors is close compared to North American custom. Frequent friendly touching on the arm or shoulder during conversation is also an appropriate way to convey warmth and sociability.
- The ability to speak articulately, even eloquently, is a prized asset among Ethiopians. Thus, they are known to speak calmly, softly, clearly, and slowly and to use metaphor and word play in their conversation. Riddles and a game of cross-examination known as *teteyeq* are popular.
- One can usually expect Ethiopians to behave with reserve and courtesy in public. Expressions of anger are rare as are frustration, pretense, and pride. Children are taught not to point at others and to be particularly respectful of older people. Speaking in a loud or high voice signals

anger or disappointment and is considered to be inappropriate. This does not mean that Ethiopians will not state their opinions when they are knowledgeable about a topic. They may even argue with those with whom they feel comfortable.

- Students are discouraged from looking the teacher directly in the eye. They are expected to stand before the teacher with their hands behind their backs and eyes on the ground when addressed by the instructor and should limit their responses to "yes" or "no."

- Although punctuality is generally observed and appreciated, the circumstances of life in Ethiopia often prevent people from keeping appointments, so moderate tardiness is tolerated. Ethiopia follows the 13-month Gregorian rather than the Julian calendar, and each day is divided into 12 daylight hours (7:00 AM to 7:00 PM) and 12 night hours (7:00 PM to 7:00 AM). Therefore, 9:00 AM on the conventional clock corresponds to 3:00 PM according to the Ethiopic clock.

- If invited to the home of an Ethiopian, expect to be treated with special care and attention. Often the host will exceed his or her budget to entertain visitors and ensure that they are comfortable. Hosts will also wait until their guests are seated before they themselves will take a seat.

FORMS OF ADDRESS

- Students address teachers with "Sir" or "Ma'am" or *Woizero* (Mrs.), *Woizerit* (Miss), or *Ato* (Mr.) plus first name rather than family name. When a woman marries, she does not take her husband's last name. As titles are important to most Ethiopians, other professionals may be called Doctor or Engineer plus last name. In general, until individuals know each other well, they retain the use of title when addressing each other.

- At birth Ethiopian children are named according to the attributes of their individuality. They are given their father's first name as a surname, so family names do not endure from generation to generation.

- The term used to refer to foreigners is *ferenji*. It is not particularly pejorative unless the speaker intends it to be.

APPROPRIATE TOPICS

- Most Ethiopians appreciate inquiries about their life, work, and families provided the conversation avoids topics that are too personal.

- Questions about one's regional origin or ethnicity are not generally welcomed since this has become a topic of controversy that has seriously undermined the unity of the Ethiopian people.

- Discussion of sex and sexuality is taboo, and directly referring to private body parts is a serious violation of etiquette. Foreigners are advised to avoid talking about religion and politics as well. There is the risk that an outsider's opinions would inadvertently cause offense. Ethiopians may be sensitive to what they perceive as criticism of their country. Soccer, on the other hand, is a popular topic, even among women and children.

- Many urban Ethiopians speak English, although as a second language.

OUTSIDE OF CLASS

- Students are responsible for cleaning the classroom and school grounds after each day's lessons. One student may be assigned to ring the bell at the beginning and end of the school day as well as to raise and lower the flag.
- Many Ethiopian children, especially those living in rural areas, have many hours of chores to do once they return home from school. Their responsibilities may include carrying water from a communal well or fountain to home, tending gardens, gathering or chopping firewood, herding animals, cleaning the house and barn, cooking for the family, burning garbage, collecting dung, building fences, making hay stacks, brewing alcohol, and babysitting. Little time is left for studying or playing.
- Favorite pastimes include soccer, basketball, volleyball, and table tennis. Both students and their teachers may tend school gardens and sell the produce as well as handmade crafts to raise funds for maintenance of the school.

Potential Adjustment Challenges

PROBLEMS/SOLUTIONS

Problem

My Ethiopian student suddenly stopped taking advantage of our free milk program. Should I ask why?

Solution

Yes, that's okay! Chances are your student is a Coptic Christian. This group is prohibited from eating meat or dairy products for six months of every year.

Problem

At a recent class picnic, I asked my Ethiopian student if she would like a hotdog. She said, "Thank you," and took the hot dog but didn't eat it. Why did she accept the hot dog if she didn't really want it?

Solution

Ethiopian students may consent to do things and agree to statements with which they do not concur in order to avoid offending authority figures such as teachers and administrators.

Problem

Outside of class, my two Ethiopian students tease each other and giggle with other students, but in class I can't get a peep out of them. How come?

Solution

Ethiopian girls in particular, but boys as well, may find active class participation to be a challenge beyond their comfort level as they have been taught that talking in class violates the code of good conduct and so they may fear a scolding from the teacher.

Liberia

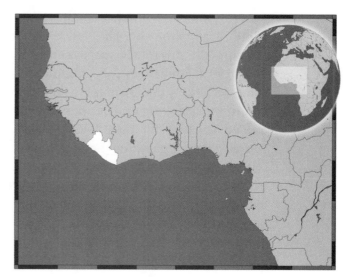

 LIBERIA Upclose

Capital: Monrovia

Population: 3,042,004 (June 2006)

Size: 111,370 sq. km. (43,000 sq. mi.) (somewhat larger than the state of Tennessee)

Location: in western Africa bordered on the east by the North Atlantic Ocean, the northwest by Sierra Leone, the northeast by Guinea, and the east by the Côte d'Ivoire

Climate: characteristically tropical (i.e., hot and humid summers with frequent heavy showers), dryer winters that are hot during the day and cool at night

Terrain: coastal plains growing to a rolling plateau with low mountains in the northeast

Monetary Unit: Liberian dollar (58.5 per U.S. dollar) (June 2006)

Religion: indigenous beliefs 40%, Christian 40%, Muslim 20%

Language(s): English, the official language (20%), plus 27 indigenous languages (e.g., Bassa, Bella, Dei, Kpelle, Gbandi, Gio, Gola, Grebo, Kissi, Krahn, Kru, Loma, Mano, Mende, Mandingo, and Vai)

Literacy Rate: total population 57.5%; men 73.3%; women 41.6% (2003)

Ethnicity: indigenous African tribes 95% (16 major ethnic groups, including Bassa, Bella, Dei, Kpelle, Gbandi, Gio, Gola, Grebo, Kissi, Krahn, Kru, Loma, Mano, Mende, Mandingo, and Vai), Americo-Liberians 2.5%, Congo people 2.5%

Per Capita Income: US$91 (2006)

Population Distribution: 47% urban, 53% rural (2003)

Population below Poverty Line: 80% (2005)

Life Expectancy: total population 39.7 years; men 37.9 years; women 41.3 years (2006)

Government: republic

PUBLIC HOLIDAYS

January 1	New Year's Day	April 12	National Redemption Day
January 7	Pioneers' Day	Friday before Easter	Good Friday
February 11	Armed Forces Day	May 14	Unification and Integration Day
February 14	Literacy Day	July 26	Independence Day
March 13	Decoration Day	August 24	Flag Day
April 11	Fast and Prayer Day	December 25	Christmas Day

◼ Personal Perspective

According to a *Worldview Magazine Online* article by Burman (2005), administrators of the Liberian Education Assistance Program (LEAP) measure the program's success in terms of everyday observations. The Ministry of Education, for example, has expressed interest in adopting some of LEAP's materials for wider distribution. Burman also notes that parents are showing more enthusiasm as many insist on identifying LEAP-trained teachers for their local schools. "But most significantly," writes Burman, "through three bouts of civil unrest, the looting of all their school supplies, teachers left unpaid, and difficult communication and travel conditions, schools continue to ask to have their teachers trained in LEAP methods and teachers continue to work because they enjoy the new methods and can provide an enriching environment for their students." One teacher, in fact, was to have claimed, "I have a problem. The kids—they don't want to go home!"

—Burman (2005)

◼ Historical Perspective

IMMIGRATION TO THE UNITED STATES

Between the years 1988 and 1998, some 17,000 Liberians legally immigrated to the United States most settling in New York, Texas, Pennsylvania, Arizona, Minnesota, Georgia, and Illinois. Virtually the entire population of Liberia, some three million people, however, fled to neighboring countries such as the Côte d'Ivoire and Ghana. Most were escaping the brutal civil war that broke out in 1989 and resulted in the death of approximately 150,000 Liberians.

In 1991, the U.S. Attorney General granted temporary protective status to approximately 14,000 Liberians. However, this initiative still obliged the immigrants to renew their status annually. Work permits were issued to those who applied and were living under temporary protective status. Most Liberians continued to process their annual status extension until 1999 when, following Liberia's introduction of democratic reforms, the U.S. government determined that temporary protective status was no longer required. Rather than calling for immediate deportation, U.S. President Bill Clinton authorized deferred enforced departure (DED) which, in essence, meant that Liberian asylees were subject to immediate deportation but that actual deportation would be deferred for one year. The U.S. government has continued to annually extend the Liberian nationals' DED but has made no moves to grant permanent residency to them. The annual renewals are accompanied by a plethora of bureaucratic paperwork and accompanying fees, including application, fingerprint, and work permit fees, which are an added financial hardship to many.

The vast majority of Liberians leaving their country escaped to refugee camps in the Côte d'Ivoire, Guinea, and Ghana. There they were provided initial basic necessities (shelter, food, blankets), but, other than that, the refugees were obliged to live by means of their own ingenuity and own propensity for hard work. Liberian refugees shun "handouts," so the relative vitality of the Liberian refugee camps in Côte d'Ivoire, for example, is testimony to their self-sufficiency and self-esteem. In such locations, it is possible to find highly skilled and educated individuals as well as those who have a minimum of formal schooling or are illiterate. While none have the opportunity, however, to work outside the camps unless their skills cannot be matched by an Ivorian national, they may take and teach classes in basic literacy, computer skills, and other subjects that will lead to employment once the refugee returns to Liberia or resettles elsewhere. Many Liberian refugees are doctors and nurses, business managers, and other professionals, and most come from rural backgrounds.

Today, three-quarters of the Liberians who initially fled the bloodshed in their country have returned home, despite their uneasiness about their safety, but approximately 200,000 are still living in refugee camps outside Liberia. Anxiety over the increase in antigovernment attacks within the Côte d'Ivoire, however, resulted in accusations by many Ivorians that the Liberian refugees were joining the ranks of the rebels. Nearly 9,000 Liberian refugees were subsequently evacuated from the camps in Côte d'Ivoire, with their safety once again compromised.

HISTORICAL SYNOPSIS

The American Colonization Society purchased land in western Africa, which would then become the Republic of Liberia in 1822. Its purpose was an attempted repatriation of former African slaves from the United States. The land was purchased from native tribal chiefs for the price of a box of beads, several pairs of shoes, a box of soap, a barrel of rum, and 12 spoons. By 1865 some 20,000 freed American slaves were settled in Liberia and elsewhere. The official language of Liberia is English, and its capital, Monrovia, is named for United States President James Monroe. The country's constitution forbids slavery, yet the Liberian government itself was accused and confirmed of enslaving native peoples of Liberia in 1930. This practice was subsequently halted in 1931.

After more than 100 years of a republic-modeled government, this somewhat peaceful country experienced a series of events, beginning in 1979, that led the country into a prolonged military dictatorship and civil war. Civilian rule was restored in 1985, and the second republic of Liberia was formed in 1986 through the acceptance of a new constitution. A comprehensive peace agreement in August 2003 ended 14 years of civil war and provoked the resignation of then president Charles Taylor, who has since been exiled to Nigeria. Though the UN mission in Liberia completed a disarmament program for former civil war combatants in 2004, security in the region remains unstable, and the process of rebuilding the social and economic institutions of this war-ravaged country is slow.

Deep Culture Perspective

DEEP CULTURE BELIEFS

- There are two major influences in Liberian culture—the traditions of the indigenous tribal groups that populated the region before nationhood and those of the ancestors of freed American slaves that founded the nation. As a result, Liberian culture is not unified but possesses strong elements of both Africa and North America, nor do its members coexist without some tension.

- Immediate and extended families are most common in Liberia. Income dictates the number of people living in a household, with the higher-income households having a correspondingly higher occupancy. Four to five children per family is typical, though in rural areas, where men commonly take more than one wife, the number of children is often appreciably higher. As many as three related families may live in a single dwelling.

- Women dominate in the kitchen, with men discouraged from stepping foot within. In addition, household chores such as washing clothes, cleaning the home, and caring for children are among those duties expected to be carried out by women. In urban areas, it is becoming more acceptable and expected to see women as part of the workforce. Though female literacy rates are still considerably lower than those of men, women's access to formal education is slowly increasing.

- Liberian men's roles are fairly traditional, with the expectation being that they be the primary breadwinner and make all major family decisions. Providing financially for children's education is seen as an important responsibility for Liberian men. Many men in Liberia see themselves as the true head of the household and, therefore, do not consider women to be their equal in any context.

- Children are seen as a blessing from God, while childlessness may be viewed as punishment due to the woman's presumed immoral lifestyle when she was a teenager. Publicly, however, the man would be held responsible for a childless marriage. Women and older siblings are the caregivers for children in Liberia. Out of necessity, girls as young as ten may be placed in charge of infants. In general, children are not always directly supervised by their parents as there are normally many adult relatives in a household or village to take responsibility for their younger kin. Relying on other members of the community to look after children is an expected and acceptable practice among Liberians. Sending a child to live with a relative or friend in another part of the country is also not uncommon. This decision is usually made in the best interest of the child (i.e., to get a better education, to avoid violence or poverty, or to allow the child to get to know distant relatives better), but sometimes it is justified on the basis of insufficient space in the original household or the necessity of the parents to travel. The practice of caring for the children of others is so valued that those who do not do so may be considered selfish. Occasionally, children who are only distantly related to the family in whose care they have been placed may be expected to take on a greater share of the household chores.

- In general, Liberian families "revolve around" the children. Nevertheless, younger members of the family are expected to respect the role of adults and to obey them. They are accustomed to physical punishment as well, a practice that is widely regarded as necessary, lest the child be spoiled, and as a sign of competent parenting. Typical punishment may involve being beaten with the belt or rattan switch, both methods often leaving telltale marks that would not be considered signs of abuse in Liberia. Some caregivers may punish children via shouting and verbal beratings, also not considered inappropriate in Liberian society. A paste made from ground hot peppers and applied to sensitive areas of the skin (e.g., the eyes and genitals) is another traditional form of punishment in Liberia, although it is less common among urban and more educated groups. Aside from their punitive function, hot peppers are also used for medicinal purposes, such as when they are applied to the lips of a woman during childbirth to help her cope with labor pains.

- Traditional Liberians might guide young boys and girls into adulthood through special initiation rites, though they are typically considered too secret to be discussed openly, especially with strangers. Girls are initiated into the Sande Society, a kind of training camp that teaches young women about their roles and responsibilities as women as well as how to perform a variety of useful skills such as making various medicines and potions out of herbs and roots. Initiation also includes ritual parading and dancing in a black raffia costume and wearing an exquisitely carved mask. Some 50 percent to 95 percent of initiates in rural areas undergo the traditional female circumcision rite. Once initiated, the girls take on a new Sande name. Boys are initiated into adulthood through the Poro Society. Common practices includes scarring the face and tattooing.

- The elderly are highly respected in Liberia and are often turned to for advice and support. Community or family disputes are frequently resolved through the counsel of one's elders. One is considered elderly around the age of 40. (The average life expectancy for the total Liberian population is 39.7 years.) Liberian elders who can no longer look after themselves are always cared for by family members.

- The age at which it is legal for a girl to marry in Liberia is 18 (21 for boys), though it is not uncommon for women to be "reserved" beforehand. Children of both sexes live with their parents until they are financially independent and married. Engaged couples generally do not live together before marriage, nor do they frequently engage in premarital sex, although increasingly men do not expect that their brides will be virgins—a change, perhaps, brought about by the use of rape as a weapon during the war and also the practice of prostitution in the absence of other means of obtaining income. It is not unusual in rural areas for women to marry at the age of 14 or 15, once they have completed their primary education. Men will commonly take more than one wife, so long as they can support them. A dowry is traditionally paid to the parents of each fiancée. Although domestic violence against wives is commonplace, divorce is nevertheless socially, if not legally, prohibited in Liberia.

- Christian churches are often filled to capacity on Sundays, with approximately 40 percent of Liberians practicing this faith. Muslims represent 20 percent of the population, with the remaining 40 percent indigenous (animist). Children follow their parents' religion until such time as they are self-sufficient and move out. Liberians by and large share strong attitudes of deference toward religion.

- The influence of the United States is omnipresent in Liberia. English is the official language, the red-white-and-blue color combination is popular, the U.S. dollar is used as the country's currency, and even the food is reminiscent of popular fare in the southern United States. Thus, collard greens, okra, cabbage, and eggplant are favorite ingredients in dishes.

PROVERBS

- Do not measure the timbers for your house in the forest.
- Though the palm tree in the jungle is big, who knows how big its yield will be?
- A little rain each day will fill the rivers to overflowing.
- Let your love be like the misty rain, coming softly, but flooding the river.
- The dog's bark is not might, but fright.
- If you try to cleanse others, like soap, you will waste away in the process.

FOLK TALE

Once upon a time, the Bassa god called *Gedepohoh* told an assembly of all the animals and people in the world to make peace and live harmoniously. Although he could have blessed his children with an abundance of food, *Gedepohoh* decided that to support this goal, humans and animals should together be responsible for growing and harvesting their own food.

First he asked for volunteers to plant a variety of poisonous grain, which, when ingested, would instantly cause death. For a long time no one spoke, but finally Chameleon stepped forward and proudly said, "Give the grain to me. I will plant it." Chameleon then made a great display of changing color, rotating his eyes, flicking his tail, flashing his eyes, and darting quickly from place to place. *Gedepohoh* gave him the grain but immediately felt regret, calling after Chameleon to stop. Instead of obeying *Gedepohoh,* Chameleon continued on with his task.

Now worried, *Gedepohoh* realized that he must plant an antidote that would inhibit the growth of the poisonous grain. Again, no one volunteered until finally Rooster said, "Let me be the one to plant the antidote. I'm stronger and faster than everyone else. I should be the one to do it." *Gedepohoh* gave him the antidote and bade him farewell. Before he reached his destination, however, Rooster spotted a lush field that was home to a huge colony of termites. Rooster gave in to temptation and spent many hours feeding on the juicy termites.

At this point *Gedepohoh* knew that Rooster would not plant the antidote, so he gave it to Dog, who dutifully went to the field and planted it. Unfortunately, his efforts failed as the whole earth by then was covered by the shafts of the poisonous grain. *Gedepohoh* sighed despondently at the realization of his dream gone awry. Said he, "Anyone who changes his appearance as frequently as does Chameleon cannot be trusted, and anyone who beats his breast with such arrogance as does Rooster should be evaluated upon the basis of his dignity and composure rather than his boasting and inflated self-concept."

Administrative Perspective

OFFICIAL EDUCATIONAL POLICY

Almost all of Liberia's educational infrastructure was destroyed as a result of more than 15 years of civil war. Many of the country's teachers were either killed or took flight. Those teachers who remain are often not paid, and there is little funding for materials and school buildings, although schools in urban areas are being refurbished at a faster pace than those in more rural settings.

In the past, it was the Liberian government's responsibility to provide free education to its people. The government's efforts were reinforced by the country's Christian churches, nearly all of which had at least one high school under their purview. With the increased arrival of practicing Muslims in Liberia, Islamic *madarasa* schools have more recently appeared, providing Islamic-based education and values. Outside companies such as LAMCO and Firestone have not only built schools for their workers' children but also sponsor scholarships for underprivileged children and provide for other educational projects for their nearby communities. Additionally, a major struggle for Liberian schools is the rehabilitation and reintegration of child soldiers who have had major gaps in their academic development. Arguably, those children who had not engaged as conscripts in civil war activities are often no further along in their academic advancement.

With a new comprehensive plan released in 2000, the Liberian Ministry of Education is attempting to address the wide range of stresses that the educational system has experienced even before, but especially since, the war. In particular, it has placed greatest attention on rebuilding and equipping schools (particularly primary schools), enrolling and keeping more girls in school, teaching students about environmentally sustainable ways to rehabilitate and reconstruct their country, designing new curricula regarding the AIDS epidemic, creating more training centers for prospective teachers, decentralizing educational policy to give communities greater control over local schools, distributing educational opportunities more broadly to Liberia's population, integrating into the new curriculum attention to peaceful conflict resolution and national unity, and introducing accelerated learning programs for overage children whose education was interrupted by war.

The Ministry, however, is reported to be chronically understaffed and bureaucratically top heavy and redundant to such an extent that many reforms cannot be realized without major adjustments within the Ministry itself. Nevertheless, the mandate for reform is aided by Liberia's tradition of community partnership in education. Parent-teacher associations, for example, are well established and considered to be effective vehicles for monitoring the educational system in general and the progress of children and effectiveness of teachers in particular.

EDUCATION AT A GLANCE

See the Education at a Glance table on page 241.

LIBERIA

Level/Age	Hours/Calendar	Language of Instruction	Compulsory Attendance	Exams	Grading System	Curriculum	Cost	Enrollment
Kindergarten ages 3–6			No, but very few kindergartens exist in Liberia.	None	None	Identification of letters of the alphabet, basic reading skills, and numeracy	No data available	No data available
Primary Grades 1–6 ages 6–12	Mar. to Dec. First shift 7:00 AM–noon Second shift 1:15–6:30 PM Some schools have a third shift as well. 45-minute classes	English	Yes	Comprehensive final exams are administered at the end of each year. Items include multiple-choice, fill-in-the-blank, and short answers, but no essay questions are assigned nor are there open-book tests.	0–100-point scale Pass/fail level: 70%	Language, mathematics, science, social studies, physical education, and reading In rural areas, boys may attend more informal schools in which they learn life skills, while girls may attend the traditional Sande schools that teach child care, cooking, and other household skills.	US$12 to US$67 per year in school fees	83.4% of primary school-age children are enrolled; 40.8% are female (47% of primary school-age girls are not enrolled). The average Liberian adult receives 2.5 years of schooling. 57.8% of age-appropriate children enroll in Grade 1. 33.3% of children reach Grade 5.
Junior secondary Grades 7–9 ages 12–15			Yes, but junior high schools are generally only found in Monrovia.	Students who pass the West Africa Examination at the end of junior secondary are eligible for admission to the senior secondary level.		Algebra, geometry, geography, physical science, chemistry Also skills-based subjects linked to the requirements of the emerging market		24.7% of secondary school-age children are enrolled; 41.4% are female.
Senior secondary Grades 10–12 ages 15–18			Yes, up to age 16, but 98% of senior high schools are located in Monrovia.	Students who pass the West Africa Examination at the end of senior secondary are eligible for admission to the university as long as they also pass a special university entrance exam.				
University ages 18+	Oct. to Aug.		No	No data available	A=90–100 B=80–89 C=70–79 D=60–69 F=fail	No data available	No data available	No data available

Surface Culture Perspective

CLASSROOMS

- Because 80 percent of Liberia's schools were destroyed during the war, classes may now be held in churches. Otherwise, the schools tend to be in disrepair (and their walls pocked with bullet holes) and poorly equipped, being neither well lit nor furnished. During the war, doors, window frames, desks, and bookshelves were often confiscated and used as cooking fuel. It is not uncommon for students to bring their own chairs to school (otherwise they sit on stones or plastic containers), and water for drinking and latrines must be carried from a distance. Many times classes are held in structures made of dried reeds, bamboo, or mud blocks, or students assemble for lessons under tents stretched over metal frames. Private schools, especially those affiliated with a religious group, are usually in better condition than public schools.

- Classes are usually large, with an average of 50 students per room, but the space allocated for learning is normally insufficient, so that classrooms are typically overcrowded. The official teacher-student ratio (no doubt heavily underreported) is 1:36 for the primary level and 1:17 for the secondary level. Because there are more students than can be accommodated in a traditional schedule, most schools have double or triple shifts (the third shift may begin at 8:00 PM). Still, within one classroom, it is not uncommon to have many children of different ages and differing amounts of formal education.

- Books, paper, pencils, and pens are in short supply—in fact, in many situations such items are scarce. Students must purchase these items as schools lack any significant support from the government to provide essential learning tools for the students. Parents pay a yearly fee of US$12 to US$67 to support the school's infrastructure and salary of the teacher.

TEACHERS' STATUS

- Pre-primary and primary school teachers receive their training at a teacher training institute and receive their Primary Teacher's Certificate/Grade C Teaching Certificate after three years. Secondary school teachers earn a Grade B Teaching Certificate in order to teach at the junior high school level. Their course work lasts four years, earning them a bachelor's degree in education. If an individual already holds a degree in another subject, a two-year course program leads to a Grade A Teaching Certificate, enabling the graduate to teach at the high school level.

- Some 80 percent of Liberian teachers are male.

- Especially in villages, teachers are treated with tremendous respect as they often work essentially as volunteers; one of the highest professional positions to which a person can aspire is that of a teacher. Peace Corps teachers are also well treated and respected for having left their homes in order to help others.
- Most Liberian teachers earn the equivalent of US$8–21 per month, though many have not received their salaries in more than a year. Many teachers have left the field, especially in central Liberia, in search of more lucrative job opportunities. Nearly all teachers report that a second job is required to survive and take care of their families. Sources for additional income include farming, tutoring, sewing, and selling clothes.

TEACHER-STUDENT RELATIONSHIP

- Students traditionally have held their teachers in very high regard and have treated them with utmost respect. However, with the deterioration of the quality of teaching in Liberia, the relationship between students and teachers has begun to erode. In light of the many problems that plague the educational system and that limit the professional development of teachers, students are increasingly indifferent to the value of their education.
- Younger students tend to be eager to learn, often believing that school is the greatest opportunity of their lives. They have generally few discipline problems as their desire to learn is so great that decorum is often maintained through internal peer pressure. Older learners, on the other hand, challenge today's teachers, who are struggling with a reversal of the once-harmonious teacher-student dynamic.

TEACHING PRACTICES

- Traditional teaching practice requires students to sit quietly, copy the teacher's lecture and blackboard notes into their copybooks, and accept a rather slow pace of teaching and learning. The conventional rote-learning ritual of memorization and recitation normally outweighs activity that involves self-expression or abstract, original, or critical thinking. In general, there is little variety in the range of learning experiences that teachers offer students.
- Without adequate teaching materials or the knowledge of how to use those that are available, many teachers are hard-pressed to plan solid lessons, and eventually many resort to little, if any, lesson planning.
- As students become increasingly discouraged about their academic progress and the quality of their education, teachers have found them harder to motivate.

TEACHERS' DRESS

- Female teachers' attire is clearly influenced by Westernized dress. Stylish, vibrant, and colorful clothing is perfectly acceptable. Still, there are some women who dress in more traditional garb, with long skirts and heads covered by wrapped bandanas.

DISCIPLINE AND CLASS MANAGEMENT

- Former Liberian President Charles Taylor flogged his 13-year-old daughter, forcing her to lie face down on the teacher's desk to reinforce the traditional belief that school is a place where discipline is learned through corporal punishment. Though such punitive measures are becoming less accepted following the war, many students who have themselves inflicted physical harm to others as child combatants appear to respond to little else. Some Liberian parents claim that every teacher should carry a stick.
- Current school policy requires unruly students to be sent home and instructed to return with a parent so that the specific nature of the offense can be discussed and the appropriate punishment meted out by the parent later at home (usually a scolding or a spanking).

STUDENTS' CIRCUMSTANCES

- Children may walk two to three miles to reach the nearest school.
- Some Liberian refugee children may have been subjected to multiple resettlements and may feel insecure in a new environment. Others have witnessed or perpetrated killings and other forms of violence; are prone to violence themselves; or do not fear rules, authorities, or punishment.
- Many children of Liberian refugees were not born or raised in their native land but have spent up to ten years of their lives in refugee camps before arriving in the United States.
- Most Liberian families live from paycheck to paycheck, with the parents working multiple jobs. Regardless of their income, they are not likely to manifest signs of affluence since much of their savings is returned to Liberia to support relatives who might otherwise starve.
- Many Liberian students have been witness to unspeakable violence, cruelty, and humiliation. Reports have surfaced, for example, of family members being forced to sing and dance while their relatives were beaten, raped, or killed.

STUDENT-STUDENT RELATIONSHIP

- Groups or pairs of students will often assemble before a major test to study together and share notes.

STUDENTS' LEARNING PRACTICES

- Students who have had the opportunity to attend school have likely been exposed primarily to the system of rote learning in which information is carefully memorized and recited without particular attention to analyzing it, generalizing it, or discussing ways to apply or evaluate it.
- Authorities believe that students should be more competitive in class and have encouraged teachers to address the situation by designing contests in class, between classes, and even between schools.
- Cheating during exams is discouraged but nonetheless not uncommon. If caught, however, the student is likely to be expelled.

STUDENTS' DRESS

- Most schools require students to wear uniforms, consisting of color-coordinated shirts and skirts or trousers. Although the cost of uniforms for a family with several children in school may be prohibitive, the practice is seen as a way of leveling the economic differences among students by making their appearance consistent.
- Oftentimes uniform requirements are waived for the initial few weeks to a few months in order to encourage parents to enroll their children in school.
- The dress code of schools extends beyond students' attire to the cleanliness and neatness of their hair and fingernails. No showy jewelry may be worn, and no rings are allowed.

GIFTS FOR THE TEACHER

- Students rarely buy gifts for teachers; however, on Teachers' Day at the end of the academic year, students may collect money to buy food for a class party.

NONVERBAL COMMUNICATION

- Instead of shaking hands, Liberians may grab the middle finger of a friend's right hand between his or her own thumb and middle finger. This practice began during years of slavery in the United States and used to function as a distinct gesture meaning freedom.
- Liberians are considered by some to have a direct and abrupt speaking style.
- Liberians generally do not offer or receive anything with the left hand as it is considered to be unclean.
- Guests are offered refreshments and a place to rest, even overnight or for an extended length of time, and will never be questioned about their day of departure.
- Raising one's voice at a parent or another adult is strictly forbidden.

- Some Liberians have a superstition that if you sweep the floors at night, the sweeper will either die, sweep away good luck, or give birth to an albino child.
- Singing while taking a bath or shower is considered bad luck.

APPROPRIATE TOPICS

- Because Liberians have become accustomed to associating the expression of political opinions with harmful consequences, they are loath to discuss politics in public and may not wish to relate their own stories.
- Children who eavesdrop on the conversation of adults are likely to be punished or at least driven from the room where adults are gathered.

OUTSIDE OF CLASS

- Students are responsible for cleaning their school and taking care of the school grounds. Some schools have associated farms, which must also be tended without financial compensation to the students.
- Children enjoy playing such games as baseball, a board game call *ludo,* marbles, hopscotch, and hide-and-seek.

Potential Adjustment Challenges

PROBLEMS/SOLUTIONS

Problem

I'm concerned about a Liberian boy in my class who bites and kicks other children. Is he suffering from Post-Traumatic Stress Disorder?

Solution

This student's behavior may or may not be attributed to the trauma of war. The exploitation of children during the civil war, especially the child soldiers who may have started using firearms by the age of five, is a troublesome concern for countless Liberian immigrants. Many were instructed to kill their own parents and were threatened with death themselves if they did not. An assessment by UNICEF in June 2003 suggests that up to 70 percent of those fighting in the civil war were children; 80 percent of these were armed combatants.

Problem

One little Liberian girl just can't seem to sit still in class. She sometimes stands up and wanders over to the bookcase or goes out into the corridor. Should she be tested for hyperactivity disorder?

Solution

Liberian children who have not attended school or who have had little exposure to formal schooling may not know about such practices as raising one's hand to go to the restroom or volunteer to speak in class. They might not even know how to write with a pencil, as slates and chalk may have been the only writing utensils in their classrooms back home or in the refugee camps.

Problem

I find the parents of some of my Liberian students disturbingly lax when it comes to disciplining their children. Does culture play a role here?

Solution

Liberian parents may not set clear rules for their children with regard to getting homework done or going to bed at a reasonably early hour nor might many appreciate the importance of helping children with homework. Many young Liberian parents have lost valuable parenting role models as a result of the war and may be unprepared to serve as the kinds of advocates for their children's education that North American parents are encouraged to be.

Somalia

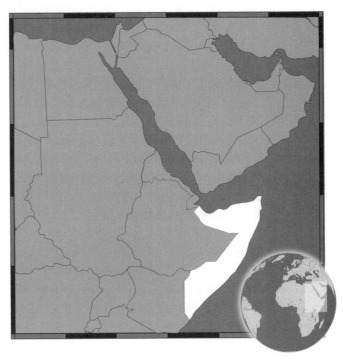

■ SOMALIA *Upclose*

Capital: Mogadishu

Population: 8,863,338 (June 2006)

Size: 637,657 sq. km. (246,201 sq. mi.) (almost the size of Texas)

Location: in east Africa, forming the area known as the Horn of Africa, bordered in the north by the Gulf of Aden, in the east and south by the Indian Ocean, in the southwest by Kenya, in the west by Ethiopia, and in the northwest by Djibouti

Climate: monsoons and moderate temperatures from December to February in the northeast; monsoons and very hot temperatures in the southwest with irregular rainfall and hot and humid periods between monsoons

Terrain: mostly flat to undulating desert plateau, with higher hills in the north

Monetary Unit: shilling (1,298 per U.S. dollar) (June 2006)

Religion: Sunni Muslim

Language(s): Somali (Maay Maay variety in southern Somalia and Af Maxaa elsewhere), Arabic with some educated Somalis speaking Italian and/or English

Literacy Rate: total population 37.8%; men 49.7%; women 25.8% (2001)

Ethnicity: Somali 85%, Bantu and other non-Somali 15% (including 30,000 Arabs)

Per Capita Income: US$600 (2005)

Population Distribution: 35% urban, 65% rural

Population below Poverty Line: No reliable data available

Life Expectancy: total population 48.5 years; men 46.7 years; women 50.3 years (2006)

Government: transitional, parliamentary federal government

PUBLIC HOLIDAYS		
	January 1	New Year's Day
	March 25*	*Eid al-Fitr* (end of Ramadan)
	May 1	Labor Day
	June 1*	*Eid-al-Adha* (Feast of the Sacrifice)
	June 26	Independence Day (Northern region)
	June 30*	*Ashura* (anniversary of the death of Husayn bin Ali)
	July 1	Independence Day (Southern region)
	August 30*	*Mouloud* (Birth of the Prophet)
		variable dates

▉ Personal Perspective

In Somalia you wore sandals, and if they broke, you fixed them. In the United States you have to wear sneakers, and other students make fun of you if you don't have the right kind of (expensive) sneakers.

—Birman, Trickett, and Bacchus (2001)

▉ Historical Perspective

IMMIGRATION TO THE UNITED STATES

The Somalis who have arrived in the United States as refugees and immigrants represent two distinct groups. The most populous is the group that traces their ancestry to the Arabs. The Somali Bantu trace their ancestry to Africans from Tanzania, Malawi, and Mozambique. They have darker skin and courser hair than their compatriots; are farmers rather than nomads; and have historically been exploited, repressed, and discriminated against in Somalia. Civil war and famine in Somalia led some 45 percent of both groups to flee their homes, and approximately 400,000 people died either from war, disease, or starvation. Reports reveal that almost half of all Somali children under the age of five died by 1993. Many died during the dangerous and difficult journey to safety. Those who found refuge filled camps in Ethiopia (500,000), Kenya (300,000), Yemen (65,000), and Djibouti (15,000), Tanzania (4,200) and some 100,000 fled to Europe.

The suffering, discrimination, and persecution of the Somali Bantu continued after reaching the refugee camps in Kenya and Tanzania. Women who left the camp to gather firewood were continually vulnerable to rape, and at night bandits regularly attacked the Bantu sections, not only stealing their belongings but also assaulting their occupants, so that eventually the Bantu were forced to erect barbed wire fences and post armed guards to protect themselves against the raids. Many times the violence perpetrated against the Bantu took place at the hands of non–Bantu Somalis.

Regardless of the obstacles they faced, many Somali Bantu used their agricultural backgrounds to support their families during the years they spent in the refugee camps. They cultivated small plots of land to grow vegetables for sale at market and were known to be reliable and diligent employees when hired by nongovernmental organizations (NGOs) as construction workers. Today around 40,000 Somali refugees have been resettled in the United States. Most live in large metropolitan centers such as Minneapolis, Columbus (Ohio), New York, Washington, DC, Boston, San Diego, Atlanta, and Detroit.

HISTORICAL SYNOPSIS

Somalia is populated by many different clans and subclans that along with outside forces have played a significant role in the country's history. During the late 19th and early 20th centuries, Somalia was under British and Italian colonial powers. In 1960, both the British and the Italian sections merged to form the United Republic of Somalia, headed by an elected president. Trouble persisted both internally with disputes between regional, clan, and subclan divisions and externally in terms of border disputes with Kenya and Ethiopia.

In 1969, Muhammad Siad Barre assumed control via a military coup, putting an end to democracy and establishing a socialist state. Over time, more and more power and wealth were concentrated in the hands of Barre's Marehan clan. The resulting anger of non-Marehan clans led to infighting throughout Somalia. Forced appropriation of property, violent repression, a massive military buildup, and a basic "divide and conquer" philosophy were all aspects of Barre's policy and led to anarchy and eventually civil war. Finally, in the 1980s, Barre's domination began to recede, and he was overthrown in 1991. After this, Somalia fell into disintegration and bitter civil conflicts, with the northwestern district of Somaliland declaring unilateral independence. The northeastern section remained fairly stable, but the south became a battlefield with various clan-based factions fighting for control. This led to a virtual stagnation of the economy, the looting of food stocks (primarily those accumulated by the Somali Bantu), the collapse of the commercial infrastructure, and the 1991–1992 famine, which, coupled with widespread violence, caused the deaths of as many as 350,000 people and the flight of nearly half a million others to Kenya, Saudi Arabia, Yemen, and Egypt. By August 1992, it was estimated that about one-quarter of the population, some 1.5 million people, were in danger of starvation. It became almost impossible to distribute food because of the activities of armed bandits often under the influence of *qat,* a mild stimulant that increases aggression. The rise of these thugs and local warlords came about as a direct result of the collapse of the central government and the absence of any organized opposition, as well as of the ready availability of weapons from the earlier arming of Somalia by both the United States and the former Soviet Union.

In November 1992, the UN sent a peace-keeping force to restore order and facilitate food distribution but left Somalia after three years having failed in its mission. In 1998, the Puntland region of northern Somalia declared independence. However, opposition and fighting continued, and rebels, sometimes with outside help, continued to seize control of some areas of the country. In April 2001, a group of warlords announced their intention of setting up a government in direct opposition to the country's transitional administration. This led to violence that killed dozens of people in the capital of Mogadishu. The situation was compounded by a serious drought in the south. The country was pushed to the edge of economic collapse after the September 11, 2001 attacks in the United States when aid workers withdrew to safety and Somalia's assets were frozen because of suspected links to al-Qaeda. Although various sections of the country have declared independence or have begun forming their own regional governments, and peace talks and cease-fires initially fed feelings of optimism, opposition still remains, the government is still unstable, and fighting and terrorist attacks still occur.

Deep Culture Perspective

DEEP CULTURE BELIEFS

Somalia is home to a variety of ethnic communities, cultures, languages, and religious beliefs and practices. The majority culture is nomadic pastoral and traces its ancestry to the Arabs. The Somali Bantu claim a traditionally African ancestry. They tend to be non-nomadic farmers, and their physical appearance differs from the non-Bantu in that they have darker complexions and coarser hair. These two very different groups represent oppressors and oppressed, yet both were compelled to escape the brutal and complex conditions of their country to find safety.

The Somali Bantu

- The ancestors of today's Somali Bantu lived in Tanzania, Malawi, and Mozambique before they were forcibly brought to Somalia as slaves in the 1800s and 1900s to serve Arab sultans. Among the many pejorative names for the Somali Bantu are the terms *adoon* and *habash*, both of which mean slave. They are also sometimes called *wagosha* ("people of the forest"), *jareer* ("kinky hair people"), or *ooji* (the Italian word for "today" and implying that the Bantu were disinterested in the future). Along with these offensive labels, the Somali Bantu have withstood discrimination and marginalization in virtually every aspect of society including education and employment, and they are openly considered second-class citizens in Somalia.
- The religious beliefs of the Somali Bantu may range from animism to Christianity. Many have converted to Islam and are considered liberal Muslims by Islamic standards, although they refrain from eating meat that is not halal (slaughtered by a Muslim in a traditional ritual) and do not consume much alcohol, except during ceremonies. Regardless of denomination or sect, it is not uncommon to find components of traditional ritual, magic, potions, trances, curses, and other mystical elements mixed into the religious practices of the Bantu. Some of these traditions find their way into health-care practices, such as the heating of a nail and placing it on a child's forehead to reduce swelling or the burning of holes in the skin to address headaches and stomachaches.

- Somali Bantu Muslim women enjoy more authority and social freedom than do many of their counterparts elsewhere. For example, they do not wear the *hijab* or headscarf that most Muslim women are required to wear in public, they work alongside men in the fields, and they participate alongside men in public ceremonies.

- The Somali Bantu are known to be resourceful and resilient. They are not averse to toiling at difficult, dirty, menial, or time-consuming jobs and are thought to be flexible and open to the changes within their environments. Many describe them as generous and excellent hosts, possessing a humble demeanor and great charm in the company of others, despite the difficulties of their personal circumstances. They are particularly obliging toward family members in need of support, but even outsiders can enjoy considerable generosity, as when they fall victim to a devastating drought and are invited to enter into a sharecropping arrangement by members of nearby Bantu villages.

- The average Somali Bantu family consists of grandparents, parents, between four to eight children, and often adult relatives and their children. Polygamy is not uncommon; as a result, many Bantu consider themselves members of more than one family. Most young people marry around age 17 or 18, and the ceremony tends to be a major event (paid for by the groom's family) involving many guests, ample food, and general merriment. Bantu couples may not stay together, however, divorce no longer possesses the stigma that it might in other parts of the world. The children of divorced parents usually live with the mother. While Bantu culture is considered patriarchal, women are respected as the head of household.

- Female circumcision (see page 267), a custom that is not mandated by the Islamic religion, is practiced by the Somali Bantu as it is with other groups of Somalis in order to discourage promiscuous behavior and thereby to protect the reputation of the family. According to a 1995 report, some 98 percent of Somali girls between the ages of eight and ten were circumcised. For many years later in life women who have been thus circumcised suffer from a variety of medical ailments directly linked to the practice of female infibulation.

The Traditional Somalis

- Unlike their Bantu compatriots, traditional Somalis, who make up 60–70 percent of the total Somali population, tend to be nomadic. Their territory (and identity) is determined by clan, a familial unit with which they identify strongly, as opposed to location of residence, as is the case with the Bantu. Thus, the question *Tol maa tahay?* ("Who are you from?") is heard more often than "Where are you from?" The clan is administered by a council of adult males, which comes to the aid of smaller groups and individuals within the clan and may also hear and resolve personal or familial crises. Perhaps also due to their nomadic lifestyle, traditional Somalis are often described as fiercely independent, flexible, and adaptable.

- Traditional Somalis are said to be governed by a strict code of ethics. Honor is the cornerstone of interpersonal activity, and retribution when wronged is taken for granted. They value psychological, spiritual, and physical strength and may boldly confront one another in the case of the perception of an affront. This boldness can be seen in the way they express themselves as well. Some claim that Somalis have an overly high opinion of themselves, but they are strong advocates of democracy, egalitarianism, and the rights of the individual. Loyalty to one's family and friends is rarely compromised, and though some contend that they are neither humble nor generous with expressions of appreciation for others, Somalis are also claimed to appreciate humor at their own expense.

- The typical Somali family is male dominated, but women have begun to exercise greater control and enjoy more liberty than in earlier times. The many deaths of men caused by the civil war accounts in large measure for this change as does the migration of husbands with their primary family to the United States while secondary wives and their children remain in refugee camps until resettlement. Another factor in the emergence of women as more powerful forces in Somali society is the economic and social reform made on their behalf by the previous socialist government.

PROVERBS

- Do not walk into a snake pit with your eyes open.
- Wisdom does not come overnight.
- In the ocean, one does not need to sow water.
- Where I make my living, there is my home.
- He who does not shave you does not cut you.
- To be without knowledge is to be without light.
- Together the teeth can cut.
- Think before you act.
- An old wound will not go away.

FOLK TALE

There once were two cousins who were traveling to a distant city where there was a school for religion. On the way they passed through a town whose leader was not particularly well educated. Because it was Friday, they went to the mosque to pray. The leader gave the sermon, but, because he was not an educated man, his words were nonsense. The two cousins continued their journey and attended the school for religion. After many months, they finished their studies and considered returning to their home. One cousin was more ambitious than the other, however, and declared that he would remain in the school to study politics. So the first cousin left alone.

On his way home, he again passed through the town with the uneducated leader. Again he went to the mosque for Friday prayers and again heard the leader talking nonsense. Unable to contain himself, the traveler interrupted the speaker and continued the sermon. He spoke so well that he shamed the leader, who became angry and threw the man in prison.

After two years, the other cousin finished his studies and started his journey home. He, too, arrived in the town with the uneducated leader in time for Friday prayers, and he, too, listened to the nonsense spoken by the leader. However, he did not interrupt but waited until the leader had finished, politely asking for permission to speak. Permission granted, the man started to lavishly praise the leader, claiming that his people were so lucky that they would be blessed just to have one hair from his head. At this everybody rushed forward to pluck a hair from the leader's head, but in their stampede, they ended up accidentally killing the leader. In his stead, the people chose the man who had studied religion and politics to be their new leader. When he learned of his cousin's fate, he immediately released his relative, and they both remarked on the advantages of education.

Administrative Perspective

OFFICIAL EDUCATIONAL POLICY

Traditionally, education in Somalia has been provided by a mixture of informal "mobile" Quranic schools called *duksi* and more formal and fixed Quranic institutions. With the advent of colonialism, some formal secular schooling was available, mostly to train clerical staff for the colonial government, but by the time of independence in 1960, few people were educated, the school infrastructure was minimal with only 233 primary and 12 secondary schools in the whole country, and most Somalis perceived such institutions as irrelevant to their daily lives. However, with the introduction of the Somali language rather than the traditional Arabic into schools and the development of its written form under the Barre regime, as well as a mass literacy campaign at that time, the education system began to be expanded. Following this there was an increase in the number of schools and in pupil enrollment. However, as funds for education dried up in the 1980s, enrollment began to fall, including the number of trained teachers, which plummeted to 611 for the whole country. Like other aspects of the Somali infrastructure, the education system virtually collapsed with the outbreak of civil war in 1991, and the country's schools shut down.

Attendance in the Quranic schools, of which there is at least one in every community, begins at age four and continues to age 15. Sometimes mobile Quranic schools follow the pastoral herdsmen. Teachers are often paid directly by the parents, and not always in monetary form. These institutions hold an important place in Somali society, attested to by their continuing existence not only in Somalia but also in three refugee camps in Djibouti where 15 Quranic schools, each with its own teacher, have been established.

After 1991, there was significant international agency support for education in Somalia, specifically on the part of UNESCO, UNICEF, the World Food Program, as well as from many other NGOs. These organizations helped with textbooks, curricula, teacher education and remuneration, the rebuilding of schools, and the dissemination of information on the importance and value of education, especially for girls. However, the absence of a national educational system has meant that reform of the curriculum is problematic if not impossible. Outside bodies such as the UN have no mandate for proposing a new curriculum or new structure, as there is not yet a body that represents the Somali community. On the other hand, there is some cause for optimism in the increased availability of educational textbooks and materials, teacher training programs, and workshops for school administrators.

Today, there are a few private secondary schools in urban parts of Somalia, but adequate educational opportunities are not available. In refugee camps, Somali children have access to basic schooling, with teacher and student numbers steadily increasing, perhaps because of the "captive" nature of the audience. Teaching methods and motivation are improving thanks to teachers' access to in-service training. There also appears to be a desire between the international agencies and people within the educational community to encourage some secular education within the Koranic schools.

EDUCATION AT A GLANCE

See the Education at a Glance table on page 256.

SOMALIA

Level/Age	Hours/Calendar	Language of Instruction	Compulsory Attendance	Exams	Grading System	Curriculum	Cost	Enrollment
Primary Grades 1–8 ages 6–14 (Many students begin primary school well beyond the age of 6.)	Due to the chronic violence in Somalia, schools often are not in session for any longer than six months at a time. Classes are held Sunday through Thursday.	Somali, but instruction may be delivered in Arabic, English, or Italian in some schools.	Yes, to age 14	No data available	100-point scale pass/fail = 60%	Reading, writing, mathematics, social studies, Arabic as a second language, some instruction in agriculture and animal husbandry.	Education is legally free, but most schools cannot function without supplements paid by parents. Subsidies from NGOs are directed to some schools.	Basic statistics for education are largely unavailable. Drop-out rate for girls is alarmingly high, especially after Grade 4. Most nomadic families send at least one of their children to school.
Secondary Grades 9–12 ages 14–18			No	National entrance exam required for university. Students are awarded the secondary school–leaving certificate upon successful completion of this level.		General schools teach all main subjects. Technical/vocational schools teach subjects that lead to development of trade skills.		10% of primary school graduates advance to the secondary level. Twice as many boys as girls attend secondary school.
University ages 19+ Students must first spend 2 years in national service; bachelor's 4 years; higher technical institutions 1–4 years; the university is introducing a master's degree.			No	Yearly exams in all subjects.	30-point scale pass/fail = 18	Bachelor's degree offered mainly at Mogadishu University. Higher technical/vocational institutions offer industrial science, public health, veterinary medicine, telecommunications, and business.	Approximately US$300–400 per year.	Most postsecondary educational institutions have disappeared as the civil war has grown more intense.

Surface Culture Perspective

CLASSROOMS

- Even before the outbreak of civil war in the early 1990s, classrooms were in a state of disrepair with few textbooks or instructional materials. During the major conflicts, about 90 percent of school buildings were either totally or partially destroyed, and all were looted; all school records were lost.
- Of the schools that remain standing, no desks, blackboards, books, or chairs can be found. Some schools, in fact, are occupied by displaced families who would have to be rehoused if the schools were to be reopened.
- Many Somali students have no experience with formal education, including common school rituals such as raising one's hand and standing in a lunch line. Their academic learning skills have not been developed, and many motor skills associated with learning, such as how to write with a pencil, have yet to be addressed.
- Since so few students attend school, the teacher-student ratio of 1:19 does not at first glance cause alarm.

TEACHERS' STATUS

- To teach at the primary school level, prospective instructors should complete one year of *Scuole Magistrali* after graduation from secondary school.
- Those who hope to teach at the secondary level receive three years of training in the National University's Faculty of Education or at the Technical Teacher Training College following graduation from secondary school.
- There were very few qualified teachers at the outbreak of the civil war, partly because of the high level of attrition toward the end of the Barre regime. This resulted from the very low and irregular teachers' salaries, often forcing teachers to find second jobs.
- Today teachers are mostly untrained and unqualified volunteers.
- The UN has designed crash courses to help teachers in Quranic schools deliver basic education in literacy, numeracy, and health.
- The majority of teachers at lower grades are men, and there are almost no female teachers at the secondary and higher levels. This discourages the presence of female students at these levels, though for other social reasons, very few girls attend these levels anyway.

TEACHER-STUDENT RELATIONSHIP

- The Quranic schools and their teachers are held in very high esteem within Somali society and are respected by both parents and children. The teachers in these schools have a great deal of influence over the lives of their students and will often discuss various personal topics with the children.
- In regular schools, teachers and students do not develop friendships but restrict their interaction to the business of learning.

TEACHING PRACTICES

- The teaching style in Quranic schools in Somalia is similar to that of such schools in other parts of the world and has not changed over time. Students basically memorize and recite sections of the Quran. Their goal is reached when they are able to recite 30 chapters from the Quran.
- While teachers in regular schools may encourage students to ask for clarification, they do not promote active classroom participation, particularly among female students, nor do they invite debate or the expression of opinions.

TEACHERS' DRESS

- Somali men tend to wear Western-style dress at work and more traditional robes for leisure activities, especially in rural areas. These consist of a white or brightly-colored cloth wrapped around them. Many Bantu men in the refugee camps, and particularly the older ones, dress in buttoned shirts or t-shirts along with the traditional wraparound cloth that other Somalis wear around their waists. Like their Somali compatriots, the Bantu may wear this clothing at home once they arrive in the United States. Younger men engaged in manual labor are more likely to wear pants rather than the wraparound cloth. Some Bantu men also put on the Muslim cap or, less often, a turban.
- Women's clothing is even more varied, from full-length dresses to sari-like white or red cotton robes. Married women tend to wear headscarves, but not the *hijab* unless they are from very conservative or fundamentalist families. Traditionally, unmarried women braid their hair and do not use headscarves, make-up, or perfume. However, increasing urbanization is blurring this distinction.
- Women often have ornate patterns painted on their feet and hands with henna or *khidaab* dyes. These are often signs of celebrations such as marriage or the birth of a child.

DISCIPLINE AND CLASS MANAGEMENT

- Parents tend to want schools to teach their children discipline. In other words, they see the process as starting at school and being reinforced at home.
- Teachers may resort to the use of corporal punishment, such as striking students with small sticks, administered in front of the entire class when students misbehave.

STUDENTS' CIRCUMSTANCES

- Most students in Somalia do not have access to an education, so those that do are very committed to it and have great respect for schools.
- Many more boys than girls enroll in school when and where education is available. Because the role of girls is seen primarily as a domestic one, the process of education is not seen as beneficial to their status. Even where an education for girls is deemed appropriate, the specific hours of instruction usually overlap with those during which household chores are undertaken.
- Schooling is often available in most of the refugee camps in which Somalis reside, and the quality of instruction is superior to that which exists in the few open schools in Somalia.

STUDENT-STUDENT RELATIONSHIP

- Somali children are very close to one another, the bond often forged through shared hardship and common experience, which may not only be the refugee camp experience but adjustment to a new and different culture in which many of their traditions and clothing are ridiculed by their North American peers.
- Many Somali households are made up of combined families where not all children are related, and yet the attachment and sense of family unity is still very strong.
- Somali children are discouraged from socializing in mixed sex groups and usually will not go out to shopping malls or movies without their families.

STUDENTS' LEARNING PRACTICES

- Students invest much of their energy in memorizing material that is presented in class.
- Most Somali students are attentive but quiet in class. They show their respect for the teacher, their classmates, and education in general by obeying rules rather than by displaying their uniqueness and creativity.
- Successful students may be rewarded by their parents with gifts of clothing or pocket money, but praise from the teacher is not expected.

STUDENTS' DRESS

- Girls normally wear simple dresses or wraparound skirts while boys' attire consists of trousers or shorts and t-shirt.
- Somali girls often wear headscarves to school.

GIFTS FOR THE TEACHER

- Gifts are rarely given to teachers by their students.
- In general, if a gift is given, it is customary to give one in return. If something is praised, it is customary to offer it to the admirer, regardless of its cost.

NONVERBAL COMMUNICATION

- When greeting acquaintances and nonacquaintances alike it is customary for people to shake hands, and it is not uncommon for men to hug and kiss on the cheek when greeting each other.
- Small talk is important, though asking about female relatives could cause offense. It is also rude to criticize a Somali openly.
- Eye contact is important during conversations, and verbal skill is highly respected.
- Somalis tend to stand close to each other when talking; about one foot of personal space is considered acceptable.
- Somalis avoid using the left hand, especially when offering and receiving food.
- It is considered very offensive to show the soles of one's feet.

FORMS OF ADDRESS

- *Aw* or Mister is used for males who are the heads of households. *Ay* or Ms. is used for older women.
- Somalis usually have three names: their given name, their father's name, and their grandfather's name. Names are often similar, given the smaller pool from which they are drawn, and, therefore, Somalis tend to use nicknames, such as *Raage,* meaning "he who delayed at birth" or *Madoowbe,* meaning "very black."
- When a woman marries, she does not take her husband's name but continues to use her father's and grandfather's names.
- A person whose name is Faduma (female name) or Mohamed (male name) is most likely the first-born child of a couple. Male twins are almost without exception named Hassan and Hussein.
- Some Somali names have an Arabic origin, such as the examples given previously, while others are Cushtic in origin. Popular Cushtic (related to the Somali language) names for girls include Awa (meaning "lucky") and Awrala ("without blemish"). Awaale ("lucky") and Waabberi ("sunrise") are popular Cushtic names for boys.

APPROPRIATE TOPICS

- While Somalis might not like to talk about their war experiences, they enjoy talking about their country.
- Politics is a subject that Somalis may broach with friends and family but may be wary of expressing their views to strangers.

OUTSIDE OF CLASS

- Most Somali children who are fortunate enough to attend school also have responsibilities at home. Girls are expected to gather firewood, cook, clean, and look after younger siblings. Boys work alongside their fathers in the fields or tend cattle.

Potential Adjustment Challenges

PROBLEMS/SOLUTIONS

Problem

One of my Somali students has barely been enrolled in my school for two months and is about ready to move again. When I asked him why his family was moving again, he appeared not to hear my question.

Solution

Personal problems or family circumstances, such as needing to move to a different location that is perhaps closer to work for one or more of the parents, may be carefully guarded by the family or community. In other words, this information is considered personal and not to be readily shared with outsiders.

Problem

Every time I attempt to compliment my Somali student, he says, "Oh no, teacher. I am not good." Is this a cultural response to praise or something more idiosyncratic to this student?

Solution

Many Somalis, especially the Bantu peoples, have known such a long history of subjugation that they may experience little self-worth and can be prone to bouts of depression and withdrawal. Because of the prolonged ethnic strife in their country and even in the refugee camps, they may feel easily threatened, unsafe, and vulnerable.

Problem

I recently met a 25-year-old Somali man who wants to enroll in a middle school in our community. Why doesn't he just register for a GED class at the community college?

Solution

Somali adults may be physically and emotionally mature, but many lack basic academic knowledge and study skills due to the closing of schools for years at a time during the war. Some have so little schooling experience that they do not qualify for GED programs, which require that enrollees meet a certain threshold of formal education. While to their North American age-mates, the prospect of studying amidst middle schoolers would be humiliating and ludicrous, to many Somalis it represents an opportunity that they already missed and may never have again.

Sudan

SUDAN *Upclose*

Capital: Khartoum

Population: 41,236,378 (June 2006)

Size: 2,505,810 sq. km. (967,499 sq. mi.) (approximately one-fourth the size of the U.S.)

Location: in central northeastern Africa, bordered on the north by Egypt and Libya; on the east by Chad and the Central African Republic; on the south by Congo, Uganda, and Kenya; and to the west by Ethiopia, Eritrea, and the Red Sea

Climate: tropical in the south and desert conditions in the north with a rainy season that may fall anywhere between April to November depending on region

Terrain: flatland desert in the north with mountains in the south, northeast, and west

Monetary Unit: dinar (234 per U.S. dollar) (June 2006)

Religion: Sunni Muslim 70%, indigenous religions 25%, Christian 5%

Language(s): Arabic, Dinka, Bedawi, Nuer, and Fur (in that order) are most common, plus approximately 130 additional distinct languages; some 400 regional dialects with English as the common second language in the south

Literacy Rate: total population 61.1%; men 71.8%; women 50.5% (2003)

Ethnicity: Black 52%, Arab 39%, Beja 6%, foreigners 2%, other 1% (in all, 19 different ethnic groups and 597 subgroups)

Per Capita Income: US$370 (2004)

Population Distribution: 39% urban, 61% rural (2003)

Population below Poverty Line: 40% (2004)

Life Expectancy: total population 58.9 years; men 57.7 years; women 60.2 years (2006)

Government: authoritarian regime

PUBLIC HOLIDAYS			
January 1	Independence Day	May 2*	*Sham el Nessim*
January 21*	*Eid-al-Adha* (Feast of the Sacrifice);		(Coptic Easter Monday)
	also called *Tabaski*	May 25	May Revolution Anniversary
February 10*	Islamic New Year	June 30	Revolution Day
March 3	National Unity Day	November 14-16*	*Eid-al-Fitr* (end of Ramadan);
April 6	Uprising Day		also called *Korité*
April 21	*Al-Mowlid Al Nabawi*	December 25	Christmas Day
	(Birth of the Prophet Mohamed)		*variable dates*

263

■ Personal Perspective

Let me provide a somewhat different, yet complementary (if humorous), example of the problem noted by Francis Deng, the illustrious international servant of the United Nations from the Sudan, which may have been a reference to his own experience when he first came to the United States. A Sudanese arriving in the States asked to see manifestations of how Blacks were mistreated in America. He was taken to and driven around Harlem. After staring out the window, block after block, he turned and asked his escort where the Blacks were. Startled and somewhat discomfited by the question, his escort replied curtly that the neighborhood that they had been driving through was almost exclusively Black. Was his guest color blind? The visitor replied, "But those are all Arabs!" For a Sudanese from the south of Sudan, the cocoa colored skin of the vast majority of American Blacks means that they are not Black but Arab, like those from the north of Sudan. For a Sudanese, Blacks have truly black and not brown skin pigmentation.

—*Metropolis Institute (n.d.)*

■ Historical Perspective

IMMIGRATION TO THE UNITED STATES

Severe ethnic and religious conflict has spawned decades of violence in Sudan and compelled thousands to flee their homes and seek safety in refugee camps in Ethiopia, Egypt, Kenya, Uganda, the Central African Republic, Chad, and the Democratic Republic of Congo. Many are children whose parents had been killed in an ethnic cleansing campaign by the pro-Arab Sudanese National Army or by anti-Arab rebel militias representing the Sudanese People's Liberation Army. Young boys, in particular, were being recruited to fight. Flight from their homes and villages meant trekking on foot thousands of kilometers over many months and sometimes years through arid and dangerous bush and enduring situations considered unthinkable by most North Americans (e.g., drinking one's own urine in order to avoid dehydration). Many died of sickness, starvation, animal attacks, or outright murder by government soldiers or rebels.

Sudan's decades-long civil war has resulted in the deaths of more than two million people, and another four million people have been displaced either inside or outside Sudanese borders. Many of these refugees spend long years in refugee camps where food and water are scarce, health care inadequate, and the fear of violence ever-present. Often the violence is perpetrated by the refugees themselves, but armed bands from outside the camps have been known to steal whatever they can, murder and rape the camp residents, and abduct men and boys into guerilla armies.

Less than 30 percent of applications by Sudanese requesting refugee status in the United States are granted. In 2002, for example, 3,680 Sudanese applied for refugee status, but only 1,054 of those applications were approved. Greater numbers of Sudanese refugees find asylum in the Netherlands, Germany, and the United Kingdom. In 2001, the United States agreed to allow 3,600 boys, girls, and young men to settle in the United States. These so-called "Lost Boys and Girls" continue to arrive with no more than the clothes on their backs. The largest numbers of Sudanese refugees have settled in Texas, Iowa, Nebraska, Arizona, and New York. They tend to be non-Arabs from southern Sudan, but some Arab Sudanese dissenters from the north have also arrived as refugees. The Sudanese refugees are known to be eager learners and hard workers, balancing academic studies with jobs in menial labor markets. This population is not known to remain on public assistance for any longer than three to four months.

HISTORICAL SYNOPSIS

While today Sudan is a desperately poor and war-torn country whose arable land is estimated at less than 7 percent and 50 percent of whose population is under the age of 18, it has a nine million–year history. Indeed, it lies in what is known as the "Cradle of Civilization"—the fertile Nile Valley region—and ancient Sudanese kingdoms competed with those in Egypt in terms of cultural achievement, economic power, military might, and political influence. Eventually, it was conquered by Egypt with later occupation by the British. Since its independence in 1956, however, Sudan has been experiencing civil war almost without interruption. The underlying cause of these conflicts is the attempted domination of the non-Muslim African Sudanese in the south by Arab Islamists in the north, but issues concerning religion, ethnicity, and natural resources have also contributed significantly to the violence.

In the late 1960s and early 1970s, both sides were being armed by outside forces—the rebel south by countries such as Israel, and the government in the north by the former Soviet Union. In 1989, the Islamists took control of the government in a military coup and joined forces with the ruling elite, imposing some aspects of *shariah* (traditional Islamic) law in 1991 (see page 267). In 1993, Omar al-Bashir was appointed president, and a new constitution was drawn up that was approved by approximately 98 percent of voters in 1998. The following year, Sudan began to export oil, and negotiations started between the president and some opposition parties, thus ushering in a period of multiparty politics. In that same year, the United States launched a missile attack against a chemical plant in Khartoum, claiming that Sudan had ties to al-Qaeda. (In the aftermath of the September 11, 2001, bombings of the World Trade Center and Pentagon, the United States imposed sanctions on Sudan for alleged continuing collaboration with al-Qaeda.)

Hostilities between government and rebel forces continued, famine struck the country in 2001, and a major Nile flood left thousands homeless. Peace talks between President al-Bashir and the rebel leader Jophn Garang began in earnest in that year, and, although these initially failed, subsequent face-to-face meetings led to cease-fires in 2002. Despite the negotiations and calls for cease-fire, however, fighting continued, with the western region of Darfur rising up against the government in 2003. The army's move to quell this uprising led to thousands of refugees fleeing to Chad and accusations that the progovernment *Janjaweed* militias were carrying out systematic killings of Africans in Darfur, which U.S. Secretary of State Colin Powell called genocide in 2004.

In January 2005, the government and southern rebels signed a peace accord, including a permanent cease-fire and the sharing of power with the southern rebel leader, John Garang, who was appointed vice president. However, accusations of systematic abuses by the government and its militias in Darfur continued, and when the vice president was killed in a helicopter crash, renewed hostilities broke out in Darfur. In March 2005, the UN Security Council sent 10,000 peace-keeping soldiers to southern Sudan, but the Darfur region remains unprotected.

■ Deep Culture Perspective

DEEP CULTURE BELIEFS

- Sudan is home to 19 different ethnic groups consisting of some 597 subgroups, but the greatest difference among the Sudanese, as far as ethnicity is concerned, is the distinction between Arabs and non-Arabs, a rough 40/60 percent divide. The largest non-Arab group (also called Blacks) are the Dinka (8% of the total population) followed by the Nuba (6%), the Nuer (between 4% and 8%), the Fur (2.7%), the Shilluk (1.6%), the Bari (1.3%), the Nubians (0.5%), and other non-Arabs (17%). Refugees coming to the United States are usually from southern Sudan, and are either Nuer or Dinka. The Nuer were primarily nomadic herders, and the Dinka, who make up the largest ethnic group in southern Sudan, were also pastoralists and farmers.
- The members of Sudan's various ethnic groups are also divided by language. Many languages and dialects of Sudan are mutually unintelligible, but Arabic is the lingua franca in the north and to some extent in the south, and rudimentary English is spoken or understood by residents of the south.
- Most Sudanese live in small communities, which typically consist of groups of related extended families. Members of these communities tend to be deeply loyal to one another and mutually supportive. They help each other rise socially or economically, and together they defend their land and village, either physically through combat or via

the institution of marriage, in which one strong family is essentially united with another of the same or greater status. Sometimes the status of a family is determined by the number of animals they keep, but often power is linked to the amount and quality of land that a family possesses. The land and the economic power that it provides is passed down from generation to generation.

- Each family is led by one of the oldest and most respected males. Lineage is traced through the male parent, and men, in general, are at the top of the social and familial hierarchy. Men are typically responsible for looking after the animals and the fields while the household and children fall under the women's purview. The relationship between the sexes tends to be more traditional in the north where men and women go about most of their lives separated from one another, whether it be at mealtime or at a special community gathering or celebration.

- Although spousal abuse is not uncommon among Sudanese couples regardless of whether they are city dwellers, rural farmers, or nomads, women in southern Sudan experience less of this kind of mistreatment and more freedoms than their peers in the northern part of the country. Unlike northern Sudanese women, for example, southern women sometimes participate in lineage councils, share many decision-making responsibilities with their husbands, and may be called upon to mediate a public conflict.

- Many Sudanese women living in the northern part of the country are subject to a traditional practice called the *zar,* a cathartic trance ceremony believed to rid a woman of evil spirits manifested as depression, infertility, or other physical or psychological afflictions. The *zar* involves animal sacrifice, the beating of drums, and frenetic dancing not only by the afflicted one but by all women present. Women usually lead these ceremonies and are typically the subject of a *zar,* but mostly male spirits are thought to possess a woman. *Zar* ceremonies were banned under *shariah* law in 1992 in Sudan, but the practice is perhaps more popular now than ever.

- Female circumcision has also been a widely accepted practice in Sudan, particularly among the Arab population. Also called infibulation, female circumcision involves removing the female genitalia of girls 12 years old or younger and stitching shut or narrowing the vaginal opening in order to prevent sexual intercourse. Despite the serious health risks immediately after the procedure and throughout the life of a woman who has been circumcised and regardless of health education programs and legislation condemning the practice, infibulation continues to be a popular custom among Sudanese Muslims.

- Most Sudanese are followers of Islam, particularly the Sunni branch of the religion, which recognizes *shariah* law, a set of principles based on the *Quran* and the pronouncements made by the Prophet Mohamed. *Shariah* law informs religious practice, governmental policy, and the day-to-day behavior of individuals. Most Sudanese Muslims do not eat pork or shellfish, but unlike many of their co-religionists, they may consume alcohol and gamble. Islam teaches that those with wealth should share it with the less fortunate, and generosity, fairness, and honesty are considered among a Muslim's most important virtues. Christianity is also practiced in Sudan, especially in the south, and many nomadic groups have held to their own multitheist traditions and beliefs despite the spreading popularity of Islam and Christianity. Many Sudanese believe in spirits, magic spells, and amulets. Fear of the evil eye is common as well.

- Not only are the Sudanese divided along religious and ethnic lines, they also diverge according to regional origin. Southerners, for example, are said to be gregarious and generous while their northern counterparts are known to be more conservative and formal in their dealings with others.

- Regardless of regional origin, Sudanese tend to see the family as the key to a successful and happy life, and they are gracious hosts to visiting relatives and friends, whether the visit is unexpected or arranged far in advance. Elaborate preparations may be made when out-of-town guests are awaited, including the slaughter of sheep or chickens, but warm hospitality is extended to visitors who drop in at midmorning or evening on Friday (the most popular visiting day). Whole families are welcomed as well. The children are usually sent away to a separate area of the house to play together, and the adults, separated by gender, enjoy tea or coffee plus light snacks. Men and women from southern Sudan may not remain segregated when families gather for more important celebrations such as weddings.

- Although most Sudanese are poor, a small upper class and middle class has developed in the cities. Regardless of economic class, wealth and power are recognized as important components of a successful life. Thus, an individual who comes from an influential and prosperous family derives benefits from that relationship beyond those that education or skill can provide, such as obtaining a government position.

- The Dinka of southern Sudan have been described as proud and even ethnocentric. Indeed, they believe that all human beings descended from their ancestors. This distinction leads them to adhere to high moral standards, to value courage, and to be sensitive to issues involving an individual's dignity and integrity. Some scholars believe that the Dinka's proud ethnic identity encourages a conservative stance toward change, particularly modernization, and a deep respect for tradition.

- The Dinka share many cultural and linguistic commonalities with other non-Arab Sudanese such as the Nuer and the Shilluk. Non-Dinka, however, are called *jur* (foreigners), and the particular type of *jur* is dictated by pigmentation. *Jur chol* are black foreigners while *jur mathiang* are lighter skinned, often Arabs.

- Cattle play a critical role in Dinka culture. They are used as currency as well as nourishment. Cattle may be sacrificed during religious or social celebrations, and dancers at such festivities often imitate them, especially with regard to the shape of their horns. From the time it is born, an ox's horns will be manipulated so that they will gradually and eventually grow to form certain predetermined shapes.

- Dinka men may have multiple wives, but they must always pay the bride price in cattle. Once the bride's family receives the cattle, they are distributed among various members of her extended family.
- Adulthood initiations may take place among the Dinka and involve the removal of the four lower canine teeth and scarring the face, a practice that is more common for males than for females.
- Although the Dinka are increasingly converting to either Christianity or Islam, their traditional belief system imbues the tribal chief with supernatural powers as well as the ability to communicate with God and the spirits of ancestors. The typical Dinka home also has a special corner where ancestors may be accommodated through the leaving of small sacrifices.

PROVERBS

- When two elephants fight, the grass suffers.
- Either I win the whole thing or leave it all.
- You can't feed your donkey only when you want to ride it.
- Your real brother is the one who comes to you when you are ill, not the one who comes to bury you.
- Health is a crown worn by those who are healthy and seen only by the sick.
- The world we live in is the world we have created.
- Even if a log lies in the water for a long time, it does not become a crocodile.
- Not all the trees in the forest make good firewood.
- We desire to bequeath two things to our children—the first one is roots; the other one is wings.
- If you think you are too small to make a difference, try sleeping in a closed room with a mosquito.

FOLK TALE

Once there was a very rich man who had everything because he could afford to buy what he wanted or needed. One day he was talking with a friend who said, "Anyone can die, and every person will eventually die." But the rich man was accustomed to control and having power over his life, so he wondered, "How can I escape death?"

That night he prayed that God would inform him of the cause and the exact date and time of his death. After he fell asleep, the rich man had a dream in which God told him he would die from a poisonous bite. Before going to bed the next night, the rich man prayed to God again, asking him for the date and time of his death. Within hours, God appeared to him in a dream and told him he would die on Thursday at 12:00 noon. Upon waking, the rich man gave thanks to God. "I will be watching," he said.

On the appointed day, the rich man gathered all his children in an open space, not too close to any trees. He cut a long pole, placed a small platform on one end, and stuck the other end in the ground. Next he climbed the pole, settled himself on the platform, and called down to his children. "If you see any snake, scorpion, or even an ant, beat it and kill it," he ordered.

Noon arrived. The rich man and his children were scouring the ground with their eyes. A hawk who was hunting in a nearby field suddenly appeared in the air carrying in its claws a live snake that it had just caught. Looking up, the rich man cried out in surprise, startling the hawk and causing it to release the snake onto the man's head. The snake bit him on the neck, and the rich man soon died.

▇ Administrative Perspective

OFFICIAL EDUCATIONAL POLICY

The educational system that prevailed before Sudan won its independence was primarily intended to educate Sudanese who would later become administrators in the colonial government. Most government schools were located in cities, but small private schools run by missionaries could be found in rural areas. Indeed, it is claimed that the colonial government virtually disregarded the education of children in the south, unloading that task on the mission schools, although the poor quality of instruction and impoverished curriculum in such schools was eventually the subject of controversy. In government schools, the size of the Sudanese teaching staff at the post-primary level was deemed insufficient as well. For this reason, foreign (mostly British) teachers were recruited, and the language of instruction became English in the British-dominated south.

After independence, efforts were made to assess and improve the quality of education in Sudan. In 1969 primary education up to Grade 6 was made compulsory, and the curriculum was to take a more vocational/technical turn. However, within ten years only one-fifth of Sudan's secondary schools had converted to the technical track, so the same problem regarding the lack of practical training among graduates persisted. Regardless of the fact that an academic education was actually less useful than a technical education, the former continued to be seen as the more prestigious. This and other failures in making education in Sudan universal and equitable led to the establishment of a new system in 1990 based on principles and teachings from the Quran and the *hadith* (a report of the Prophet Mohamed's teachings and activities).

Despite efforts to reform the system of education in Sudan, girls were nonetheless discouraged from attending school as the formal educational environment was thought to expose them to potentially immoral and harmful influences. Moreover, it was seen as unnecessary and ineffective in preparing girls for marriage. Millions of boys and girls, especially those in the south, lost precious years of schooling due to the continuing civil war. Those who eventually reached refugee camps found schools there to be even less adequate than those they had attended before the violence forced them to flee. As a result, many young Sudanese arriving in North America have little or no formal education.

The Sudanese government is still trying to reform the educational system. Among its goals are to strengthen religious faith of students, to develop a moral and self-reliant society, to promote patriotism and loyalty to country, to encourage innovation through modern technology, and to raise the environmental awareness of young people.

EDUCATION AT A GLANCE

See the Education at a Glance table on page 272.

SUDAN

Level/Age	Hours/Calendar	Language of Instruction	Compulsory Attendance	Exams	Grading System	Curriculum	Cost	Enrollment
Primary Grades 1–8 ages 6–14	July–Apr. The school year has been extended from 180 days to 210 days to compensate for the interruption of schooling experienced by most Sudanese students.	Local language during first two years of primary school with Arabic or English serving as the language of instruction through the end of secondary school	Yes, to age 14	To advance to secondary level, students must pass the Basic Education Certification Examination.	100-point scale A=80–100 B=70–79 C=60–69 D=50–59 F=0–49	Schools are currently not operational in Sudan. However, in refugee camps in Kenya, Sudanese students may study their mother tongue, English, Kiswahili, Arabic, mathematics, science, agriculture, religion, home science, arts and crafts, social studies, music, physical education.	Legally education is free in Sudan, but with the inability of the government to fund schools and teachers, parents are increasingly being pressed to pay portions of salaries and for upkeep of schools.	10% of primary school-aged girls are enrolled. Girls make up 45% of total primary level attendance. The average Sudanese has an average of 2.1 years of schooling (the lowest rate in the world).
Secondary Grades 9–11 ages 14–17 General secondary and technical schools: 3 years Vocational training centers: 2 years			No	At the end of the secondary cycle, students must sit for the Sudan School Certification Examination. Results determine entry to higher education. A score of 50% or higher qualifies a student for admission to non-university institutions. To enter the University of Khartoum, a score of 73% is needed; 88% for medicine.		Before the closing of schools in Sudan, students took languages (Arabic, English, and French), mathematics, physics, biology, geography, chemistry, environmental studies, history and social sciences, engineering, agriculture and animal production, commerce, physical education, family education, arts and design, military education, and computers. New curricula include modules on HIV/AIDS and life skills. In the final year students choose between arts and sciences stream. Technical secondary schools include industrial, commercial, and agricultural schools for boys and home economics schools for girls.		81% of primary school graduates advance to secondary level. Female share is 61.7% (second in the world for female share of enrollment at the secondary level).
University ages 18+		Arabic	No	No data available	A+ to F	Several national universities operate in the northern part of Sudan, while education has virtually shut down in the south. Several universities specialize in the training of clerics and religious scholars, and others focus on scientific and technical fields.		Overall enrollment is 6.9%.

Surface Culture Perspective

CLASSROOMS

- Sudan ranks last in the world in terms of government funding of education. School buildings are frequently no more than mud brick structures or single mud hut classrooms with thatch roofs, which are often destroyed by weather or termites within a year of their construction. In locations where no such "bush schools" are available for classes, lessons may be conducted under the shade of a tree. Whether under a tree or under the thatched roof of a mud hut, most students will sit on the ground as desks are considered luxuries. Where walled classrooms exist, their size is often too limited to accommodate the enrolled students, so some students must participate in the lessons standing outside the windows of the classroom. In some locations, classes cannot be held during the rainy season. No bathroom facilities, running water, or electricity are available in most schools. Nonetheless, many students will walk several hours one way to attend school.
- Neither students nor teachers may have books, they may be forced to share pencils, and sometimes they must cut their notebooks into smaller pieces in order to extend the "life" of the notebook. In some locations slates are available for students to write on during the lessons.
- In addition to the lack of school supplies and facilities, Sudan still suffers from a severe shortage of qualified teachers and an inadequately developed curriculum.
- It is not at all unusual for children of different ages to study together in the same grade.
- In addition to academic lessons, school children will often tend school vegetable gardens. Not only can the produce be sold at the market or used to pay teachers, but the students learn some basics of agriculture by planting and tending the gardens.

TEACHERS' STATUS

- In order to teach in the pre-primary and primary schools, prospective teachers, in theory, should attend colleges of basic education from which they receive a teaching certificate. After several years of teaching, they may return to college to study for a bachelor's degree in education.
- Those hoping to teach at the secondary level should study for a bachelor's degree in education within the College of Education in a university. The University of Khartoum now offers a graduate diploma in Teaching English at the Secondary Level (DIPTEASL).
- The Sudanese Ministry of Education reports that 43 percent of its primary-level teachers have been professionally trained to teach, and 39 percent of secondary school teachers have benefited from formal teacher preparation.

- For the most part, Sudanese teachers receive no pay from the government for their service. Instead, they are offered "incentives." That is to say, parents are relied upon to collect enough money to pay the teacher, but frequently they fail to scrape together sufficient funds, so the teacher either works essentially as a volunteer, demonstrates little commitment to the school and is frequently late or absent, or leaves the school as soon as he or she finds another job.
- In some villages where no teacher is available, an itinerant instructor will arrive periodically with some teaching materials, ready to offer lessons to whichever children choose to attend.

TEACHER-STUDENT RELATIONSHIP

- The Sudanese revere their teachers and do their best to please them. Their general demeanor toward the teacher is one of humility and utmost politeness. In this way, they believe not only that the teachers will receive the honor they deserve but also that the teachers will do their best in return to offer high-quality instruction.

TEACHING PRACTICES

- In situations in which students have no textbooks, the teacher may read from the only book available, lead the students in discussion, or use drawings or everyday objects and biological specimens as the basis for discussion. Thus, most lessons are not print based.
- Group activities are not common. Lessons are primarily teacher centered, although learners are encouraged to participate in discussion.
- Teachers will generally not move through instructional material quickly but linger on concepts in order to compensate for the lack of elaboration or reinforcement outside of class.

TEACHERS' DRESS

- In the northern cities, men may either wear Western shirts and trousers or the more traditional long white robes *(jalabia)* with accompanying turbans *(imma)*. Women wear long dresses plus a headscarf *(hijab)* or veil *(tarha)*.
- In the south, Western dress is more popular and acceptable for both men and women. Although women still dress modestly, they are more prone than their northern counterparts to wear plenty of jewelry in public.

DISCIPLINE AND CLASS MANAGEMENT

- Behavior that is considered worthy of punishment includes fighting, failing to pay attention in class, being late for school, or skipping school.

- On the rare occasion that a Sudanese student misbehaves in class, the teacher will generally send a note home to the parents inviting them for a special consultation. Once assembled, the parents and teacher discuss the child's situation, with the teacher typically offering advice to the parents and the parents apologizing to the teacher and to the principal and promising that the incident will not be repeated.
- Sudanese teachers consider corporal punishment beneath them; thus, they will never hit their students. However, they may require students to come to their homes to cut their grass or weed their gardens.
- A student may be expelled from school after receiving three warnings without a change in behavior.

STUDENTS' CIRCUMSTANCES

- Most Sudanese children receive a great deal of physical affection at home from all members of their extended families. Caregivers teach children to be quiet and obedient and may try to discourage curiosity and activity. Rambunctiousness on the part of children is often answered with punishment.
- Many Sudanese children grow up expecting to be rebuffed when they approach parents for assistance with resolving a problem. Indifference or telling children that they must solve their own problems leads many to develop resilience and independence, but for others this distance between parents and children may result in depression or anger.

STUDENT-STUDENT RELATIONSHIP

- Sudanese students are generally eager to help each other with their studies. Thus, one student may go to the home of another student who is having problems in school and help the weaker student with his or her homework.
- Although students are required to sit far away from one another during an exam, when the teacher leaves the room or if there is a break, someone may ask "Who understands?" and thereby solicit the help of stronger students in order to perform better on the test. This type of interaction among students is marked neither by coercion nor shame.

STUDENTS' LEARNING PRACTICES

- Younger students tend to be more willing to participate actively in class than their older peers, who are reported to be rather cautious and passive.
- The lack of opportunity to attend school makes many Sudanese children all the more eager to take advantage of the educational opportunities in North America once they have resettled. They tend to be hardworking and persistent with a high commitment to doing their best and getting the most out of school.

STUDENTS' DRESS

- Despite the impoverished conditions under which Sudanese children study, many schools require students to wear uniforms. Some schools change the uniform every year, and in some schools each grade has a different uniform. In such cases, many families simply cannot afford to comply with the uniform requirement and must keep their children out of school for this reason.

GIFTS FOR THE TEACHER

- A class of students may take up a collection and present a gift to a teacher they consider especially kind and effective. Such gifts are usually presented on graduation day and typically carry some symbolic value, such as a lamp for its ability to provide "light."
- Sudanese students rarely bring food to the teacher.

NONVERBAL COMMUNICATION

- In the south, Sudanese greetings are extended and elaborate, involving several exchanges inquiring about all members of each person's family (whether they are *tamtam,* or well), the shaking of hands and/or nudging each other's shoulders, and smiling broadly. Men and women will frequently greet each other with a handshake, contrary to the prohibition against this practice in the north.
- In the north, people gently shake the hand of friends of the same sex, or close friends may hug. These gestures are accompanied by greetings of *salaam alaykum* (peace be upon you) to which the other answers *alaykum salaam* (and upon you). Hosts may exclaim *ahlan wasahlan* (welcome).
- It is considered rude to point to another person using the index finger.
- Sudanese, especially those from the north, will not eat, pass food, or accept objects with the left hand. Often a person will extend both hands to offer or receive.
- Like other Muslims, Sudanese Arabs find exposure of the bottom of the feet or shoes to be the height of offense.
- In some parts of Sudan, nodding the head repeatedly in a downward direction implies affirmation, but nodding in the upward direction can mean "no."
- When greeting a friend or stranger who has just entered a room, anyone who was initially seated is expected to stand up.

FORMS OF ADDRESS

- Students typically address their teachers by Mr. or Mrs. or just "teacher," but these titles are never followed by the teacher's name, primarily because only schoolmates can use each other's names.
- It is not unusual for Sudanese to have nicknames. These are used among friends and for children. For elders it is more appropriate to use auntie or uncle. Older relatives who have made the pilgrimage (or *haj*) to Mecca will be called by *haji* plus first name. Women will not address their husbands by their given names. Government workers and professionals are called by title plus family name.
- Because cattle play such an important role in Dinka culture, the names of children are often inspired by the color of special cattle. Ayen and Yar (the color of cows) would be appropriate names for girls while Mayom, Mayen, and Malith (the color of bulls) would suit boys. The Dinka also assign special names to twins. Typical twin names are Ngor, Chan, and Bol.

APPROPRIATE TOPICS

- There are numerous taboo topics among the Sudanese. They include any discussion of sexuality (including female circumcision), bride sharing, child marriage, or polygamy. Religious debate is out of the question, and women's rights are virtually untouched as a topic of public discussion. In conversation with foreigners, broaching topics that may reflect negatively on the nation or culture (e.g., selling women and children into slavery) is considered extremely offensive.

OUTSIDE OF CLASS

- Most Sudanese males enjoy playing or watching soccer, and the country produces some of the best soccer players in Africa. Occasionally, men and boys play basketball and volleyball, and they are particularly adept at wrestling. Sudanese females are fond of dancing, jumping rope, and playing a form of hopscotch called *arika*. They also spend as much time as possible socializing with friends and, particularly, family. Men may meet their friends and relatives in a special hut called a *diwanya*.
- Whether they attend school or not, girls are expected to do heavy housework, including walking perhaps two hours one way to stand in line to fetch water, carrying up to five gallons at a time back home on their heads, grinding corn, cooking for the family, and looking after younger siblings.

Potential Adjustment Challenges

PROBLEMS/SOLUTIONS

Problem

My principal asked if I would work one-on-one with a new Sudanese student who doesn't seem to be making much progress in school. I'm happy to do this, but I have lots of other refugee students, too. Why should this particular student get special attention?

Solution

As survivors of trauma, Sudanese refugees may experience memory impairment, a relatively short attention span, a propensity for aggression, and anxiety associated with adjustment to a formal school environment, especially for those who have never attended school before. Individualized coaching may help allay some of the students' anxieties and promote the development of better learning strategies.

Problem

I am surprised that my new nine-year-old Sudanese students can't read or write. Aren't there schools in the refugee camps in Kenya where she lived before she came here?

Solution

Schools in refugee camps are often overcrowded or experience constant teacher attrition and, thus, cancellation of classes. Frequently, no school supplies are available, either. Students who have no school background and are illiterate may need help with basic motor activities such as holding a pencil, practicing the shape of letters, and understanding the left-to-right direction of writing in English.

Problem

If Arabic is the official language of Sudan, why do my Sudanese students only speak Dinka?

Solution

The cultural, ethnic, and linguistic diversity of Sudan is so pronounced that shared nationality may mean little in terms of understanding the background and needs of Sudanese learners.

Language ————————————

Pronunciation Key

ă	rat		ō	rat
ā	race		ô	draw
ä	father		o͞e	noise
b	boy		ū	goose
ch	church		û	took
d	day		ŭ	cat
ĕ	pet		ou	now
ē	Pete		p	perfect
f	fun		r	right
g	good		s	sin
h	hope		sh	shin
ĭ	in		t	tin
ī	ice		th	*(voiced)* bathe
j	judge		th	*(voiceless)* bath
k	kick		v	voice
kh	*(German) ich* rockhard		w	wide
l	lake		y	yawn
m	make		z	zebra
n	none		zh	pleasure
ng	ring		ə	about *(schwa)*

◼ Amharic

Amharic is the national language of Ethiopia with more than 17 million native speakers and four million speakers of Amharic as a second language. There are numerous speakers of the language in Egypt, Israel, and Sweden as well. Amharic is an Afro-Asiatic language closely related to another language commonly spoken in Ethiopia (Oromo) and less directly related to Arabic.

GRAMMAR

- Amharic uses suffixes to convey notions that, in English, would be expressed via separate words. For example, the Amharic word *betitu* in English translates into the small house; in Amharic, *bet* means "house," *it* means "small," and *u* is the definite article "the."
- Negatives and some conjunctions are marked as endings on verbs, whereas separate words are used in English to convey negation and conjunction.
- Nouns in Amharic can have either masculine or feminine gender, with the feminine gender also used to express smallness, tenderness, or sympathy.
- The subject in Amharic is added to the verb, and the direct object can be marked on the verb as well as some prepositional phrase complements and negatives. Because of this, a verb can stand alone as a sentence. This means that students will have trouble making the complex verb forms in English that require auxiliary verbs. For example, *they resembled us* would be expressed in Amharic as one word *messel-u-n* or *resemble* (past) + *they* + *us*.
- Plurals can be formed either by the plural marker *-oc* or by repeating the noun or adjective root.
- As in English, adjectives appear before the noun.
- Typical word order is subject-object-verb, which differs from the English subject-verb-object.

PRONUNCIATION

- Amharic has 38 separate sounds, which include 7 vowel sounds and 31 consonant sounds.
- Amharic includes some sounds not found in English, such as glottalized consonants *p, t, k, ch, s* (somewhat akin to a cough)—the stream of air coming from the lungs is shut off by the glottis—and sharp clicks (made by sucking in air while the tongue makes contact with a particular part of the vocal tract, such as when imitating the popping of a cork or saying *tsk-tsk*).
- Amharic also has some ejective sounds that are not features of English. Ejective sounds are produced by releasing a burst of air while the tongue makes contact with various parts of the vocal tract.

- Amharic has a close sound-symbol correspondence. In other words, it is pronounced as it is written. Each symbol consists of a consonant and a vowel sound.
- Nearly all the consonants in Amharic are pronounced with a slight rounding of the lips.
- Amharic makes frequent use of the gemination, or lengthening, of consonants to distinguish between the meaning of one word with another, and a single word may have up to five lengthened consonants as in *la<u>mm</u>e<u>nn</u>e<u>tt</u>ama<u>mm</u>ana<u>bb</u>at,* meaning "to the one in whom we have confidence."
- Through a process of consonant weakening, *w* and *g* may become *y.*
- Amharic has no initial consonant clusters. Thus, *sport* may become *esport.*
- Amharic distributes stress equally over every syllable in a word.
- The Amharic *r* is flapped or trilled as in the North American pronunciation of the word *butter* or the Spanish word *gracias.*
- Amharic makes greater use of the glottal stop (as in *uh-oh*) than does English.

English Expression	Amharic Equivalent	Amharic Pronunciation
yes	awo	ou
no	aye	ī
please	ibakkih (m) ibakkish (f)	ĭ-bä-khĭ ĭ-bä-khĭsh
thank you	amessagganalo	ä-mə-sə-gə-n ä´-lō
you're welcome	minim aidel	mĭ´-nĕm ī´-dĕl
hello	selam	sä -läm´
good-bye	dehna wal (m) dehna wai (f)	dä-hə-nä´ wäl dä-hə-nä´ wī
do you understand	yi gebahal (m) yi gabashal (f)	yĭ gə-bä-häl´ yĭ gə-bä-shäl´
I don't understand	alegebagnem	äl-gə-bä´-nyəm
how are you	indemin alleh (m) indemin allesh (f)	ĭn-dĕm-ĭn ä´-lĕ ĭn-dĕm-ĭn ä´-lĕsh
sit down	kuchebal (m) kuchebai (f)	kū-chə-bäl´ kū-chə-bī´
listen	sema (m) semi (f)	sə-mä´ sə-mē´
are you okay	dehena newi (m) dehena neshwi (f)	də-hə-nä´ nə-wē də-hə-nä´ nəsh-wē
good	tiru	tĭ´-rū
correct	liknau	lēk´-nou
homework	bet sira	bĕt sē´-rä
teacher	astemari	äs-tə-mä´-rē
happy birthday	ankwan desali (m) ankwan desalesh (f)	ən-kwän´ dɛs ä-lĕ ən-kwän´ dɛs ä-lĕsh
excuse me	yekireta	yĕ-kə-rə-tä´
I'm sorry	aizo izosh	ou-zō´ ē-zēsh´
what is your name	simih man new (m) simish man new (f)	sə-mĭ´ mä´-nou sə-mĭ´ shmä´-nou
Amharic	Amareegna	ä-mä-rē´-nyə
English	Ingleezigna	ĭn-glē´-zĭ-nyə

◼ Dinka

There are several mutually intelligible varieties of Dinka and dozens of Dinka dialects spoken in Sudan, primarily in the south, with close to two million native speakers. Arabic is the official language of Sudan, however. A Nilo-Saharan language, Dinka is related to many of the languages spoken in nearby Chad, Ethiopia, Niger, Uganda, and the Democratic Republic of Congo.

GRAMMAR

- In Nilo-Sahara languages such as Dinka, both nouns and verbs use endings for case (e.g., subject, object, etc.), tense, number, and location.
- Word order in Dinka is usually subject-verb-object but can vary as in a sentence that is topic-verb-comment *(e.g., The jar open it which is on the top shelf)*.
- Pronouns (such as *you, he, we*) appear as prefixes in Dinka. For example, *tomaye* means "I did not drink."
- Dinka nouns carry information regarding case—nominative, accusative, genitive, dative, locative, and so forth.
- Dinka verbs carry information regarding person, number, tense, aspect, mood, and voice. Additional features may imply whether the verb is negative, causative, or dative.

PRONUNCIATION

- Dinka has 13 vowels plus additional vowel features such as breathiness, vowel lengthening, creakiness, pushing the root of the tongue forward in the mouth, and vowel harmony. The latter refers to the stipulation that all vowels in a word must be from the same category (i.e., either creaky or breathy, or not creaky and breathy). These features contribute to differentiation in meaning.
- In Dinka, the word stem does not change to indicate tense or number; instead, noun and verb inflections are indicated by voice quality (breathiness, etc., as noted above).
- Dinka has 20 consonants, some of which are categorized as implosives as when air is drawn into the oral cavity and contact between the lower lip and the top teeth produce a unique sound.
- Dinka is a tonal language, possessing two levels and three contours. Thus, word meaning changes according to whether a syllable or word is high falling, low falling, or rising.
- Most Dinka words follow the consonant-vowel-consonant pattern.

English Expression	Dinka Pronunciation
yes	gäm
no	rēch
please	yēn kä lōng
thank you	ə´-pəth
no problem	ə-chēn´-kä-rē´-yə
hello	chē-bäk´
see you tomorrow	ō-wä´-bɛn rōm´-nē-äk
do you understand	shä-dɛ´-dēch
I don't understand	ä-shä-dɛ´-dēch
how are you	lō´-kä-dä
sit down	ngyō´-ē pyēng
listen	pyē´-nyə
are you okay	pē-äl´ ē-kwäp´
good	ə´-pəth
correct	shä´-pēn-yə
homework	lō´-ē nyō´-ē-dū
teacher	rän-pyūj´
happy birthday	myɛd-pō´ kō´-dē-rēn
excuse me	dō´-gäzh
I'm sorry	mä-lāsh´
what is your name	shä´-rē-ɛn kūn´-gō
Dinka	dēn-kä
English	lēn´-glēth

<u>Note</u>: There is often not agreement among Dinkas as to the correct spelling of many words. Indeed, most Dinkas are not literate in their mother tongue, and few formal publications in Dinka are available to them in Sudan. Thus, only the pronunciation of the English to Dinka translations are provided here.

Farsi/Persian/Dari

Farsi, the official language spoken in Iran, is also called Persian, and its eastern variety, spoken as the official language in Afghanistan, is known as Dari. Farsi is spoken in Pakistan as well. All tolled, there are more than 61 million native speakers of Farsi. Like English, Farsi is an Indo-European language, though it is closer to Hindi and Urdu than to English, and it makes use of the Arabic rather than the Latin script. Note, however, that Arabic and Farsi belong to different language families. Arabic is an Afro-Asiatic language.

GRAMMAR

- Farsi adheres mainly to subject-object-verb word order. However, case endings (e.g., for subject, object, etc.) expressed via suffixes may allow users to vary word order. Verbs agree with the subject in person and number.
- Almost 50 percent of Farsi words come from Arabic, but it has also borrowed words from English, French, and Turkic languages.
- Pluralization in Farsi is produced via suffixes.
- Farsi nouns do not indicate gender via grammar.
- In Farsi the question word *aya,* which indicates the posing of a yes/no question, appears at the beginning of a sentence.
- Adjectives generally follow the nouns they modify.
- Verbs in Farsi have two basic stems—one present and one past—and tend to be regular.
- Pronouns are not essential in a Farsi sentence, as verb endings provide information about the subject. *Goes home* would be an acceptable utterance in Farsi.
- The verb system in Farsi allows for subtle meanings to be expressed through prefixes and suffixes rather than through modals.

PRONUNCIATION

- Farsi has 6 vowel sounds and 23 consonant sounds. The writing system, however, does not necessarily reveal the sounds of vowels. In other words, the vowel sound may be contained within a letter, so that the name *Mohamed* may be represented in English somewhat like *Mhmd.* Consonants that appear at the beginning versus the middle or the end of a word will usually take on a different shape.
- Most syllables in Farsi are made up of a consonant-vowel-consonant order.
- Farsi does not allow for two vowels to be placed adjacent to each other. They must be separated by glottal stop (the sound between syllables in *uh-oh,* represented by the symbol "?") or *y* as in *mi-gu-?i* or *mi-gu-yi* ("you are saying").
- Stress falls on either the derivational suffix or the base word as in *dast* "hand" to *dast-é* "handle" or on the plural marker (*ketab* or book to *ketabhá* or books).
- The last syllable of a word in Farsi usually receives the stress.

English Expression	Farsi Equivalent	Farsi Pronunciation
yes	بلی	bă´ lē
no	نه	nä
thank you	متشکرم	mô-thĕ´-šä-kĕr´-äm
you're welcome	خواهش میکدم	khä-hĕsh´ mē kô´-näm
good	خوب	khūb
hello	سلام	sä-lä m´
good-bye	خداحافظ	khô´-dä hä´-fĕz
do you understand	می فهمی؟	mē fäh´-mē
I don't understand	من نمیفهمم	män nē-mē-fäh´-mäm
how are you	حال شما چطور است	hä lĕ-tän´ chē-tōr´ äst
sit down	بنشین	bĕ´-shēn
listen	گوش بده	gūš bĕ´-dĕ
are you okay	خوبی؟	khū´-bē
correct	صحیح	sä-hē´
homework	مشق	mäshgh
teacher	معلم	mô-lĕm´
happy birthday	تولدت مبارک	tä´-vä-lō-dät mô-bä-räk´
excuse me	ببخشید مرا	bə-bäkh´-shēd mä-rô´
I'm sorry	معذرت میخواهم	mə-zĕ-rät´ mē´-khä-həm
what is your name	اسم شما چیست؟	ĕs´-mĕ shō´-mä chēst
Farsi Dari	فارسی دَري	făr-sē´ dä´-rē
please	خواهش میکنم	khä-hĕsh´ mē-kō´-näm
English	انگلیسی	ĕn-glē-sē´

Hindi

Hindi is the official language of India (along with English and 21 other languages). It has approximately 180 million native speakers mostly situated in the northern part of the country and 120 million second language speakers throughout the country. As an Indo-European language, Hindi is a distant relative of English, but most of its vocabulary is derived from Sanskrit, minus words from Arabic and Persian.

GRAMMAR

* Hindi verbs are inflected for number, gender, tense, aspect, and honorifics (e.g., intimate, familiar, respect).
* Hindi has two grammatical genders, masculine and feminine, but there is no neutral *it*. The rule of thumb is that nouns ending in –*a* are masculine while those ending in –*i* are feminine.
* The language also has two forms of the second person pronoun *you*—one formal and one informal. There are also two cases—direct and indirect (used when a noun is followed by a postposition).
* Hindi verbs tend to be placed at the end of the sentence, following the subject-object-verb word order pattern as in *you Hindi speak*. Hindi speakers also use postpositions rather than prepositions (subject-object-postposition-verb) rendering *I eat at school* into *I school at eat*.
* Where English speakers place the adverb at the end of a negative imperative sentence *(Don't write it quickly)*, Hindi speakers will use adverb-negative-verb construction *(Quickly not write it)*.

PRONUNCIATION

* Standard Hindi possesses 11 vowels and 35 consonants.
* Many vowels carry both nasal and non-nasal contrasts that can change the meaning of a word.
* The sounds /*f*/, /*z*/, and /*rd*/ only occur in Hindi as a part of loanwords.
* Voiced, unaspirated consonants such as the /*g*/ in *get*, the /*b*/ in *bet*, and the /*d*/ in *debt* have voiceless, unaspirated counterparts, so /*g*/ almost becomes /*k*/ to produce *ket* rather than *get*. There are aspirated voiceless consonants such as the /*p*/ in the English word *pat* and aspirated voiced consonants that are produced by following the consonant with a strong /*h*/ sound.
* Hindi has retroflex consonants produced by placing the tip of the tongue on the hard palate.
* The Hindi /*r*/ is a tap, much like the flapped /*r*/ in the Spanish word *pero*.

English Expression	Hindi Equivalent	Hindi Pronunciation
yes	हाँ	hān
no	नहीं	nə-hīn´
please	कृप्या	kri-pä´-yā
thank you	आपका धन्यवाद	āp kā dhän´-ya-vād
you're welcome	आपका स्वागत है	āp kā svā´-gät hai
hello	नमस्ते	nä-mä´-ste
good-bye	अलविदा	äl´-vi-dā
do you understand	क्या आप समझते हैं	kyā āp sä´-mäjh-te hain
I don't understand	मैं नहीं समझता हूँ	main nä-hīn´ sä-mäjh-tā hūn
how are you	आप कैसे हैं	āp kai-se´ hain
sit down	बैठिए	bai-thi´-ye
listen	सुनिए	su-ni´-ye
are you okay	क्या आप ठीक हैं	kyā āp thīk´ hain
(very) good	(बहुत) अच्छा	(ba-hut´) ac-chā´
correct	ठीक	thīk
homework	घर का काम	ghär kā kām´
teacher	शिक्षक	shik´-shäk
happy birthday	जन्म दिन मुबारक हो	jän-mä-din´ mu-bā-rak ho
excuse me	क्षमा करें	kshä-mā´ kär-en
I'm sorry	मुझे खेद है	mu-jhe khed´ hai
what is your name	आप का नाम क्या है	āp kā nām´ kyā hai
Hindi	हिंदी	hin´-dī
English	अंग्रेजी	äng´-re-zī

Hmong

"Hmong" is often used to refer to any one of three related languages and approximately 15 mutually unintelligible dialects spoken by some eight million Hmong people, residents of northern Laos, some parts of southern China, Vietnam, and Thailand. The most common Hmong languages spoken by immigrants in the United States are White Hmong (Hmong Daw) and Blue Hmong (Hmong Njua), the names derived from the primary color of the garments worn by their speakers.

GRAMMAR

- Most Hmong sentences follow the subject-verb-object word order.
- There are no suffixes or declensions in Hmong nor grammatical gender.
- There is no distinction in pronouns between male and female in Hmong.
- In Hmong, the adjective generally follows the noun.
- A classifier is used to introduce a noun in Hmong (e.g., *one person of child*).
- One subject in Hmong can be attached to several different verbs (e.g., *I ran picked brought back some berries.*)

PRONUNCIATION

- The word *Hmong* is spelled by its speakers as *Hmoob,* the double *oo* indicating nasality and the *b* indicating high tone.
- Hmong consonants may be aspirated in linguistic environments in which they would not be aspirated in English. For example, the *hm* in the initial position in the word *Hmong* is produced by closing the lips and breathing out through the nose without using the voice.
- Consonant sounds such as *th, z, w, b,* and *g* do not exist in Hmong.
- Hmong can have up to 60 consonant sounds if consonant clusters are included in the count, such as the cluster *nplh.*
- There are very few vowel initial words in Hmong.
- Hmong words generally are one syllable in length and consist of a consonant and a vowel or diphthong.
- Syllables rarely end with a consonant sound. Thus, the English word *book* could be shortened to *bû.*
- Hmong has seven distinct tones; use of the tones can change the meaning of a single word. For example, *pó* (high) means *lump, po* (mid) means *pancreas,* and *pò* (low) means *thorn.* Other tones include high rising, mid rising, low falling (or creaky), and mid-low (or breathy).

English Expression	Hmong Equivalent	Hmong Pronunciation
yes	yog	yô
no	tsis yog	chē yô
please	thov	tə-hô
thank you	ua koj tsaug	ōr kô chou
you're welcome	tos txais koj	tô khī kô
hello	nyob zoo	nô zông
good-bye	mus zoo	mū zông
do you understand	koj puas to taub	kô pū-a tô tou
I don't understand	koj puas nyob zoo	kū chē tô tou
how are you	koj puas nyob zoo	kô pū-ä nô zông
sit down	zaum tsawg	zou chĕr
listen	mloog	mə-lông
are you okay	koj puas ua li cas	kô pū-ä u-ä lē chä
alright / okay	ua li	ōr lē
(very) good	zoo (heev)	zông (hĕng)
correct	yog	yô
homework	hauj lwm hauv tsev	hou lū hou chä
teacher	xib fwb	sē fū
happy birthday	zoo siab hnub yug	zông shä nū yū
excuse me	zam txim rau kuv	zä khē dou kū
I'm sorry	kuv thov txim	kū tô khē
what is your name	koj lub npe hu li cas	kô lū bā hū lē chä
Hmong	Hmoob	mông
English	Askiv	ä-kē

Serbo-Croatian

Serbo-Croatian is the language (or group of closely related languages and dialects) spoken in most of Bosnia-Herzegovina and Croatia. It has more than six million native speakers and is on the South Slavic branch of the Indo-European family of languages.

GRAMMAR

- Serbo-Croatian is a highly inflected language, with very flexible word order.
- Nouns can take several cases (i.e., nominal, accusative, genitive, locative, dative, vocative, and instrumental).
- There are no definite or indefinite articles (*a, the*) nor are there auxiliary verbs (*have, has, is, was*).
- Serbo-Croatian possesses three genders (masculine, feminine, neuter) and two numbers (singular, plural).
- There are seven verb tenses in Serbo-Croatian plus three moods (indicative, imperative, conditional—only used for writing) and two aspects (perfective, imperfective).
- Because American names do not have an ending to show which is male and which is female, as they do in Serbo-Croatian, learners may also have problems recognizing male and female names.
- In Serbo-Croatian, adjectives agree with nouns and verbs agree with subjects in terms of case, gender, and number. Students may therefore try to put plural endings on adjectives (*bigs houses*) and may also have trouble with the English verb system.
- Croats use only the Latin script to write their language while Serbians and Bosnians use either the Latin or Cyrillic alphabet.
- Serbo-Crotatian usually has a subject-verb-object word order, which is the same as in English.

PRONUNCIATION

- Serbo-Croatian, with 25 consonants and 5 vowels, has fewer distinct sounds than other Slavic languages. There are no diphthong sounds in Serbo-Croatian.
- Vowel sounds can be long or short and also can vary in pitch or accent to alter the meaning of a word.
- As in English, stress can occur on any syllable of a word and varies between dialects.
- In Serbo-Croatian, there are no silent letters, such as the *k* in *knife* in English.

English Expression	Serbo-Croatian Equivalent	Serbo-Croatian Pronunciation
yes	da	dä
no	ne	nĕ
please	molim	mō´-lēm
thank you	hvala	hvä´-lä
you're welcome	nema na čemu	nĕ´-mä nä chĕ´-mū
hello	zdravo	zdrä´-vō
good-bye	dovidjenja	dō-vē-jĕn´-yä
do you understand	da li razumiješ	dä lē rä-zūm´-ē-yĕsh
I don't understand	ja ne razumijem	yä nĕ rä-zūm´-ē-yĕn
how are you	kako si	kä´-kō sē
sit down	sjedi	syĕ´-dē
listen	slušaj	slū´-shī
are you okay	da li ste u redu	dä lē stĕ´ ū rĕ´-dū
(very) good	(vrlo) dobar	vrlō dō´-bär
correct	ispravno	ēs´-präv´-nō
homework	domaći zadatak	dō-mä´-shē zä-dä´-täk
teacher	učitelj *(m.)* učiteljica *(f.)*	ū-chē´-tĕl ū-chē-tĕl-ēt´-sä
happy birthday	sretan rodzendan	srĕ´-tän rōzh´-ĕn-dän
excuse me	oprostite	ä-prō´-stē-tĕ
I'm sorry	žao mi je	zou´ mē yĕ
what is your name	kako se zoveš	kä´-kō sĕ zō´-vĕsh
Serbo-Croatian	Srpsko-Hrvatski	srəp´-skō hvrät´-skē
English	engelski	ĕn-gĕl´-skē

▌Somali

Somali is the official language of Somalia, although Arabic and Italian are used widely in this country as well. In Somalia alone there are almost eight million native speakers of the language, but the number rises to 12.5 million if speakers are counted in Djibouti, Ethiopia, Kenya, Oman, Saudi Arabia, the United Arab Emirates, Yemen, and even Finland, Italy, and Sweden. Somali is an Afro-Asiatic language and more specifically a Cushtic language like several of the languages spoken in Ethiopia.

GRAMMAR

- Number (singular, plural) and gender (masculine, feminine, neuter) are marked by using tones as well as some endings, but there are no cases in Somali. Tones are also used to indicate past tense and imperative aspect.
- There are no indefinite articles in Somali (e.g., *a, an*).
- Somali word order usually follows the object-subject-verb pattern, but subject-verb-object is also possible under certain circumstances.
- Prepositions (or more accurately, postpositions) occur at the end rather than at the beginning of a prepositional phrase.

PRONUNCIATION

- The Somali language has a very complex sound system, with 22 distinct consonant sounds, 20 pure vowel phonemes, and 20 diphthongs. The language also has a tone system.
- Vowels in Somali may be either short or long (doubled in length), the variation affecting the meaning of words. Some consonants, too, may be doubled without this effect changing meaning.
- The interdental sound *th* is always voiced in Somali (i.e., *th* as in *this* as opposed to *thin*).
- The bilabial consonant *p* only occurs in the middle of words in Somali.
- There is a fixed one-to-one correspondence between each letter of the Somali alphabet and the sound it represents.
- Unlike Arabic, Somali has no glottal stops (as between the syllables in *uh-oh*) or pharyngeal sounds such as *kha*.
- Somali may be written in one of three alphabets—Latin, Arabic, or Osmanya.

English Expression	Somali Equivalent	Somali Pronunciation
yes	haye, haa, hee	hä-yĕ, hä, hē
no	maya	mī´-yä
please	fadlan	fäd-län
thank you	waad mahadsantahay	wäd mä-häd-sän-tä-hī
you're welcome	adaa mudan	ä-dä mū-dän
hello	iska warran	ē-skä wä´-rän
good-bye	nabadgelyo	nä-bäd-gɛl-yō
do you understand	ma fahantay	mä fä-hän-tī
I don't understand	ma fahmin	mä fä-mēn
how are you	iska warran	ē-skä wä-rän
sit down	fadhiiso	fäd-hē-sō
listen	dhegaysad	dhe-gē-sō
are you okay	ma fiican tahay	mä fē-kän tä-hī
(very) good	(aad u) fiican	(äd ū) fē-kän
correct	sax	säkh
homework	shaqo guri	shä-khō gū-rē
teacher	macalin	mä-kä-lēn
excuse me	raalli iga ahow	rä-lē ē-gä ä-hou
I'm sorry	waan ka xumahay	wän kä khū-mä-hī
what is your name	magacaa	mä-gä-kä
Somali	soomaali	sō-mä-lē
English	ingiriisi	ēn-gē-rē-sē

▌Spanish

Spanish is the official language of most countries in Latin America. It is also spoken in parts of the Caribbean, in the Canary Islands, and, of course, in Spain. Worldwide, it has a total native speaker population of 358 million. As an Indo-European Romance language, it has many similarities to English. However, be aware that even in the Spanish-speaking world, significant variations in vocabulary and sometimes in morphology exist.

GRAMMAR

- Spanish has a highly inflected verb system, with most of the tenses found in English. In Spanish, there are no modal auxiliaries.
- In Spanish, it is common to use the combination *have* + noun to express what in English would be *be* + ADJECTIVE. For example, whereas a Spanish speaker might say *tengo hambre* ("I have hunger"), an English speaker would say *I am hungry*.
- The endings *–ing* and *–ed* do not have active or passive meanings in Spanish. In Spanish there are no *–ing* nouns. Instead, the infinitive is used as a noun.
- When generalizing, the definite article is often used in front of mass and plural nouns as in, *the corn grows in Iowa*.
- Spanish word order is much freer in Spanish than in English. Adjectives are normally placed after the nouns they modify. Adverbs can be placed in several positions in the sentence.
- Adjectives and nouns show gender and number. The ending *–s* is used in Spanish to show plural number in adjectives, articles, possessives, and nouns.
- Since Spanish is a pro-drop language, personal pronouns are normally not used because the ending of the verb indicates person and number. Learners may omit the subject pronoun.

PRONUNCIATION

- Spanish has five vowels and five diphthongs.
- There are no lax vowels in Spanish, and, therefore, no distinction between /ē/ (as in *beat*) and /ĭ/ (as in *bit*) or between /ā/ (as in *bait*) and /ĕ/ (as in *bet*). In addition, there is no /ə/ sounds (as in *putt*), no /ă/ (as in *pat*), and no /û/ (as in *put*).
- The sound /z/ has no correspondence in Spanish and is usually substituted with /s/ (so *lose* becomes *loose*).
- Spanish speakers often have problems pronouncing the *y* as in *Yale*, using the sound /dz/ (*jail*) instead.

English Expression	Spanish Equivalent	Spanish Pronunciation
yes	sí	sē
no	no	nō
please	por favor	pōr fä-vōr´
thank you	gracias	grä´-sē-äs
you're welcome	de nada	dā-nä´-thə
hello	hola	ō´-lä
good-bye	adios	ä-dē-ōs´
do you understand	entiendes	än-tē-ĕn´-dĕs
I don't understand	no entiendo	nō än-tē-ĕn´-dō
how are you	como estás	kō´-mō ĕs-täs´
sit down	sientese	sē-ĕn´-tĕ-sä
listen	escuche	ĕs-kū´-chä
are you okay	estás bien	ĕs-täs´ bē-ĕn´
(very) good	(muy) bien	(mū´-ē) bē-ĕn´
correct	correcto	kō-rĕk´-tō
homework	tarea	tä-rā´-ä
teacher	professór (m.) professóra (f.)	prō-fĕ-sōr´ prō-fĕ-sōr´-ä
happy birthday	feliz cumpleaños	fā-lēs´ kūm-plā-än´-yōs
excuse me	perdon	pĕr-dōn´
I'm sorry	lo siento	lō sē-ĕn´-tō
what is your name	como te llamas	kō´-mō tā yä´-mäs
Spanish	español	ĕs-pän-yōl´
English	inglés	ēn-glās´

⬛ Ukrainian

The official language of Ukraine is Ukrainian, an east Slavic Indo-European language with more than 31 million native speakers in Ukraine alone. Speakers of Ukrainian can also be found in Armenia, Azerbaijan, Belarus, Estonia, Georgia, Hungary, Poland, Romania, Russia, Bosnia-Herzegovina, Slovakia, Turkmenistan, Uzbekistan, and even in Argentina. It is similar in vocabulary and structure to Russian, Polish, and Slovak.

GRAMMAR

- Ukrainian is a richly inflected language, with nouns of three grammatical genders (masculine, feminine, neuter) declined in seven cases (nominative, accusative, genitive, dative, instrumental, prepositional, and vocative).
- Subject pronouns are only used for emphasis, as verbs are marked for first, second, and third persons, plus singular and plural.
- In Ukrainian, there is a fundamental distinction between perfective (completed actions) and imperfective (ongoing actions). This distinction is integrated into the structure of the verb itself, usually via suffixation.
- Ukrainian word order is fairly free, but often subject-verb-object is the norm.
- Ukrainian does not use definite and indefinite articles *(a, the)*.

PRONUNCIATION

- There are 6 vowel sounds and 32 consonant sounds in Ukrainian. The semi-vowel *y* is sometimes combined to create additional phonemes such as *ya, yu, ye,* and *yo*. There are no diphthongs in Ukrainian.
- Most consonants in Ukrainian are close in pronunciation to those that exist in English, but certain combinations can occur in Ukrainian where they would not in English. The combination of *t+s* as in *bits,* for example, frequently appears in word-initial position in Ukrainian. On the other hand, Ukrainian has no interdental /*th*/ sound, nor does the consonant cluster /*ng*/ exist.
- Ukrainian makes use of a variant of the Cyrillic alphabet. Sometimes people use a Romanized form of the alphabet.
- There is typically a one-to-one sound-symbol correspondence in Ukrainian.

English Expression	Ukrainian Equivalent	Ukrainian Pronunciation
yes	так	täk
no	ні	ngē
please	прошу (US) будь ласка (UKR)	prō´-shū būd lä´-skä
thank you	дякую	jyä´-kū-yū
you're welcome	прошу	prō´-shū
good day good morning	добри день добри ранок	dō-brē´-dēng dō-brē´-rä´-nōk
good-bye	до побачення	dō pō-bä-chĕn´-gyä
do you understand	розумієш	rō-zū-mē´-yĕsh
I don't understand	я не розумію	yä nĕ rō-zū-mē´-yū
how are you	як справи	yäk sprä´-vē
sit down	прошу сісти	prō´-shū sē´-stē
listen	слухай	slū´-khī
are you feeling okay?	чи ти добре чуєся	chē tē dō´-brē chū´-yĕ-syä
alright / okay	добре	dō´-brĕ
(very) good	(дуже) добре	(dū´-zhĕ) dō´-brĕ
correct	добре	dō´-brĕ
homework	домашнє завдання	dō-mä´-shnĕ zouv-dän´-gyä
teacher	учитель *(m.)* учителька *(f.)*	ū-chē´-tĕl ū-chē´-tĕl-kä
happy birthday	з днем народження (UKR) многая літа (US)	z dnĕm nä-rō´-jĕn-gyä mnō´-gä-yä lē´-tä
excuse me	перепрошую	pĕ-rĕ-prō´-shū-yū
I'm sorry	я вибачаюсь	yä vē-bä-chä´-yūs
what is your name	як твоє ім'я	yäk tvō-yĕ´ ēm-yä´
English	англійська мова	än-glē´-shkä mō´-vä
Ukrainian	Український	ū-krī-ēn´-skē

Select Bibliography

▮ Websites Frequently Consulted

Country Studies
www.allrefer.com

Centre for Intercultural Learning
www.intercultures.ca

Creative Proverbs
www.creativeproverbs.com

Cultural Profiles Project
www.cp-pc.ca

Folktales and Values
www.flameghana.org/ictprojects/folktalevalue

Global Income Per Capita
www.finfacts.com

Migration Information Source
www.migrationinformation.org

Nationmaster
www.nationmaster.com

Office of Refugee Resettlement
www.acf.hhs.gov/programs/orr

The World Factbook 2005
www.cia.gov/cia/publications//factbook

U.S Citizenship and Immigration Services
http://uscis.gov

U.S. Committee for Refugees and Immigrants
www.refugees.org

World Education Forum Country Reports
www.unesco.org/education/efa

World Wide Colleges and Universities
www.globaled.us

Yahoo Currency Converter
http://finance.yahoo.com/currency

Yearbook of Immigration Statistics
http://uscis.gov

▨ Additional References

Refugees by numbers
www.unhcr.org

Adler, Beatrice
www.peacecorps.gov

Bavolek, Stephen

Briton Putman, Diana
www.culturalorientation.net

Bognar, Ladislav
www.gewi.kfunigraz.ac.at/csbsc

Boyson, Beverly
www.cal.org

Burman, Erica
www.worldviewmagazine.com

Camarota, Steven
www.cis.org

Coskran, Kathleen
www.peacecorps.gov

Duffy, John
www.culturalorientation.net

Dunn-Marcos, Robin
www.culturalorientation.net

Eannarino, Rosalind
www.ucis.pitt.edu/clas/publications

Education for all
www.logos-net.net

U.S. Immigration and Naturalization Service
http://uscis.gov

Fix, Michael
www.urban.org

Garyantes, Dianne
www.peacecorps.gov

Grieco, Elizabeth
www.migrationpolicy.org

Office of Homeland Security
www.uscis.gov

Kang, Hee-Won
www.ncela.gwu.edu

Kobayashi, Audrey
http://institute.metropolis.net

Madden-Shephard
http://rosella.apana.org.au/~mlb/cranes/reslink1.htm

Manners, Lynn
www.culturalorientation.net

McCabe, Donald
www.lib.washington.edu

Metropolis Institute
http://institute.metropolis.net

Meyers, Deborah
www.migrationinformation.org

Morse, Ann
www.ncsl.org

LaBrack, Bruce
www.sikhpioneers.org

Nakamura, Tetsu
www.rmaf.org.ph

National report
www.bologna-berlin2003.de

O'Brien, Penny
www.peacecorps.gov

Office of Homeland Security
http://uscis.gov

Rich, Angela
www.peacecorps.gov

Robson, Barbara
www.culturalorientation.net

Schmidley, A. Diane
www.census.gov

Thomsen, M.
www.peacecorps.gov

Tranfiae, Anela
www.onestopenglish.com

World refugee survey 2004
www.refugees.org

Yang, Schwa
www.jefflindsay.com

Additional References

Adler, Beatrice. "Someday I Will Miss…" Peace Corps World Wise Schools. n.d. *www.peacecorps.gov/wws/adayinthelife/guatemala1.html*

Axtel, Roger. *Do's and Taboos of Humour around the World.* New York: John Wiley and Sons, 1999.

———. *Gestures: The Do's and Taboos of Body Language around the World.* New York: John Wiley and Sons, 1998.

Bavolek, Stephen. *Multicultural Parenting Education Guide.* Park City, UT: Family Development Resources, Inc., 1997.

Birman, Dina, Edison Trickett, and Natalia Bacchus. "Somali Refugee Youth in Maryland: Needs Assessment, 2001." *www.dhr.state.md.us/ mona/pdf/somali.pdf*

Bognar, Ladislav. "Problems and Perspectives in the Development of Schooling in Croatia." Grasz, Austria. Center for the Study of Balkan Societies and Cultures, 2000. *www-gewi.kfunigraz.ac.at/csbsc/country_ reports/Education_Croatia.htm*

Boyson, Beverly, Bronwyn Coltrane, and Deborah Short, eds. *Proceedings of the First National Conference for Educators of Newcomer Students.* Washington, DC: Center for Applied Linguistics, 2002. *www.cal.org/ projects/newcproceedings.pdf*

Bras-Car, Misela. "Education for All: The Year 2000 Assessment." United Nations Educational, Scientific and Cultural Organization, 2000. Paris, France. *www.unesco.org/education/efa/*

Briton Putman, Diana, and Mohamood Cabdi Noor. "The Somalis: Their History and Culture." Washington, DC: Center for Applied Linguistics, 1993. *www.culturalorientation.net/somali/index.html*

Burman, Erica. "Without Blackboards." *Worldview Magazine Online* 18, no. 1 (2005). *www.worldviewmagazine.com/issues/article.cfm?id=151&issue=37*

Camarota, Steven, and Nora McArdle. "Where Immigrants Live: An Examination of State Residency of the Foreign Born by Country of Origin in 1990 and 2000." Washington, DC: Center for Immigration Studies, 2003. *www. cis.org/articles/2003/back1203.html*

Coskran, Kathleen. "So This Is Paris." Peace Corps World Wise Schools, 1994. *www.peacecorps.gov/wws/stories/ethiopia-coskran.html*

Deupree, John. "Afghanistan: Shaking Off the Dust." *International Educator* 12, no. 4 (2003): 6–9.

Duffy, John, et al. "The Hmong: An Introduction to Their History and Culture." Washington, DC: Center for Applied Linguistics, 2004. *www.cultural orientation.net/hmong/index.html?ID=299*

Dunn-Marcos, Robin, et al. "Liberians: An Introduction to Their History and Culture." Washington, DC: Center for Applied Linguistics, 2005. *www. culturalorientation.net/liberians/liberian_050406_1.pdf*

Eannarino, Rosalind. "Nicaragua: People, Culture, and History." *Las Noticias* 3, no. 1 (2003). *www.ucis.pitt.edu/clas/publications/LAS_NOTICIAS_ SPRING_2003.pdf*

Education for All: (EDUCATODOS)—Honduras. International Labour Office, 2002. *www.logos-net.net/ilo/195_base/en/init/hon_2.htm*

Fix, Michael, and Jeffrey Passel. "Immigration and Immigrants: Setting the Record Straight." Washington, DC: Urban Institute, 1994. *www.urban. org/url.cfm?ID-305184.html*

Flaitz, Jeffra. *Understanding Your International Students: An Educational, Cultural, and Linguistic Guide.* Ann Arbor: The University of Michigan Press, 2003.

Garyantes, Dianne. "Not Just Any Other Day." Peace Corps World Wise Schools, n.d. *www.peacecorps.gov/wws/stories/notjustanyotherday.html*

Grieco, Elizabeth. "What Kind of Work Do Immigrants Do? Occupation and Industry of Foreign-Born Workers in the United States." Washington, DC: Migration Policy Institute, 2004. *www.migrationpolicy.org/pubs/five_ industry_occupation_foreign_born.pdf*

Igoa, Cristina. *The Inner World of the Immigrant Child.* Mahwah, NJ: Lawrence Erlbaum, 1995.

Kamyab, Shahrzad. "Education in Iran: An Overview." *College and University Journal* 79, no. 4 (2004): 57–60.

Kang, Hee-Won, Phyllis Kuehn, and Adrienne Herrell. "The Hmong Literacy Project: A Study of Hmong Classroom Behavior." *Bilingual Research Journal* 18, nos. 3 and 4 (1994): 63–83. *www.ncela.gwu.edu/pubs/nabe/ brj/v18/18_34_kang.pdf*

Kobayashi, Audrey. "Race and Racism in Canada." Ontario Administration of Settlement and Integration Services, 2002. *http://institute.metropolis.net/ cours/005_introduction-e.pdf*

LaBrack, Bruce. "Dr. Bruce LaBrack's Study of South Asian Immigrants, 1997." *www.sikhpioneers.org*

Madden-Shephard, Janice. "Paper Cranes." Thousand Cranes Peace Network, 2005. *http://rosella.apana.org.au/~mlb/cranes/reslink1.htm*

Maners, Lynn. "The Bosnians: An Introduction to Their History and Culture." Washington, DC: Center for Applied Linguistics, 1995. *www.cultural orientation.net/bosnia/index.html*

McCabeam, Donald. "Student and Faculty Perspectives on Plagiarism and Academic Dishonesty." Seattle: University of Washington, 2004. *www.lib. washington.edu/about/events/academic/McCabeam.ppt*

Metropolis Institute. "Race and Racism in Canada." n.d. *http://institute. metropolis.net/cours/005_introduction-e.pdf*

Meyers, Deborah, and Jennifer Yau. "U.S. Immigration Statistics in 2003." Washington, DC: Migration Policy Institute, 2004. *www.migration information.org/USfocus/display.cfm?ID=263*

Morrison, Terri, Wayne Conaway, and George Borden. *Kiss, Bow, or Shake Hands: How to Do Business in Sixty Countries.* Holbrook, MA: Adams Media Corporation, 1994.

Morse, Ann. "A Quick Look at U.S. Immigrants: Demographics, Workforce, and Asset-Building." Washington, DC: National Conference of State Legislatures Immigrant Policy Project, 2004. *www.ncsl.org/programs/immig/ Demographics2000Census.htm*

Nakamura, Tetsu. "Transcending Ethnicity, Religion, and Politics towards Peace." Magsaysay Awardees Lecture Series, 2003. *www.rmaf.org.ph/ Awardees/Lecture/LectureNakamuraTet.htm*

"National Report." Republic of Croatia, Ministry of Science and Technology, n.d. *www.bologna-berlin2003.de/pdf/Croatia.pdf*

O'Brien, Penny. "Local Genorisity 'Nose' No Limits." Peace Corps World Wise Schools, n.d. *www.peacecorps.gov/wws/stories/Dominica_essay.html*

Office of Homeland Security. "Immigration by Region and Selected Country of Last Residence: Fiscal Years 1820–2004." In *Yearbook of Immigration Statistics 2004.* Washington, DC: Office of Homeland Security, n.d. *http:// uscis.gov/graphics/shared/statistics/yearbook/2004/table2.xls*

———. "Refugees and Asylees Granted Lawful Permanent Resident Status and Selected Country of Birth: Fiscal Years 1946–2004." In *Yearbook of Immigration Statistics.* Washington, DC: Office of Homeland Security, 2004. *http://uscis.gov/graphics/shared/statistics/yearbook/2004/ Table21.xls*

Rich, Angela. "Work Days." Peace Corps World Wise Schools, n.d. *www. peacecorps.gov/wws/cybervol/2002/let1fall.html*

Robson, Barbara, and Juliene Lipson. "The Afghans: Their History and Culture." Washington, DC: Center for Applied Linguistics, 2002. *www.cultural orientation.net/afghan/index.html*

Schmidley, A. Diane. "Profile of the Foreign-Born Population in the United States: 2000." Washington, DC: U.S. Census Bureau, n.d. *www.census. gov/prod/2002pubs/p23-206.pdf*

Suarez-Orozco, Carola, and Marcelo Suarez-Orozco. *Children of Immigration.* Cambridge, MA: Harvard University Press, 2001.

Thomsen, Moritz. "The Student Arrives at the Door." Peace Corps World Wise Schools, n.d. *www.peacecorps.gov/wws/stories/Ecuador_essay. html*

Tranfiae, Anela. "Don't Ask Too Many Questions." One Stop English.com, 2004. *www.onestopenglish.com/magazine/anecdotes/sad/sad2.htm*

United Nations High Commissioner for Refugees. "Refugees by Numbers." Geneva, Switzerland: United Nations High Commissioner for Refugees, 2005. *www.unhcr.org/cgi-bin/texis/home?id-search*

U.S. Immigration and Naturalization Service. Office of Policy and Planning. "Estimates of the Unauthorized Immigrant Population Residing in the United States: 1990 to 2000." Washington, DC: Office of Homeland Security, 2003. *http://uscis.gov/graphics/shared/statistics/publications/ Ill_Report_1211.pdf*

"World Refugee Survey 2004." U.S. Committee for Refugees. Washington, DC. *www.refugees.org/article.aspx?id=1156*

Yang, Schwa. "The Rising Generation of Hmong." In *The Hmong People in the U.S.,* 2001. *www.jefflindsay.com/Hmong_tragedy.html*